D1757195

Midwest Studies in Philosophy
Volume XXVI

MIDWEST STUDIES IN PHILOSOPHY

EDITED BY PETER A. FRENCH
HOWARD K. WETTSTEIN

Many papers in MIDWEST STUDIES IN PHILOSOPHY are invited and all are previously unpublished. The editors will consider unsolicited manuscripts that are received by January of the year preceding the appearance of a volume. All manuscripts must be pertinent to the topic area of the volume for which they are submitted. Address manuscripts to MIDWEST STUDIES IN PHILOSOPHY, Department of Philosophy, University of California, Riverside, CA 92521.

The articles in MIDWEST STUDIES IN PHILOSOPHY are indexed in THE PHILOSOPHER'S INDEX.

Midwest Studies in Philosophy Volume XXVI Renaissance and Early Modern Philosophy

Editors

Peter A. French
Arizona State University

Howard K. Wettstein
University of California, Riverside

Consulting Editor

Bruce Silver
University of South Florida

BLACKWELL PUBLISHING • BOSTON, MA & OXFORD, UK

Copyright © 2002 Blackwell Publishing, Inc.

Blackwell Publishing, Inc.
350 Main Street
Malden, MA 02148 USA

Blackwell Publishing, Ltd.
108 Cowley Road
Oxford OX4 1JF
United Kingdom

Library of Congress Cataloging-in-Publication Data is available for this publication at the Library of Congress

ISBN 0-631-23382-2 (pbk.: alk.paper)

MIDWEST STUDIES IN PHILOSOPHY
Volume XXVI
Renaissance and Early Modern Philosophy

Thomas Malory (ca. 1405–1471)
"Always to do ladies, damosels, and gentlewomen succour": Women and the
Chivalric Code in Malory's *Morte Darthur* . . . . Felicia Ackerman   1

Nicholas of Cusa (1401–1464)
Nicholas of Cusa (1401–1464): First Modern Philosopher? . . . . . Jasper Hopkins   13

Marsilius Ficino (1433–1499)
Marsilio Ficino on *Significatio* . . . . Michael J. B. Allen   30

Pietro Pomponazzi (1462–1525)
Pomponazzi: Moral Virtue in a Deterministic Universe . . . . John L. Treloar   44

John Pico della Mirandola (1463–1494)
The Secret of Pico's *Oration*: Cabala and Renaissance
Philosophy . . . . Brian P. Copenhaver   56

Niccolo Machiavelli (1469–1527)
Between Republic and Monarchy? Liberty, Security, and the Kingdom of
France in Machiavelli . . . . Cary J. Nederman and Tatiana V. Gómez   82

Michel de Montaigne (1533–1592)
Montaigne, *An Apology for Raymond Sebond*: Happiness and
the Poverty of Reason . . . . Bruce Silver   94

Giordano Bruno (1548–1600)
The Natural Philosophy of Giordano Bruno . . . . Hilary Gatti   111

Francis Bacon (1561–1626)
Francis Bacon and the Humanistic Aspects of
Modernity . . . . Rose-Mary Sargent   124

Thomas Hobbes (1588–1679)
Hobbes's Atheism . . . . Douglas M. Jesseph   140

Pierre Gassendi (1592–1655)
New Wine in Old Bottles: Gassendi and the Aristotelian Origin of
Physics . . . . Margaret J. Osler   167

Rene Descartes (1596–1650)
Descartes, Mechanics, and the Mechanical Philosophy . . . . Daniel Garber   185

Antoine Arnauld (1612–1694)
"Presence" and "Likeness" in Arnauld's Critique of
Malebranche . . . . Nancy Kendrick   205

Blaise Pascal (1623–1662)
Pascal's Wagers . . . . Jeff Jordan   213

Baruch Spinoza (1632–1677) and Levi ben Gershon (Gersonides)
Eternity and Immortality in Spinoza's *Ethics* . . . . Steven Nadler   224

Nicolas Malebranche (1638–1715)
Occasionalism and Efficacious Laws in Malebranche . . . . Nicholas Jolley   245

Pierre Bayle (1647–1706)
What Kind of a Skeptic Was Bayle? . . . . Thomas M. Lennon   258

Charles de Montesquieu (1689–1755)
From Locke's *Letter* to Montesquieu's *Lettres* . . . . Edwin Curley   280

Contributors   307

Midwest Studies in Philosophy 1976–2004

Midwest Studies in Philosophy
Volume XXVI

Midwest Studies in Philosophy, XXVI (2002)

"Always to do ladies, damosels, and gentlewomen succour": Women and the Chivalric Code in Malory's *Morte Darthur*

FELICIA ACKERMAN*

There once was a Knight named Sir Lancelot
Who couldn't keep it in his pantsalot
One day he got caught
His king was distraught
And he had to go off to Francealot.

Medieval chivalry involves a distinctive sort of moral code, one that is far loftier than what the above limerick suggests. This sort of code, however, is unlikely to appeal to most present-day philosophers. Progressive people are apt to dismiss chivalry as oppressive to women. This essay will subject that attitude to critical examination through a discussion of one particular chivalric code, the code in Sir Thomas Malory's *Morte Darthur*. I will argue that in addition to its obvious limitations, Malory's chivalric code holds some currently unrecognized advantages for women. First, however, some background about Malory's *Morte Darthur* is in order.

The *Morte Darthur* is an English prose compilation, compression, adaptation, and supplementation of medieval French (in Malory's translation) and English Arthurian romances. Written by Sir Thomas Malory, it was first published (as well as edited) by William Caxton in 1485.[1] This essay focuses on the two-

* I am indebted to many people, especially Dorsey Armstrong, Shannon French, and Kenneth Hodges, for helpful discussions of this material. An early version of this essay was read at the Thirty-Sixth International Congress on Medieval Studies. This article is dedicated to the glorious memory of Nina Lindsey.

1. A different edition of Malory, the Vinaver edition, is based mainly on the Winchester manuscript, a Malory manuscript (believed to be in the handwriting of scribes rather than of Malory himself) discovered at Winchester College in 1934 and subsequently edited by Eugène Vinaver—

volume Penguin Classics edition, which is based on the Caxton edition (and from which my Malory excerpts are taken, unless otherwise indicated), as the Penguin basically preserves the language of the Caxton edition but modernizes the Middle English spelling.[2] The distinction between changing the language and changing the spelling obviously has borderline cases, but the net effect of focusing on the Penguin is to make the quoted Malory material readily accessible to philosophers. In this essay, I take the Penguin text largely as a given and use such expressions as 'Malory's world' without going into such questions as to what extent the relevant aspects of Malory's world come from his sources or what editing Caxton did. Of course, when I speak of Malory's world, I mean the fictional fifth-century world of Malory's *Morte Darthur*, not the fifteenth-century world of Malory's actual life. This fictional world is fundamentally a world of the aristocracy; it does not have the full range of people found in the actual world. Also, although there are many writers of Arthurian material and hence many versions of Arthurian chivalry, for simplicity of exposition I will confine myself to Malory, as he is the greatest of all Arthurian writers and also the medieval Arthurian writer most widely read today.[3]

"[P]erhaps the most complete and authentic record of M[alory]'s conception of chivalry"[4] is found in Malory's version of the Round Table Oath (also called the Pentecostal Oath), to which "all the knights . . . of the Table Round, both old and

---

a sequence of events that, unsurprisingly, transformed Malory scholarship. Although the Winchester manuscript and Caxton's edition contain basically similar material, they also have significant differences, and debate continues over which is more authentic, in the sense of being closer to what Malory actually wrote. (For discussion of this issue, see Walter Kendrick, "Which Malory Should I Teach?" in Maureen Fries and Jeanie Watson [eds.], *Teaching the Arthurian Tradition* [New York: Modern Language Association of America, 1992, pp. 100–105]; Ingrid Tieken-Boon van Ostade, *The Two Versions of Malory's Morte Darthur* [Cambridge, UK: D. S. Brewer, 1995]; and Eugène Vinaver [ed.], *The Works of Sir Thomas Malory*, Third Edition, revised by P. J. C. Field [Oxford: Oxford University Press, 1990], especially Vinaver's preface to his first edition and chapters 2–4 of his introduction.) Reflecting his (highly controversial) view that Malory wrote eight separate romances rather than one unified work, Vinaver called his edition not *Le Morte D'Arthur* (Caxton's title), but *The Works of Sir Thomas Malory*. The general term "the *Morte Darthur*," which I use in this essay, covers both versions. Vinaver's edition uses unmodernized Middle English spelling, and there is no unabridged edition based on the Winchester manuscript and using modernized spelling.

2. For the sake of Malory scholars (whom I hope this essay will also interest, despite the practical necessity of my including background information already familiar to them), I include references to Vinaver's three-volume *The Works of Sir Thomas Malory* for all quoted Malory passages. I am using a three-way reference system, giving first the volume and page numbers in the Penguin Classics volumes (e.g., v.2, 227), then the book and chapter numbers in the Caxton edition (e.g., C XIV, 2), then the volume and page numbers of the corresponding (and not always identical) passages in the third edition of Vinaver's three-volume *The Works of Sir Thomas Malory* (e.g., V 2: 907). The spelling of all proper names is from the Penguin Classics volumes.

3. For discussion of other versions of the chivalric code in the work of other medieval Arthurian writers, see Beverly Kennedy, *Knighthood in the Morte Darthur*, Second Edition (Cambridge, UK: D.S. Brewer, 1992), pp. 67–68 and Thomas L. Wright, "'The Tale of King Arthur': Beginnings and Foreshadowings," in R. M. Lumiansky (ed.), *Malory's Originality* (Baltimore: Johns Hopkins University Press, 1964), p. 36 ff.

4. Vinaver, Commentary on *The Works of Sir Thomas Malory*, 3: 1335.

young . . . every year were . . . sworn at the high feast of Pentecost."[5] The Caxton edition's version of the Round Table Oath goes as follows:

> never to do outrageousity nor murder, and always to flee treason; also, by no mean to be cruel, but to give mercy unto him that asketh mercy, upon pain of forfeiture of their [the knights'] worship and lordship of King Arthur for evermore; and always to do ladies, damosels, and gentlewomen succour, upon pain of death. Also, that no man take no battles in a wrongful quarrel for no law, ne for no world's goods.[6]

The version in the edition of Malory described in footnote 1, the Vinaver edition, goes as follows:

> never to do outrage nor murder, and always to flee treason, and to give mercy unto him that asketh mercy, upon pain of forfeiture of their [the knights'] worship and lordship of King Arthur for evermore; and always to do ladies, damosels, and gentlewomen and widows succour; strengthen them in their rights, and never to enforce them, upon pain of death. Also, that no man take no battles in a wrongful quarrel for no love, nor for no worldly goods.[7]

The clause mentioning ladies (unsurprisingly known as the ladies' clause) is my focus in this essay. Malory's terminology here for women illustrates the point that he is writing about the aristocracy. I will go along with this restriction (although, for simplicity of exposition, I will sometimes use the general terms "woman" and "women"), as nonaristocratic women scarcely even appear in Malory's world. Malory can obviously be faulted for his dismissive attitude toward the lower classes; however, this issue is outside the scope of my essay.

What does the ladies' clause require knights to do? Of the various roles knights of the Round Table have in Malory's world, two are important here.[8] First, Round Table knights function as quasi-policemen and keepers of the peace, who prevent and investigate crimes, rescue victims and potential victims, and, unlike policemen in our society, lawfully sometimes mete out summary, even capital, punishment. (The benefits of such knightly police action are not limited to female victims and potential female victims. Knights often rescue their beleaguered or imprisoned fellow knights, as well as damsels in distress.) Examples of knightly police action on behalf of women include killing a serial rapist (Book VI, chapter

---

5. Sir Thomas Malory, *Le Morte D'Arthur* (London: Penguin, 1969), v.1, 116; C III, 15; V 1: 120.

6. Ibid., v.1, 115–116; C III, 15.

7. *The Works of Sir Thomas Malory*, 1: 120. I have used the modernized spelling in Sir Thomas Malory: *Le Morte Darthur: The Winchester Manuscript*, abridged and edited with an introduction and explanatory notes by Helen Cooper (Oxford: Oxford University Press, 1998), p. 57, although I have not followed her substitution of 'nor' for 'ne.'

8. For a discussion of other knightly roles, see my " 'Never to do outrageousity nor murder': The Code of the Warrior in the World of Malory's *Morte Darthur*," in Shannon E. French, *Code of the Warrior* (New York: Rowman and Littlefield, forthcoming).

10) and interceding for a woman against a homicidally jealous husband (Book VI, chapter 17). In the jealous husband case, Launcelot even ignores the husband's attempts to justify his behavior. Women, however, can also be victims of summary justice. When a lady Arthur has spurned tries to strike off his head with his own sword in revenge, Arthur beheads her, following another lady's advice, "Let not that false lady escape."[9]

Is Arthur violating the oath? If not, how should oath be understood? I will return to this question after outlining the second pertinent role of a Round Table knight, a role likely to strike the modern reader as bizarre. Nowadays, we are apt to take for granted our modern system of criminal justice, where (at least in the absence of plea-bargaining) the guilt or innocence of someone accused of a crime is determined by presenting the evidence to a jury of his peers. In Arthur's kingdom, however, guilt or innocence is determined by a trial by battle between the accuser (or a knight fighting on his behalf) and the accused (or a knight fighting on his behalf). In a sense, the judge is taken to be God, who is expected to "speed the right"[10] by providing victory to the side of the accused if he is innocent and to the side of the accuser if the accused is guilty. Women do not have the option of fighting on their own behalf in trials by battle in Malory's world. But the ladies' clause keeps women from being "helpless before the law so long as legal quarrels could be settled only by means of battle,"[11] any more than nonlawyers in our world are helpless before the law to the extent that our legal quarrels can be settled only by means of lawyers. Just as nonlawyers in our world gain legal power by having lawyers represent them, women in Malory's world gain legal power by having knights fight on their behalf in trials by battle. Similarly, just as police power protects civilians against crime in our world, knightly power protects women against crime in Malory's world. The analogy between knights and lawyers or policemen is—to put it mildly—hardly perfect, but it is a corrective to the exaggeration of the subjugation of women in Malory's world. In fact, since the oath *requires* Round Table knights always to do ladies, damsels, and gentlewomen succor, such women have an automatic claim on the prowess of even the strongest knight. It is as if present-day Americans had an automatic claim on the free services of the likes of Johnnie Cochran and Alan Dershowitz. It might even be argued that in this respect, women are more powerful than men in Malory's world, as the Round Table Oath does not require stronger knights to provide succor to lesser knights.

Dorsey Armstrong has argued that "the knightly understanding of women as powerless ironically renders them powerful."[12] This insight is just part of the story. What makes women powerful in Malory's world is not just the knightly understanding of women as powerless, but this understanding *in conjunction with*

---

9. Malory, *Le Morte D'Arthur*, v.1, 409; C IX, 15; V 2: 491.

10. Ibid., v.2, 379; C XVIII, 4; V 2: 1051.

11. Kennedy, *Knighthood in the Morte Darthur*, p. 39.

12. Dorsey Armstrong, "Gender and the Chivalric Community: The Pentecostal Oath in Malory's 'Tale of King Arthur,'" in *Bibliographic Bulletin of the International Arthurian Society* (Madison, WI: A-R Editions, Inc., 2000), p. 303.

the moral imperative that knights of the Round Table do ladies, damsels, and gentlewomen succor. Without this imperative, the knightly understanding of women as powerless could be a basis for overpowering and taking advantage of women rather than for protecting and serving them.

At this point, some qualifications are in order. First, just how much more powerful (in the indicated way) are women than lesser knights in Malory's world? Round Table knights certainly do hold themselves obligated to aid their fellow knights, as well as to aid women. For example, Launcelot's rationale for rescuing Kay from three knights who "lashed on him at once with swords"[13] is "if he be slain I am partner of his death."[14] And in a much later incident, Arthur says, in praising Gareth, "For ever it is a worshipful [honorable] knight's deed to help another worshipful knight when he seeth him in a great danger."[15]

A second possible objection to what I have said so far is that the oath's final clause—prohibiting battles in a wrongful quarrel—indicates a restriction on the succor owed to ladies. There is an obvious tension between the two clauses: what if doing a lady succor requires fighting for her in a wrongful quarrel? This possibility is not just theoretical. In the final tale (Book XX), Launcelot saves Guenever from being burned to death when he knows she is guilty and offers to prove her innocence in a trial by battle. But in an earlier episode, where Guenever is (falsely) accused of poisoning a knight at a feast, the remaining knights who were present at the feast refuse to fight for her in a trial by battle because "all they have great suspicion unto the queen"[16] and Launcelot, who has promised Guenever "ever to be her knight in right other in wrong,"[17] is (initially) absent. A problem thus arises: sometimes a woman may need to *appear* to be in the right in order to get a knight to fight for her to *prove* she is in the right. Women who do appear to be in the right, however, have the power I have mentioned: every Round Table knight is obliged to defend them. Note also that it is not only men from whom women may need protection in Malory's world. The possibility that a woman may need protection from another woman is recognized in a forerunner of the Round Table Oath, administered only to Gawain, which includes the provision that "he should never be against lady ne gentlewoman but if he fought for a lady and his adversary fought for another."[18] As Malory tells us, "there by ordinance of the queen there was set a quest [judgment] of ladies on Sir Gawain, and they judged him"[19] to swear to this oath. Recognizing the judicial role of women to "set a quest" to advance their interests is another corrective to the exaggeration of the subjugation of women in Malory's world.

When the ladies' clause conflicts with other clauses of the oath, Malorian values frequently favor the former. Malory clearly approves of Launcelot's above-mentioned support of Guenever. Another clause that may conflict with the ladies'

13. Malory, *Le Morte D'Arthur*, v.1, 214; C VI, 11; V 1: 273.
14. Ibid.
15. Ibid., v.2, 425; C XVIII, 24; V 3: 1114.
16. Ibid., v.2, 378; C XVIII, 4; V 2: 1050.
17. Ibid., v.2, 386; C XVIII, 7; V 2: 1058.
18. Ibid., v.1, 104; C III, 8; V 1: 109.
19. Ibid., v.1, 104; C III, 8; V 1: 108.

clause is the mercy clause, which requires that a knight accept a surrender and refrain from slaying a knight he has overcome in combat and who has yielded to him and asked for mercy. This situation can arise when the victorious knight is in either of the knightly roles I have mentioned: quasi-policeman and keeper of the peace or combatant in a trial by battle, and in other potentially homicidal situations as well. Mercy is a Christian virtue. Requiring mercy shows the religious underpinnings of Arthurian knighthood as embodying Christian virtues, rather than resting on brute force.[20] In order to see how such a requirement may conflict with the ladies' clause, we need to consider what the ladies' clause might require of knights beyond the already mentioned quasi-police and trial-by-battle functions.

Doing women succor does not entail automatically granting whatever they may request. Sexual requests are clearly exempt. For example, when Elaine of Astolat (who may be more familiar to philosophers as Tennyson's Lady of Shalott) implores Launcelot to "have mercy upon me, and suffer me not to die for thy love"[21] by marrying her or at least becoming her lover, he is not in violation of the ladies' clause (or, for that matter, the mercy clause) when he refuses. Nor does giving women succor invariably override other considerations in Malory's world. If it did, female transgressors could hardly be punished. But the scope of the ladies' clause may be surprisingly broad. Malory scholars often take it to include adherence to the so-called "rash boon" tradition, where a lady asks for a "gift," and a knight is expected to grant her request before even knowing what the gift will turn out to be.[22] Armstrong uses this tradition in order to argue that there is a way in which the outlook underlying the ladies' clause *unintentionally* gives power to women. She employs an example involving a damsel in an early, pre-oath episode, which is part of how, as Thomas L. Wright puts it, "Malory's rules of chivalry [i.e., the clauses of the Round Table Oath] are ... determined empirically."[23] In this episode, a damsel "asks *first* for a gift, which request [Tor] in adhering to the already demonstrated and soon to be made lawful rule about behavior to ladies [i.e., the ladies' clause], grants."[24] But the damsel, taking advantage of what Armstrong calls "the helplessness of a knight when confronted by a lady asking favors,"[25] is pursuing a personal vengeance. Her requested "gift" turns out to be the head of Abellus, who, she tells Tor, killed her brother, *and* who yields and asks Tor for mercy. Interestingly, in an earlier "rash boon" episode, where the "gift" turns out to be the head of Balin or the damsel who gave him a sword, Arthur is not helpless when confronted by a lady asking favors. He blamelessly refuses to grant this gift to the Lady of the Lake, saying, significantly, "I may not grant neither of their heads *with my worship* [honor],"[26] despite the fact that he previously

---

20. For qualification here, see my "'Never to do outrageousity nor murder ...'"
21. Malory, *Le Morte D'Arthur*, v.2, 411; C XVIII, 19; V 2: 1089.
22. Knights (including King Arthur) sometimes agree to fill unspecified requests from men as well.
23. Wright, "Beginnings and Foreshadowings," p. 42.
24. Armstrong, "Gender and the Chivalric Community," p. 301. (Italics in original.)
25. Ibid., p. 303.
26. Malory, *Le Morte D'Arthur*, v.1, 64; C II, 3; V 1: 65. (Italics added.)

agreed to give her "what gift ye will ask"[27] in return for her giving him his sword Excalibur and, unlike Abellus, no potential target is asking for mercy. As Mark Lambert has observed in another context, Malory's outlook has "internal contradictions . . . He has not thought the whole thing out."[28] Tor's and Arthur's pre-oath dilemmas foreshadow the oath's incompatible requirements.[29] But these incompatibilities do not prevent the oath from functioning as a moral code in practice in cases where the incompatibilities are irrelevant.

Armstrong's article does not mention the case of the Lady of the Lake, but she offers this analysis of Tor and the damsel:

> The damsel in this episode performs as a knight would expect her to, miming feminine behavior and thus transcending her categorization as such: although in a sense a helpless, needy female, she capitalizes on her position to effectively make [Tor] her instrument. Here we can see how the rigid conception of gender categories and the attributes that mark these categories actually create a space in which women may wield some measure of power and influence within the patriarchal social project of chivalry. While the Arthurian community understands and indeed, values the catalytic effect the feminine has in encouraging feats of bravery and prowess, it fails to anticipate the use of that catalytic effect for ends other than the glorification of the community and of the individual knights who comprise it. In this instance, her brother's death provides the damsel with the impetus to act for her own 'selfish' interests, rather than subsuming her personal desire into that of the communal good (i.e., a test of knightly ability that would bring renown back to [Tor] and his community).[30]

I will consider this account in relation to the oath's mercy clause, which has important parallels with the ladies' clause. Here are three parallels. First, both clauses have penalties attached: death for violating the ladies' clause and social death (forfeiture of worship and lordship of King Arthur for evermore) for violating the mercy clause. The oath does not rank-order the clauses. But the fact that Arthur and Guenever "made great joy"[31] upon hearing Tor "tell of his adventures"[32] (on a quest including the episode discussed above) suggests that at least in this instance they value service to ladies over mercy to knights. Whatever the damsel's intentions, Tor's adventures do, in fact, "bring renown back to [him] and

27. Ibid., v.1, 56; C I, 25; V 1:53.

28. Mark Lambert, *Malory: Style and Vision in Le Morte Darthur* (New Haven: Yale University Press, 1975), pp. 195–196.

29. For more discussion of this problem, see my "'Never to do outrageousity nor murder . . . ,'" as well as Bonnie Wheeler, "Romance and Parataxis and Malory: The Case of Sir Gawain's Reputation," *Arthurian Literature* 20 (1993), pp. 117–118 and Wright, "Beginnings and Foreshadowings," pp. 62–66.

30. Armstrong, "Gender and the Chivalric Community," p. 302.

31. Malory, *Le Morte D'Arthur*, v.1, 109; C III, 11; V 1: 114.

32. Ibid., v.1, 109; C III, 11; V 1: 113.

his community"—precisely because this community places such high value on knights providing service to women.

Second, both clauses deal with relations between the strong and the weak. On the one hand, the two clauses support Elizabeth Pochoda's claim that the Round Table Oath "is specifically directed at eliminating the tyranny of one individual over another, at protecting the weak from the strong."[33] On the other hand, the existence (or creation) of such weakness is essential to chivalry. Knights who yield as overcome are "passive, powerless object[s],"[34] "vulnerable and helpless"[35]—precisely the qualities Armstrong identifies the Arthurian community as ascribing to women. Her claim that "a demonstration of knightly prowess is impossible without the presence of the subjugated feminine"[36] should be applied to the presence of the defeated, subjugated knights. A disanalogy is that the position of the defeated knight is (to use the sort of social-science jargon that would make Malory turn over in his grave) achieved rather than ascribed, as well as relative to a particular context of a particular combat. But just as Arthurian society ascribes roles to women, it establishes conditions for knightly combat. Both the ladies' clause and the mercy clause, like the clause prohibiting battles in a wrongful quarrel, deal with specifically knightly duties, as opposed to general human duties. All people are supposed to refrain from committing murder, "outrageousity," or treason, but the oath's remaining three clauses are unique aspects of the knightly role in Arthurian society.[37]

The third parallel is the most important for my purposes. It is that both clauses can be manipulated by the weak. Beverly Kennedy has suggested that the mercy clause "can be interpreted either as an ethical imperative applicable to the behavior of an adventurous knight errant [which includes the quasi-policeman role] or as a rule applicable to the behavior of combatants in trial by battle."[38] The victorious knight is often free to set his terms for granting mercy. Knights who receive mercy from a knight in his quasi-policeman role are often required to go and yield themselves at King Arthur's court. Other terms for granting mercy also occur. In an early tournament in Ireland, Tristram extracts these terms from the defeated Palomides: "that ye forsake my lady La Beale Isoud, and in no manner wise that ye draw not to her. Also this twelvemonth and a day that ye bear none armour nor none harness of war. Now promise me this, or here shalt thou die."[39] Neither Tristram nor Palomides is yet a knight of the Round Table, but Tristram's

---

33. Elizabeth T. Pochoda, *Arthurian Propaganda: Le Morte Darthur as an Historical Ideal of Life* (Chapel Hill, NC: University of North Carolina Press, 1971), p. 84.

34. Armstrong, "Gender and the Chivalric Community," p. 297.

35. Ibid., p. 298.

36. Ibid., p. 300 n17.

37. For an interesting discussion of the relation between moral rules and social roles, see P. F. Strawson, "Social Morality and Individual Ideal," *Philosophy* XXXVI, no. 136 (1961): 1–17.

38. Kennedy, *Knighthood in the Morte Darthur*, p. 38.

39. Malory, *Le Morte D'Arthur*, v.1, 320; C VIII, 10; V 1: 388. It may seem ludicrous that a tournament could come to this, but it is an illustration of the blurred line between sport and battle in Malory's world. See the discussion in my " 'Never to do outrageousity nor murder . . .' " Note also that the condition against bearing armor or harness is not unique to Tristram. Alisander le Orphelin also employs it (Book X, chapters 36 and 39).

requirement would be acceptable in one. Later, King Mark, also not a Round Table knight, swears (upon yielding to Gaheris) never to be against errant knights and to befriend Tristram if Tristram ever comes into Cornwall (Book IX, chapter 38). But just as women can use the ladies' clause for their own personal ends, defeated knights can do likewise with the mercy clause, swearing to terms they have no intention of keeping. This possibility is also not just theoretical. Neither King Mark nor Palomides keeps his promise. But then a question arises. What does the mercy clause indicate: that the Arthurian community cannot anticipate the possibility of insincere promises accompanying appeals for mercy or that the community values mercy so highly that it is willing to take that risk? Now consider the parallel question of whether Armstrong is correct in claiming that the ladies' clause indicates the community's inability to admit or even conceive of "the possibility of female agency"[40] that goes against the community or whether this clause indicates that the community places such high value on doing succor to women that it is willing to take that risk. Consider also that even before the promulgation of the Round Table Oath, we encounter masculine acknowledgment of particular cases of perfidious women following private, antisocial agendas. This casts doubt upon Armstrong's claim that "the masculine agents of the chivalric community cannot, of necessity, allow for or conceive of any resistance to gender categories as constructed by the Arthurian society."[41] When Balin justifies his beheading of the Lady of the Lake on the grounds that she destroyed many good knights and caused his mother to be burnt "through her falsehood and treachery,"[42] Arthur's reply is "Which cause soever ye had, ye should have forborne her in my presence."[43] This reply indicates open-mindedness about this lady's true character, rather than inability or unwillingness to conceive of "the possibility of female agency" that could choose to work against knights.

So far I have been discussing Malorian chivalry in relation to views of Malory scholars who are not professional philosophers. I now turn to an explicitly philosophical treatment of a related notion, Linda Bell's discussion of gallantry. Bell does not specifically discuss Malorian chivalry. Gallantry, as she conceives it, is not identical with Malorian chivalry. But it is worth considering to what, if any, extent Bell's criticisms of gallantry apply to Malorian chivalry. Bell characterizes gallantry as follows: "First, gallantry involves a generosity that goes beyond what is required by good manners. Gallantry, like good manners, is praised; but unlike a breach of manners, a lack of gallantry is not usually condemned . . . no . . . negative judgment [as rude] greets the man who does not go out of his way to open the door for a woman."[44] This overlooks the traditional requirement of a certain degree of gallantry as part of good manners. For example, *Drebett's Etiquette and Modern Manners* says, "Courtesy has long *demanded* that a man should open a door for a

40. Armstrong, "Gender and the Chivalric Community," p. 312.
41. Ibid., p. 311.
42. Malory, *Le Morte D'Arthur*, v.1, 65; C II, 3; V 1: 66.
43. Ibid.
44. Linda A. Bell, "Gallantry: What It Is and Why It Should Not Survive," *Southern Journal of Philosophy* 22 (1984), p. 165.

woman."[45] In support of her claim, Bell points out that "Sir Walter Raleigh's [spreading his cloak over a puddle in the path of his queen] received mention . . . in history books,"[46] while mere good manners would not. But this shows only that Sir Walter Raleigh's extreme gallantry counted as supererogatory to the point of being noteworthy, not that all gallantry did. Certainly, the chivalry embodied in the ladies' clause is obligatory in Malory's world; it is part of an *oath* knights swear to.

Bell also claims that gallantry involves "a feigned inferiority"[47] and hence a duplicity, involving a kind of irony that is really an insult on the part of the man. While Bell cites men whose rationales for gallantry support this claim, its general applicability to Malory's world is dubious. Vowing to do women succor is not inherently duplicitous, nor, as I shall argue presently, does it entail any insult. Of course, Malorian chivalry, like virtually anything else, can be used in a duplicitous way. In an early episode, Gareth, his true identity concealed, gets King Arthur to let him answer a damsel's plea for succor. But that damsel despises him, mocks him for being a "kitchen knave," and denigrates his success at knightly pursuits. When a knight he defeats asks for mercy, Gareth tells him, "thou shalt die but if [unless] this damosel that came with me pray [ask] me to save thy life."[48] This episode fits Bell's account of gallantry: Gareth, in granting the damsel's grudging request that he give the knight mercy and telling the damsel, "your charge is to me a pleasure,"[49] is feigning inferiority and subjugation to her will. He has actually has gotten this scornful damsel to make a request for mercy that only he can grant, *after* she has already made it clear that she despises him too much to be willing to request this of him. (After all, her repeated requests that this "kitchen knave" go away are not to him a pleasure; he refuses to grant them.) But this is an atypical situation in Malory's world.

Another philosophical critic of gallantry, Marilyn Frye, faults gallant men for "commonly [making] a fuss about being helpful and providing small services when help and services are of little or no use [but rarely being] at hand when substantial assistance is really wanted either in mundane affairs or in situations of threat, assault, or terror."[50] Whatever the merits of such criticism of the twentieth-century society about which Frye is writing, it is obviously false of Malorian chivalry. In Malory's world, knightly assistance to women characteristically comes in response to women's practical requests, often in situations of threat, assault, or terror. Note also that women in Malory's world can act as judges of knightly behavior (as in the already mentioned episode involving an oath administered only to Gawain). This undermines the applicability of Bell's claim that "the recognition of gallantry

---

45. Elsie Burch Donald (ed.), *Drebett's Etiquette and Modern Manners* (London: Pan Books, Ltd., 1982), p. 232. (Italics added.)

46. Bell, "Gallantry," p. 165.

47. Ibid., p. 167.

48. Malory, *Le Morte D'Arthur*, v.1, 245; C VII, 8; V 1: 306.

49. Ibid.

50. Marilyn Frye, *The Politics of Reality: Essays in Feminist Theory* (Trumansburg, NY: The Crossing Press, 1983), p. 6. Frye grants that her essays in this book "are timebound and culture-bound" (ibid., ix).

as a civilizing factor requires an acknowledgment that the physically stronger and mentally superior have a right to rule those who are physically and mentally weaker."[51] Malorian chivalry does rest on a blanket assumption that women are physically weaker than men, overlooking social causes of and possible exceptions to such "weakness." But requiring knights to use their presumed physical strength in the service of women hardly constitutes acknowledging the right of the strong to rule the weak, nor does Malorian chivalry assume women's mental inferiority at all. And although physical prowess is a knightly virtue essential for the knightly role, the assumption that it is lacking in women is not an insult. Women in Malory's world are not judged by that standard or devalued because of the assumption that they cannot meet it.

But who is stronger? Who is weaker? Why? Such questions lead to Bell's criticism that is most applicable to Malorian chivalry: "Gallantry is not . . . reversible."[52] In particular, "the sexes of the two participants in gallantry are not irrelevant."[53] The same is true of Malorian chivalry. Men can be providers, but women can only be recipients (although, as I have indicated, knights can also be recipients of knightly succor and mercy). Some women in Malory's world have magical powers, however, which Geraldine Heng characterizes as "a woman's equivalent of a knight's skill at arms,"[54] and which are sometimes used to benefit knights in a sort of reverse chivalry (for example, Book IV, chapters 10 and 22). There is no suggestion that this assistance insults knights. Admittedly, such reverse chivalry is much rarer than standard chivalry in Malory's world, in part because knights outnumber women with magical powers, let alone women who use such powers in order to benefit knights. There are also anomalous instances where women do wield knightly weapons (for example, the already mentioned case of a spurned lady who attempts to decapitate Arthur with his own sword). Armstrong holds that "even as the [Round Table] Oath seems to offer explicit protection to women in the ladies' clause . . . it also simultaneously and deliberately constructs them as 'feminine' in the chivalric sense—helpless, needy, rape-able."[55] Seems to offer? In what sense is the protection illusory? Part of the problem is presumably that women are being made dependent *on* knights for protection from rape *by* knights.[56] An obvious alternative would be to "empower" women to protect themselves, thereby revising what Catherine Batt calls "the *Morte*'s sexist (and of course

---

51. Bell, "Gallantry," p. 169.

52. Ibid., p. 166.

53. Ibid., p. 167.

54. Geraldine Heng, "Enchanted Ground: The Feminine Subtext in Malory," in Thelma S. Fenster (ed.), *Arthurian Women: A Casebook* (New York: Garland, 1996), p. 112 n39.

55. Armstrong, "Gender and the Chivalric Community," p. 298. See also Catherine Batt, "Malory and Rape," *Arthuriana* 7: 3 (1997), p. 85. Armstrong is referring to the Vinaver edition's version of the oath, which has an explicit prohibition against rape ("never to enforce them"). Vinaver suggests that Caxton deleted the explicit prohibition because "it must have seemed to [him] singularly incongruous in an Arthurian context" (Commentary on *The Works of Sir Thomas Malory*, 3: 1335), i.e., it was an unacceptable insult even to suggest that Arthurian knights could be guilty of rape (although it was presumably acceptable to suggest that they could be guilty of murder). See also Batt, "Malory and Rape," p. 96 n17.

56. See the discussion in Batt, "Malory and Rape," p. 85.

unequal) terms of individual social integrity—women are rapeable, men risk defeat in battle."[57] But why is it bad for women to need recourse to knights for protection? I will consider two possible answers.

The first possible answer is that dependence is inherently degrading. This sort of claim is prominent in present-day philosophical justifications of assisted suicide. For example, Ronald Dworkin approvingly notes that some people "think it degrading to be wholly dependent [because of the] impact . . . on their own dignity,"[58] and M. Pabst Battin cites a sick old woman's "dependence" as one reason why her "[s]uicide . . . may be constitutive of human dignity in [that] it leaves one less example of human degradation in the world."[59] By contrast, other philosophers, including feminist philosophers such as Susan Wendell, question independence as an ideal and point out that no one is completely independent and that "'independence' . . . is defined according to a society's expectations about what people 'normally' do for themselves and how they do it."[60] Anita Silvers notes that independence need not "be compromised by having others execute, on one's behalf, physical activities one cannot or does not wish to engage in one's self [provided that this does not involve] being controlled by the caregiver."[61] Such views are both more logical and more humane than the view that "dependence" is characteristic of only some people's lives or is inherently degrading.

But this does not let Malorian chivalry off the hook. Sex-role rigidity has obvious disadvantages. Although not inherently degrading, reliance on knightly prowess does not always work well for women in practice. Some knights mistreat women. And knights do not always spring to a lady's assistance, as Guenever discovers in the poisoning episode previously mentioned, where she has to engage in some genuinely degrading begging for help. Furthermore, given the opportunity, some women might prefer to fight for themselves, some might be good at it, and some might welcome the opportunity to explore new, nonbellicose means of conflict resolution, as might some men. Malorian chivalry has genuine weaknesses for women.[62] This essay has focused on its strengths.

---

57. Ibid., p. 90. Batt grants that this dichotomy is not absolute, but space limitations prevent me from going into this or discussing Batt's treatment of additional complexities concerning rape in Malory's world.

58. Ronald Dworkin, *Life's Dominion* (New York: Vintage, 1994), p. 210.

59. M. Pabst Battin, "Suicide: A Fundamental Human Right?" in M. Pabst Battin and David J. Mayo (eds.), *Suicide: The Philosophical Issues* (New York: St. Martin's Press, 1980), p. 274. See the discussion in my "Death, Dying, and Dignity," in K. Brinkmann (ed.), *The Proceedings of the Twentieth World Congress of Philosophy, v.1: Ethics* (Philosophy Documentation Center, 1999), pp. 189–201.

60. Susan Wendell, *The Rejected Body: Feminist Philosophical Reflections on Disability* (New York: Routledge, 1996), p. 145.

61. Anita Silvers, Review of Susan Wendell, *The Rejected Body: Feminist Philosophical Reflections on Disability, American Philosophical Association Newsletter on Philosophy and Medicine* 97.2 (1998), p. 123. See also Wendell, *The Rejected Body*, pp. 146 and 148.

62. There are additional problematic constraints on women in Malory's world. For example, some women, such as Guenever, are subjected to arranged marriages (although others are not). Space limitations restrict this essay to a discussion of the ladies' clause of the Round Table Oath.

Midwest Studies in Philosophy, XXVI (2002)

Nicholas of Cusa (1401–1464): First Modern Philosopher?

JASPER HOPKINS

Ever since Ernst Cassirer in his epochal book *Individuum und Kosmos in der Philosophie der Renaissance*[1] labeled Nicholas of Cusa "the first modern thinker," interest in Cusa's thought has burgeoned. At various times, both before and after Cassirer, Nicholas has been viewed as a forerunner of Leibniz,[2] a harbinger of Kant,[3] a prefigurer of Hegel,[4] indeed, as an anticipator of the whole of

1. Leipzig: Teubner, 1927, p. 10: "But this contrast [between the being of the absolute and the being of the empirical-conditioned] is now no longer merely posited dogmatically; rather, [according to Cusanus] it is to be grasped in its ultimate depth; it is to be conceived from out of the conditions of human knowledge. This position on the problem of knowledge determines Cusanus as the first Modern thinker" ["... charakterisiert Cusanus als den ersten modernen Denker"]. All translations are mine.

2. Robert Zimmermann, "Der Cardinal Nicolaus Cusanus als Vorläufer Leibnitzens," pp. 306–328 of *Sitzungsberichte der philosophisch-historischen Classe der kaiserlichen Akademie der Wissenschaften*, 8 (Vienna, 1852).

3. Richard Falckenberg, *Grundzüge der Philosophie des Nicolaus Cusanus mit besonderer Berücksichtigung der Lehre vom Erkennen* (Breslau: Koebner, 1880), p. 3: "That which Nicholas wanted, Leibniz, Kant, and Kant's successors brought about." See also Josef Koch, *Die Ars coniecturalis des Nikolaus von Kues* (Cologne: Westdeutscher Verlag, 1956), pp. 47–48. See n. 73 below.

4. Edmond Vansteenberghe, *Le Cardinal Nicolas de Cues (1401–1464)* (Paris, 1920; reprinted in Frankfurt am Main: Minerva, 1963), p. 282: "The great discovery of the Cardinal, the discovery that constitutes the basic originality of his system, is—to use modern terms—his critique of the faculty of knowledge. 'The principle of contradiction has validity only for our reason.' Isn't all of Hegel germinally present in this affirmation? And doesn't the fact alone of having formulated it make of Nicholas of Cusa one of the fathers of German thought?"

Note also Josef Stallmach's citation (p. 243): "According to Erwin Metzke 'no one has come closer to the thinking of Nicholas of Cusa than has Hegel'." Stallmach, "Das Absolute und die Dialektik bei Cusanus im Vergleich zu Hegel," pp. 241–255 in *Nicolò Cusano agli inizi del mondo moderno* (Atti del Congresso internazionale in occasione del V centenario della morte di Nicolò Cusano. Bressanone, 6–10 settembre 1964). Florence: Sansone, 1970.

German Idealism.[5] Joachim Ritter, gathering together various comments made by Edmond Vansteenberghe, points to the latter's view that decisive stimuli went out from Nicholas "to the Academy of Ficino, to Leonardo da Vinci, to Bruno, to Galileo, to French Platonism as it concerns Margaret of Navarre, to Pascal, to Kepler, to Copernicus, to Leibniz"; moreover, "in the latently but lastingly influential world of the German-Dutch *devotio* and mysticism his [intellectual] spirit . . . [was] alive."[6] Heinrich Ritter sees Nicholas in even more grandiose terms: "In the very first years of the fifteenth century a child was born whose life and influence can be seen as a foreshadowing of almost all that the subsequent centuries were to bring."[7]

The foregoing appraisals are motivated by modern-sounding themes in Cusa's writings, so that it becomes easy to perceive Nicholas—if not as the Father of Modern Philosophy, a title usually reserved for Descartes—at least as the prime mover of the period that intervenes between the end of the Middle Ages and the time of Descartes.[8]

I. CUSA'S MODERN THEMES

One can identify at least sixteen Cusan themes that have a peculiarly Modern ring to them and on the basis of which Nicholas has been deemed to occupy a special relationship to Modernity. (*1*) One such theme is found in his dialogue *De Mente*, chapter 10: "A part is not known unless the whole is known, for the whole measures the part." This theme resurfaces in German Idealism, where the whole's determining of the part takes ontological precedence over the part's determining of the whole. (*2*) A corresponding tenet is found in *De Mente* 3 (69): "If someone had precise knowledge of one thing: then, necessarily, he would have knowledge of all things." Here again Nicholas so interrelates part and whole that when the part is wholly known, then the whole is known, just as when the whole is known,

---

5. Frederick Copleston lends credence to this view, without himself actually endorsing it, in Vol. III, p. 245 of his *History of Philosophy*. Note also Heinrich Rombach's appraisal: "It is scarcely possible to over-estimate the importance of Cusa for the development of the modern branches of learning . . . The horizon of his thought not only encompasses the sphere of Descartes' thinking and contains the most important impulses for the metaphysics of Spinoza and of Leibniz but also is exemplary and fundamental for the Kantian turn in philosophy and, therewith, for German Idealism too." *Substanz, System, Struktur. Die Ontologie des Funktionalismus und der philosophische Hintergrund der modernen Welt* (Munich: Alber, 1965), p. 150 of Vol. I.

6. Joachim Ritter, p. 111 of his "Die Stellung des Nicolaus von Cues in der Philosophiegeschichte. Grundsätzliche Probleme der neueren Cusanus-Forschung," *Blätter für Deutsche Philosophie*, 13 (1939–40), 111–155. Ritter also (p. 111) understands Vansteenberghe to be teaching that Cusa "stands with Eckhart, with Böhme, Kant, and Hegel in a single movement, being equal to them in creative, philosophical power, in depth of probing, in breadth and universality of philosophical conception."

7. Heinrich Ritter, *Geschichte der Philosophie*. Vol. IX: *Geschichte der neuern Philosophie* (Hamburg: Perthes, 1850), p. 141.

8. Richard Falckenberg speaks of Cusanus as "der Reigenführer jenes vorbereitenden Zwischenraumes": "the dance-leader of that preparatory intermediate-period." *Geschichte der neueren Philosophie von Nikolaus von Kues bis zur Gegenwart* (Leipzig: Viet, 1905), p. 12.

so too is the part: there is cognitive reciprocity. (*3*) Another such theme is introduced in Cusa's *De Beryllo*, viz., the Pythagorean notion that "man is the measure of all things" in that he is the measuring scale for all things. Some interpreters have construed this ancient doctrine, as it reoccurs in Cusa's writing, to constitute a preview of Kant's "Copernican Revolution."[9]

(*4*) Similarly, Nicholas's distinction between *ratio* (reason) and *intellectus* (understanding)—the latter being the higher mental faculty—has been thought to resemble, in relevant respects, Kant's distinction between *Verstand* (understanding) and *Vernunft* (reason),[10] so that for the most part nowadays the Germans translate Cusa's word "*ratio*" by "*Verstand*" and his word "*intellectus*" by "*Vernunft*," even though Nicholas himself used the reverse translations: "*ratio-Vernunft*" and "*intellectus-Verstand*." Nicholas claims that the principle of noncontradiction applies only at the level of *ratio*, not at the level of *intellectus*. And, as we have already seen (n. 4 above), Vansteenberghe understands this doctrine to have become the crux of Hegelianism. (*5*) Nicholas claims that what is caused cannot be fully or satisfactorily known unless its cause is also known[11]—a doctrine that, once again, sounds anticipatory of Idealism. (*6*) Nicholas, under the influence of Leon Battista Alberti, emphasizes that human knowledge is perspectival, so that all empirical knowledge is imperfect, incremental, and subject to

9. Cassirer, *Das Erkenntnisproblem in der Philosophie und Wissenschaft der neueren Zeit* (Berlin: Verlag Bruno Cassirer; Vol. I, 2nd ed., 1911), p. 38: "*Genuine* rational concepts must not constitute the product and the end of the cognitive process but must constitute its *beginning* and its presupposition." Cassirer, ibid., pp. 35–36: "From *similitudo* Cusa moves on to *assimilatio*: from the assertion of a similarity present in the *things*—a similarity that furnishes the basis for their comprehension and their generic characterizing—he moves to representing the process by virtue of which the *mind* first must produce and create a harmonious connection between the objects and itself. At this point, the self no longer recognizes the objects in conforming itself to them and in copying them; on the contrary, the self recognizes them in apprehending and comprehending them in accordance with the likeness of its own being. We understand outer-objects only insofar as we are able to re-discover in them the categories of our own thought. All 'measuring' of objects arises, fundamentally, only from the mind's singular desire to arrive at the measure of itself and its powers." Falckenberg, *Grundzüge*, op. cit. (n. 3 above), p. 139: "Nevertheless, it remains a pleasure to see, on the threshold of the Modern Age, the doctrine already advanced by Plotinus and Scotus Eriugena, renewed [by Cusa] so forcefully that time, numbers, spatial figures, and all categories . . . are brought forth out of the creative power of the mind."

10. Josef Koch, *Die Ars coniecturalis*, op. cit. (n. 3 above), p. 48. See n. 73 below.

11. Cusa, *De Possest* 38. *Sermones* (contained in Vol. II of *Nicolai Cusae Cardinalis Opera* [Paris, 1514]; reprinted in Frankfurt am Main: Minerva Verlag, 1962), folio 146ᵛ, lines 17–18. *Sermo* CXXXV (3:13) (Vol. XVIII, fascicle 1 [1995] of the Heidelberg Academy edition of *Nicolai de Cusa Opera Omnia* [Hamburg: Meiner Verlag]). All references to Cusa's works are to the Latin texts. References to *De Docta Ignorantia; De Coniecturis; De Filiatione Dei; Apologia Doctae Ignorantiae; De Pace Fidei; De Beryllo* (1988 edition); *Cribratio Alkorani; De Ludo Globi*; and *De Venatione Sapientiae* are to the editions in the series *Nicolai de Cusa Opera Omnia* (Hamburg: Felix Meiner Verlag). Other references are to my editions: *De Aequalitate* (in *Nicholas of Cusa: Metaphysical Speculations: Volume One*); *De Sapientia I* and *II*; *De Mente* (in *Nicholas of Cusa on Wisdom and Knowledge*); *De Visione Dei* (in *Nicholas of Cusa's Dialectical Mysticism* [1988, 2nd ed.]); *De Possest* (in *A Concise Introduction to the Philosophy of Nicholas of Cusa* [1986, 3rd ed.]); *De Li Non Aliud* (in *Nicholas of Cusa on God as Not-other* [1987, 3rd ed.]); and the *Compendium* (in *Nicholas of Cusa on Wisdom and Knowledge*).

degrees of certainty and of uncertainty. (*7*) The Infinite, writes Nicholas, is manifest (symbolically) in and through the finite. Some interpreters have compared Cusa's notion that the Infinite is present in, and is manifest through, the finite as anticipatory of Hegel's notion of an intensive (vs. an extensive) infinity. According to Nicholas, the Divine Mind is symbolically "reflected" in and through the human mind, so that all knowledge of the Infinite Being is metaphorical, not analogical. "Infinite goodness is not goodness but is Infinity. Infinite quantity is not quantity but is Infinity. And so on."[12] Yet we not unfittingly speak of God, metaphorically, as good, immense, etc.

(*8*) In other words, there is no comparative relation between the finite and the Infinite,[13] so that the medieval view of *analogia entis* as a route for discerning God's nature is foreclosed.[14] (*9*) Human minds are likened unto living mirrors that mirror one another and all of reality[15]—a comparison adopted also by Leibniz. (*10*) Mind "performs all [its operations] in order to know itself."[16] Yet the human mind, Nicholas is said to teach, cannot know itself as it is in and of itself, cannot know its own quiddity. Nicholas is here said by various interpreters to take up a theme—viz., self-knowledge—that later became central to figures such as Locke, Berkeley, Hume, and Kant. (*11*) Nicholas maintains that the earth *moves*, although he does not state that it rotates about its own axis or that it revolves about the sun. Still, the fact that he at all ascribes movement to it constitutes a break with the Ptolemaic theory, so that some historians of philosophy have named him "Copernicus before Copernicus."[17] (*12*) Also contributing to that name and also Modern-sounding is his notion of relativity, with respect to his teaching that to someone situated on the earth, the center of the universe seems to be the earth but to anyone located on the sun, the sun would seem to be at the center of the universe.[18] (*13*) Likewise, he holds that there is life on other planets, an idea that has even a familiar contemporary ring. (*14*) And he emphasizes the importance of mathematics as a symbolism for approaching not only the empirical domain but also both the theological and the nontheological metaphysical domains. (*15*) He

---

12. Cusa, *De Visione Dei* 13 (58).

13. This doctrine will be referred to hereafter as the doctrine of *nulla proportio.* Cusa, *De Docta Ignorantia* I, 3 (9) and II, 2 (102).

14. Cassirer, *Individuum und Kosmos in der Philosophie der Renaissance* (Leipzig: Teubner, 1927), p. 11: "However, in these concise and simple opening sentences of the work *De Docta Ignorantia* a decisive turning is now already completed. For now, with a single sharp cut there is severed the cord that previously bound together scholastic theology and scholastic logic: logic in its previous form stopped being an instrument of the speculative doctrine of God."

15. Cusa, *De Filiatione Dei* 3 (65–67).

16. Cusa, *De Mente* 9 (123:7).

17. Joachim Ritter, "Stellung," op. cit. (n. 6 above), p. 112, quoting other interpreters.

18. Cassirer claims a connection here with Cusa's doctrine of learned ignorance: ". . . the thought of 'docta ignorantia' is what first enlightened Cusanus about the relativity of all spatial location and therewith made him the forerunner of the Copernican world-system." *Das Erkenntnisproblem,* op. cit. (n. 9 above), p. 29. Or, again, on p. 32 Cassirer writes: "Cusanus here [i.e., with respect to his interest in empirical details] indicates the *historical turn of Platonism*—a turning which leads to *Kepler* and *Galileo*."

self-consciously raises the issue of the relationship of language to reality, so that some interpreters have viewed him as heralding a nominalistic theory of names, whereas others have taken him to be promoting a realistic theory of names, howbeit with nominalistic overtones. According to such nominalism, names do not name the essence of a thing but are only conventional designators;[19] and the definitions of things are not definitions that accord with their quiddity. (*16*) Cusa is said to prefigure Leibniz when he asserts that the universe is as perfect as it can be. Even though God could have created an infinite number of better and better universes, He created this present universe to be as perfect as was possible for *it* to be.[20] Something similar holds true, Nicholas teaches, of each being within the universe.[21] This harmony is so intrinsic to the universe that unless the earth and each heavenly body were as it is, "it could neither exist nor exist in such a place and with such an order—nor could the universe exist."[22] This doctrine-of-harmony has seemed to some historians of philosophy to foretell of Leibnizianism and even of Hegelian and post-Hegelian Idealism.

Some combination of these sixteen tenets appeared to Cassirer, and to certain others before him or after him, to constitute Nicholas of Cusa as a distinctively Modern philosopher—one who partly broke with the High Medieval Aristotelian Scholasticism of Albertus Magnus and Thomas Aquinas, as well as with the Late Medieval Scholasticism of William of Ockham. Indeed, to Cassirer it seemed that Nicholas's very doctrine of *nulla proportio inter finitum et infinitum* undercut the entire foundation of medieval thought[23] and paved the way for a new cosmology, a new (non-Aristotelian) physics, a new epistemology, and a new theology. Little wonder, then, that Heinrich Rombach labels Cusa "the Aristotle of Modern thought"[24] and that others can exalt him as the equal of Kant and Hegel "in creative, philosophical power, in depth of probing, in breadth and universality of philosophical conception."[25]

II. CUSA'S THEORY OF KNOWLEDGE

It is impossible here to examine the many facets that have contributed to Nicholas's being construed as a "Modern" philosopher. However, let us examine the one facet that Vansteenberghe speaks of as the keystone of Nicholas's philosophy[26] and of which Norbert Herold writes: Some interpreters observe

---

19. Cusa, *De Mente* 2 (58).

20. Cusa, *De Docta Ignorantia* II, 1 (97).

21. Cusa, *De Docta Ignorantia* II, 2 (104) and II, 10 (154).

22. Cusa, *De Docta Ignorantia* II, 13 (178).

23. Cassirer, *Individuum*, op. cit. (n. 14 above), pp. 11–13.

24. Heinrich Rombach, *Substanz, System, Struktur*, op. cit. (n. 5 above), p. 150, note 4: "Es wäre nicht falsch, wurde man Cusanus den Aristotles des neuzeitlichen Denkens nennen."

25. See n. 6 above.

26. Edmond Vansteenberghe, *Le Cardinal*, op. cit. (n. 4 above), p. 279: "The keystone of Nicholas of Cusa's philosophical system—and in this respect Nicholas is quite modern—is his theory of knowledge."

that the reorienting-of-thought that finds its expression in Kant's giving new meaning to the concept of subject, takes its departure, as regards its essential features, from Cusanus. The turning back to one's own subjectivity is generally understood as what is new about, and characteristic of, Modern philosophy, so that Modern philosophy can be described as the history of a progressive self-reflection. Hence, the reckoning of Nicholas of Cusa as belonging to the Modern Age, or to its beginnings, depends on how far one sees as present in him this turning back, which is represented as transcendental reflection.[27]

Let us follow Herold and Vansteenberghe in construing the central issue in assessing Nicholas's Modernity as the issue of Nicholas's theory of knowledge. It is not a question of the Cusan doctrine of learned ignorance or of the doctrine of *nulla proportio*. Rather, the central question is that of how close Nicholas comes to advancing a Kantian-like transcendental idealism, according to which the forms of space and of time, along with certain universal concepts, or categories, are imposed by the mind on an unordered sensory-manifold, so that in this way the "given" becomes synthesized and constructed by the knowing mind, which makes the objects-of-experience conform to it, rather than its conforming to them, when it combines sensory-images of them, compares the images, and abstracts from the images mental concepts.

Interpreters who see Nicholas as a proto-Kantian are prone to call attention to seven supposed features of his thought.

a. *Time.* In *De Ludo Globi* II (93) Nicholas puts into the mouth of Albert, his discussant, the words: "How greatly it pleases me to have understood that if the rational soul were removed, then time (which is the measure of motion) could neither be nor be known, since the rational soul is the measuring-scale of motion, or the numerical-scale of motion! And how greatly it pleases me that things conceptual, insofar as they are conceptual, have this fact from the [rational] soul, which is the creator of things conceptual, even as God is the Creator of things really existent!"[28] Kant, too, interpreters remind us, makes the point that if the knowing subject were removed, then time (and space) would also disappear.[29] Like Kant, Nicholas is said to maintain that our mental conception of time makes possible empirical succession.[30] For he declares: "Since time is the measure of motion, it is the instrument of the measuring soul. Therefore, the form (*ratio*) of the soul does not depend on time, but, rather, the form of the measure-of-motion, which is called time, depends on the rational soul. Therefore, the rational soul is not subject to

27. Norbert Herold, *Menschliche Perspektive und Wahrheit. Zur Deutung der Subjektivität in den philosophischen Schriften des Nikolaus von Kues* (Münster: Aschendorff, 1975), pp. 2–3.

28. "ALBERTUS: Quantum mihi placet intellexisse tempus, quod est mensura motus, sublata rationali anima non posse aut esse aut cognosci, cum sit ratio seu numerus motus; et quod notionalia, ut notionalia sunt, ab anima hoc habent, quae est notionalium creatrix sicut deus essentialium."

29. Immanuel Kant, *Critique of Pure Reason* A 42.

30. Norbert Henke, *Der Abbildbegriff in der Erkenntnislehre des Nikolaus von Kues* (Münster: Aschendorff, 1969), p. 60.

time but exists antecedently to time, just as sight exists antecedently to the eye . . .”[31] Furthermore, Nicholas teaches that “the rational soul enfolds the enfolding-of-time, which is called *the now* or *the present*; for time is found to consist only of the now.”[32] So, according to certain of Cusa's interpreters, time, which consists only of the now, resides in the mind. And in order to differentiate and to measure time, the rational soul likens itself to the now that is within it.[33]

b. *Space*. Likewise, various interpreters construe Cusa as anticipating even Kant's doctrine that space is a transcendental ideal that the mind contributes to the apprehending of the empirically real; that is, they understand Cusa to speak not in Kant's way about space as a form of intuition but to speak in a more general and vague way about space as a product of the understanding (*Verstand*).[34] Cassirer regards even Cusa's conception of mathematical space as pointing in the direction of Modernity:

> The spatial change-of-place of a point is not anything other than the law-like consequence and ordering of its infinitely many states of rest: motus est *ordinata quies seu quietes seriatim ordinatae*. With these words Cusanus anticipated not only the thought but even the *language* of the new mathematics as it would unfold itself with Descartes and Leibniz. [With Cusanus] the marking of co-ordinates, of lines applied in an ordered way, is in [a state of] preparation, while, on the other hand, the universal conception which leads to the foundation of the integral calculus already prevails.[35]

However, the parallels between Cusa and Kant are said to go even further, for a similar interpretation besets Nicholas's doctrine of the categories.

c. *Categories*. In *De Ludo Globi* II (93) Nicholas writes: “The ten categories are enfolded in the rational soul's conceptual power. So too [are enfolded] the five predicables and whatever logical principles and other things are necessary for perfect conceiving (whether they exist independently of the mind or not), since without them no discernment and conception can be perfectly possessed by the

---

31. Cusa, *De Ludo Globi* II (94).
32. Cusa, *De Ludo Globi* II (92).
33. Henke, op. cit. (n 30 above), p. 60. Note also Cassirer's somewhat less extreme judgment (*Individuum*, op. cit., n. 14 above), p. 44: “As origin and creator of the branches of learning, the mind is not only in time, but, much rather, time is in it.” Note also Cassirer's further judgment, on pp. 44–45: “Just as the eye is related to sight, so too time is related to the soul: time is the instrument that the soul uses in order to be able to fulfill its basic function, viz., the function of ordering and classifying what is manifold and what is dispersed in various ways. Just as Cusanus by means of this idealistic conception lays the ground for the Modern mathematical-physical notion-of-time that later appeared with Kepler and Leibniz, so too he therewith simultaneously opened a new view of history and a new appraisal thereof.”
34. Falckenberg, *Geschichte*, op. cit. (n. 8 above), p. 20: “Furthermore, the thought upon which Cusa bases his proof of immortality seems thoroughly modern: viz., the thought that space and time are products of the understanding [*Verstand*] and that, therefore, they cannot harm the mind, which produces them. For the producer stands above, and is more powerful than, his product.”
35. Cassirer, *Das Erkenntnisproblem*, op. cit. (n. 9 above), p. 43.

soul." Likewise, in *De Mente* 8 (108) he speaks of the mind as *making* the predicables: viz., genera, differentiae, species, proprium, and accident.[36] And, according to Henke, "the transcendental starting-point is manifest in Cusa very clearly in his conception that the categories do not exist outside the mind."[37] Henke also claims that, for Cusa, "the unfolding of the categories out of the mind's oneness anticipates, in its point-of-departure, Kant's transcendental deduction, even if the unfolding's systematic development is lacking."[38]

d. *Productive Imagination.* Interpreters such as Henke, in emphasizing Cusa's philosophical kinship with Kant, also emphasize Cusa's ascribing to the mind a spontaneity and a normativeness whereby the mind determines the measure of things. For Nicholas considers mind (*mens*)—whose name derives, he says, from "measuring" ("*mensurare*")[39]—as measuring both itself and other things. In the very first chapter of *De Mente*, he asserts: "mind is that from which derive the boundary and the measurement of every [respective] thing." Moreover, "multitude and magnitude derive from mind."[40] And "from the power of multitude quantities, qualities, and the other categories descend and furnish a knowledge of things."[41] So mind, says Henke on behalf of Cusa, is active through an innate spontaneity,[42] an innate power-of-judgment (*vis iudiciaria*)[43] that sets norms, so that the mind, in receiving sense-impressions, actively structures[44] them in accordance with its own productive (vs. reproductive) imagination[45] and categories. Thus, the mind's concepts are not measured by how well they conform to objects, but, rather, the objects are measured by how closely they conform to the mind's universal concepts[46]—much as a circular object is judged to be more or less circular in conformity to the mind's concept of a circle.[47]

---

36. These are the five predicables, or second-order predicates, according to Porphyry, who substituted "species" for "definition," thus modifying Aristotle's enumeration. "Proprium" indicates a permanent property that is uniquely characterizing (of a species) but that is not an essential property. For example, it is a proprium of human beings to be *capable of laughter.*

37. Henke, op. cit. (n. 30 above), p. 115.

38. Henke, ibid., p. 121.

39. Cusa, *De Mente* 1 (57). Nicholas takes this point from Albertus Magnus.

40. Cusa, *De Mente* 9 (116).

41. Cusa, *De Mente* 10 (128).

42. Henke, op. cit. (n. 30 above), pp. 109–115.

43. Cusa, *De Mente* 4 (77).

44. Henke, op. cit. (n. 30 above), pp. 52, 58–59, 96–97. Cf. Cassirer, *Das Erkenntnisproblem*, op. cit. (n. 9 above), p. 37: "The soul itself sends forth through the intermediary of the peripheral organs decidedly different 'species', which in accordance with the influence of the objects are changed in many ways. Thereby they bring about the changing plurality of the impressions. Thus, in general, not only the nature of the outer-object but also the nature of the receiving medium determines the kind of sense-perception."

45. Henke, ibid., pp. 38, 66–68, 70–71, 76, 86.

46. Henke, ibid., pp. 42, 61, 112.

47. Ekkehard Fräntzki, *Nikolaus von Kues und das Problem der absoluten Subjektivität* (Meisenheim: Hain, 1972), p. 51: "In that Cusa considers the understanding [*Verstand*] or the human mind as that which gives the measure [of a thing], he already completes, in the domain of knowing-as-a-measuring, . . . that 'Copernican Revolution' which Kant was later to conceive of for knowing-in-general."

e. *Analogy with Mathematics*. Interpreters such as Cassirer see an analogy between what Cusa says about mathematical knowledge and what he comes to hold regarding empirical knowledge. For example, our knowledge of what, by definition, a true circle is is superior to the perception of the imperfect circularity of any given thing.[48]

> The "circle in the mind" is the singular pattern and *measure* of the circle that we draw in the sand. Analogously, with respect to each content that presents itself to us we can distinguish a *twofold mode of being*: viz., insofar as we consider it once in all the contingency of its concrete existence and consider it again in the purity and the necessity of its exact concept. The *truth* of things is found first of all in this second kind of conception. Moreover, Cusanus applies the viewpoint of assimilation to this conception. But now it is no longer a matter of the mind's turning itself to, and conforming itself to, the sensible object but is rather a matter of the mind's turning itself to, and conforming itself to, the objects' pure mathematical definition, which represents the objects' entire cognitive content.[49]

f. *Assimilation*. Accordingly, in measuring an object, the mind assimilates itself, that is, likens itself, not to the object itself but to the concept that the mind has formed of the object. Hence, what is known is neither the object itself nor the object in itself but only the object insofar as it appears to the mind through the apparatus of the productive power of imagination, the discriminating power of reason (*ratio*), and the synthesizing power of intellect (*intellectus*). Hence, Nicholas states: "mind has within itself that unto which it looks and in accordance with which it judges about external objects."[50] However, according to this interpretation, the categories and the predicables are not concreated with the mind but are "unfolded" from the mind's innate natural propensity to think in exactly these normative ways.

g. *Mind as Pattern for the Empirical*. Another way of expressing the foregoing points is given by Cassirer when he declares: "Thus, the human intellect is indeed [for Cusanus] an image of the Absolute Being but is also a model and a pattern of all empirical being: mens per se est dei imago et omnia post mentem, non nisi per mentem."[51] This is Cassirer's way of interpreting Nicholas to mean that the mind imposes its forms upon a partly unorganized sensory manifold.

III. CONSEQUENCES OF THE PROTO-KANTIAN INTERPRETATION

Because those who interpret Nicholas of Cusa to be a proto-Kantian cannot dismiss the passages in which he alludes to the human mind as assimilating itself

---

48. Cusa, *De Mente* 7 (103).
49. Cassirer, *Das Erkenntnisproblem*, op. cit. (n. 9 above), pp. 38–39.
50. Cusa, *De Mente* 5 (85).
51. Cassirer, *Das Erkenntnisproblem*, op. cit. (n. 9 above), p. 37. Cusa, *De Mente* 3 (73).

to the object,[52] alludes to truth as an adequation of the mind and the thing,[53] and alludes to the intellect's knowing by way of abstracting an intelligible representation from what is a perceptual likeness,[54] they conclude, necessarily, that Nicholas's theory of knowledge is inconsistent.

> Thus Nicholas attempts to merge the metaphysical viewpoint [according to] which the mind (1) as intermediary between infinite and finite stands above the things or (2) as that which, being directed at infinity, develops its ideas from out of itself (the concept is better than the thing)—to merge it with the empirical viewpoint, which lets mind, which is a thing among other things, find an outer-world that cannot be adequately imaged (the concept is worse than the thing). This attempt could not possibly succeed, because *complicatio* [enfolding] and *similitudo* [likeness], when thought-through consistently, simply exclude each other.[55]

IV. RESOLUTION OF THE PERCEIVED CONTRADICTION

There is, indeed, a tension between one's picturing Cusa as a proto-Kantian and one's picturing him as someone who holds a more Albertistic-Thomistic theory of empirical knowledge, according to which the categories-of-thought correspond to categories-of-being, so that in the course of knowing the world, the human mind must liken itself to an object that is known by way of abstracting *species intelligibiles*, or concepts, from *species sensibiles*, or sensory-images. According to this latter theory, the categories-of-thought are not such that they enable the mind to *transform* the manifold of experience but are such that they enable the mind to *conform itself* to the instantiated categories-of-being, so that the mind can "reflect," or represent, the outer-world realistically, even if with some degree of imprecision and even though qualities such as colors do not characterize the world

---

52. E.g., Cusa, *De Mente* 7 (99:7–8) and 7 (104:6–8). Cusa, *Compendium* 10 (32): "Knowledge occurs by means of a likeness." Cusa, *De Visione Dei* 20 (90): "For a thing is understood by a man only by means of a likeness." Cusa, *De Venatione Sapientiae* 17 (50): "Hence since knowledge is assimilation, the intellect finds all things to be within itself as in a mirror that is alive with an intellectual life." Cusa, *De Mente* 3 (73:1–3): "All things are present in God, but in God they are exemplars of things; all things are present in our mind, but in our mind they are likenesses of things." (When Nicholas states that all things are present in our mind, he means that they are present in the mind's power, they are present in the mind potentially, since the mind has the power to make concepts of whatsoever real things.)

53. E.g., Cusa, *Compendium* 10 (34:20–22). *De Aequalitate* 39:1–2.

54. Cusa, *De Venatione Sapientiae* 36 (107).

55. Falckenberg, *Grundzüge*, op. cit. (n. 3 above), pp. 110–111. See also Henke, op. cit. (n. 30 above), pp. 123–124. Henke concludes, regarding the relationship (in Cusa's theory of knowledge) between the mind's spontaneous-structuring operation and its copying operation that Nicholas (inconsistently) holds onto both of them by situating them next to each other: "Daher bleibt es bei einem Nebeneinander von Schöpferischem und einem Abbilden" (p. 124). Cf. p. 66: "Es zeigt sich erneut der Widerstreit zwischen der Abbildtheorie und einem Apriorismus in der Erkenntnislehre des Nikolaus von Kues."

apart from a perceiver. These two different schools of thought—the Kantian-like and the Thomistic-like—are in and of themselves unreconcilable, so that if a thinker were to subscribe to both of them, he would do so inconsistently. However, Nicholas of Cusa does not, in fact, subscribe to them both, for he does not adopt the theses alleged by the interpreters who desire to link his epistemology with Kant's.

(a) Nicholas does not adopt the view that time is but a form of the human mind—the view that time is unfolded from the mind so as to condition the world. What Nicholas means in *De Ludo Globi* II (93) is not that in the absence of rational souls there would be no time. What he means is that there would be no observer-measurer of succession—succession that would continue on, as would also change and plurality. Since there would still be succession, there would still be time insofar as there would remain change that could be measured and that God Himself could measure. For God would know of the succession and would be able to measure it by means of an infinite number of measuring-scales. When Nicholas says that "the Eternal Mind understands, without successiveness, all things at once and in every manner of understanding,"[56] he means to include (among the things that the Eternal Mind understands) the fact of successiveness; and he means to include (among "every manner of understanding") the way in which the human mind would apprehend successiveness. Accordingly, the Divine Mind, which is without successiveness, understands *the way in which* a human mind would apprehend successiveness but does not apprehend successiveness *in the way in which* a human mind would apprehend it. In Cusa's view time began to exist with the created, changing world, not merely with the creation of the human mind. Time depends upon the human mind only insofar as the human mind sets up measuring-scales for time. It marks off periods into years, months, weeks, days, hours, and so on. But it could just as well adopt a different scale, one whereby a day would last forty-eight hours and an hour would last thirty minutes. Or it could change the definition of a minute's length, should it choose to. Indeed, the soul "is the creator of things conceptual" in just this sense (as well as in the sense of formulating empirical concepts by way of abstracting them). Finally, interpreters have mistranslated one of Nicholas's sentences in *De Ludo Globi* II (94): "Non igitur dependet ratio animae a tempore, sed ratio mensurae motus, quae tempus dicitur ab anima rationali dependet . . ." This sentence does not mean "Therefore, the form (*ratio*) of the soul does not depend on time, but, rather, the form of the measure-of-motion, which is called time, depends on the rational soul," a translation that favors the view that time is a form of the soul and depends on the soul for its existence. Rather, what Nicholas means is better captured by the translation: "Therefore, the soul's measuring-scale (*ratio*) does not depend on time; instead, the scale for the measuring of motion—a measuring that is called time—depends on the rational soul." And, indeed, according to Nicholas, the measuring-scale for time does depend on the rational soul, in the way explained above.

(b) Moreover, Nicholas nowhere teaches that space is a mental form whereby spatial-relations are constructively read into an unorganized sensory-

---

56. Cusa, *De Mente* 11 (133:22–24).

manifold. Most interpreters who take him to propound a doctrine of space that makes it transcendentally ideal do so as a further inference from their conviction that he maintains that time is transcendentally ideal. But in his works there is no passage where he expresses doubt about the existence of space and spatial relations independently of the human mind. Yet he does recognize the relativity of our perception of spatial relations and of motion, as when he cites the illustration of the moving ship (*De Docta Ignorantia* II,12) aboard which one would not perceive himself to be moving if he did not see the shoreline or other such markers.

(c) Furthermore, Nicholas does not regard the twelve categories and the five predicables as present only in the mind. Henke is mistaken when he asserts the opposite.[57] For there is nothing in Cusa's *De Mente* 11 or in his *De Ludo Globi* II (93)—the texts cited by Henke—that denies the reality of extramental categories or that denies the extramental reality of species, genera, accidents, etc. Nonetheless, Nicholas rejects a Platonistic theory of universals.[58] Indeed, he holds a Thomistic "moderate realistic" theory of universals;[59] in accordance with this theory, as he espouses it, differences of genera are not simply marked off normatively by the human mind; instead, they are realities existing independently of the human mind but not independently of God's Mind.[60] Similarly, although Nicholas states that "multitude and magnitude derive from mind,"[61] he means to include the *Divine Mind* when he there speaks of *mind*—a point that is clear from *De Mente* 9 (117).[62] Likewise, when in *De Mente* Nicholas, speaking through the literary figure of the Layman, affirms that "number and all things derive from mind,"[63] the dialogue's Philosopher immediately asks: "Is there, then, no plurality of things apart from our mind's consideration?" To this query the Layman replies: "There is. But it is from the Eternal Mind. Hence, just as with respect to God the plurality of things is from the Divine Mind, so with respect to us the plurality of things is from our mind. For only mind numbers." Thus, another mistake made by those who interpret Cusa as a proto-Kantian is the mistake of failing to see that sometimes (but not always) his use of the word "*mens*" encompasses both "*mens humana*" and "*mens divina*." According to Nicholas as well as according to Thomas, categories characterize the world, even apart from the human mind. For example, things are substances[64] and undergo causal influences apart from the presence or even the existence of any human observer-measurers.

57. See n. 37 above.

58. Cusa, *De Mente* 11 (136). Cf. *De Beryllo* 56.

59. Cusa, *De Docta Ignorantia* II, 6 (126).

60. Cusa, *De Mente* 5 (85:4) and 3 (73:1–3). *De Sapientia* I (23).

61. Cusa, *De Mente* 9 (116:13).

62. Cusa, *De Mente* 9 (117:5–9): "Thus, the measure or end-point of each thing is due to mind. Stones and pieces of wood have a certain measurement—and have end-points—outside our mind; but these [measurements and end-points] are due to the Uncreated Mind, from which all the end-points of things derive."

63. Cusa, *De Mente* 6 (92:25).

64. Nicholas holds that number, multitude, and plurality would cease if the One (viz., God) were removed, not if the rational soul were removed (*De Venatione Sapientiae* 21 [61]). Moreover, he endorses Pseudo-Dionysius's judgment that nothing is corruptible according to its nature and substance (ibid., 22 [66]) And he likewise endorses Pseudo-Dionysius's affirmation that "God

(d) Likewise, Nicholas nowhere distinguishes imagination into a reproductive and a productive power. Ascribing to Nicholas a quasi-Kantian conception of imagination's productive determining of objects is an example of eisegesis. Although Nicholas does maintain that the mind can conceive of a perfect circle, which nowhere exists independently of the mind, he nowhere attributes to the power of imagination, rather than to the power of reason (*ratio*), this idealized abstracting from visual circles. Nor does he anywhere claim that such concepts become patterns and models through which we actually experience objects as perfectly circular, etc. Rather, through these ideal concepts, once we have formed them, we speak of and measure objects in their varying degrees of imperfect circularity. But these concepts do not *constitute* the objects as circular (or as triangular, square, etc.).

(e) We dare not follow Cassirer in drawing an analogy between arithmetical and geometrical concepts, on the one hand, and empirical concepts, on the other hand.[65] For although Nicholas maintains that geometrical figures are idealizations that we form when we are stimulated by the perception of imperfectly shaped figures, nevertheless such a consideration does not apply to empirical concepts. That is to say, although mathematical concepts are declared by Nicholas to be precise concepts, because they are derived from reason alone (*ratio*) when it is properly stimulated by the senses, the opposite is true of empirical concepts: all of them are imprecise, because they are imperfectly abstracted from imperfect sensory-images. And even though the human mind makes numbers, so that in this respect (conceptual) multitude and (conceptual) magnitude can be said to derive from the mind,[66] nevertheless the numbers that proceed from our minds are said by Nicholas to be images of number that proceeds from the Divine Mind,[67] so that conceptual multitude and conceptual magnitude would remain even if there were no human minds; similarly, there would remain the multiple real-objects that have magnitude; for Nicholas states unequivocally that plurality would remain.[68]

(f) Moreover, Nicholas endorses the view that empirical knowledge is the knowledge of objects by way of their likenesses. He does not teach that the mind knows only the likenesses, never the objects themselves. According to Nicholas, as also according to Thomas, the images and the concepts (both of which he calls likenesses)[69] are intentional: that is, they point beyond themselves to the objects of which they are likenesses. And the conceptual likenesses are abstracted from (and, in the case of mathematical concepts, are idealized from) sensory-images, which themselves are more proximate likenesses of the material objects. According to

---

is the Ordering of all ordered things," (ibid., 30 [90]), so that a thing's being ordered and harmonious does not depend upon the knowing human mind. Finally, Nicholas evidences his proximity to Aristotle (and Aquinas) in this late work *De Venatione Sapientiae* (viz., at 21 [61]), just as he also evidenced it in his early work *De Docta Ignorantia* (viz., at I, 18 [53]: "Wherefore Aristotle was right in dividing all things in the world into substance and accident").

65. Note especially the quotations from Cassirer in n. 9 above.
66. Cusa, *De Mente* 9 (116:12–13).
67. Cusa, *De Mente* 6 (88:19–20) and 6 (95:11–13).
68. Cusa, *De Mente* 6 (93:1–3).
69. Cusa, *De Mente* 7 (100) and 8 (108:11–12).

Nicholas the making of *a priori* concepts—such as the concept of oneness or the concept of fairness—is done by the mind on the occasion of the stimulation of the senses. *A priori* concepts, on his view, are not concreated with the soul.[70] What is concreated is a power-of-judgment (*vis iudiciaria*), together with an aptitude (*aptitudo*) for recognizing instances of rudimentary unfairness, etc., and for making a corresponding concept. For example, as soon as the mind hears of and understands the principle "Do unto others as you would have others do unto you," it assents to it, recognizing it as a principle of justice; and out of its own creative spontaneity and its own concreated aptitude, the mind proceeds to make a concept of justice, even though an imprecise (but *a priori*) one.[71] Thus, not all *a priori* knowledge has the precision of *a priori* mathematical knowledge.

(g) Finally, according to Cusa, mind is not a pattern for the empirical. The text alluded to by Cassirer[72] in his claiming the opposite is *De Mente* 3 (73:12–15), which may be compared with *De Mente* 4 (76:1–7).[73] But these passages indicate only that nonhuman animals, vegetables, and minerals are formed in the image of God insofar as they partake of *mind*—by which Nicholas here means not the human mind but mind understood generally as intelligence. For he views all of nature as ordered and purposive, so that in this respect nature is pervaded by intelligible principles, that is, by "mind." Nicholas is not here making a point about the human mind's legislating and prescribing its categories to nature. Cassirer has misapprehended the text's meaning.

V. OUTCOME

So, in final analysis, Nicholas of Cusa is not an anticipator of Kant's theory of knowledge, nor does his theory even come close to resembling Kant's theory. Rather, interpreters such as Cassirer, Falckenberg, Henke, and Josef Koch[74] are

---

70. Cusa, *De Mente* 4 (78:8–11) and 4 (77:20–22).

71. See my discussion of Nicholas's view of *a priori* knowledge, in my *Nicholas of Cusa: Metaphysical Speculations: Volume Two* (Minneapolis: Banning, 2000), pp. 121–139.

72. See n. 51 above.

73. Cusa, *De Mente* 4 (76:1–4): "*Philosophus*: Videtur quod sola mens sit dei imago. *Idiota*: Proprie, ita est, quoniam omnia quae post mentem sunt, non sunt dei imago nisi inquantum in ipsis mens ipsa relucet . . .":"*Philosopher*: It seems that only the mind is an image of God. *Layman*: So it is, properly speaking. For all things [ontologically] subsequent to mind are an image of God only insofar as mind shines forth in them . . ." See further.

Cf. Cusa, *De Venatione Sapientiae* 29 (86): "Granted that our mind is not the origin of things and does not determine their essences (for this [ontological] prerogative belongs to the Divine Mind), it is the origin of its own operations, which it determines; and in its power all things are enfolded conceptually."

74. Josef Koch, *Die Ars coniecturalis*, op. cit. (n. 3 above), pp. 47–48:

With regard to the subsequent effects of the work [*De Coniecturis*] further questions arise. I will mention only two thinkers: Leibniz and Kant. In Leibniz's philosophy, especially in the *Monadology*, we find much that reminds us of *De Coniecturis*: the monad as basic concept, the representation of the universe in each thing in that thing's particular manner, the law of continuous continuity, which Leibniz in his *New Essays on Human Understanding* so strongly emphasizes . . . Much more interesting is the line that can be drawn

guilty of what borders on *Schwärmerei*: they are overeager to detect in Nicholas's genius signs of Modernity. Over and above the fact of this gushing overeagerness is the further fact that Nicholas did not always express himself clearly. Many of his works were written in haste; others of them attest to his being a *speculative*

> from *De Coniecturis* to Kant's *Critique of Pure Reason*, although here it is evident, from the start, that Kant had no knowledge of Cusa. Yet, the theory of knowledge developed in *De Coniecturis* exhibits an astonishing kinship with the *Critique's* moving from [a consideration of] the unordered sensory-impressions all the way to the unknowable God, by way of the understanding and reason. The Cusan concept of enfolding becomes, with Kant, the *a priori*. The distinction between understanding as the faculty of concepts and reason as the faculty of Ideas is found in both [philosophers]. Of course, the concept of Idea changed. Cusa's view (1) that the understanding orders sensory-impressions and conducts them to itself qua higher unity and his view (2) that reason is the unity for the understanding become, with Kant, the theory that knowing is a synthetic function. Finally, both men conceive of the principle of non-contradiction as a pure law of the understanding. To be sure, Kant is far removed from the view of the coincidence of opposites; for, with Kant, it is not the case that a pre-given absolute unity is the highest factor that produces unity; rather, [the highest such factor] is the transcendental apperception.

All of these claims about Cusa's intellectual lineage in Leibniz and Kant are grossly exaggerated by Koch. For example, it is not unqualifiedly true that Cusa's doctrine of *complicatio* (enfolding) becomes Kant's doctrine of the *a priori*. For Cusa speaks of all concepts—including empirical concepts—as enfolded in the mind (*De Mente* 2 [58:11–13] and 3 [72:15–16]). However, empirical concepts are enfolded in the mind only after the mind abstracts them from sensory images. And *a priori* concepts are enfolded in the mind only after the mind forms them, by its innate power-of-judgment and recognition, on the occasion of stimulation from sensory-impressions. Even Koch himself sees that the comparison between Cusa's notion of the difference between *ratio* (Koch's translation: *Verstand*, i.e., *understanding*) and *intellectus* (Koch's translation: *Vernunft*, i.e., *reason*) and Kant's distinction between *Verstand* and *Vernunft* is farfetched, for he hastens to add that the concept of Idea changed. Moreover, for Kant, speculative metaphysics breaks down, because *Vernunft* encounters the antinomies—a view completely foreign to Cusa. Moreover, Cusa does not regard *intellectus* (*Vernunft*) to be an illicit extension of *ratio* (*Verstand*); nor does he speak of *intellectus* as misapplying categories such as *substance* and *cause* directly to reality and apart from the mediation of percepts. On the contrary, Nicholas says that there is nothing in the intellect that was not first in the senses (*De Visione Dei* 24 [107:14–15]) and that the human mind has no concreated concepts (*De Mente* 4 [77]).

Furthermore, Koch sees that Nicholas has no doctrine that resembles Kant's doctrine of the transcendental unity of apperception or no doctrine of the transcendental deduction of the categories, no distinction between the phenomenal self and the noumenal self such that the latter, but not the former, is free. Nor is Koch's comparison between Cusa and Kant regarding the principle of noncontradiction at all significant, given that the framework in which the principle plays a role is totally different for Cusa and for Kant. On Nicholas's view, the fact that nothing can both be and not be the case in the same respect and at the same time holds true whether or not there are any human minds, even though that principle is a prerequisite of all *rational* thinking (vs. *intellectual* thinking) and is assented to by all rational minds as soon as it is heard (*Compendium* 11 [36]). According to Kant, the principle of noncontradiction obtains for *Verstand* but not for *Vernunft*, so that *Vernunft* does not arrive at knowledge, whereas for Nicholas there is no claim that *intellectus* does not attain knowledge. Sometimes Nicholas seems to be suggesting that the principle of noncontradiction does not fully obtain even for the domain of *ratio*. For example, he states that just as in God contradictories coincide (*De Docta Ignorantia* I, 22 [67]), so also opposites can be affirmed (by *ratio*) even of a finite object, with regard to certain given properties: "For since all things are singular, they are both *similar*, because they are singular, and *dissimilar*, because they are singular; [and they are *not similar*, because they are singular], and *not*

philosopher—one who generates many different ideas but one who does not patiently take the time to work out their implications. Just as Nicholas does not anticipate, prefigure, foreshadow, etc., Kant, so also he does not anticipate Copernicus or Spinoza or Leibniz[75] or Berkeley or Hegel. Several of his insufficiently qualified expressions have created a gap between what he means and what he says, so that one must interpret his unclear passages in terms of his other, clearer passages, rather than leaping to spectacular conclusions, as, say, Kurt Flasch has recently done.[76]

Is, then, Nicholas of Cusa the first Modern thinker, the first Modern philosopher, as Cassirer and his followers are wont to proclaim, all the while admitting that

> Nicolaus Cusanus, in the whole of his thought and his writings, is still very firmly rooted in the total outlook of the medieval mind and of medieval life. The cord that linked together the conceptualizations of the centuries [that intervened] between Christianity's content of faith and the theoretical content of the Aristotelian and the Neoplatonic systems was a tight cord—much too tight for it by means of a single stroke to have become severed for a thinker [such as Cusanus,] who stood so firmly and assuredly within that content of faith.[77]

In truth, Nicholas is *not* the first Modern thinker. For his "Modern themes" are not sufficiently developed for him to warrant this title. Moreover, certain of those themes are not really Nicholas's but are ascribed to him out of misunderstanding. In retrospect, Nicholas must be regarded as a transitional figure some of whose ideas (*1*) were *suggestive* of new ways of thinking but (*2*) were not such as to conduct him far enough away from the medieval outlook for him truly to be called a Modern thinker. Spinoza, Kant, and Hegel never mention him, although Kepler, Descartes, and Leibniz do. His ideas were given a boost by the printing of his collected works (Paris, 1514) by Jacques Lefèvre d'Étaples. They were given a further boost by Giordano Bruno's appropriating some of them. Nevertheless, Emerich

---

dissimilar, because they are singular. A corresponding point holds regarding *same* and *different*, *equal* and *unequal*, *singular* and *plural*, *one* and *many*, *even* and *odd*, *concordant* and *discordant*, and the like, although this [claim] seems absurd to the philosophers who adhere—even in theological matters—to the principle that each thing either is or is not [the case]" (*De Venatione Sapientiae* 22 [67]). However, since, here, the respects differ, Nicholas is not really disavowing the principle of noncontradiction for the domain of *ratio*. For example, one thing is similar to another thing because both things belong to the *species* of singular things; but the respect in which the two things are dissimilar is that each differs individually (not *specifically*).

Koch's entire comparison between Cusa and Kant is far too facile and tendentious.

75. See my brief discussion of Cusa and Leibniz on pp. 139–144 of my *Nicholas of Cusa: Metaphysical Speculations: Volume Two*, op. cit. (n. 71 above).

76. Kurt Flasch, *Nikolaus von Kues. Geschichte einer Entwicklung* (Frankfurt am Main: Klostermann, 1998). See my critique of Flasch on pp. 78–121 of my *Nicholas of Cusa: Metaphysical Speculations: Volume Two*, op. cit. (n. 71 above).

77. Cassirer, *Individuum*, op. cit. (n. 14 above), p. 19.

Coreth's judgment remains cogent: "Cusa's direct influence on Modern thought is small; an immediate common-bond is scarcely confirmable."[78]

Nicholas's intellectual influence on his own generation and on subsequent generations remained meager. Nevertheless, as Cassirer discerns, Nicholas commands our respect—though for reasons less pronounced than Cassirer himself gives. Looking back on Cusa, we find in his corpus of writings certain ideas that were developed by his Modern successors, without his having directly influenced most of those successors through his own writings, of which they had scarcely any firsthand knowledge. The proper metaphor for assessing Cusa's historical role is that of *das Türöffnen*: Nicholas opens the door to Modernity—without himself ever crossing over the threshold that distinguishes the Middle Ages from Modernity. Thus, he does not help "legitimate" the Modern Age, to borrow Hans Blumenberg's title.[79] Instead, the reverse is true: the Modern Age helped "legitimate" certain of his ideas (with or without knowing them to be his)—for example, his notion of learned ignorance, his notion of the infinite disproportion between the finite and the infinite, his notion of the coincidence of opposites in God, his notion of the mobility of the earth, and his notion of the earth's being privatively infinite (i.e., its being finite but unbounded). By themselves these five notions—being more in resonance with the Modern Age than with the medieval world—evidence for us that Nicholas's thought is, indeed, an unmistakable major boundary-marker on the pathway to Modernity. That is why these five themes, in particular, have been so intently explored by today's philosophers.[80]

78. Emerich Coreth, p. 15 of his "Nikolaus von Kues, ein Denker an der Zeitwende," pp. 3–16 in Nikolaus Grass, editor, *Cusanus Gedächtnisschrift* (Innsbruck: Universitätsverlag Wagner, 1970).

79. Hans Blumenberg, *Die Legitimität der Neuzeit* (Frankfurt am Main: Suhrkamp, 1966). The 1976 edition was translated by Robert M. Wallace as '*The Legitimacy of the Modern Age*' (Cambridge, MA: MIT Press, 1983). Blumenberg attacks Karl Löwith's notion that the Modern Age was somehow "illegitimate" because it was but a deformed secularization of medieval Christianity's eschatology and doctrine of *Heilsgeschichte*.

See, pp. 50–93 of my *Nicholas of Cusa's Dialectical Mysticism* for my appraisal of Blumenberg's depiction of Cusa.

80. For example, in several of my books see the bibliographies that list articles on Cusa by philosophers, theologians, and historians from many different nations. Also contained in these books are English translations of all of Nicholas's major philosophical and theological works. These treatises, in English translation, are freely available on the webpage: http://www.cla.umn.edu/jhopkins/.

Midwest Studies in Philosophy, XXVI (2002)

Marsilio Ficino on *Significatio*

MICHAEL J. B. ALLEN*

Several scholars, beginning with Allison Coudert,[1] and including Brian Vickers[2] and more recently James Bono,[3] have argued that the Florentine Neoplatonist Marsilio Ficino (1433–1499) espoused a magical view of language, identifying the powers of names with their referents and in general adopting the position that Socrates and his respondent Hermogenes attribute to Cratylus in his eponymous Platonic dialogue.[4] All three have used as their starting point the arresting passages in the *Philebus* Commentary 1.11,12 which speak to the power of divine names.[5] Here I will not address the onomastic issue directly, but rather point out some of the complex metaphysical and theological issues that should give us pause, whether we distinguish, in the Hermogenean, Aristotelian, and modern scientific manner, between an object and its name, holding the latter to be the result of convention, or whether we expound, as Socrates himself does for a while, what

---

* This essay will also appear in the volume *Res et Verba* (Herzog August Biliothek: Wolfenbüttel, Germany) under the title "In principio: Marsilio Ficino on the Life of Text."

1. "Some Theories of a Natural Language from the Renaissance to the Seventeenth Century," in *Magia Naturalis und die Entstehung der modernen Naturwissenschaften: Studia Leibnitiana*, Sonderheft 7 (Wiesbaden, 1978), pp. 56–114 at 65.

2. "Analogy versus Identity: The Rejection of Occult Symbolism, 1580–1680," in *Occult and Scientific Mentalities in the Renaissance*, ed. B. Vickers (Cambridge, 1984), pp. 95–163 at 117–123. See Vickers' important introduction, and cf. Plato's *Theaetetus* 231A, which alerts us to the dangers of analogy.

3. *The Word of God and the Languages of Man: Vol. 1: Ficino to Descartes* (Madison, 1995), chap. 2, p. 31.

4. 383Aff. and 390Dff. Diogenes Laertius, *Lives* 3.6, says Hermogenes was a pupil of Parmenides and a teacher of Plato; see Ficino's *Vita Platonis* and his *Cratylus* epitome (*Opera*, pp. 764.1, 1310).

5. Ed. and trans. M. J. B. Allen (Berkeley and Los Angeles, 1975), pp. 138–145.

S. J. Tambiah perhaps too glibly designated the "more primitive" notion that a real connection exists between the two.[6]

For a Platonist, the intelligible Ideas are the *res verae*. The *res/verba* problem is the problem, therefore, of how to talk about what is, though intelligible, humanly ineffable and hence how to deploy the *via analogica* and the *via negativa*: the consideration both of negative propositions and of symbols, metaphors, figures, the modalities of likeness. Can we have symbols or figures indeed that function as negative propositions, and if so what are their defining characteristics? Conversely, can negative propositions be analogues, predicating figures? And in a Platonic-Plotinian context what would these alternatives look like? Obviously myths of violence or disorder—Uranus' castration, Saturn's devouring of his children, Zeus's rape of various women, the theomachies, the dismemberment of Dionysus, the Titans' rebellion, the flaying of Marsyas, the various incestuous unions among the gods—occur throughout Greek and Roman mythology. The Platonic tradition, influenced doubtless by the ancient allegorizing of Homer's epics, interpreted such myths theologically as figurative presentations of being's origin in the One, its emanation into the many, its conversion and return to the One. As Edgar Wind,[7] Robert Lamberton,[8] and others have justly remarked, the violence or immorality of these myths—antithetical it would seem to the figuring forth of what is truly divine and at first glance impious and blasphemous—functions apotropaically to repel those uninitiated in the mysteries and in their correct interpretation. The more profound or fundamental the mystery, the more apposite or appropriate the violence of the story: the more precious the fruit, the uglier, the more repellent the rind. But violent or unruly myths are not myths about negation per se. Rather, the myths and figures of concealment, of silence, of night, of chaos are those that point to the paradoxes investing the notion of the One as being beyond being and non-being: as being not being and as not being being. For the Neoplatonic One transcends our every notion of a *res*, though the origin, cause, and end of all *res*.

In considering the problematics of Plato's intelligible *res* and thus of his theory of the Ideas, several thorny issues confront us. The *Sophist* postulates six super Ideas, pairs of which are binary and therefore defined by opposition:

---

6. "The Magical Power of Words," *Man*, n.s. 3 (1968), 175–208, as cited in Vickers, pp. 96–97. Vickers, pp. 97–100, appropriately warns us against identifying Plato or for that matter Socrates with the essentialist view. The *Cratylus* is a complex study of language. In general, see Marie-Luce Demonet's brilliant book *Les voix du signe. Nature et origine du langage à la Renaissance (1480–1580)* (Paris, 1992); also M. M. Slaughter, *Universal Language and Scientific Taxonomy in the Seventeenth Century* (Cambridge, 1982); Michel Foucault, *The Order of Things: An Archaeology of the Human Sciences* (London and New York, 1973); Richard Waswo, *Language and Meaning in the Renaissance* (Princeton: Princeton University Press, 1987); Martin Elsky, *Authorizing Words: Speech, Writing, and Print in the English Renaissance* (Ithaca, NY, 1989); and Judith H. Anderson, *Words that Matter: Linguistic Perception in Renaissance English* (Stanford, CA, 1996).

7. *Pagan Mysteries in the Renaissance*, rev. ed. (New York, 1968), pp. 133–138.

8. *Homer the Theologian: Neoplatonist Allegorical Reading and the Growth of the Epic Tradition* (Berkeley and Los Angeles, 1986), pp. 207–208, 245, citing Pseudo-Areopagite, *Celestial Hierarchy* 2.3; and Wind, *Pagan Mysteries*, pp. 12–13, citing the same Areopagitian text but 2.5.

Identity v. Difference, Rest v. Motion, and more contentiously Essence v. Existence.[9] In what sense can these be Platonic *Res*, since they are above or more fundamental than the other Ideas? Moreover, can there be an Idea of an individual or for that matter of individuals, a *Res* of a *res* or of many *res*?[10] Can there be a *Res* of Cosmos and correspondingly of Chaos? Does the language of *res* with which we define chaos and cosmos "participate in" truth, just as the species of sensible things participate in their intelligible Ideas? Is there an Idea or *Res* of language corresponding to the Idea of Truth? Can one *Reify* Truth in this special Platonic sense?

From the onset Platonism has been a dualistic philosophy and has always had a dual sense of language. The philosopher's words serve as midwives to the birth of truth, while the sophist's words deceive and confuse, and poetic texts are not sacred or profane in themselves so much as open to sacred or profane readings, to allegorical and anagogic interpretations. The instability in the sense of the polysemy or plurisignification of words is of course an ancient philosophical and rhetorical topos, but it is central both to the Platonic tradition and to the Pythagorean tradition from whence it grew. Moreover, the notion of words has always been potentially what the Schoolmen called a universal; that is, a paradigm that can configure or reticulate reality in the manner that Panurge's notion of debt or the Elizabethan poet John Davies' notion of the dance configure the entire ordering and functioning of natural, human and social life, of the cosmos itself. Medieval and Renaissance thinkers could toy with the interrelated notions of the night sky as words, nature as words, death as words, man or his body or his soul as texts, nations or institutions or communities as texts, almost anything complex as text. In part this was a game, albeit a serious one; in part it was the consequence of the conviction that analogy and correspondence govern the relationships between the disparate spheres and orders of being; in part it was an acknowledgement of the Hebraic emphasis on the authority of the Bible as the Word that God has given to man as a guide for his salvation; and in part, as we shall see, it spoke to the Greek and Judeo-Christian fascination with the idea of the Divine Logos, the Divine Word, creating and ordering the world as text.

Interestingly, and despite the primacy in the Hebreo-Christian tradition both of a sacred text and of a logos theology and cosmogony, our word *text* began as an image of something quite different. In the majority of the European languages, it is etymologically derived from the Latin verb *texere* meaning to weave or plait, a *textus* being literally something that is woven, a product of the goddess of

---

9. *Sophist* 248A–256D. For Ficino's analysis, see my *Icastes: Marsilio Ficino's Interpretation of Plato's "Sophist"* (Berkeley and Los Angeles, 1989), pp. 49–82.

10. While Plotinus recognized Ideas of individual men in his *Enneads* 5.7 (cf. 4.3.5, 4.5.7, 5.9.12, 6.4.4.34–46, 6.7.12), though whether he consistently held to the doctrine is unclear, Proclus denied there were Ideas of individuals in his *In Parmenidem* 824.13–825.35 (ed. V. Cousin in *Procli philosophi Platonici opera inedita*, Paris, 1864, repr. Frankfurt, 1962, cols. 617–1258). In a letter to Francesco da Diacceto of 11 July 1493 (*Opera*, p. 952.1), Ficino writes that "the Ideas of individuals are not mutually distinguished in the prime Mind absolutely, but relatively," and that this reconciles Plotinus's views with Proclus's.

weaving, Athene.[11] In the *Statesman* 274C ff. Plato refers to the various gifts humankind received in the beginning from the gods, chief among them being the art of forging metals from Hephaestus (preeminently a male activity), and the arts of weaving and sewing from Athene (preeminently a female one).[12] Without these two master sets of skills, humankind could not have survived, given its lack of horns, claws, wings, and other animal attributes. Whereas Hephaestus remained the god of metallurgy and a mythological sport as Aphrodite's cuckolded husband who had netted his wife in the arms of Ares to his own public humiliation, Athene was the virgin goddess of wisdom, born parthenogenetically from the head of her divine father, Zeus. Her attributes were the little owl that sees in darkness, the aegis with the boss of Medusa's Gorgonizing head, the spear of truth, and the helmet of invincibility. In other words, whereas Hephaestus's gift enabled man to dig and wound the earth, and thus to forsake the fabled, irenic ages of gold and silver for the bellicose ages of bronze and iron, metals being used for money and for weapons, Athene's gifts first protected us from the cold without and then supplied garments for the inner self, provided a *textus* for the soul. Every fifth year of the Panathenaea, the annual festival to celebrate the union of Attica under Theseus, a *peplos*, an outer robe or shawl worn by the women of Athens, was woven for the statue of Athene. It was then carried in the triumphal procession to her sanctuary on the Acropolis, commentary as it were, the warp and woof of her intellectual and spiritual life, brought in tribute to the originary deity of Athens, to the virgin of the city's sacred text, to the armed virgin who could vanquish Ares, accoutred though he was in armor forged by Hephaestus.

Later in the *Statesman* 279B–283B, Plato took up the notion of weaving a fabric, a *textus*, in order to use it as an example of the kind of correct divisions and subdivisions which Dialectic as the "capstone of the sciences"[13] must learn to deploy if she is ever to attain an understanding equally of the relationship of genus to subgenus to species and subspecies, and of the role of the Ideas in structuring— in reifying—the world. This image was not selected at random. For the *Statesman* 308D ff. goes on to speak of the "royal science"—the knowledge of the ruler—as being analogous to the art of weaving. Ruling must expertly weave together the citizens of the commonwealth, republic or *polis* as though they were various strands and threads, just as the dialectician must weave our concepts into a web of philosophical arguments, and just as "the central element of the soul itself" must be bound "with a divine cord to which it is akin" (309C1–3).

---

11. See John Scheid and Jesper Svenbro, *The Craft of Zeus: Myths of Weaving and Fabric*, trans. Carol Volk (Cambridge, Mass., 1996); original title *Le métier de Zeus*. Starting with Ernst Robert Curtius' chapter "The Book as Symbol" in his *European Literature in the Latin Middle Ages*, tr. Willard R. Trask (Princeton, 1953), pp. 302–347, the notion of the human heart as text, codex, or book has a rich scholarly history; see, for example, Jesse M. Gellrich, *The Idea of the Book in the Middle Ages: Language Theory, Mythology and Fiction* (Ithaca, NY, 1985); Mary J. Carruthers, *The Book of Memory: A Study of Memory in Medieval Culture* (Cambridge, 1990); and Eric Jager, *The Book of the Heart* (Chicago, 2000).

12. Cf. *Protagoras* 320D ff.

13. This famous phrase occurs in the *Republic* 7.534E; cf. 6.498A.

Weaving thus constitutes one of the images which in the Latin tradition informs and even at times controls, at least in part, our notion of verbal communication, orally and in writing: we weave semantic threads. Interpretation is thus the careful unravelling and reweaving of the weft, a procedure open to the tangles, the sophistry, of misinterpretation, and therefore, *ante rem*, deconstruction. But presiding over the text as woven fabric is the goddess to whom Paris should have awarded the golden apple on the slopes of Mt. Ida, the goddess to whom Socrates and after him all the philosophers in the occidental tradition have been devoted. Athene in effect valorizes the notion of text as she does the notion of weaving, being the *arche*, the origin and cause, of both.

Socrates, however, who entered death with the pious certainty of crossing the threshold into another and immortal life, was deemed impious in his mortal life for creating uncertainty; for urging the youths he loved to question their assumptions about loving, and to become steadfast in their doubting of what unquestioning men upheld too steadfastly. Moreover, Socrates had deliberately distinguished between the oral and the written media, and in particular had eschewed writing and rejected the notion of handing down his wisdom in a written text, however dexterously woven by the skills of Athene. This refusal of writing, ironically, links him with Pythagoras, though in terms of metaphysics it was Plato, one of the sublime creators of text, who was the more deeply and obviously indebted to the Pythagoreans.[14] For Pythagoras reputedly had refused to let his disciples record his *verba*, though in later antiquity his school had compiled a series of cryptic *aurea dicta* that they attributed to him.[15] But in the beginning, and for many subsequent centuries, it was said of the Pythagoreans that they would attribute their wisdom only to what the master had said, using a formula that is still famous as theirs, *autos epha*, in Latin *ipse dixit*. Here the enemy is not the sophist with his sleights of logical hand, but the notion itself of writing down, of weaving a signifying warp and woof of *textus*, even of a tributary *peplos*.

Plato's *Phaedrus* 274C–275B refers to the story of the Egyptian deity Thoth or Theuth, the god of ingenuity and interpretation. Associated with him, Plato writes, following Egyptian lore, are such clever beasts as the sacred ibis (and Ficino adds hunting dogs and apes), along with such taxing games of skill as draughts and dice. He was the inventor, more importantly, of the intellectual "disciplines" of arithmetic, geometry, and astronomy and above all of writing that he introduced

14. Plato's debts to Pythagoras and the Pythagoreans were recognized as early as Aristotle's *Metaphysics* A.6.987a29 ff. But it is everywhere in the Platonic tradition, e.g. Diogenes Laertius, *Lives* 3.6 ff.; Porphyry, *Vita Pythagorae* 53; Iamblichus, *De vita Pythagorica* 27.131, 30.167, 31.199; Proclus, *Theologia Platonica* 1.5; idem, *In Timaeum* 1.1.11–25, 1.2.29 ff., 1.7.19–25; idem, *In Alcibiadem* 317.11 ff., 18 ff. In particular, see Cornelia J. De Vogel, *Pythagoras and Early Pythagoreanism* (Assen, 1966); and for Ficino, Christopher S. Celenza, "Pythagoras in the Renaissance: The Case of Marsilio Ficino," *Renaissance Quarterly* 52.3 (1999), 667–711; also my *Icastes*, pp. 73–81, and *Synoptic Art: Marsilio Ficino on the History of Platonic Interpretation* (Florence, 1998), pp. 43–47.

15. Ficino's translation of these and the Pythagorean *Symbola* conclude his *Opera omnia*, pp. 1978–79; see Paul O. Kristeller, *Supplementum Ficinianum*, 2 vols. (Florence, 1937), I, pp. cxxxviii–cxxxix; II, pp. 98–103. Pico, in his *Heptaplus*, proem 1, claimed on the other hand that Philolaus, not Pythagoras, was the author of the dicta.

as an aid to wisdom and a prop to the memory. In Plato's tale, Theuth journeyed from his own city of Naucratis (Hermopolis) to the Upper Egyptian city of Thebes, where Jupiter was worshipped as Ammon, and revealed his inventions to the king of Thebes, Thamus. The king then questioned whether the arts should be passed on to the Egyptian people in general, and proceeded "to condemn what he thought were the bad points and to praise what he thought were the good," marshalling for each art "a number of views for and against." But when it came to writing, Thamus distinguished between the skill necessary to invent an art and the judgement needed to determine the measure of profit or harm it would bring to those exercising it. He then rejected writing on two counts: first, that it would implant forgetfulness in men's souls so that they would cease to rely on, and thus to exercise, their memory; and second, that in the process of telling men about many things without truly educating them, Theuth would enable them to seem to know much, while for the most part they knew little or nothing. As sophists filled, not with wisdom, but with the conceit of wisdom, they would become a burden to their fellows (275AB); or, in Ficino's gloss, "writing would make them careless about finding things out (*ad inventionem negligentiores*), inasmuch as they would rely on the acuity (*ingenium*) of their superiors and not on their own."[16] Note that these twin reservations are keyed to writing alone, and thus to the perceived disjunction between words and things, and not apparently to Theuth's inventions of the three mathematical skills. Presumably mathematics is not subject to the same kind of callow, self-deceiving appropriation.

In interpreting this passage, Ficino clearly thinks of Plato as having ethical or theological truths in mind. For he notes in his *In Phaedrum* 3.3 that "In the manner of the Pythagoreans, Socrates affirms that the contemplation and transmission of truth occurs in souls rather than in books"; and then in summa 50 that Socrates prefers "living discourse which has been impressed by the teacher on the pupil's soul and not merely written down in texts (*scriptis*),"[17] the implication being that *scripta* in themselves are dead or at least moribund discourses. Picturesquely, in summa 49, Ficino had borrowed a gloss from the ancient *Phaedrus* commentator, Hermias, in referring to the appropriateness of the ibis as Mercury's bird: "it advances with uniform steps and gives birth to eggs from its throat, just as Mercury too produces his offspring from the mouth."[18] However, in the *Phaedrus* 275DE, Plato has Socrates compare writing to painting on the grounds that both merely seem to be alive; and yet, "if you question them, they maintain a most majestic silence . . . ; written words seem to talk to you as if they were intelligent, but if you ask them anything about what they say, from a desire to be instructed, they go on telling you just the same thing for ever. And once a thing is put in writing, the composition, whatever it may be, drifts all over the place, getting into the hands not only of those who understand it, but equally of those who have no business with

16. *In Philebum* 1.29.273 (ed. Allen); cf. Ficino's *In Phaedrum*, s. 49 (ed. Allen as *Marsilio Ficino and the Phaedran Charioteer*, Berkeley and Los Angeles, 1981, p. 211).

17. Ed. cit., pp. 81, 83, 211. Jacques Derrida has an influential reading of this text in "Plato's Pharmacy, I," in his *Dissemination*, tr. Barbara Johnson (Chicago, 1981), pp. 65–119.

18. Ed. cit., p. 211; cf. Hermias, *In Phaedrum*, p. 254 (ed. Couvreur).

it; it doesn't know how to address the right people, and not address the wrong. And when it is ill-treated and unfairly abused it always needs its parent to come to its help." Writing here is inanimate, is "dead discourse" as Phaedrus himself puts it, or, at the most, is in suspended animation as "a kind of image" of "living speech" (276A).

Although it might contribute to, or enhance, the lethal effects of Lethe, the river that souls sipped upon their entry into the world and that made them dead to their former lives, Plato's story does not say that Thamus absolutely commanded Theuth to forego his invention. "Socrates does not forbid us to write," Ficino notes circumspectly, "but he does condemn our putting any confidence in writing,"[19] our assuming that "instruction (*disciplina*) will be clear and secure (*perspicua tutaque*) in writing."[20] After all, in Ficino's Neoplatonic interpretation, Theuth had been inspired to discover the *disciplinae* by the high god Ammon, that is, by Jupiter himself. Socrates is advocating in effect a compromise. To entrust doctrine to writing is to cultivate what Socrates calls at 276B "a garden of Adonis," that is, a garden cultivated for the sake of flowers, not fruit or produce.[21] Cultivating such a garden may be "the most beautiful of all pastimes or games"—an act of remembering and of memorializing the dead Adonis in the flower named after him, with "flowers" being the favored trope for the ornaments of rhetoric. Nevertheless, he who entrusts the various disciplines, "the lawful offspring of understanding," to the minds of people worthy to receive them, "to souls worthy of the mystery," is practicing "a better agriculture, one that is serious and worthy of the highest study." Interestingly, Ficino refuses to take up Socrates' analogies between written words and first a painting and then a helpless child constantly in need of protective parents.

Ficino's interpretation of Theuthian writing involves, I would argue, a radical departure from Socrates' little story. For he was drawn to identifying Theuth variously, even simultaneously with the Greek god Mercury, with one of his principal daimon followers, and with the sage Hermes Trismegistus, the founder of Egyptian religion and cult and one of the first, if not the first, of the *prisci theologi* culminating in Plato.[22] Hence, his invention of Egyptian writing, writes Ficino in his *In Philebum* 1.29, was the invention of hieroglyphs (we recall we are in the era of Horapollo not of Champollion). Here the shapes (*figurae*) of animals and plants

---

19. *In Phaedrum*, s. 50 (ed. cit., p. 211).

20. Ibid., s. 52 (ed. cit., p. 213).

21. Ibid., s. 51 (ed. cit., p. 213). Anna de Pace writes, "Durante le Adonie, feste in onore di Adone, il primo giorno le donne esponevano vasi con piante che presto germogliano e sfioriscono (appunto i "giardini di Adone"), i quali nell'ultimo giorno venivano buttati giù dai tetti. Il rito fa riferimento al giovinetto morto nel fiore dell'età, e l'espressione "giardini di Adone" è assunta a significare "ciò che è effimero" (private communication). See Marcel Detienne, *The Gardens of Adonis: Spices in Greek Mythology*, tr. from the French by Janet Lloyd, with an introd. by J.-P. Vernant (repr. Princeton, 1989), with all the relevant literary and iconographical sources.

22. For Hermes as the second in the line of six ancient theologians, see my *Synoptic Art*, pp. 24–31, with further refs.; also Eugenio Garin, *Il ritorno dei filosofi antichi* (Naples, 1983), pp. 67–77. In his *In Phaedrum*, s. 49, however, Ficino allegorizes Theuth both as a human being and as a demon, and Thamus both as an actual king and as the planetary god Mercury or even as the Intellect Mercury in the realm of pure Mind; see my *Platonism*, pp. 36–38.

were used as the principal characters, the object of such sacred writing being to keep the mysteries contained therein concealed from the vulgar gaze.[23] Thus, Theuth's invention was a clever one. Rather than inventing something "for the Egyptians in general," as Plato's myth had implied, Theuth had invented something for the elite, or more properly for those few *purgati* worthy of initiation into the secrets of the ancient theology.

Plato's myth and its Renaissance interpretation point to an ambivalence, an anxiety even, about the authority and role of words separated from the mind of the teacher, taken as it were out of his mouth. Truth for the many resides in words only when they are orally transmitted from teacher to disciple and are part of an ethical and axiological exchange, the transmission of knowledge in the context of ultimate values, a living discourse of the heart. As Ficino notes in his commentary on Romans 1.1–2 and 2.14, Christ had never written his teachings down in any tablet or book, but only in the hearts and souls of those who believed in him.[24] For ambivalence about humankind's encounter with writing and thus with text is associated not only with the loss of innocence, the departure from the golden age of the pastoral, and the taking up of the survival gifts of Hephaestus and Athene, but also, more provocatively, with the onset of transcription, with the entombing of sacred mysteries in the living grave of astromorphological and zoomorphological hieroglyphs. There, moribund, they await the coming of the theologian-interpreter who will resurrect and revivify them, lead them out of the mouth of their long silence.

Ostensibly a myth cautioning against the dangers of inventing writing at all, the Theuth story became for Ficino the story of the beginning specifically of sacred writing, of the protective veiling, the warping and woofing, the textualization of truths, and thus of words requiring not only meditation by the righteous but careful interpretation and transmission by a line of hermeneut-masters. Writing was now, in the time-worn simile, like a winter seed, apparently dead and buried in the earth, but awaiting a vernal, blossoming life when watered and tended by a learned gardener and illumined by the Sun of Truth. Although Thamus had warned against the giving of writing to the people, Jupiter Ammon, writes Ficino, had been the inspiration behind Theuth's invention; and Plato seems in fact to be identifying Thamus with Ammon or identifying him with an attribute of Ammon, witness the reference at 275C to "Ammon's utterance."[25]

In any event we have a typically sacred paradox wherein the deity both attracts and repels, excites and forbids, gives and takes away his *verba* and his *res*. The originary written text, like the *peplos* woven with the art given us by Athene,

---

23. Ed. cit., p. 271. For the separate problem of Zoroaster's priority as the inventor of writing using the stars and constellations as the "letters," see my *Synoptic Art*, pp. 35–36.

24. *In epistolas divi Pauli* 1, 15 (*Opera*, pp. 428, 450).

25. Indeed, the text is often emended here to identify Thamus with Ammon. Ficino, however, retained the reading *theon* while acknowledging that Socrates's words seem "to include Thamus and Ammon under the same person," even though "reason in its precision" should continue to distinguish between Jupiter in himself and the mercurial qualities in Jupiter which we can refer to as Thamus. Again see the subtle Proclus inspired analysis in his *In Phaedrum*, s. 49 (ed. cit., p. 209).

emerges as a malediction and a blessing. From the old Pythagorean viewpoint, it is words in a grave, but from the Ficinian it is a secluded garden memorializing the untimely rape of Aphrodite's untimely consort, a virgin's floral defloration, a March's transformation into cruellest April. Here the written text must be viewed *sub mysterio mortis*, as possessing a complementary if another kind of life than the life of *oratio*, of living speech. No longer seen as a shroud however beautiful, however cunningly woven, testifying to the loss of true converse between soul and soul, and thus to a sacrificial love, it has become a seminary, a hortulan source of metamorphosis and the new life.

Hence, instead of recalling the Pythagorean and Socratic tradition with its distrust of all but living instruction, it recalls the Bible as the *scriptum sacrum*, the book with supreme sovereignty over the *verba sacra* of the individual prophets in the post Mosaic line of prophets. For the Scriptures are the living word testifying to the Living Word made flesh, the incarnate Christ. He is the master text of creation, the alpha and omega of God's scheme for man's redemption, the eternal *Verbum* who entered once and forever into flesh and time, into the *res* and *verba* of man's post-lapsarian worlds and alphabets. The three Abrahamic religions attribute a unique authority to certain words as the instrument of God and as the way to eternal life. If man's words by analogy are participating commentary, his life for a Christian is a participation in the text of the Lord and the Redeemer, is the life of that living text, that *oratio eterna*.

In Plotinian metaphysics also "life" has a special status. Given the famous passage in the *Sophist* on the need for life to be present in the realm of intelligible being,[26] Plotinus emphasizes the presence of "life" among the intelligibles in the well-known triad of being-life-intellect,[27] and upholds the notion that as souls we participate in the "life" of Truth and therefore in absolute Life, in the Idea of Life, the middle term in the definition of absolute Being. Indeed, for a Neoplatonist, the distinction between *res* and *verbum* slips out of focus when we cross the conceptual threshold signalled by life. For it is "life" that haunts the metaphysics of the Platonists not the Aristotelians; and it is "life" that also preoccupies Christian theology, given Christ's central exhortation that we search for a more full, a more perfect life, a life of the spirit liberated from the death of the sensible world, of the shadowy earthly *res* which are alien to the luminous *verbum* of heaven. For man and his thoughts participate, however variously, in eternal Life; and by virtue of that participation are endowed with the eternal being of the Word. This Johannine-Pauline theology, fraught as it is with paradoxes, and grafted onto the transcendental, idealist metaphysics of Platonism, inevitably problematizes the traditional schemata of logical analysis by contraries, including, as we have seen, analysis by way of any *res/verba* distinction, which is anchored in a materialist

---

26. *Sophist* 248E–249D; for Ficino's analysis, see my *Icastes*, pp. 56–59.

27. See R. T. Wallis, *Neoplatonism* (London, 1972), pp. 67, 106, 124–25, 130, 132–33, 149–51; the important article by P. Hadot, "Etre, vie, pensée chez Plotin et avant Plotin," in *Entretiens Hardt V: Les sources de Plotin* (Vandoeuvres-Geneva, 1960), pp. 107–57; and A. H. Armstrong, "Eternity, Life and Movement in Plotinus' Accounts of *Nous*," in *Le Néoplatonisme* (Paris, 1971), pp. 67–76.

metaphysics, and specifically in Aristotelian form-matter theory. At first glance it might even appear to elevate *verba* over *res*. But Platonism is a philosophy that seeks to recover and to validate as the supreme realities the *res exemplares* as the *verba exemplaria*: to point to their union in the transcendental realm as the ideal objects, the Ideas, and to recover an understanding of their unitary relationship. At the core of Plotinian epistemology and semiotics is the mystery of how either *res* or *verbum* can signify at all in the realm of what is "here" in the illusory non-signifying world, when "there" *res* is *verbum*, and to participate in *res* there is to participate in *verbum*. It is one of Ficino's contributions that he explored not only, or not particularly, the essentialist notions of language, and preeminently of names, advanced for a while in the *Cratylus*, but these broader notions of signification and participation—what we might call the existentialist dimensions of language as the product of *actus*, and of *verba* consequently as the actuation, the unfolding life of enfolded thoughts.

Insofar as both *verba* and *res* "here" participate in the Ideas "there," both are *umbrae* here.[28] For inferior or impaired participation—itself a problematic notion—results in false, umbratile opinions and not in the truth or in the true opinions that result from full, from luminous participation, however defined. Correspondingly, the more impaired the participation and the more material the condition of the *res*, the darker they are as *umbrae*. Does this mean that our perception of such *umbrae* must always depend on vagrant opinions, or can we know the constant truth about the inconstant shadows? And what then about the sophists, the jugglers with their adumbrations, the conjurors of shadow play and manipulation, the protean shape-changers in the murk of opinions? Must we suppose their words brazen when compared to the golden words of a Pythagoras? And do love (*eros*) and strife (*eris*) contend in the oceanic realm of *verba* as they do perpetually in the realm of *res*? Can we effect a compromise between a Heraclitian and a Democritean view of *verba*? Can we imagine ourselves in our own linguistic *Aeneid*: on a journey, that is, which leads us away from the Troy of *verba voluptuosa* to the Carthage of *verba activa* and thence to the Italy of *verba contemplativa*; from the *verba mortua mundi*—for Virgil's Christian allegorists like Landino—to the *verba viva Dei vivi*?[29] And does this correspond to a journey from non *res* to *res* to *Res*, from nothingness, matter and penumbral illusion to the sunlight of the Ideas? And finally in this run of speculative questions, what is a non *verbum* and what could be the relationship between a non *res* and a non *verbum*? Any answer must turn to consider the antithesis of life, the death that lurks in the valley of shadows, in the sophist's opinions. For dead words and dead things, *verba*

28. The fundamental passage is of course the *Republic*'s allegory of the cave in books 6 and 7; and the most famous shadow image is the Twenty-Third Psalm's "the valley of the shadow of death." Renaissance shadow lore, skiagraphy and skialogy, is a science, but not merely a science, since it has far reaching imaginative and religious associations.

29. See Cristoforo Landino's *Disputationes Camaldulenses* (c. 1472), books 3 and 4, where one of the principal characters, Alberti, interprets the *Aeneid* 1–6 Platonically: that is, as the story of the hero's arrival at contemplative perfection (Italy), having conquered the vices and passions of the *vita voluptuosa* (Troy) and the *vita activa* (Carthage). See, too, Landino's commentary on the *Aeneid*.

mortua atque res mortuae, are scattered like Ezekiel's dry bones in the world as a dead text, a dead *verbum*, a dead *res* awaiting resurrection and rebirth as a living word inseminated and animated by the living Word. Indeed, no correspondence can truly exist between the dead *res* and the dead *verbum*, since death is itself defined by non-correspondence, by the death of the love that binds *verbum* to *res*, like to like. All becomes *eris* instead of *eros*, eristic instead of truth.

By contrast, the paradigmatic life, Life itself, consists in the union of *res* and *verbum* in the words of the seven Sacraments, above all in the words of the eucharistic transubstantiation of the wafer and the wine into salvific body and blood in Christianity's central act of hylomorphic magic. It is here clearly that the *res/verba* problem becomes a sacred mystery, given the analogy of the body with the word (Eph 4:4, 5:30 etc.)—of Christ the perfect *res* with the Son who is the perfect *verbum*—and the theological extensions of the Platonic notion of participation in an Idea. For we participate in Christ and therefore in the Word that Simeon in St. Luke's Gospel cradled in his arms in the temple as he acknowledged that at last the promise, the prophetic word had been fulfilled. He had lived to see the coming of the light to lighten the Gentiles, the child "set for the fall and the rising again of many in Israel; and for a sign which shall be spoken against" (2:34),[30] the Messiah that was and is the Idea of Man.[31]

Prophecy, however, raises complex issues. For the *verba* of an authentic prophet forewarn us of coming events and in certain permitted instances enable us to avoid the dangers attending them, to avoid *res adversas*, or rather to fashion for ourselves a new set of *res prosperae et secundae*. The *verba* determine, in a propitious context (*pro re*), their own *res* to our advantage (*nostra re*) and can be said to have priority and therefore control over them.[32]

In the opening remarks of a letter written to Giovanni Cavalcanti late in his career—it is dated 12 December 1494—Ficino attempts to justify the existence of evil as ultimately serving the cause of good: "Divine providence wished our souls while on earth to be troubled by hosts of violent perturbations."[33] He cites Plato's *De scientia* (i.e., the famous passage in the *Theaetetus* 176A) to the effect that it is impossible to root out evils entirely, "for evil is necessary always for someone as a contrary to the good." The disease makes us appreciate the doctor more, the storm-whipped seas make the sailors admire the prudence of the pilot. At this point Ficino introduces an opportunistic variation on this ethical Stoicism, arguing

---

30. See Ficino's sermon on Simeon's "Nunc dimittis," *Opera*, pp. 491.2–492.

31. The question as to whether Plato had postulated an Idea of Man is complicated. Parmenides asks, in his eponymous dialogue, "And is there a form (*eidos*) of man, apart from ourselves and all other men like us—a form of man as something by itself?" (130C). Socrates admits to being puzzled about this. Proclus takes up this passage in his commentary and establishes a chain of different levels of man descending from the Idea of Man (812.10–16). Thus, Ficino accepts the Idea of Man as *idea hominis*, as *homo idealis*, and as *ipsa humanitatis idea* in his own *In Parmenidem* 5, 21 (*Opera*, pp. 1139–40, 1144.2), while Pico also refers to the "Idea of men" as being in the hypostasis Mind in his *Commento* 1.6. There are obvious Christological implications.

32. It is difficult not to pun on the many idioms in Latin employing *res* and thus to *res*tore their weft!

33. *Opera*, pp. 961.2–963.

that "sometimes" God allows us by way of prophecy to avoid imminent evils; witness, he says, the following notices in Plato. In the *Symposium* [201D] "the priestess" Diotima warned the Athenians about a pending plague ten years before it actually struck, and thus enabled them to sacrifice to the gods in order to delay its onset. Likewise in the *Phaedrus* [244A–E] Plato refers to the sibyl and others endowed with prophecy: "the ancients testify that prophecy is the result of a divine fury and is much more eminent than human conjecture and human prudence . . . the divine fury comes to certain among the gentiles from elsewhere, enabling them to predict future events." When they then turn to prayers and divine worship, to expiations and propitiations, they are rendered safe and whole. In the *Laws* 1 [642DE], Epimenides of Crete, inspired by an oracle of God, warned the Athenians ten years before the outbreak of the Persian war that the Persians would not come for ten more years and that they would depart with their goal unaccomplished. Such prophecies are frequently greeted with incredulity, continues Ficino recalling the *Phaedrus* 244A–D, inasmuch as the authentic prophet, "who has rightly used divine meditations and always is imbued with the perfect mysteries," is thought a fool by the many who suppose him a man beside himself (*extra se positus*). For even though he is inspired by God and clings to the divine (*divino inhaerens*), he is cut off from ordinary human studies and enthusiasms, from ordinary *res*. Prophecy so far exceeds human wisdom that we must account the prophetic mind a mind on fire with divine love, as rapt in amatory ecstasy. A fury and an alienation, prophecy excels not only human wisdom but all other divine gifts: hence St. Paul's words "but greater than these is charity" (I. Cor. 13:13). For the words of the prophet ultimately proceed from love, from the heat and the light of the Holy Spirit.

Prophets are sent by God, Ficino advises Cavalcanti, as the instruments of His pity (*misericordia*); for we are fated to encounter adversities because of the sin of our first parents. However, as Plato too had declared [in the *Phaedrus* 244E], "God, moved as it were with pity, often inspires the prophets to predict coming afflictions, so that warned by the prophets we might seek refuge in prayers and sacred expiations. When we perform these as we should, often we escape the scourges unharmed." Interestingly, Ficino instances Savonarola as having been "elected divinely" to perform this monitory task; a view of the Dominican he was to abandon a few years later when he vehemently turned against the friar after his execution. God's pity for mankind thus validates the prophet's words if they excite the hearer to prayer, to repentance and to acts of propitiatory devotion, expiation and purification. This is a special instance of the divinizing of *verba* and it follows naturally on the notion of the creative divine Word—"And God said, 'let there be light' " (Genesis 1.3). But in this theological context it does point to the verbalizing of *res* and to the reifying of *verba*, that is, to the interweaving of the Logos in the unfolding of the things of nature, the *res creatae* that depend for their very existence on the divine utterance. This is more than the magic of names or spells. It looks to a logology, that is, to an understanding, however partial or contingent, of an eternal creating and sustaining *verbum* that gives life to all *res*, and lends its authority to the lesser *verba* of the divinely inspired prophet in his amatory ecstasy—*verba* that sustain our lives of action and contemplation alike, inspire us to more fervent devotion, and shield us providentially from the blows of an inimical Fate and from the endless vicissitudes of Fortune.

A theological vision of this kind blurs to the point of nullifying the distinctions we customarily draw between *res* and *verba*. For it is predicated on a radically different conceptual set, which at first glance seems to invert the values with which we normally invest the two terms, but which is ultimately transvaluative. In Ficino's exalted conception, the philosopher is a lover of the divine Word, which is the word of the Father consubstantial with the Word, His Son, and whose Holy Spirit in its procession breathes the Word into the hearts and souls of all who truly worship and believe in Him, endowing them with the fullness of life. Man in this salvation context is thus a newly living text, a living *verbum*, a prayerful *oratio*. But since a living word is by definition prophetic, anticipating the world to come, anticipating the *dies novissimi* and the *res publica nova* of the heavenly Jerusalem, the paradigmatic man is the prophet prophesying the heavenly life to come. Such a man shares in the primacy of the word over things, being created in the likeness and image of the Logos, the Word that was with God and was God in the *in principio* that opens both Genesis and the Gospel of St. John.

But the theology of *verba* and of non *verba* is itself trinitarian. In commenting on a section in the memorable opening chapter of the Areopagite's *De mystica theologia* (*De Trinitate*), Ficino writes:

> It seems the mind uses three steps to approach God. Firstly it uses as many words as possible, secondly as few as possible, thirdly none. It uses as many as possible when the mind affirms and denies equally—using the same words but in a different sense—whatever men may adduce concerning God. It uses as few words as possible when it refers to [just the causal] relationships, that is, refers things to God as to [their] principle, end, and mean, and as their conserving, converting, and perfecting [cause]. But the mind uses no words at all, when it neither refers things to God or the reverse by way of analogy, nor denies anything [of Him], nor restores to Him by way as it were of affirmation anything that depends on Him. But when it is about to affirm something of God Himself, the mind breaks off inner speech and falls immediately silent, lest by setting a limit to God by affirming this something, it might insolently predicate the finite of Him instead of the infinite. Therefore, if speech is remitted to the degree that the love of the Good is intensified, immediately (as we said) in this blazing fire in the presence of the Good the light of the Good blazes forth; and it exhales the Good.[34]

---

34. *Opera*, p. 1018.3: "Mens circa Deum tres (ut videtur) gradus agit. In primo verbis quam plurimis utitur; in secundo paucis; in tertio nullis. Quam plurimis, inquam, ubi quotcunque occurrunt de Deo affirmat pariter atque negat, paribus quidem verbis, sed ratione diversa. Paucis autem ubi relationibus utitur, referendo videlicet res ad Deum tanquam ad principium, finem, medium, conservantem, convertentem, perficientem. Nullis [*Op.* Nullus] autem quando nec ulterius res ad Deum refert neque vicissim, neque negat quicquam, neque dependens a Deo aliquid Deo quodammodo reddit affirmans. Sed ipsum Deum mox affirmatura, sermonem rumpit intimum siletque protinus, ne affirmando finiens insolenter reportet pro infinito finitum. Tunc igitur si quatenus sermo remittitur eatenus intenditur amor boni, statim (ut diximus) in hoc ipso incendio penes bonum effulget boni lumen spiratque bonum."

Here Ficino defines three ways of approaching God, three deployments of *verba*, though the third is their suspension, the abandonment of all discourse, whether affirmative, negative or analogical. As the love of God intensifies and the soul enters the presence of the Good, the Harpocratean act of falling silent sets a term to the first breaking into words, which signalled both The Creation and our creation by the divine Word. Here the sense of an ending, the sense of having allowed discourse to run its course, of allowing speech to return to silence, signals the return of the many to the One, of the radiating lines back to the center's point, of the emanated splendor back to its luminous source. It also signals the perfection of *verba* and of *res* equally, or rather a perfection that transcends the distinction. The Bible has been opened, read, and closed, returned to the beginning, ended in its genesis: its sacred Word falls silent in the fullness, in the fulfilment of meaning, all *res* perfected both in its opening "beryshit" and in its final "Amen," in the alpha and omega, the aleph and tav of the divine alphabet.

Correspondingly, we, too, are the three conditions of utterance. We are subject to the manifold fullness of predication, negation, and analogy. We are stark simplicity. We are silence. We are the many *res* and *verba* rejoicing in the mystery of the Holy Spirit. We are the single *res* and *verbum* gathered into the mystery of the Son. We are eventually the non *res* and the non *verba* annihilated in the mystery of the Father. In such paradoxical formulations the quotidian alternatives of *res* and *verbum*, non *res* and non *verbum*, quasi *res* and quasi *verbum*, fall away as we approach the Janus-guarded gateway into the supramundane realm. We pass through to the time before the semantic fall and the expulsion from meaning, before the curse of Babel's many tongues with their *verba*'s diverse significations of many *res*. And we pass beyond Eden with its naming to the pre-Adamic, genesis moment when darkness was upon the face of the deep and the earth was without form and void. For then even the language of God was "in the beginning," in the sublime obscurity of the divine night from which proceeded the creation command "fiat lux." In this deep but dazzling darkness—to quote Henry Vaughan's most famous poem—temporal man was not yet a lucid, an enlightened text, neither an affirmation nor a negation, not a figure, not a thread, neither a living word nor a dead thing, even as the Idea of Man had already been begotten eternally of the Father full of grace and truth.

Midwest Studies in Philosophy, XXVI (2002)

Pomponazzi: Moral Virtue in a Deterministic Universe

JOHN L. TRELOAR

Prometheus vere est philosophus qui, dum vult scire Dei archana, perpetuis curis et cogitationibus reditur.

—Pietro Pomponazzi, *De fato*, III, 7[1]

I. INTRODUCTION

Few philosophical problems have so vexed thinkers as the inherent conflict in the assertion that we exist in a universe with preestablished laws and the claim that human beings have a capacity for free choice. The present study will examine the unity of Pietro Pomponazzi's work *Libri quinque de fato, de libero arbitrio, et de praedestinatione.*[2] One should note several things about the complete title of this work. First, Pomponazzi's title seems to indicate that he sees the problems of fate, free choice, and predestination as related problems. And it has often been the case that commentators on this work have emphasized one aspect of this work to the detriment of the coherence of Pomponazzi's work; or they have come to the work with a kind of a priori prejudice that Pomponazzi rejects certain ways of doing philosophy because of some of his rhetoric. Thus, despite the fact that the title indi-

---

1. "Prometheus, truly, is the philosopher who, because he wishes to know the secrets of the gods is gnawed perpetually by cares and worries," quoted in Martin L. Pine, *Pietro Pomponazzi: Radical Philosopher of the Renaissance* (Padua, Editrice Antnore, 1986), 343.

2. Pietro Pomponazzi, *Libri quinque de fato, de libero arbitrio, et de praedestinatione.* Richard LeMay, Ed. (Lucca: In Aedibus Thesauri Mundi, n.d.). As the critical edition of *De fato*, all future references to this work will indicate the book, chapter, and page of this edition (e.g. Bk. 3, ch. 12, 287). In accord with the somewhat deceptive English language custom, we will refer to the work simply as *De fato*, but the reader must keep in mind that this is simply shorthand for the longer title.

cates that there are five books, the work as a whole is a unity detailing a complex of problems. Secondly, it has become customary to refer to this work simply as *De fato*, and as such has probably led commentators to think of Pomponazzi's view as simply deterministic. Third, the word *fato* can be translated into English simply as fate, but what Pomponazzi really indicates is a universe of set physical laws. This is a naturalistic version of fate, not some preordained determination by a god or goddess. Pomponazzi deals with the latter preordination in Books 4 and 5, where he treats the problem of predestination.

Pomponazzi grapples with the conflict of human freedom, moral choice, and moral development in a law-governed universe. In this struggle, he serves as something of a bridge between medieval thought and early modern philosophy. He knows classical authors such as Cicero and Plutarch well; carries on disputation with Aquinas, Scotus, and Ockham; respects the work of his contemporaries such as Pico and Ficino; and is conscious that the Ptolemaic view of a law-governed universe must change radically in order to preserve scientific thought.[3] Situated on the cusp of the modern age, Pomponazzi gives his readers a snapshot of one age collapsing and a new era ascending.[4] He is the philosopher who wants to know the secrets of God and who is cursed with perpetual cares and worries.

The problem of freedom and determinism facing Pomponazzi may best be summarized by examining the place that moral virtue has to play in his thought. It is quite common for commentators to claim that Pomponazzi has a Stoic view of virtue.[5] This picture is essentially deterministic in nature. That is, the gods set up

3. Pomponazzi and Copernicus (1473–1543) are almost contemporaries of each other. Pomponazzi was already teaching at the University of Padua when Copernicus became a student of canon law at that university. Even though Copernicus developed his own theory of a heliocentric universe only later in his life after he returned to Poland, the difficulties inherent in the Aristotelianism of Padua, as we shall see, could have given him some impetus for a new theory of the physical universe.

4. John Herman Randall, Jr. in *The School of Padua and the Emergence of Modern Science* (Padua: Editrice Antenore, 1961) summarizes Pomponazzi's place in the change of world views saying, "[Pomponazzi is] Called 'the last Scholastic and the first man of the Enlightenment' he did indeed partake of the natures of both; of the latter in his fiery zeal against theologians, his scorn for all comfortable and compromising modernism in religion and his sober vision of the natural destiny of man; of the former in his refusal to leave the bounds of the Aristotelian tradition, in his meticulous use of the medieval method of refutation, and in his painstaking attention to the reasons by which a position was defended. But as the Renaissance man between the two, he shared the spirit of his age: its concentration on man and his destiny, its view of human nature as the link between heaven and earth, its reverence for the authority of the ancients—for him, Aristotle—and despite all theory, its Stoic temper of mind" (87–9).

5. See Paul Oskar Kristellar, "Pomponazzi, Pietro," *Encyclopedia of Philosophy*, Paul Edwards, Ed. (New York: The Macmillan Co. and The Free Press, 1967), V. 6 who reads the *De fato* as Pomponazzi's Stoic stand against Alexander of Aphrodisias. After quoting a long passage from chapter 14 of *De Immortalitate Animae* concerning reward and punishment, Randall says, "This striking statement and defense of a thoroughly naturalistic ethics owes more to the Stoics than to Aristotle" (99). But see *De fato*, Book 2, ch. 7, 190–221, where Pomponazzi in typical medieval style lays out all the benefits and deficits of the Stoic position. He concludes Book 2 by saying, "Sic itaque mihi videtur esse dicendum in sequendo Stoicorum opinionem, quamquam ut in sequenti libri dicam, haec opinio sit falsa, quoniam religioni Christianae quae verissima est

the universe according to predetermined laws and the virtuous person accepts one's lot in life simply by living according to these laws. Pomponazzi, however, also follows Aristotle's theory of virtue as a good habit developed by consistent good choices made in freedom. Because of his devotion to Aristotle, then, Pomponazzi must sort out the meaning of virtue as having both Stoic and Aristotelian elements—a combination seeming to have many inherent and perhaps irreconcilable contradictions.

One way to begin a study of *De fato* is by considering varying opinions scholars have had concerning this work. One can ask whether one can find an essential unity concerning Pomponazzi's position that depends on a knowledge of the whole work. Martin L. Pine in *Pietro Pomponazzi: Radical Philosopher of the Renaissance* has great sensitivity to this issue; by examining all five books of *De fato*, he manifests the movement of Pomponazzi's thought in detail. Since Pine implies rather than explicitly states that the book is a unity, it is important to make this fact more explicit. If one is to understand fully Pomponazzi's position concerning a determined universe and freedom of the human being, one must follow his conversation with his predecessors and his contemporaries as he structures it in the whole work. The study that follows intends to point out the movement of this conversation—why he finds a position unsatisfactory, what the subsequent position has to offer that the earlier one did not, and finally how Pomponazzi resolves the problem.

The focus of this present discussion will use as its ground Pomponazzi's work *Libri quinque de fato, de libero arbitrio, et de praedestinatione.*[6] As Pine points out, he deals in Book 1 with the determined universe of the Stoics, producing an argument that looks as if he denies human freedom simply on the basis of the natural laws of a determined universe set in motion by God. Books 4 and 5 give his arguments against the theologians and his own final resolution of the problem of God's predestination of human beings with the doctrine of human freedom. Finally, Book 3 provides a kind of bridge between the early parts of the work and the latter books. In Book 3 he tries to solve the problem concerning the human will's capacity to manipulate things and events to its own end.

The following discussion aimed at verifying the essential unity of *De fato* has three sections that will prove, by looking at the issue of moral virtue, especially justice, that Pomponazzi is neither simply Stoic in his ethics nor Aristotelian, nor Christian. Rather, he attempts to provide a synthesis of these three positions that respects not only the philosophic implications of moral virtue, but also the theo-

---

adversatur" (221). Two things must be noted about this quotation. Many have thought that statements similar to this are simply Pomponazzi's manner of covering his tracks because of his troubles with the Church of Rome. If one, however, takes the statement at face value, one sees that Pomponazzi's later struggle with providence and its treatments by his medieval predecessors has much more meaning. It also explains his own solution much more adequately.

6. In this scheme I follow Pine's general treatment of the division of *De fato* in the last chapter of his *Radical Philosopher of the Renaissance* (275–343). One should note, however, that Pine's scheme generally ignores Book 2. In that book Pomponazzi treats six positions that thinkers have taken with respect to the matter of fate. Three of these positions are especially germane to the topic of this paper—those of Cicero, Aristotle, and the Stoics.

logical ones and all of this in a law-governed universe. Section II provides a meta-physical discussion of three possible positions confronting Pomponazzi concerning the possibility of a coherent doctrine of virtue. Section III looks at Pomponazzi's respect for the human will and his attempt to reconcile a predestining God with human virtue. Finally, Section IV indicates some ways in which Pomponazzi anticipates later positions in his struggle with fate, predestination, and free choice.

II. POMPONAZZI'S METAPHYSICAL PROBLEMS

Among the commentators, one finds three possible interpretations of Pomponazzi's doctrine of moral virtue. First, it is basically Stoic, for he takes the notion of virtue as living according to the general and enduring order of the universe. If one accomplishes this, one will arrive at a state of *eudaimonia*, a state of happiness resembling that of the gods. The four Stoic cardinal virtues of intelligence, bravery, justice, and self-control are the methods one uses to achieve such a goal. Secondly, one can look at Pomponazzi's system as Aristotelian. In such a system there is a conflict between the ordered universe of Aristotle's *Physics* and his doctrine of virtue as set forth in the *Ethics*, which demands free choice and the capacity to form habits. Moral virtue for Aristotle is a state of character having as its abiding disposition the choice of the mean.[7] Aristotle lists the cardinal moral virtues as courage, temperance, and justice. Finally, one could take the position that Pomponazzi makes appropriate adjustments to the Christian doctrine of virtue to bring it into line with the philosophical theory of virtue. In its crudest form, the Christian doctrine of virtue can be interpreted in such a way that virtuous acts lead to reward after this life and vicious acts lead to punishment. Pomponazzi himself has little patience with people who act virtuously only for the sake of a future reward. Even though the Christian position relies on many sources for its doctrine of virtue, the standard virtues for Christian theology seem to be courage, temperance, justice, and prudence (sometimes called practical wisdom). Even from this brief summary, one can notice that justice appears in each of the lists as a cardinal or chief virtue. Therefore, justice can serve as an exemplar for each of the three interpretative positions of Pomponazzi's resolution of the matter of human freedom in a deterministic universe.

Is Pomponazzi's notion of moral virtue Stoic? Martin L. Pine gives the best account of this position when he shows that Pomponazzi has a naturalistic interpretation concerning the workings of the universe. According to the ancient Stoics who view the universe almost entirely in light of efficient causality, there is little room for human free choice. God (or the Unmoved Mover) has set the universe in motion according to fixed laws of action, interaction, and reaction. Everything that happens in the universe happens according to these laws without exception. Such a position, then, obviously denies any possibility for human freedom of choice or hope that one can change the outcome of the universe. The virtuous person acknowledges this real situation and manifests virtue by simply accepting the way

---

7. See Aristotle, *Nichomachean Ethics*, Bk 2, chs. 5–7, 1105ᵇ, 19–1108ᵇ, 10.

the universe runs. Pine points out that any supposed autonomy is simply an illusion.[8] Humanity, in the Stoic view, is simply governed by the divine ordering of causes, hence the first portion of the title of original title of *Libri quinque de fato, de libero arbitrio, et de praedestinatione*—Fate. Two things should be noted. First, in Book 1 Pomponazzi gives an entirely naturalist interpretation of fate. Second, if he is, indeed, simply Stoic in his ethics, he will have to explain moral virtue without a genuine notion of human choice. Critics and scholars who stop with Book 1 and/or Book 2 naturally claim that his position concerning moral virtue is basically Stoic.

The second position commentators have taken with respect to the overall plan concerning *De fato* has to do with the fact that Pomponazzi himself cannot make any philosophical sense of a moral universe if his position is basically a Renaissance version of Stoicism. Aristotle, then, is the favored philosophic candidate who provides some hope for resolving the issue. Pomponazzi is well aware of the fact that Aristotle's physical theory is largely deterministic in nature. He is also cognizant that Aristotle's ethical theory of moral virtue as a habitual disposition requires genuine human freedom for its initial development. The question can be put as a dilemma resident in the very thought of Aristotle himself—Is the universe determined? If that is the case, then, what sense does it make to talk of moral virtue as freely chosen and developed by repeated actions of the person? Pine points out that Pomponazzi is not entirely successful in his attempt to resolve these Aristotelian issues that also bear the inherent contradictions of the Stoic position.[9]

Depending on whether one reads Aristotle from an Averroist view point or from the perspective of Alexander of Aphrodisias, one will come to different conclusions concerning Aristotle's own text. Alexander seems to emphasize the ethical context. The strict Averroist interpretation stresses the physics and metaphysics of causality. Consequently, the notion of free choice would have little place in Aristotle despite the existence of Aristotle's ethics.[10] In a word, the Aristotelian theory

8. Pine, *Radical Philosopher of the Renaissance*, 277.

9. The matter of Pomponazzi's relationship to Aristotle is quite complex. He certainly esteems the basic Aristotelian texts, but there are also various commentaries on Aristotle that he neither approves nor disapproves. Sometimes it is difficult to determine whether he objects to the commentator's interpretation of Aristotle or to the text of Aristotle itself. For example, at the end of Book 1 of *De fato* (12–18), Pomponazzi provides a long discussion of the position of Alexander of Aphrodisias showing the weaknesses of Alexander's position. In effect, he shows his approval of Averroes' more naturalistic interpretation of Aristotle. But one can ask where the Aristotelian text is in all of this discussion. For an argument concerning Pomponazzi's relationship to Latin Averroism, see Armand Maurer, "Between Reason and Faith: Siger of Brabant and Pomponazzi on the Magic Arts," *Medieval Studies*, 18, 1–18.

10. Ibid. Maurer shows in his analysis of Siger of Brabant, probably the most famous of the Parisian Averroists, that all extraordinary physical events often called magic and miracles can be explained by purely natural but perhaps unknown causes. Such happenings never result simply from words spoken by a human being or from the free choice of a human. Whether Pomponazzi actually read Siger's texts is not clear, but he was conscious of Siger's positions, for as Pine points out, "Within the limits of reason alone, Siger denied the existence of demons, ascribed miracles to the influence of the Intelligences, and held for the cyclical return of all events . . . All these positions would later be explicitly accepted by Pomponazzi." *Radical Philosopher of the Renaissance*, 269–70.

of the governance of the Intelligences supercedes human free choice. There is, however, the interpretation of Aristotle that emphasizes the notion of free choice provided by Alexander of Aphrodisias. Alexander has three points that indicate the existence of free choice. First, one cannot deny the occurrence of chance and accidental events. Secondly, everyone has personal experience of deliberation concerning a problem. Third, there are evil results, such as the inability to assign responsibility for a human action, that flow from accepting determinism as a philosophical position.[11] Some read Pomponazzi's treatment of fate as a response to Alexander's attack on the Stoic doctrine and the source of Pomponazzi's own discussion of contingency.[12] Pine concludes that the situation of Pomponazzi's Aristotelianism is very much up in the air. Following the Paduan school, Pomponazzi certainly esteems Averroes and his follower Siger of Brabant. A superficial reading of the early parts of *De fato* looks like Pomponazzi simply rejects any talk of freedom, but as Pine points out and as a quick look at the chapter headings of Book 3 indicates the work actually tries to reconcile the conflicting trends surrounding a deterministic universe and free choice. "Unable to resolve the contradiction, Pomponazzi decides that Cicero was right when he said that Aristotle was a determinist who believed in fate. The position taken in the *Ethics*, Pomponazzi concludes, is intended to hide determinism out of fear of persecution. So Aristotle said one thing and believed another."[13]

If one feels some discontinuity between Pomponazzi's dealing with Aristotle's theory of the physical universe and his theory of human free choice in ethics, then the issues become even more complex as Pomponazzi attempts to deal with the position of Christian faith and moral virtue. Pomponazzi is often read as having no use for the speculations of theologians, but the issues are considerably more complex than that.

Here the major question is whether God as provident and omnipotent predestines the human soul. In the Christian view the concept of 'predestination' performs the same function as the purely deterministic universe in the naturalist's version of a fully set universe. The problem may be phrased in a question—How can God know everything and still leave room for the human to make choices that are either just or unjust? It would seem that if one holds the doctrine of an omniscient God, then one cannot at the same time hold that humans can genuinely work out their own salvation by means of the free choices they make. Now there are many texts in which Pomponazzi simply seems to dismiss out of hand all theological discussion such as the issue of predestination and free choice. The particular targets of these attacks often seem to be the Thomists of his own time and place.[14] But, he also has problems

11. See Pine, *Radical Philosopher of the Renaissance*, 287–90.

12. Ibid., 286–7.

13. Ibid., 339–40.

14. See my earlier article "Pomponazzi's Critique of Thomas Aquinas's Argument for the Immortality of the Soul, *The Thomist*, Vol. LIV (July 1990), 463–70 in which I try to point out that much of what Pomponazzi objects to in the arguments for the immortality of the soul are not genuinely teaching of Thomas Aquinas but rather of later Thomists who have slipped into a dualistic interpretation of the relationship of body and soul.

with both Scotus's and Ockham's solutions to the issue of predestination and free choice.[15]

Having rejected the Thomist, Scotist, and Ockhamist positions on predestination and free choice, Pomponazzi presents his own solution in Book V of *De fato*. Pine mentions that this explanation sharply separates Pomponazzi from his medieval predecessors.[16] Pomponazzi holds that as long as one attempts to answer questions concerning the relationship of determinism and free will in the context of Christian theology by beginning with divine omnipotence, one will never reach an adequate solution to those questions. Instead, he suggests that divine omnipotence must itself have some limitation. This limitation, however, can never come from outside the divinity itself, since that would make divine omnipotence itself a contradictory notion. Pomponazzi then suggests that God willingly limits or masks both omniscience and omnipotence in order truly to grant the human being freedom of choice.[17]

Given the fact that he expends this kind of effort on the issues of predestination and free choice, both of which have philosophical and theological implications, one can hardly say that Pomponazzi simply dismisses theological problems. Nor can one say that he is cynical or flippant about these issues. Rather, he sees the philosophical problems from the Stoic and Aristotelian views as concern for a doctrine that respects universal causation or predestination in the universe. But both Stoicism and Aristotelianism must still bear in mind the claim that human beings have free choice within that universe. These are issues needing reconciliation. From the fact that he provides his own solution for the issue of God's omnipotence and free will, one can see not only his desire for natural explanation but also his sensitivity to theological issues. Is there some way that Pomponazzi can provide a "theological" solution that at the same time respects the canons of natural reason?

III. A PREDESTINING GOD AND HUMAN VIRTUE

The discussion in the previous section attempted to show that Pomponazzi himself saw the metaphysical difficulties of a Stoic or Aristotelian determined universe when one comes to a discussion of human virtue. Even though neither Stoicism nor Aristotelianism speaks of an omnipotent God, in both systems one finds an

---

15. Pine in *Radical Philosopher of the Renaissance* gives a good summary of both Scotus's and Ockham's approaches to the issue of predestination and free choice (325–30).

16. Ibid., 330.

17. From a theological rather than a philosophical perspective, one finds strong foundations for the notion that God can and does mask the omnipotence inherent in the divinity. In the concept of the Incarnation, the Word of God became fully human, as the *Letter to the Hebrews* states referring to Christ as the high priest, ". . . we do not have a high priest who is unable to sympathize with our weaknesses, but one who has similarly been tested in every way" (New American Bible, 4:15). Theologians have spent much time speculating on the self-knowledge of Jesus as the Word of God and as Savior of the World. Since, as has been shown earlier in this article, Pomponazzi sharply separates philosophical and theological speculation, he cannot directly refer to this revelation of divine masking in *De fato*.

apparent contradiction of a totally determined universe standing side by side with a doctrine of human virtue as something under the control of and important to the human person. The most notable of the so-called cardinal virtues in this difficult situation is justice. Since justice is not only individual but also social in nature, one can speak of this virtue either in the context of a good person or more generally in the context of a good society. That is, to be just is in the power of both the individual and the community. It also seems that justice both individual and societal must necessarily be directly under the control of human free choice.

Does it make any meaningful sense for the Stoic to speak of justice? Pomponazzi seems to pick up some of his views of Stoicism from Cicero's treatment of that system, for in *De Officiis* Cicero gives a firm exposition of the Stoic position regarding justice. In Book I Cicero says, ". . . it is the chief province of justice to restrain man from doing evil to his neighbor, unless provoked by evil; moreover, it teaches us to use common property for the common good and only our personal possessions for our own."[18] But, contrary to the more generally held Stoic position of a determined universe, this description of justice certainly implies a measure of free choice. In the slightly later work, however, Cicero seems less committed to the Stoic position. In *De Natura Deorum* the conversation between the Epicurean, Cotta, and the Stoic, Balbus, manifests that Cicero is reexamining the Stoic position. In Book II of this work, Balbus lays out the Stoic doctrine of a completely ordered universe. In his response to Balbus, Cotta in Book III answers each point raised by Balbus and finally concludes by citing the basic contradiction of Stoicism in rather poetic terms. ". . . do you hold . . . it is righteous for us to bind ourselves with vows? But vows . . . are made by each man for himself, it follows, then, that the divine intelligence is attentive to the aspirations of everyone of us."[19] In other words, how can one have both individual choice and gods who look out for the welfare of the whole universe? Since one's aspirations may contradict the general welfare of the universe, either the gods cannot be provident or aspirations are mere illusions and dreams.[20] The end, then, of Cicero's *De Natura Deorum* seems to reject the Stoic position.[21]

If it is true that Pomponazzi takes some of the Stoic argument from Cicero, then this classical Latin source itself shows the contradictions embedded in Stoicism when one tries to reconcile metaphysics and ethics. Pomponazzi is certainly aware of these problems and therefore sees in his examination of the six positions of Book 2 of *De fato* that Stoicism in and of itself cannot solve the problem of providence and human freedom. Either one must reject providence as the Epicurean Cotta does or one must accept providence to the detriment of a free choice to act justly. As Pine demonstrates, all of the teeth have been taken

18. *De Officiis*, Book 1, 7, 473 in Marcus Tullius Cicero, *Brutus, On the Nature of the Gods, On Divination, On Duties*, Hubert M. Poteat, trans. (Chicago: University of Chicago Press, 1950). Further references to this volume of Cicero's treatises will simply indicate the individual work with its appropriate references. In all cases the final number is the page number of this edition.
19. *De Natura Deorum*, Book 3, 39, 332.
20. Ibid.
21. Cf. *De fato*, I, 12, 76 for some of Pomponazzi's comments on Cicero and his summary of Augustine's views on the Ciceronian position.

from justice if one follows the Stoic position.[22] It is therefore entirely facile to say that Pomponazzi has basically a Stoic position with respect to determinism and free choice.

People often think of Pomponazzi as one of the chief advocates of Aristotelianism at the University of Padua. Even though there is no doubt about his devotion to Aristotle, Pomponazzi finds something of the same conflict in Aristotle that he found in the Stoic position concerning the matter of justice and an ordered universe. The *Physics* of Aristotle certainly speak of a completely determined universe. The *Nichomachean Ethics*, however, has a long exposition of the virtue of justice that necessitates free choice on the part of the human agent. In Book 1 of *De fato*, Pomponazzi wrestles with the Aristotelian quandary, especially the version of Alexander of Aphrodisias and by implication Averroes, concerning the problem of determinism and free choice.[23] Aristotle himself says, "The necessary in nature, . . . is plainly what we call by the name matter, and the changes in it."[24] But, ". . . none of the moral virtues arises in us by nature; for nothing that exists by nature can form a habit contrary to its nature."[25] Justice would be such a habit, and as such seems contrary to nature as Aristotle understands it.

It appears, when one looks to the specific moral virtue of justice, that Aristotle is not in a much more satisfactory position than the Stoics. For, according to Aristotle, ". . . all men mean by justice that kind of state of character which makes people disposed to do what is just and makes them act justly and wish for what is unjust; and similarly by injustice that state which makes them act unjustly and wish

22. "It is crucial to understand that the great variety in human dispositions is just another instance of the variety in nature. This variety is necessary to the coherence of nature, no less than the diversity of animal, plant, and mineral natures. There can be no question here of justice or injustice, cruelty or kindness for two reasons: the universe requires this diversity for its order and the fixed compositions of all natures indicates again that God cannot alter the smallest aspect of the universal order. Thus within human history the oppression of the poor by the rich, the weak by the aggressor, the martyr by the tyrant is all a necessary working out of human dispositions. A balance is nevertheless achieved by historical cycles which will insure that one day the oppressed will be oppressors, the strong weak and so on. Each will get his turn." *Radical Philosopher of the Renaissance*, 299. While Pine's summary of Pomponazzi's position is certainly accurate, the actual text is much more poetic and graphic than Pine indicates. For example, Pomponazzi says, "[some act] as innocent animals some as serpents, some as tigers, some as lions, some as wolves" etc. to indicate the variety in human existence. This also indicates a difference in choice of activity that seems to be against a purely deterministic universe. Pine refers to *De fato*, 2, 7, 196, 193–5, and 205.

23. Cf. *De fato*, Book 1, in which Pomponazzi does an extended commentary on the position of Alexander of Aphrodisias. From the location and extent of this commentary, one might be tempted to surmise that Alexander is Pomponazzi's chief opponent in the matter of a deterministic universe. Even though there are many aspects of Alexander's thought that Pomponazzi dislikes, this early discussion sets up the context for the treatment of the other ancient positions in Book 2.

24. Aristotle, *Physics*, Bk 2, ch. 9, 200ᵃ, 30–1.

25. Aristotle, *Nichomachean Ethics*, Bk 2, ch. 1, 1103ᵃ, 20. See also 26–35, where Aristotle says, ". . . of all the things that come to us by nature we first acquire the potentiality and later exhibit the activity . . . ; but the virtues we get by first exercising them, as also happens in the case of the arts as well. Fort the things we have to learn before we can do them, we learn by doing them."

for what is unjust." The implication here is that one has the power within oneself to determine one's own actions through free choice.[26] How can one speak of the voluntary in a completely ordered universe as described in the *Physics?* It would seem that Pomponazzi's mentor, Aristotle, does not give him much guidance to resolve the issue of determinism and freedom in virtuous action.

The only appropriate solution, then, appears to be some kind of theological resolution. This forces Pomponazzi to look toward the Thomists, Scotus, and Ockham. Commentators have generally thought that Pomponazzi is excessively harsh on theologians because they step outside of the purely rational and use revelation as a crutch to solve every difficult problem. One can also read Pomponazzi, however, not merely as a sarcastic critic of the theological position, but rather as an advocate of rigorous honest inquiry. This inquiry can indeed be theological but must meet all the canons of any rational discourse. His critique of the Thomist, Scotist, and Ockhamist positions shows how they are unsatisfactory for a variety of reasons as a solution to the determinism and justice issue. Pomponazzi then turns to his own more theological perspective. The previous section of this article gave a brief summary of the manner in which Pomponazzi attempts from a rational theological point of view to solve the issue of a providential God who knows every human action. Since Pomponazzi does not directly appeal to revelation as a source for his position, one can look at his solution as an attempt to obey the canons of reason alone.

One must examine God's own free decision to block providential knowledge and the effects this would have on the virtue of justice. Since God is omnipotent, God certainly has the power of free choice to block his knowledge of the future for the sake of freedom among humans. If it is, indeed, the case that God blocks foreknowledge of human choices in order to avoid completely determining the universe, then one can posit a capacity in the human being for free choice.[27] When one acts justly, then, one can really be that just person who knows how to give everyone what belongs to him/her as advocated by the Stoics. One can also be Aristotle's just person who acts voluntarily to be lawful and fair. Finally, one can be the Christian who works out justice not simply for the sake of reward at the end of life, but rather because justice is the virtue par excellence of genuine freedom both individually and socially. Hence, Pomponazzi's willingness to acknowledge a God who blocks His own providential oversight in favor of free choice solves the problem of justice as a moral virtue. Such a virtue would be a disposition formed by repeated choices in accord with Aristotle's more general theory of all virtues as habits.

---

26. Ibid., Bk 5, ch. 1, 1129^a, 7–10.

27. Pine in the final pages of the chapter called "Man and Freedom" gives an extensive analysis and critique of Pomponazzi's attempt to reconcile providence and free will. Pine points out a number of aspects of the argument, but two of the most noteworthy are that, first, Pomponazzi changes the emphasis from his medieval predecessors on God's omnipotence to the freedom of the human being, and, second, Pomponazzi's final solution is the only way he could rescue human freedom from the deterministic universe without an appeal to revelation. Pine concludes that Pomponazzi is only partially successful in his attempt to solve the problem of freedom and determinism. Cf. 315–43.

IV. CONCLUSION

In this final section, it is important to look at the renewed interpretation of Pomponazzi as first proposed by Pine in *Pietro Pomponazzi: Radical Philosopher of the Renaissance*. Pine noticed in a way that others have not that Pomponazzi was really dealing with a related set of problems in the *De fato*. This set of problems surrounding a deterministic universe and moral virtue seems to resist solution on merely philosophical grounds. This is especially galling to Pomponazzi, since he clearly wants to avoid theological intrusion into the realm of philosophical speculation. In the end, however, he must turn to his medieval predecessors who are both philosophers and theologians for help in solving the problem. He develops a rather sophisticated rational theology that ultimately helps him out as he struggles with freedom and determinism. In this sense, he follows Cicero who ultimately concludes with Cotta's statement in *De Natura Deorum*, "I have now said substantially what I had to say on the matter of the gods, my words were spoken, not to destroy belief but to give you some conception of the obscurity of the whole matter and of the difficulties involved in any attempt to explain it."[28] Pomponazzi's Renaissance and early modern background, however, allow him to see that the emphasis in the problem of freedom and determinism should be on human freedom rather than on divine omnipotence. In this he differs from Aquinas, Scotus, and Ockham. Finally, there is an astute sensitivity on the part of Pomponazzi to the development and cultivation of moral virtue, most notably justice, as the quintessential virtue of freedom. In this he firmly rejects the Stoic position of some kind of general justice that provides equality throughout the career of the universe rather than as a result of human action. He is firmly in the Aristotelian camp that advocates justice as a virtue that can be learned and acted upon by the free human being.

While others have readily admitted that Pomponazzi's *De fato* is extremely difficult, it is helpful to see the text as a unified disputative discussion in the medieval tradition of looking at all possible positions of a problem prior to providing a solution unique to the author. For this reason, it is necessary when one reads the work not to stop at Book 1 and Book 2 and claim that he is basically Stoic in his ethics. Neither is he basically Aristotelian, Thomist, Scotist, or Ockhamist. His final solution shows how God cooperates with humans to assure their freedom to develop virtuous ways of acting. In this sense, he is modern and seems to step outside of the medieval approach by providing a new look at natural theology and human freedom.

Pomponazzi does not provide a final solution to the problems of *De fato*. Indeed, the discussion will become even more intense during the Enlightenment. It is possible at this point only briefly to indicate one philosopher who had equal struggles with the issues of determinism and free will. In Immanuel Kant one sees the progress of his thought as an attempt to move from a view of the necessity embedded in a doctrine of physical causality as advanced in *Critique of Pure Reason* to reestablishing freedom as a special kind of intelligible causality under

---

28. Bk 3, 39, 332.

the control of the rational agent in *Critique of Practical Reason*. Like Pomponazzi, Kant felt a need to allow both philosophy and science to stand on their own. When one comes to morality, however, one must introduce elements that do not easily coincide with deterministic science. Pomponazzi was not yet separated completely from his medieval predecessors and only moves slightly from his predecessors' theological solutions for the problem. Kant, because of Hume's devastating critique of the idea of cause and his Enlightenment background, provides a solution that is totally philosophical. But the stage for such a solution was not yet set during Pomponazzi's generation.

A comparison of Kant and Pomponazzi on these matters would be an especially enlightening exercise for three reasons. First, both philosophers esteem but also see the limitations of Stoic ethics. Secondly, both deal with theories of a deterministic universe and the relationship of that universe to free choice. Third, both are situated in particularly fertile times concerning the place of reason in human affairs. In Pomponazzi's case, the Scientific Revolution is just beginning; in Kant's case, that revolution has become the accepted intellectual way of talking about our physical universe and our relationship to that world.

Contemporary readers of Pomponazzi can find in this author the seeds, even if unsuccessful, of a truly modern approach to the issues of determinism, freedom, and moral virtue. At the beginning of the "Epilogue or Peroration" of the *De fato*, Pomponazzi says that he has given six opinions concerning the issues of determinism and freedom. He points out that each of these positions has its good points but that each position also has its overwhelming difficulties. He cautions that if one considers each of these arguments and is moved only by reason, then none of the positions is totally satisfactory.[29] It would appear that one must either allow God's omnipotence in some form and do away with moral virtue, or that in preserving moral virtue one must limit God's omnipotence, which prima facie appears to be contradictory. In the issue of freedom and determinism Pomponazzi has shown what it means to be a Prometheus who struggles with the major philosophical problems.[30]

29. *De fato*, Epilogus sive Peroratio, 1, 451.

30. I would like to thank Ms. Noureen Ahmed who as my research assistant in the Philosophy Department of Marquette University during the academic year of 2000–2001 helped a great deal with some of the basic research for this paper.

The Secret of Pico's *Oration*: Cabala and Renaissance Philosophy

BRIAN P. COPENHAVER

The work of Renaissance philosophy best known in our time is the *Oration* written by Giovanni Pico della Mirandola in 1486. More than half a century after he wrote it, Pico's speech came to be called the *Oration on the Dignity of Man*, and under that title it has been celebrated as the great Renaissance proclamation of a modern ideal of human dignity and freedom.[1] I have argued elsewhere, however, that both the fame of the *Oration* and its attachment to this ideal are products of the Kantian revolution that transformed philosophy and its historiography. Although the celebrity that Pico earned during his brief and dramatic life never waned, it had little to do with the *Oration* before the end of the eighteenth century. For three centuries after he died in 1494, the *Oration* was little more than an entry in lists of Pico's books until post-Kantian historians invented the first elements of the interpretation now common in college textbooks.[2]

The root opposition in Kant's philosophy is between phenomenal nature and noumenal freedom, a polarity that gives rise to many others, including the distinction between price, on the one hand, and worth or dignity, on the other. Things have their prices, but only people have dignity, and without freedom there can be no dignity. The centrality of such ideas in Kant's thought and the prominence of similar notions in the first few pages of Pico's *Oration* invited post-Kantian historians to read the speech in terms of the critical philosophy, a response that culminated in the extravagantly Kantian story told by Ernst Cassirer in the *Erkenntnisproblem* and later works: Cassirer saw transcendental idealism as the

---

1. Paul Oskar Kristeller, *Eight Philosophers of the Italian Renaissance* (Stanford: Stanford University Press, 1964), pp. 54–67; Eugenio Garin, *Italian Humanism: Philosophy and Civic Life in the Renaissance* (Oxford: Blackwell, 1965), pp. 105–8.
2. Copenhaver, "Magic and the Dignity of Man," in press.

telos of post-Medieval philosophy and Pico's speech as early progress toward that goal. Another Kantian, but a more judicious one, was Paul Kristeller, who created the study of Renaissance philosophy in the United States and in the process brought the Anglo-American picture of Pico into better alignment with history. But Kristeller's Pico, who became the Pico of the textbooks, is still a hero of human dignity and freedom.[3]

Kristeller first expressed his views on Pico in a work of wide readership in 1948, long before Frances Yates added another page to the philosopher's dossier in 1964. Yates's Pico is a Hermetic freedom-fighter whose advocacy of natural magic anticipated the Scientific Revolution, with all its liberalizing and progressive implications. Yates used the term 'Hermetic' broadly to name a 'tradition' whose main commitments were to types of philosophy (Platonic), theology (gnostic), occultism (natural magic and Cabala), and eirenic, syncretist historiography (the ancient theology). Pico's original contribution to this mixture was Christian Cabala, which he adapted from mystical Jewish approaches to biblical hermeneutics, theological speculation, and practical spirituality that emerged after the twelfth century.[4]

Elsewhere (again) I have argued that Yates misapplied the term "Hermetic" to Marsilio Ficino, one of the key figures in her justly renowned book on the *Hermetic Tradition*, and I will also claim (though I will not argue here) that Pico was even less Hermetic than Ficino.[5] His *Oration* is not about Hermetic magic, though the practice of natural magic is one of its major recommendations. The speech also promotes Cabala, as Yates recognized. But if Pico was really a champion of human

3. Ernst Cassirer, *Gesammelte Werke, Hamburger Ausgabe*, ed. Birgit Recki, *Vol. 2: Das Erkenntnisproblem in der Philosophie und Wissenschaft der neueren Zeit*, Vol. I (Hamburg: Felix Meiner, 1999), pp. 81–3, 120–42; "Giovanni Pico della Mirandola: A Study in the History of Ideas," in *Renaissance Essays from the Journal of the History of Ideas*, ed. P. O. Kristeller and Philip P. Wiener (New York: Harper and Row, 1968), pp. 11–60; Kristeller, *Eight Philosophers*, pp. 65–8, 70–1.

4. Kristeller, "Introduction," in *The Renaissance Philosophy of Man*, ed. Cassirer, Kristeller, and J. H. Randall, Jr. (Chicago: University of Chicago Press, 1948), pp. 215–22; Frances A. Yates, *Giordano Bruno and the Hermetic Tradition* (London: Routledge and Kegan Paul, 1964), pp. 84–116. For an introduction to Cabala, whose basic ideas will be assumed but not explained here, see Gershom Scholem, *Major Trends in Jewish Mysticism* (New York: Schocken Books, 1946); *Kabbalah* (Jerusalem: Keter, 1974); Moshe Idel, *Kabbalah: New Perspectives* (New Haven: Yale University Press, 1988).

5. Copenhaver, "Scholastic Philosophy and Renaissance Magic in the De vita of Marsilio Ficino," *Renaissance Quarterly*, 37 (1984), 523–54; "Renaissance Magic and Neoplatonic Philosophy: Ennead 4.3–5 in Ficino's *De vita coelitus comparanda*," in *Marsilio Ficino e il ritorno di Platone: Studi e documenti*, ed. G. C. Garfagnini (Florence: Olschki, 1986), 351–69; "Hermes Trismegistus, Proclus and the Question of a Philosophy of Magic in the Renaissance," in *Hermeticism and the Renaissance: Intellectual History and the Occult in Early Modern Europe*, ed. Ingrid Merkel and Allen G. Debus (Washington: The Folger Shakespeare Library, 1988), pp. 75–110; "Hermes Theologus: The Sienese Mercury and Ficino's Hermetic Demons," in *Humanity and Divinity in Renaissance and Reformation: Essays in Honor of Charles Trinkaus*, ed. John W. O'Malley et al. (Leiden: Brill, 1993), pp. 149–82; "Lorenzo de' Medici, Marsilio Ficino and the Domesticated Hermes," in *Lorenzo il Magnifico e il suo mondo: Convegno internazionale di studi*, Firenze, 9–13 giugno 1992, ed. G. C. Garfagnini (Florence: Olschki, 1994), pp. 225–57; below, n. 49.

dignity and freedom, as Yates, Kristeller, Cassirer, and many other post-Kantian critics have maintained, how should we account for his occultism, which is not a habit of mind that would seem to promote dignity and freedom?

My answer is that the *Oration* is not about dignity and freedom as any modern or post-modern reader would understand these terms. If the *Oration* does not really deserve the title that Pico did not give it—*On the Dignity of Man*—what should it be called? What is his famous speech about? What follows is a short and simplified answer to this question, supported by only a minimum of documentation and leaving the full case to be made in a book on Pico and his *Oration*.

*   *   *   *   *

Pico wrote the *Oration* when he was in his early twenties and at the peak of the powers of mind and speech that dazzled his peers in Renaissance Florence. He meant it to introduce a public debate in Rome on 900 theses that he drafted for the occasion, but the debate was quashed by the Church, Pico was disgraced, and the *Oration* was never published in his lifetime, though the theses were printed as the *Conclusiones DCCCC* in 1486.[6] The rest of this essay interprets parts of the *Oration* to show how it makes the case for something quite unlike human dignity and freedom.

"Man is a great wonder, Asclepius." By placing this phrase near the start of his speech and by linking it with Asclepius, one of the voices of Hermetic wisdom, Pico might have been announcing the human miracle as his theme and his account of this miracle as Hermetic.[7] But if he meant these words as clues, what follows in the body of the speech makes us ask if they are false clues—not impossible in a text explicitly described as esoteric, as written both to conceal and to reveal.[8] Although Pico names "the ancient theology of Mercurius Trismegistus" as a source for the 900 theses introduced by his speech, he identifies no other person or idea in the *Oration* as Hermetic; his only other use of the Hermetic writings is silent, and its message makes the human condition repulsive, not miraculous.[9] After its famous opening, the rest of the speech advises humans to become angels, to leave human nature behind in a flight to union with the divine.

Sages of the Orient and ancient Egypt have said that man is the greatest wonder, Pico declares, pointing to the central and mediating place of humanity in the cosmic order. But he doubts the ancient arguments. Why should angels not amaze us more, he asks, finding his answer in a new story of Genesis, an audacious

6. The standard work on Pico is Eugenio Garin, *Giovanni Pico della Mirandola: Vita e dottrina* (Florence: Felice le Monnier, 1937); for a recent summary of the life and works see Copenhaver, "Pico della Mirandola, Giovanni," in *Encyclopedia of the Renaissance*, ed. Paul F. Grendler (New York: Charles Scribner's Sons, 1999), V, 16–20; for the philosophy, see Copenhaver and Charles B. Schmitt, *A History of Western Philosophy*, Vol. 3: *Renaissance Philosophy* (Oxford: Oxford University Press, 1992), pp. 163–76.

7. My translation of Pico's *Oration* is based on the Latin text in *Oratio de hominis dignitate*, ed. Eugenio Garin (Pordenone: Edizioni Studio Tesi, 1994), p. 3; *Asclepius* 6.

8. Below, nn. 42, 66.

9. Pico, *Oration*, pp. 18, 56; *Asclepius* 12.

myth of his own construction. Having brought all other creatures into being, God made Adam last to assess and admire his work. But before this final stage of world-making, as Pico tells the story, the Creator had used up his models and filled every vacancy in the universe. Lacking a unique form for this last of his creatures, God took something from all the others, and having no special place to put him, he let Adam find his own location.[10]

At first God stations this labile Adam at the center of the universe, not to fix him in the hierarchy but to let him rise—or fall. The prelapsarian Adam is not yet heavenly or earthly, mortal or immortal. His nature is undefined. "You will determine that nature by your own choice," says the divine Craftsman: "on your own, as molder and maker, duly appointed to decide, you may shape yourself in the form that you prefer." To crawl with the animals or climb to the gods is the "supreme and wondrous happiness of man, to whom it is given to have what he chooses, to be what he would be!" From "the supreme liberality of God the Father" Adam gets the gift of choice. Unlike spirits on high or beasts of the earth, whose natures confine them, he cultivates the mix of seeds planted in him by the Divine Gardener, selecting from miscellaneous natures assembled in him by the Divine Builder.

Plant, animal, heavenly being, and angelic being—these are Adam's first four options, arising from the nutritive, sensitive, rational, and intellectual powers of his soul. But a fifth choice remains "if he is not content with the lot of any creature," if he wants to exceed the limits of what God has given him from what was meant for every other thing. The way to this fifth level is inward as well as upward: if he "draws himself into the center of his unity, becoming a spirit and one with God, this being who has been placed above all things will transcend them all in the lonely darkness of the Father." Thus, at the peak of a climb that starts with free choice and rises through terrestrial, celestial, and supercelestial natures, Adam's last movement is withdrawal into himself, and his final goal is mystical extinction in the godhead.[11]

Ascending sequences of three, four, or five steps give the *Oration* its world-escaping rhythm. Pico introduces this motif in a passage about vegetal, sensual, rational, and intellectual faculties of the soul, perhaps taking it from the *Protrepticus* of Iamblichus, part of that philosopher's exposition of the Pythagorean life.[12] This educational program and spiritual regimen was nearly 900 years old when Iamblichus wrote in the third or fourth century CE. Plato had probably learned it long before from teachers whose teachers were Pythagoreans of the sixth and fifth centuries BCE. But Pico, like Ficino, condenses this epoch of vast changes into a unity, a coherent ancient wisdom of Chaldaean, Orphic, Hermetic, Pythagorean, Platonic, and other philosophies, a *prisca theologia* of Greek and barbarian doctrines to support the revelations of the Bible. Iamblichus, third of the Neoplatonist masters after Plotinus and Porphyry, shaped the last phase of this tradition. After Iamblichus, its last great pagan voice was Proclus, who laid the groundwork

10. Pico, *Oration*, pp. 2–6.
11. Pico, *Oration*, pp. 6–8.
12. Iamblichus, *Protrepticus* 5 (Des Places 66.9–25).

for its Christian culmination in the mystical and angelic theologies of Dionysius the Areopagite, the name given to a fifth or sixth century writer whom most Christians of Pico's day thought to be a companion of St. Paul.[13]

For the Greek side (there is also a Hebrew side) of the project promoted by the *Oration*, Pico took his primary inspiration from Dionysius and the Neoplatonists. His morality is ascetic, his novel practices are magical (or theurgic), and his aim is mystical, what Dionysius and his predecessors called perfection (*teleiosis*), contemplation (*theoria*), or unification (*henosis*). Because this project requires a curriculum as well as a regimen, philosophy is part of it—but as a means, not an end, a way of purifying the soul and enlightening it before it sinks into the divine abyss at the peak of its spiritual progress. The Christian Dionysius still thought of the soul's perfection or *teleiosis* as the climax of a rite of initiation, like the old pagan cult of Eleusis. The blessing earned by the Eleusinian initiate was to gaze on (*theorein*) a sacred sight, foreshadowing the beatific vision of Christian bliss. For pagan theurge and Christian mystic alike, the ultimate reward was a loss of self, absorption into the divine by becoming one (*henosis*) with God.[14]

Having presented the human marvel as striving to enter "the lonely darkness of the Father," Pico next asks "who would not wonder at this chameleon?" The obvious point of amazement is that man can alter his nature as the animal changes its color. According to ancient sources that Pico knew, it looks and behaves like a lizard, combining features of a fish, pig, viper, tortoise, and crocodile into a horrific appearance that masks its harmlessness. Is man such a monstrosity, assembled from parts of other creatures? The reptile's changing colors signified timidity or inconstancy, and ancient magicians found a whole pharmacy of magical substances in its limbs, though the authorities called most of them fakes.[15] With one exception, Pico's other examples of mutability in this section of the *Oration* are as negative or ambiguous as the chameleon—transmigration of criminal souls into animals or plants and the shapeshifting of Proteus, the Old Man of the Sea who fights the noble Menelaus in the *Odyssey*. The only clearly positive transformation is angelic, that of the biblical Enoch into the angel of the *Shekinah* or Divine Presence, an aspect of divinity hypostasized and personalized in Cabalist texts that Pico knew.[16]

In the end, says Pico, if one's ambitions are angelic, it is not bodily assets or defects that matter but those of soul and mind. Hence, those who are bound to

13. Pico, *Oration*, p. 56; D. P. Walker, *The Ancient Theology: Studies in Christian Platonism from the Fifteenth to the Eighteenth Century* (London: Duckworth, 1972), pp. 1–21; R. T. Wallis, *Neoplatonism* (London: Duckworth, 1972), pp. 94–110; Andrew Louth, *The Origins of the Christian Mystical Tradition From Plato to Denys* (Oxford: Clarendon Press, 1981), pp. 1–17, 159–64; *Denys the Areopagite* (London: Geoffrey Chapman, 1989), pp. 1–16.

14. Dionysius, *Celestial Hierarchy* 3.1–3, 7.1; Louth, *Origins*, pp. 22–3, 52–60, 162–4; Walter Burkert, *Ancient Mystery Cults* (Cambridge: Harvard University Press, 1987), pp. 7–11, 43, 69, 88–102, 113–4.

15. Pico, *Oration*, p. 8; Aristotle, *Nicomachean Ethics* 1100^{b}4–6; *History of Animals* 503^{a}15–^{b}29; *Parts of Animals* 692^{a}20–5; Pliny, *Natural History* 8.120–2; *Desiderii Erasmi Roterodami adagiorum chiliades quatuor et sesquicenturia* (Lyon: Gryphius, 1558), cols. 817–8.

16. Pico, *Oration*, pp. 8–10; Homer, *Odyssey* 4.383–572; Plato, *Ion* 541E; Erasmus, *Adagia*, cols. 480–1; below, nn. 59–65.

the body's sensitive functions, "scratching where it itches and enslaved by the senses," are like Calypso's pigs, bewitched, and those limited to mere feeding are even less human, like plants. But the philosopher's reason lifts him to heaven, while the "pure contemplator, unaware of the body, withdrawn to the sanctuary of the mind, . . . is neither earthly nor heavenly but more majestic, a divinity cloaked in human flesh." Through these four grades, passing beyond nutrition and sensation to reason and contemplation, this being "who transforms, forges and fashions himself in the shape of all flesh" strives to transcend the way of all flesh. He begins with "no image of his own," only a plurality of images that are "many, alien and accidental," as his nature too is "variable, multiple and inconstant." Human mutability is a marvel, declares Pico, but it is also unreliable.[17]

Having offered new proof for the old thesis that man is the greatest wonder, having made the case for mutability and choice at the start of the *Oration*, Pico then sets forth the purpose of this choice. It is to exercise "a holy ambition," he says, to "scorn the things of earth, . . . despise those of heaven, and then, leaving behind whatever is of the world, . . . [to] fly up to the hypercosmic court nearest the most exalted divinity, . . . [with the] Seraphim, Cherubim, and Thrones." The right choice, he asserts, is to despise the earth and flee it, disdaining the heavens as well, to reach for the realm of the angels beyond and "be their rivals for dignity and glory." Man finds his dignity by emulating the angels.[18]

Introducing this pivotal point is an elliptical passage that begins clearly enough: man's privileged position and power of choice should not tempt him to forget that the dullest cattle are his relatives; their shepherd and his, as the Psalmist teaches, is death. Less clear is Pico's claim that misapplication of the words of the prophet Asaph—"You are all gods and sons of the Most High"—might abuse God's gift of free choice and make it harmful. Perhaps he means simply that humans must treat this verse as a command to join their angelic kin and rise above their animal cousins. Or perhaps, keeping the Pythagorean rule of silence, Pico has in mind the larger message of Psalm 82, where an angry God judges the angels for their sins:

> God stood in the synagogue of the gods,
> In their midst to judge among them . . .
> But these gods know nothing nor do they understand,
> They walk in shadows . . .
> I have declared: you are all gods,
> and sons of the Most High,
> Yet you shall die as men die,
> And you shall fall as one of the princes.[19]

Pico praises the angels as godlike with words from a Psalm that condemns them. He also knew a Cabalist text that contrasts man's nearness to the angels in one

17. Pico, *Oration*, pp. 10–12.
18. Pico, *Oration*, p. 12.
19. Ps. 49:10–21; 82.

Psalm with his tie to the animals in another. Whatever this meant to him, his larger aim was to rival the heavenly hosts in their glory. With this purpose established, the *Oration* next asks how to achieve it. "Let us see what . . . life they live," exhorts Pico, speaking of the angels closest to God, "and if we live that life . . . , we shall have made our chances equal to theirs."[20]

These highest angels are the Seraphim, Cherubim, and Thrones. Only the first two are named in the Hebrew Bible, where they protect, praise, purify, and expiate, mainly in ritual and eschatological contexts. Thrones appear in the Epistles of the New Testament; the elaborated angelology of the Epistles helps explain why Paul came to be linked with Dionysius, whose *Celestial Hierarchy* is the main Christian account of the subject. Others before Dionysius had named nine ranks of angels, but he was the first to organize them in three orders of three, with Thrones, Cherubim, and Seraphim at the top.[21]

Pico focuses on this highest order and arranges its three ranks in a rising hierarchy according to their ways of being (active, contemplative, unitive), their psychological functions (judgment, contemplation, love) and their types of substance (solidity, light, fire). Humans "committed . . . to the active life and concerned . . . with lower things" may aspire to live like Thrones, who are angels of judgment. Others "not . . . employed in active matters" rise higher to contemplation and "gleam with Cherubic light," while those who reach the summit of love burn with a Seraphic fire that consumes them. The Seraphs are nearest to the God who sits above the Thrones of judgment and hovers over the Cherubs of contemplation, "for the Spirit of the Lord is borne upon the waters . . . above the heavens." Pico alludes here not only to the first mention of the Spirit in the book of *Genesis* but also to a reading of *shamayim*, the Hebrew word for 'heavens,' as containing fire (*esh*) and water (*mayim*), so that the waters of the "Cherubic minds" are above the visible heavens but below the supercelestial fire of the Seraphim. The judgment of Thrones is a great force, and Seraphic love is the greatest of all, "but how can anyone judge or love what is unknown?" asks Pico. Judgment and love both require knowledge, so "the Cherub with its light both prepares us for the Seraphic fire and also enlightens us for the judgment of Thrones."[22]

Thus, the Cherub is the knot that ties the other "primary minds" together. Its angelic order is that of Pallas, goddess of wisdom, and it is the "guardian of contemplative philosophy." These are the angels that Pico wants us to emulate. "We are to form our lives on the model of the Cherubic life": this is the conclusion to which the opening sections of the *Oration* lead. This is the point of the free choice that makes humankind a miracle. In principle, the Cherubic life prepares us to move up or down from the level of contemplation, "to be carried off to the

20. Pico, *Oration*, pp. 12–14; Ps. 8:6; 49:21; *Expositio secretorum punctuationis* in Chaim Wirszubski, *Pico della Mirandola's Encounter with Jewish Mysticism* (Cambridge: Harvard University Press, 1989), p. 222.

21. Gen. 3:24; Exod. 25:18–22; Ps. 18:10–11; Ezek. 9:3, 10:2–22, 11:22; Isa. 6:1–7, 14:29, 30:6, 37:16; Col. 1:16; Karel van der Toorn et al., eds., *Dictionary of Deities and Demons in the Bible* (Leiden: Brill, 1999), pp. 189–92, 742–4, 864–6; Louth, *Denys*, pp. 36–7.

22. Pico, *Oration*, pp. 14–16; Gen. 1:2; Wirszubski, *Pico*, p. 180; Scholem, *Origins of the Kaballah* (Princeton, NJ: Princeton University Press, 1987), p. 144.

heights of love and then to descend . . . [to] the duties of action." The rest of the *Oration* confirms, however, that what Pico wants is the journey up to the Seraphim, where even contemplation ends in an ecstatic blaze of assimilation to the deity: "One who is a Seraph—a lover—is in God, and God is in him; or rather, he and God are one." The final miracle of the human condition is to be exalted and consumed in divinity.[23]

*   *   *   *   *

Meanwhile, because we "are flesh and smell of the earth," even the lesser life of the Cherubs is beyond our reach; for help we must look to the "ancient fathers." This advice opens the longest part of the *Oration*, occupying a quarter of its length, a seven-part exposition of the Cherubic life as curriculum and regimen, as preparation for Seraphic consummation. At this point, with most of his speech still to come, Pico has finished with the topic of human freedom. He now proposes a method to direct man's choices outside the body, above the world and ultimately beyond the choosing subject toward the holy abnegation of union with God.[24]

The seven "ancient fathers" whom Pico wants his hearers to consult are Paul, Jacob, Job, Moses, the ancient theologians, Pythagoras, and the Chaldaeans, all of them assisted by other voices of wisdom. In each of these sages or schools, Pico finds instructions for a graded ascent to God, usually in four steps but sometimes in three or five. Partly the idea derives from ancient treatments of the divisions of philosophy that were much debated by the Stoics, and partly it comes from theories of the soul's levels, functions, and destiny derived from Plato. The combined framework was a favorite of the pagan Neoplatonists and their Christian contemporaries.[25] Clement of Alexandria, for example, applied it to "the Mosaic philosophy," which he

divided into four parts, into the historical and legislative properly so called, which pertain precisely to ethical activity, while the third part is ritual (*hierourgikon*) and has to do with natural contemplation (*phusikes theorias*), and finally the fourth is theological, the contemplation (*epopteia*) that Plato says belongs to the great mysteries.[26]

Although the basic idea is triadic—moral purification and mental illumination leading to theological perfection—the initial catharsis often comes in two phases, one to cleanse a lower level of the soul, closer to the body, the other to purify a

23. Pico, *Oration*, pp. 14–16.
24. Pico, *Oration*, p. 16.
25. A. A. Long and D. N. Sedley, *The Hellenistic Philosophers*, Vol. I: *Translations of the Principal Sources with Philosophical Commentary* (Cambridge: Cambridge University Press, 1987), pp. 160–2; Proclus, *Platonic Theology* 1.2 (Saffrey and Westerink 1.10.11–11.26); *Commentary on I Alcibiades* 245.6–246.15 (Segonds); W. K. C. Guthrie, *A History of Greek Philosophy*, Vol. IV; *Plato, The Man and His Dialogues: Earlier Period* (Cambridge: Cambridge University Press, 1975), pp. 421–6; Louth, *Origins*, pp. 52–74.
26. Clement of Alexandria, *Stromata* 1.28.176–9.

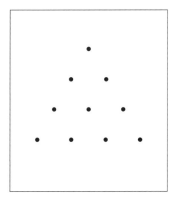

Figure 1. The teractys.

higher level. The resulting process of four steps claimed an ancient pedigree, represented by the triangular amulet or *tetractys* of the Pythagoreans (Figure 1) and described in a doxography ascribed to Plutarch:

> The nature of number is the decad, but the power of ten . . . is in the four and in the tetrad, and the reason is that when one ascends from the monad and adds the numbers up through four, the sum is the number ten . . . This is why the Pythagoreans declared that the tetrad is the mightiest oath and [swore by] . . . "the one who gave our soul the *tetractys* . . ." Our soul is also composed of a tetrad . . . : contemplation (*noun*), knowledge (*epistemen*), opinion (*doxan*), sensation (*aisthesin*).[27]

Thus, four stages of spiritual ascent correspond to four levels or functions of the soul. In Clement's scheme, which is both biblical and philosophical, the ethical stage has two phases, historical and legislative, reflecting the travails of ancient Israel and their resolution in the Law, while the third stage is 'hierurgic' or ritual and the fourth is theological and mystical.

Clement's language, based on a tradition that goes back to Plato, respects the pagan mysteries. The *mystes* underwent purification and performed a ritual in order to enjoy the culminating *epopteia*—watching or observing the divine, "the sight of divinity by the light of theology," in Pico's words. The ritual stage that Clement calls "natural contemplation" is a kind of natural theology, understanding the Creator by philosophizing about the created universe and thus preparing for mystical contemplation, whose point is intuitive rather than discursive. But the climax of *epopteia* is also the end of a curriculum that progresses from ethics through natural philosophy to theology.[28] In fact, the two earlier phases of ethical activity (historical and legislative) in Clement correspond to the first two types of

27. Ps.-Plutarch, *Opinions of the Philosophers* 877A–B.
28. Pico, *Oration*, p. 28; Plutarch, *Isis and Osiris* 382D–E; Louth, *Denys*, p. 40; above, n. 14.

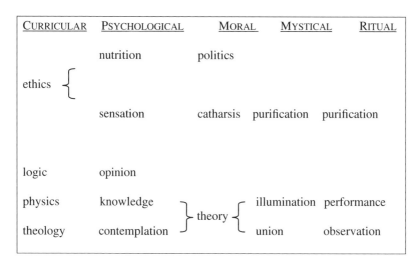

Figure 2. Types of ascent.

virtue (political and cathartic) in the curriculum that the Neoplatonists used to teach Plato's dialogues.

In the first cycle of this *paideia*, after the introductory *I Alcibiades*, students began with a pair of <u>ethical</u> dialogues, the *Gorgias* for political virtue and the *Phaedo* for cathartic. Then, leading up to a summative treatment of the Good in the *Philebus*, they read three pairs of <u>logical</u> (*Cratylus* and *Theaetetus*), <u>physical</u> (*Sophist* and *Statesman*) and <u>theological</u> (*Phaedrus* and *Symposium*) texts, all interpreted as teaching theoretical virtue to those who had moved beyond politics and catharsis. The clearest presentation of this curriculum survives in an anonymous *Prolegomenon* to Platonic philosophy, probably written in the sixth century and much influenced by Iamblichus.[29] The curricular, psychological, moral, mystical, and ritual aspects of this conception may be summarized as shown in Figure 2.

In this framework, the body and its activity in this world are at best points of departure for a higher journey, at worst obstacles to that ascent. From the curricular and psychological points of view, the goal is a kind of action, whereby the soul looks upon God in *theoria*—in a theology not so much examined as experienced. From the mystical perspective, however, action ceases for the human agent when *theoria* becomes the final peace of union (*henosis*) or assimilation (*apho-moiosis*) with God.[30]

29. L. G. Westerink, ed. and trans., *Anonymous Prolegomena to Platonic Philosophy* (Amsterdam: North Holland Publishing, 1962), pp. xxxix–xl, 48–9; B. D. Larsen, *Jamblique de Chalcis: Exégète et philosophe* (Aarhus: Universitetsforlaget in Aarhus, 1972), pp. 322–40; Lucas Siorvanes, *Proclus: Neo-Platonic Philosophy and Science* (New Haven, CT: Yale University Press, 1996), pp. 114–8.

30. Dionysius, *Celestial Hierarchy* 3.1, 7.1; Louth, *Denys*, pp. 38–9; *Origins*, pp. 164, 172.

This is the mystical perfection (*teleiosis*) taught by Paul and Dionysius in the first of Pico's seven accounts of the Cherubic life. "As we emulate the Cherubic life on earth," he urges, "checking the impulses of the emotions through <u>moral knowledge</u>, dispelling the mists of reason through <u>dialectic</u>, let us cleanse the soul, . . . [and] then . . . flood [it] . . . with the <u>light</u> of <u>natural philosophy</u> so that finally we may <u>perfect</u> it with <u>knowledge of divinity</u>." In Dionysius, where everything is triadic, this curriculum is the mystic's ascent through purgation (*katharsis*), illumination (*photismos*), and perfection (*teleiosis*), which is also Pico's reply to the question about Paul that opens this part of the *Oration*. Asking what Paul "saw the Cherubim doing when he was raised to the third heaven," Pico learns from Dionysius "that they are cleansed, then enlightened and finally perfected."[31]

The project that Dionysius defines at the start of the *Mystical Theology* is to move inward as well as upward to the divine "darkness of unknowing," a voyage that demands "unqualified and unconditional withdrawal" from the world and finally from the self. The aim of this experiential theology is to be something, not to know something. The mystic forsakes knowledge, abandoning even the light of the Cherubim, to enter God's nameless shadows and enjoy the ecstasy of divine love. Yearning for the divine can be satisfied only by leaving the knowing self behind.[32] Although *epopteia*—gazing, contemplating, perceiving, or learning in the Dionysian texts—is the apex of the mystical way, all this activity of the subject dissolves in the assimilation that motivates the various hierarchies. The celestial hierarchy of angels, like the ecclesiastical hierarchy of priests, guides the mystic up to the peace of deification. Disagreements and distinctions fall away as peace comes near. Since Dionysius treats theology as a discipline in the ascetic (not the pedagogical) sense, it is no surprise that he also applies the Neoplatonist term *theourgia*—ritual god-work as opposed to theological god-talk—to the Christian sacraments. Like the pagan mystics, he also regards his theology as an 'occult tradition (*kruphia paradosis*)' open only to the initiated. To publish the deity's unutterable secrets would be to cast sacred pearls before swine. The Dionysian program is an esoteric, ascetic, theurgic, eirenic, and ecstatic mysticism, terms that apply also to Pico's advocacy of the Cherubic life.[33]

Having made the mystical theology of Dionysius the basis of his angelic regimen, Pico derives it again from three Bible heroes—Jacob, Job, and Moses. His exposition of their familiar stories links the patriarchs with ancient gentile sages but also with the later speculations of the Cabalists, which were completely unknown to Christians in Pico's day and may seem obscure even now. For this reason, it will be useful to review Pico's words about Jacob as an example of his exegesis:

31. Pico, *Oration*, p. 16; Dionysius, *Celestial Hierarchy* 3.2, 7.3, 10.1; *Ecclesiastical Hierarchy* 5.1.3; *Divine Names* 4.2; Louth, *Origins*, p. 163.

32. Dionysius, *Mystical Theology* 1; *Celestial Hierarchy* 3.1, 7.1; *Divine Names* 1.5, 7.3, 13.1; Louth, *Denys*, p. 38; *Origins*, pp. 164, 172; above, n. 14.

33. Dionysius, *Celestial Hierarchy* 1.2; 2.2–3,5; 3.3; 4.1,4; 7.2–3; 15.9; *Ecclesiastical Hierarchy* 1.1; 2.3.8; 3.3.4–6; 7.3.1,3; *Divine Names* 1.1,4,8; 2.1; Louth, *Denys*, pp. 38–40; *Origins*, p. 169; Gregory Shaw, *Theurgy and the Soul: The Neoplatonism of Iamblichus* (University Park; Pennsylvania State University Press, 1995), pp. 4–5; below, n. 42.

Let us consult the patriarch Jacob, whose gleaming image is carved in the seat of glory. As he sleeps in the lower world and watches in the world above, this wisest of fathers will advise us. He will use a figure (everything used to depend on them) to give us his advice: that there is a ladder reaching from earth below to the sky above, marked off in a series of many steps, with the Lord seated at the top. Up and down the ladder angels of contemplation move back and forth. But if we are to do the same as we aspire to the angelic life, who (I ask) will touch the Lord's ladder with dirty feet or hands unclean? If the impure touches the pure, it is sacrilege, as the mysteries teach. What are these feet and hands, then? The foot of the soul, surely, is that worthless part that relies on matter as on the dirt of the ground, a nutritive and feeding power, I mean—tinder for lust and mistress of voluptuary softness. As for the hands of the soul, why not call them the wrathful part that battles to defend the appetites, plundering in heat and dust to snatch something to gorge on while snoozing in the shade? These hands, these feet—the whole sensual part where, so they say, the lure of the body hangs like a noose round the neck of the soul—let us wash them in the living waters of moral philosophy lest we be turned away, desecrated and defiled, from the ladder. But if we want to join the angels speeding up and down Jacob's ladder, this washing will not be enough unless we have first been instructed and well prepared to advance from stage to stage as the rites require, never leaving the way of the ladder nor rushing off two ways at once. After we have completed this preparation through the art of speaking or reasoning, then, animated by the Cherubic spirit, philosophizing through the rungs of the ladder (or nature), passing from center to center through all things, at one moment we will be descending, using a titanic power to tear the one—like Osiris—into many, while at another moment we will be ascending, using the power of Phoebus to gather the many—like the limbs of Osiris—into one, until at last, resting at the top of the ladder in the bosom of the Father, we shall be perfected in theological bliss.[34]

The later Neoplatonists who influenced Dionysius had described the mystical ascent as "a bridge or a ladder." Pico's account of Jacob's ladder grounds this metaphor in familiar biblical imagery but also attaches it to strange Cabalist ideas. Jacob sleeps low to the ground but sees angels on high, dreaming of "a ladder standing above the earth with its top touching the sky, and angels of God . . . going up and down it."[35] Thus, he counsels us to forget the lower world and wake to a higher destiny. Like the angels of contemplation, the Cherubim, we may move up or down, but we must first wash the dirty hands and feet that would defile the Lord's ladder. In Pico's terms, we must purge the soul's lower limbs, its nutritive and irascible powers, with moral philosophy. Loathing for the soul's "sensual part" is the message of Pico's vivid phrases, one borrowed from the Hermetic *Asclepius*,

---

34. Pico, *Oration*, pp. 18–20.

35. Gen. 28:10–22; Iamblichus, *Protrepticus* 1 (Des Places 41.11–24); Synesius, *Dion* 9 (Treu 28.16–30.10).

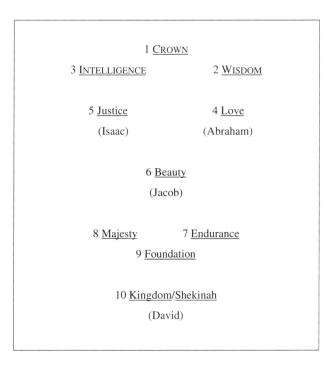

Figure 3. The *Sefirot*.

where "the lure of the body hangs like a noose round the neck of the soul." Cleansed of such pollutions, we may mount the celestial ladder, which gives a way of proceeding, a logic, to the uninstructed. Overcoming his confusion, the contemplator rises next to physics, and through the myth of Osiris—a cycle of death by division and resurrection by reunification, as Plutarch and Macrobius tell it—he understands the cosmic strife of Titanic plurality against Apollonian unity. Theology is the final stage of the climb, and the reward is peaceful perfection.[36]

Jacob woke from his dream of angels shouting that he had seen "the house of God and heaven's gate (*porta caeli*)," a vision that Pico knew from the Bible but also from the *Gates of Justice* by Joseph Gikatilla, a Cabalist work of the thirteenth century translated for him as the *Portae iustitiae*. Here and in the *Gates of Light*, Gikatilla's more famous work, Jacob stands out among the patriarchs whose stories reveal the secrets of the *Sefirot* (Figure 3), the ten aspects of supernal

36. Plutarch, *Isis and Osiris* 354A,F; 357F–358E; 360E–F; 364E–F; *The E at Delphi*, 388E–89A; Macrobius, *Commentary on the Dream of Scipio* 1.12.12; Idel, "The Ladder of Ascension: The Reverberations of a Medieval Motif in the Renaissance," in *Studies in Medieval Jewish History and Literature*, vol. 2, ed. Isadore Twersky (Cambridge: Harvard University Press, 1984), p. 88; Edgar Wind, *Pagan Mysteries in the Renaissance* (Harmondsworth: Penguin Books, 1967), pp. 133–5, 174–5; above, n. 9.

divinity that constitute the basic framework of Cabalist theosophy.[37] In Gikatilla's version, one of these biblical tales begins

> when Adam sinned [and] a blemish was placed upon him and he was made susceptible—like dough—to all the ministers, and even the powers of impurity on the outside, for all of them spewed their acid on him, and this is the same filth that the primordial snake spewed on Eve, . . . [and] this pollution did not separate from Adam's body until it was gradually refined from the righteous of subsequent generations.

The seventy ministers who bedevil Adam's heirs are constellations in the heavens and nations on the earth. They afflict Israel, but their power wanes as the six generations after Adam (Seth, Enoch, Noah, Shem, Abraham, and Isaac) become gradually purer. Still,

> there is some pollution found in Abraham and in Isaac which gives the ministers a place to connect, and that is why you find Abraham and Isaac on opposite sides facing the ministers on the right and on the left . . . Jacob, however, who is pure and without refuse, is in the middle between Abraham and Isaac.

Right, left, and middle here are directions in theosophical space, regions in the standard deployment of the *Sefirot*, where Gikatilla connects Abraham with the fourth *Sefirah* (Love, Compassion, or Greatness) on the right, Isaac with the fifth (Justice, Fear, or Power) on the left, and Jacob with the sixth (Beauty, Truth, or Knowledge) between them. Although the promise of a covenant lets Abraham foresee where his seed will spread, Jacob hears a stronger pledge in his dream when God tells him that his seed will "burst forth" in every direction. His inheritance breaks the bounds that confine his less sanctified forefathers. In mystical terms, Jacob as Beauty or the sixth *Sefirah* is "the only one that ascends . . . to reach *Keter* (Crown)," while Isaac (Justice) and Abraham (Love) stay hemmed in below by the seventy ministers.[38]

In one grouping, Jacob and his two ancestors form "a throne for the divine constellation"; the middle triad of *Sefirot*, in other words, supports the supreme triad. In another configuration, all seven of the lower *Sefirot* make up the chariot (*Merkabah*) in which the higher triad rides or the throne on which it sits. Knowing that "the patriarchs are the chariot," Cabalists thought of Abraham, Isaac, and Jacob in their linkage with Love, Justice, and Beauty. To supply a fourth wheel for

---

37. Gen. 28:17; Scholem, *Kabbalah*, pp. 96–116. For Gikatilla's *Gates of Justice*, one of the Cabalist texts translated for Pico by Flavius Mithridates, see Wirszubski, *Pico*, pp. 13, 56–7, 74–5, 111–12; the *Gates of Light* is available in a complete English translation: *Sha'are Orah: Gates of Light*, trans. Avi Weinstein (Walnut Creek: Altamira Press, 1994).

38. Gikatilla, *Gates of Light*, pp. 8, 209, 223–31, 235, 326; Fischel Lachower, Isaiah Tishby, and David Goldstein, ed. and trans., *The Wisdom of the Zohar: An Anthology of Texts* (London: The Littman Library of Jewish Civilization, 1949), I, 348.

the chariot or a fourth leg for the throne, they also connected David with Kingdom. But this last of the *Sefirot*, through which the Creator touches his creation, is also his Presence (*Shekinah*) in the world. Since emanation from the Infinite terminates in the divine Presence, the *Shekinah* can stand for the whole of the seven lower *Sefirot*, the Throne of Glory in its entirety. Jacob as Beauty, also called the husband of the *Shekinah*, stands at the center of the throne, governing the "middle line" that goes straight up through the Crown toward the Infinite. The *Shekinah* ascends through this middle line or "central pillar, and her descent was also that way . . . It is, therefore, called 'a ladder'." On earth she dwells in the place where Jacob had his dream, called Beth El or the House of God.[39]

When Pico writes that Jacob's "image is carved in the seat of glory," he is using a Cabalist metaphor (*galaph*, carving) for the Sefirotic emanation of divinity out of its hidden depths, and he is describing the patriarch's privileged position among the *Sefirot*. Jacob's theosophic primacy gave Pico reason to put him first among the biblical elders who show the way to the Cherubic life. Since Pico's goal was to climb "to the top of the ladder in the bosom of the Father," the direct route from Jacob's central place to the Sefirotic summit—where a Cherub rides the chariot—was an attractive path. On these points, Pico could have learned from the earliest work of Cabala, called the *Bahir*, from earlier *midrashim*, as well as from Gikatilla and, directly or indirectly, from the *Zohar*. These authorities along with other Cabalists that Pico knew in Latin translation were of great help to him, but so were the Jewish mystics of his own day.[40]

One of them was Yohanan Alemanno, who offered other perspectives on the ascent. Like Pico, he saw philosophy as preliminary to a curriculum whose advanced stage is theurgy, and he believed that theurgy enables the mystic to unite with divinity itself. He departed from the program of the *Oration* not in the method of his mysticism but in its aim, which was altruistic, concerned less with elevating and transforming the human person than with redeeming the entire universe. From one point of view, he imagined the worlds of mind, soul, and matter as a hierarchy of concentric spheres, with matter at the bottom. From another, he used an alternative geometry that depicts soul or nature as a ladder used by angels and humans to move up and down between matter and mind. This latter image of "two circles and a straight line," which Alemanno took from an Arabic source, appears cryptically in the *Oration* as "philosophizing through the rungs of the ladder (or nature) [and] passing from center to center through all things, at one moment . . . descending, . . . at another . . . ascending." The learned inquiries of Moshe Idel have revealed this to modern scholars, but to Renaissance Christians such secrets were sealed until Pico himself began to open them.[41]

This pattern holds throughout Pico's presentation of the Cherubic life: various Cabalist authorities support his program, but they are obscure or invisible

39. Lachower et al., *Zohar*, I, 288, 402, II, 571–2, 588–90.

40. *The Bahir*, ed. and trans. Aryeh Kaplan (York Beach: Samuel Weiser, 1979), pp. 49–50, 75 (135, 190); Scholem, *Origins*, pp. 144–6, 213, 267, 317; *Trends*, p. 113.

41. Pico, *Oration*, p. 20; Idel, "Ladder," pp. 84–7; "The Anthropology of Yohanan Alemanno, Sources and Influences," *Topoi*, 7 (1988), 201–20.

to the Christian audience of the *Oration*, which is in keeping with Pico's esoteric intentions. When he finally makes his Cabala explicit toward the end of the speech, what he reveals is its history and its habit of concealment. "To disclose . . . the more secret mysteries, the arcana of supreme divinity," he insists, would be "to give the sacrament to dogs and to cast pearls before swine. Hence it was a matter of divine command, not human judgment, to keep secret from the populace what must be told to the perfect."[42]

Like the vision of Jacob, the tale of Job holds keys to hidden Cabalist treasures, including the notion of *gilgul* or transmigration of souls, understood by Pico as showing human nature to be polymorphous, "lifting us up to heaven" or "plunging us down to hell." The conclusion that Pico draws from the story of "Job the just" is that the goal of theological peace is actually a kind of death—in Cabalist terms the holy "death of the kiss" bestowed by God on Jacob and other patriarchs. Pico closes his treatment of Job with a line from Psalm 116, the scriptural source of this idea, that "the death of the saints is most precious" in the sight of God. Dionysius cites the same text to show that the saints are dead only to this world, having risen to the "peaceful oneness of the One" by discarding the earthly lusts and enmities that excluded them from the "unified and undivided life." In this respect, Dionysius had learned from Plato and his successors that the body is a tomb for the soul, that the world is a prison from which the soul escapes, and that philosophy is a preparation for the death that the wise man desires. "We should make all speed to take flight from this world to the other": these words of Plato's also describe Pico's purpose in proposing a Cherubic *askesis* based on Greek, Jewish, and Christian wisdom.[43]

The same fugitive program, visible to Christians at one level but veiled in the enigmas of Cabala at another, is what Pico derives from Moses, the third Hebrew patriarch in his elucidation of the Cherubic life. Dionysius treats Moses as ascending toward "the darkness of unknowing" but never really seeing God in his theophanies of physical vision and cognitive contemplation. Pico presents Moses in a different role, as hierophant rather than initiate, the guide of souls through the chambers of the Tabernacle as described in Exodus. In Cabalist terms, "the Tabernacle and its instruments are . . . material images in which may be contemplated superior images which are their models . . . It consists of three parts: within the veil, without the veil, and the court." Accordingly, Moses first gives the moral law to souls dwelling in "the lonely desert of the body"; then admits them by logic and natural philosophy to various grades of ritual service within the sanctuary but outside the veil; and finally conducts them by theology inside the veil to the Tabernacle's Holy of Holies. After purifying themselves ethically like gentile "priests of Thessaly" outside the court of the Tabernacle and then mastering

42. Pico, *Oration*, p. 70; Matt. 7:6; Dionysius, *Celestial Hierarchy*, 2.5.

43. Pico, *Oration*, pp. 20–6; Ps. 116:15; Dionysius, *Ecclesiastical Hierarchy* 3.3.9; Plato, *Phaedo* 64A, 81A–B, *Theatetus* 173D–174A, *Phaedrus* 250C, *Gorgias* 493A, *Republic* 515C–17C; Wirszubski, *Pico*, pp. 153–60; Scholem, *Origins*, p. 385; *On the Mystical Shape of the Godhead: Basic Concepts in the Kabbalah*, ed. J. Chipman, trans. J. Neugroschel (New York: Schocken Books, 1991), pp. 208–19, 226–8.

dialectic inside as "diligent Levites," the elect join the priesthood of philosophy to complete their preparation for a "journey to the heavenly glory to come."[44]

Having extracted this message four times from the "Mosaic and Christian mysteries" in Paul (or Dionysius), Jacob, Job, and Moses, Pico turns next to the ancient pagan theologians to examine "those liberal arts that we have come to debate" and to interpret them as "stages of initiation . . . in the secret rites of the Greeks." The goal of this next exposition of the Cherubic regimen remains the same, a "fast trip . . . to the heavenly Jerusalem" after purification through moral and dialectic arts, ritual performance through natural philosophy, and then "the sight of divinity by the light of theology."[45]

"These are the reasons," Pico writes, "that have not only excited me to study philosophy but have also forced me to it." He must learn philosophy because moral, logical, and physical lessons are prerequisite to theology, the highest form of discursive knowing that leads in turn to the experience of contemplation and union. As angels of contemplation, the Cherubs live at this summit of divinity, but their way of life reaches down to the first ethical exercises required of those who emulate them. Thus, having chosen the Cherubic life as the best way to form a formless human nature, Pico finds himself at the lower philosophical stages of an ascetic and mystical ascent to ecstasy. Once he has made this choice, philosophy is his obligation: this is his answer to those who condemn his commitment to it.[46]

*   *   *   *   *

About halfway through the speech, having explained what the Cherubic life is and how philosophy prepares the way for it, Pico's purpose changes to a defense of his claim to the title of philosopher. He pledges himself to an ambitious and original program of philosophizing. Not content with the "common doctrines," he boasts of using arcane material from Hermetic, Chaldaean, Pythagorean, and Cabalist sources and adds "many things that I have discovered and devised on topics natural and divine." The fullest expression of this plan survives in the *Nine Hundred Conclusions*, but the *Oration* provides a partial preview, summarizing several new themes:

- "the concord between Plato and Aristotle"
- "novel concepts in physics and metaphysics . . . using a method much different from the philosophy . . . read in the schools"
- "another novel method that philosophizes with numbers"
- "theorems about magic"
- "the ancient mysteries of the Hebrews . . . [that] confirm the . . . Catholic faith"
- "views on interpreting the poems of Orpheus and Zoroaster."[47]

---

44. Pico, *Oration*, p. 26; Exod. 25–7, 35–6; Lachower et al., *Zohar*, III, 867–78; Dionysius, *Mystical Theology* 1.3; Wirszubski, *Pico*, pp. 247–8, translating a passage from a *Commentary on the Pentateuch* by Bahya ben Asher at Exod. 25:9; Louth, *Origins*, p. 173.
45. Pico, *Oration*, p. 28.
46. Pico, *Oration*, p. 38.
47. Pico, *Oration*, pp. 56–62, 68, 76.

Two of these subjects—magic and Cabala—occupy most of the remainder of the *Oration*.

Pico's novel theorems about *magia* apply that word in two senses: one corresponds to *goeteia* (sorcery) in Greek and must be repudiated as the work of evil demons; the other, called *mageia* by the Greeks, is to be revered as wisdom and piety. As the one is vain, fraudulent, and shameful, banned by governments and ignored by the learned, so the other is solid, honest, and honorable, prized by sages and supported by their authority.

Plotinus, the last of twenty experts on magic whom Pico names, "mentions it when he shows that the magus is nature's minister, not her artificer." Pico refers here to the most extensive discussion of magic in the *Enneads*, where Plotinus claims that magic is always already there in nature. Magicians, who cannot cause magical effects, know where to find them in the world and how to exploit them for good or ill. Although Plotinus recognizes the fact of magic, he regards it as a detour from the ascent, a distraction that leads down to the world of matter. Natural magic is a reality, but it does no good for salvation. By the same token, "contemplation (*theoria*) alone stands untouched by magic," while the soul that stays involved in nature is prey to sorcery. Since the only escape from nature and magic is philosophical ascent to contemplation and union, Plotinus neither used ritual (theurgy) as a way up to the One nor feared magic as a snare for the philosopher. In fact, theurgy had no place in Neoplatonic spirituality until Porphyry, a student of Plotinus, introduced it as an alternative to the risky practice of sorcery (*goeteia*) and to the rigor of education in the virtues. But he still confined real magic to the world of nature and thought it useless for reaching the realm above.[48]

For Plotinus, then, philosophy was the only way to ascend, and for Porphyry it was still primary. But Iamblichus had less confidence in philosophy. The contemplation (*noesis*) that philosophy can sustain by itself will not lead to union, he concluded; *noesis* is necessary for the ascent but not sufficient, and it is less effective than theurgic ritual, which touches the higher soul. Theurgy—literally, "god-working"—is the work of gods who reach down through actions (rites) and objects that transmit divine energy on their own: they are always linked to the gods by the force of amity (*philia*) that these higher beings project through lower things. Amity from on high also causes the sympathy (*sympatheia*) that operates in nature. Some rituals are merely a lower theurgy that taps this sympathy but cannot lead the soul up to union. Only a higher theurgy empowered by divine amity can make the final leap. But amity also causes the sympathy that mortals perceive as natural magic, which is like lower theurgy, and both these lesser practices may be steps toward higher theurgy and eventual union. Unlike Porphyry's theurgy, which is an alternative to virtue, the higher theurgy of Iamblichus requires prior education in the virtues. Although such a theurgy based on divine friendship must be good in

48. Pico, *Oration*, p. 64; Plotinus, *Enneads* 4.4.40–4; Wallis, *Neoplatonism*, pp. 70–2, 108–10; Andrew Smith, *Porphyry's Place in the Neoplatonic Tradition* (The Hague: Nijhoff, 1974), pp. 70, 74, 122, 128, 134–40, 147–8.

itself, Iamblichus admits that it can also be dangerous if the impure attempt it or if evil demons interfere.[49]

To make his case for natural magic, Pico cites Porphyry but not Iamblichus, and it is Plotinus who gets most of his overt attention. The disdain of Plotinus for lesser demons, celebrated in Porphyry's *Life* of his master, reinforces the antithesis between natural and demonic magic, which is Pico's theme. One is bondage, the other mastery. One is neither art nor science, "while the other is full of the deepest mysteries, . . . leading at last to the knowledge of all nature." Stressing another point from Plotinus, Pico emphasizes that this knowledge is applied "not so much by working wonders as by diligently serving nature as she works them." The forces that the magus uses are already at play in the world.[50]

Pico's account of natural magic so far is Plotinian, but then he makes a Christian point about grace and the virtues. By uncovering the world's marvels, natural magic "excites man to that wonderment at God's works of which faith, hope and a ready love are sure and certain effects." Thus, while the old pagan magic had come to depend on the four natural virtues, as Plato taught, the three theological virtues are within reach of Pico's new Christian magic that "by a constant contemplation of God's wonders" will move us to a love so ardent that "we cannot hold back the song, 'Full are the heavens, full is the whole earth with the greatness of your glory'." This hymn that natural magic compels us to sing is the music of the Seraphim, part of the triple blessing chanted by the fiery angels in the book of Isaiah. Magic—at least the good natural magic that Pico defends—drives us up to join these highest angels in their hymn of blazing, self-consuming love. Natural magic thus plays the same role as natural philosophy in Pico's angelic curriculum, preparing us for theology and ultimately for union. This is what Pico means when he says that magic is "the final realization of natural philosophy." Reflecting the aims of the later Neoplatonists, his goal is not to control the world of nature but to escape and rise above it.[51]

Accordingly, what closes his account of magic is the supernal song of the Seraphim, and what comes next is Cabala. Since we are now near the peak of theology and contemplation, raised to this height by natural magic and headed for mystical union, the place of Cabala in the ascent ought to be higher than magic, and so it is. What Pico discovers in the books of the Cabalists is "a stream of intellect, or an ineffable theology of supersubstantial divinity; a fount of wisdom, or an exact metaphysics of intelligible and angelic forms; and a river of knowledge, or a most certain philosophy of nature." Here he embellishes the end of the seventh vision in *2 Esdras*, where God tells Ezra how he had instructed Moses on Sinai in

49. Wallis, *Neoplatonism*, pp. 99–100, 120–3; Smith, *Porphyry's Place*, pp. 59–61, 83–98, 105–10, 134–40, 148; Shaw, *Theurgy*, pp. 4–5, 85, 110–12, 123, 129, 150–5, 169; "Copenhaver, Iamblichus, Synesius, and the *Chaldaean Oracles* in Marsilio Ficino's *De vita libri tres*: Hermetic Magic or Neoplatonic Magic?" in *Supplementum Festivum: Studies in Honor of Paul Oskar Kristeller*, ed. J. Hankins et al., "Medieval and Renaissance Texts and Studies" (Binghamton: Center for Medieval and Early Renaissance Studies, 1987), pp. 448–50.

50. Pico, *Oration*, pp. 64–6; Porphyry, *Life of Plotinus*, 10.

51. Pico, *Oration*, pp. 62, 66–8; Isa. 6:2–3; Plato, *I Alcibiades* 121E–122A; Smith, *Porphyry's Place*, pp. 59–61, 134–48.

"the secrets of the ages and the end of time, and . . . what to make public and what to keep hidden." Ezra receives a revelation whose public part fills twenty-four books, "but the last seventy books are to be kept back and given to none but the wise."[52]

Most of what Pico says about Cabala in the *Oration* is historical or apologetic. The history recounts and justifies the distinction between exoteric and esoteric revelation, the latter transmitted by Jewish tradition and reinforced by pagans and Christians. Pico's apologetic (and prudential) motive is "to do battle for the faith against the relentless slanders of the Hebrews." To convince Christians to turn the alien force of Cabala against the Jews, he puts it on the level of Pythagorean and Platonic philosophy. Even more compelling is its theological authority, which Pico describes schematically in his brief elaboration of Ezra's vision. Explicating the prophet's simple promise of "a stream of intellect and a fount of wisdom and a river of knowledge" flowing from the seventy secret books, Pico finds in them his "ineffable theology . . . , exact metaphysics . . . , and . . . most certain philosophy of nature." Whatever he meant to convey by his compressed account of this arcane and abstruse topic, the progression from physical nature through metaphysical forms to the inexpressible godhead mirrors the program of mystical ascent that his speech recommends. Moreover, if Cabala was a theurgy as well as a theosophy, as indicated by the distinction between practical and speculative Cabala in Pico's *Conclusiones*, its grounding in a preparatory magic would confirm the similar ideas of the later Neoplatonists. In fact, a major influence on Pico's Cabala was the thirteenth century mystic, Abraham Abulafia, whose work was available to him in Latin, and Abulafia's Cabala was aggressively theurgic.[53]

Abulafia centered his Cabala on prophecy and divine names: 'prophecy' is his term for the ecstasy that culminates in mystical union; meditation on the sacred names is the technique recommended to achieve this goal. Repeating the letters that make up the names of God, either in speech or in writing, combining them with other letters from other words of power, chanting their sounds, breathing correctly, moving the head in certain patterns, matching the numerical values of letters and words with their meanings—such practices are Abulafia's way to ecstasy, starting with God's holiest name, the unutterable Tetragrammaton. "Begin by combining this name," he writes, "namely, YHWH, at the beginning alone, and examine all its combinations and move it and turn it about like a wheel returning around, front and back, like a scroll, and do not let it rest." Abulafia called this practice *Ma'aseh Merkabah* or the 'Work of the Chariot', a term used by other Cabalists

---

52. Pico, *Oration*, p. 74; 2 Esdras 14:3–6, 42–8.

53. Pico, *Oration*, pp. 68, 74; Matt. 13:11; Lk 8:10; Origen, *Against Celsus* 1.7; Plato, *Phaedo* 69C–D, *Phaedrus* 249C–50C, 209E–11D; Iamblichus, *Protrepticus* 21 (Des Places 131.16–135.10); *The Pythagorean Life* 103–5; Guthrie, *History*, IV, pp. 348–40; Dominic J. O'Meara, *Pythagoras Revived: Mathematics and Philosophy in Late Antiquity* (Oxford: Clarendon Press, 1989), p. 39; Burkert, *Lore and Science in Ancient Pythagoreanism* (Cambridge: Harvard University Press, 1972), pp. 176–80; Wirszubski, *Pico*, pp. 60–5; Scholem, *Trends*, pp. 56–7, 144–6; Idel, *Kabbalah*, pp. 41–2, 101; *The Mystical Experience in Abraham Abulafia*, trans. J. Chipman (Albany: State University of New York Press, 1988), pp. 18–19.

to denote theosophical speculation on the highest mysteries of revealed divinity, as distinct from *Ma'aseh Bereshit* or the 'Work of Genesis' indicating the cosmological secrets of creation. What Pico calls "revolving the alphabet" in the *Conclusiones* corresponds to Abulafia's use of the sacred names and letters for ecstatic meditation, and Abulafia's designation of this practice as *Ma'aseh Merkabah* accords with Pico's presentation of alphabetic meditation as the first of four divisions of speculative Cabala, the other three being the "triple Merchiava, corresponding to a triple philosophy in parts dealing with divine, intermediate and sensible natures."[54]

Meditation to induce ecstasy is the use of the holy names characteristic of Abulafia, but he and other Cabalists taught that the names also enlarge theological understanding and reveal sources of magical power: theory and practice both start with the names. Since Pico also describes Cabala as both practical and speculative, linking the former with divine names and the latter with the *Sefirot*, he may have been making a concession to a magical application of Cabala. In any case, that the names of God and the letters of the sacred language have a role to play in his speculative Cabala is plausible.[55]

The nature of Pico's practical Cabala is less clear. He says in the *Conclusiones* that it "puts into practice all of formal metaphysics and lower theology." The latter might be a theology inferior to 'supersubstantial divinity', the former an 'exact metaphysics of intelligible and angelic forms', two of the three terms in the *Oration*'s definition of Cabala. The third term is missing, however: 'a most certain philosophy of nature'. Its absence implies that Pico's practical Cabala was not a magic meant to act on the natural world. Moreover, setting 'intelligible and angelic forms' apart from a 'lower theology' indicates that the practice of Cabala aims high—perhaps as far as the *Sefirot*. Another possibility is that Pico meant to bring both the *Sefirot* (a theology expressed in names and hence lower than the 'ineffable' theology) and the *Merkabah* (forms, angels, intelligences, what Maimonides called 'metaphysics') into his practical Cabala.[56]

In the end, Pico's telegraphic taxonomy of Cabala raises more questions than it answers, but whatever he learned from Abulafia and other Jewish mystics must have seemed both enticing and forbidding. Like Plotinus, who "lived as if he were ashamed of being in the body," like the *Hermetica* in their many world-hating moments, like Christians who sometimes forgot that the Word was made flesh, Abulafia understood prophetic ecstasy as salvation *from* a degraded and defiled human condition:

We are born through harlotry and lust and menstrual blood and urine. And we are a fetid drop at the time of our creation, and so we are today, fetid

---

54. Pico, *Conclusiones nongentae: Le novecento tesi dell'anno 1486*, ed. Albano Biondi (Florence: Olschki, 1995), p. 126; Wirszubski, *Pico*, pp. 137–8; Idel, *Abulafia*, pp. 8–9, 14, 21; Scholem, *Kabbalah*, pp. 6, 11–12, 23.

55. Wirszubski, *Pico*, p. 139.

56. Pico, *Conclusiones*, p. 126; Wirszubski, *Pico*, pp. 137, 140; above, n. 52.

and besmirched with filth and mud and vomit and excrement so that there is no clean place . . . And we shall be dead carcasses, putrid and crushed in fire, like rubbish . . .

Although his technique was ecstatic rather than ascetic, Abulafia demanded that the mystic abandon this repulsive world in order to be saved from it. The aim of his Cabala was "that human beings shall turn into separate angels" by reaching the ecstatic state called prophecy "and . . . be saved by this from natural death on the day of [their] . . . death and live forever." "The Torah is not preserved except by one who kills himself in the tents of wisdom": for Abulafia this maxim from Maimonides was the equivalent of the Platonic directive to practice death and of the Neoplatonic desire for the soul to exit the body deliberately.[57]

"One who works in Cabala without mixing in the extraneous and stays at the work a long time," according to Pico's *Conclusiones*, "will die the death of the kiss." What sounds like an admonition is actually an invitation, for this is the good death that Pico wants, while avoiding the ghastly end of the magus who makes mistakes in Cabala. If he "goes wrong in the work or comes to it unpurified, he will be devoured by Azazel," warns the second half of the same conclusion. Frightful demons lurk where angels sing, which is why Pico needs the proper technique to protect his ascent to the One. A righteous theurgy, cleared of demonic snares, will summon the good angel Metatron to fight his fallen cousins, even the sinister Samael, the Cabalist counterpart of Satan. One use of practical Cabala, then, is for counter-magic against unclean spirits, a magic powered by Abulafia's theories about the letters of the Hebrew alphabet.[58]

The secrets of the sacred letters shape the numerological architecture of Pico's *Conclusiones*, whose terse assertions are often obscure in themselves and connect with one another even more obscurely. To be worth reading, Pico believed that he had to write in riddles, and the *Oration* describes his Cabala in just such teasing terms, as "divine matters that are published and not published." Pico intended his account of Cabala to be enigmatic, requiring his hearers to make what they could of the puzzles set for them. Even before introducing Cabala toward the end of the *Oration*, he had left a clue to its mysteries near the start of the speech while discussing the problematic mutability of the human chameleon: "the Hebrews with their more secret theology," he writes, "sometimes transform the blessed Enoch into an angel of divinity, which they call *malach haShekinah*, and sometimes they change others into other divine powers." From the latter part of the speech, we learn that this "more secret theology" is Cabala. The words *malach*

57. Porphyry, *Life of Plotinus* 1; Copenhaver, *Hermetica: The Greek Corpus Hermeticum and the Latin Asclepius in a New English Translation with Notes and Introduction* (Cambridge: Cambridge University Press, 1992), pp. xxxix, lii, 24, 74, 102–3, 144–6, 152–3; Idel, *Abulafia*, pp. 141–5; above, n. 9.

58. Pico, *Conclusiones*, p. 128; Wirszubski, *Pico*, pp. 159–60; Copenhaver, "Number, Shape and Meaning in Pico's Christian Cabala: The Upright *Tsade*, the Closed *Mem* and the Gaping Jaws of Azazel," in *Natural Particulars: Nature and the Disciplines in Renaissance Europe*, ed. Anthony Grafton and Nancy Siraisi (Cambridge: The MIT Press, 1999), pp. 25–76.

haShekinah mean the "angel of God's presence," the divine height to which Pico taught that humans must ascend.[59]

In one way, then, practical Cabala was a defense, to invoke the mighty Metatron as protection against Azazel, the malign demon who invented magic and waited to devour any who used that art wrongly. But Cabala could do more, Pico believed. He even claimed in the *Conclusiones* that "no knowledge gives us more certainty of Christ's divinity than magic and Cabala," though the Church condemned this conclusion, despite the pains that he took to distinguish his good magic and salvific theurgy from demonic magic.[60] Like Ficino, he wished to base a learned and beneficial occultism on the remains of ancient wisdom, sacred and secular, so the threat of dying in the jaws of Azazel was a matter of special risk for him. The aid that he sought from Metatron, however, was not just to protect his life. What he wanted was the good ecstatic death, the death of the kiss, that frees the soul from the body for its angelic destiny and divine union.

The great risk in Pico's project was not bodily death but loss of the soul from the theurgic excesses of the Cabalists, who dared not only to call spirits down from heaven and turn humans into angels but even to change the configuration of the Godhead by causing the *Sefirot* to rearrange themselves. That Pico wished to redraw the blueprint of divinity is unlikely, though he knew that Cabala presented such temptations. Danger lay closer in the magic needed to summon Metatron, the angelic prince described by Abulafia in a Latin text available to Pico:

> What takes our intellect from potency to act is an intellect separated from all matter and called by many different names in our language ... For it is called *hu saro sel aholam* or 'he is the prince of the world' and it is 'Mattatron prince of the faces,' in Hebrew ... *mattatron sar appanim* ... And his real name is just like the name of his master, which is *sadai* ... And the wise ... call him ... *sechel appoel* or 'agent intellect' ... , and he has many other names besides, ... and he rules over the hierarchy of angels called *hisim* ... Therefore the intellect or intelligence in our language is called ... *malach* or 'angel' or *cherub* ... Therefore our wise men often call him ... Henoch, and they say that Henoch is Mattatron.[61]

In its least provocative form, the entity described here is the agent intellect of Aristotelian philosophy, usually treated in the Greek and Latin tradition as an internal faculty of the human psyche that activates higher mental processes. Moslem and Jewish philosophers, however, moved the agent intellect from the human microcosm to the macrocosm and placed it last (hence closest to the lower world) among ten emanations from the One. In this cosmic and hypercosmic framework, contacting the agent intellect is no longer just an act of human psychology. It is a theological adventure—the metaphysical basis of prophecy for

59. Pico, *Oration*, pp. 8–10, 70; Copenhaver, "Number," pp. 41–60; above, n. 16.

60. Pico, *Conclusiones*, p. 118.

61. Wirszubski, *Pico*, p. 231; Idel, *Messianic Mystics* (New Haven: Yale University Press, 1998), pp. 88–9.

Abulafia, whose usual name for the agent intellect is Metatron. Pico knew the sources of this idea: conventional scholastic Aristotelianism; the Averroist challenge to that philosophy; and the Cabalist apotheosis of the agent intellect.[62]

To become Metatron in Abulafia's Cabala is a type of mystical union and thus an eradication of the self. The self withers away not only in the One but also in favor of the other because Abulafia's prophecy is Messianic as well as ecstatic. The agent intellect is the *Mashiyah*, the Anointed, and through angelic ecstasy the Messianic mystic becomes a savior. The physical force of this transformation penetrates Abulafia's imagery when he describes the mystic's experience: "it will appear to him as if his entire body . . . has been anointed with the oil of anointing, . . . and he will be called 'the angel of the Lord' [*mal'akh ha-'elohim*]." Numerological calculation (gematria) also relates this supreme angel's name "to that of his Master, which is Shaddai," one of the names of God in the Hebrew Bible. Metatron, Messiah, Shaddai—these and other sacred names raise Abulafia's Cabala to the highest levels of spirituality and thereby expose its practitioner to the gravest danger.[63]

According to the Latin Abulafia, another of Metatron's names is "*ruuah accodex* or 'Holy Spirit' and . . . *xechina*, which means 'divinity' or 'dweller'."[64] The *Shekinah* or Presence of God acts as the Creator's lowest attribute and first point of contact with creation. This commonplace of Cabala was a discovery for Pico but a riddle to his Christian contemporaries. Thus, when he mentioned Enoch's becoming the angel of the *Shekinah* or Metatron, the allusion could only mystify Christians, though it was well known to Jews since the early medieval period:

> R. Ishmael said: 'I asked Metatron and said to him: "Why art thou called by the name of thy Creator, by seventy names?" . . . He answered: . . . "Because I am Enoch, the son of Jared. For when the generation of the flood sinned and were confounded in their deeds, . . . then the Holy One . . . removed me from their midst to be a witness against them . . . Hence the Holy One . . . lifted me up . . . [and] assigned me for a prince . . . among the ministering angels . . . In that hour three of the ministering angels, 'Uzza, 'Azza and 'Azzael came forth and brought charges against me . . . [But] the Holy One . . . answered: . . . "I delight in this one more than in all of you, and hence he shall be a prince . . . over you in the high heavens . . ." When the Holy One . . . went out and went in . . . to the Garden of Eden then all . . . beheld the splendour of his Shekina, and they were not injured until the time of Enosh who was the head of all idol worshippers . . . And they erected the idols . . . and . . . brought down the sun, the moon, planets and constellations . . . to

62. Wirszubski, *Pico*, pp. 86, 101, 193, 200; Idel, *Mystics*, p. 85; Oliver Leaman, *An Introduction to Medieval Islamic Philosophy* (Cambridge: Cambridge University Press, 1985), pp. 87–107; *Averroes and His Philosophy* (Oxford: Clarendon Press, 1988), pp. 82–103; John Marenbon, *Later Medieval Philosophy (1150–1350)* (London: Routledge, 1987), pp. 94–128.

63. Idel, *Mystics*, pp. 65–8, 72, 85.

64. Wirszubski, *Pico*, p. 232.

attend them . . . They would not have been able to bring them down but for 'Uzza, 'Azza and 'Azziel who taught them sorceries.'[65]

Man's angelic potential was a great prize to Pico, but it was also a great peril, for Cabalist (and earlier) speculations on Metatron not only confirmed Pico's fear of demonic magic and ratified his confidence in angelic theurgy but also reached into regions that good Christians must reserve for orthodox theology and the spirituality sanctioned by the Church. That Enoch becomes Metatron, that practical Cabala turns humans into angels, is astounding enough. Beyond astonishment is Metatron's appearance as Shaddai, Messiah, and *Shekinah*, an angelic appropriation of the Trinity.

The safer consequence of Pico's Cabala, the Christianized Jewish mysticism sketched so faintly in his great speech, is that using secret names of God in Abulafia's ecstatic method is another application of the moral theory of the *Oration*, where the best choice is to choose the Cherubic life in order to die the best kind of death. No wonder that Pico passes over the worst dangers of a Christian Cabala, the temptations of a Trinitarian theurgy. Rather than betray the hazards of his project, he devotes most of his account of Cabala to justifying its secret ways. The sphinxes of Egypt, the silence of Pythagoras and the riddles of Plato support the wisdom of the Jews who treat the books of Cabala with such reverence that "they permit no one below the age of forty to touch them"—a caution that Pico in his early twenties ignored.[66]

*   *   *   *   *

What might the practice of philosophy achieve? Does it create a body of wisdom that ought to be a public good? Or does it build a body of learning whose technical difficulty makes it the private property of philosophers? The latter state of affairs, whether asserted or conceded, seems to be the condition of philosophy in post-modern times. If philosophy ends up being private, however, in the sense that few people know much about it, it still has no secrets. On the contrary, like other kinds of higher learning, philosophy authenticates itself by offering itself in print and in speech to public scrutiny. Without this test, open in principle to anyone, philosophy cannot be authentic. A secret philosophy in our day is no philosophy at all.

Our commitment to public examination is itself not much examined. We take it for granted that philosophy has no secrets to keep, taking little notice, for example, of the deeper meaning of the verb "to publish." Pico made no such assumptions. He did not publish the *Oration*, and he lodged his claim to be a philosopher in this same speech that makes so much of secrecy. He meant the speech to introduce a public event, a scholastic disputation on a grand scale, but his plan failed, keeping the *Oration* out of wide circulation during his lifetime. This

---

65. *3 Enoch or the Hebrew Book of Enoch*, ed. and trans. Hugo Odeberg (New York, Ktav Publishing House, 1973), pp. 8–16 (chaps. 4–5).

66. Pico, *Oration*, pp. 70–4.

temporary silence, an accident of his remarkable biography, is less important than the purposeful, Pythagorean silence that Pico practices as a first principle of his way of philosophizing.

Pico's speech, as noted above, has been called the most famous product of Renaissance philosophy. But that part of Western philosophy—the period between Occam and Descartes—is the least studied and the least understood in the whole of the discipline's history. Much about the *Oration*, given its status in this context, might explain why post-Cartesian philosophers have taken so little account of their immediate pre-Cartesian ancestry: written in Latin, expressed in recondite allusions to classical and biblical texts, and dependent on sources even more arcane, the *Oration* could be read as the antithesis of what Descartes wanted philosophy to become: divorced from history and philology and obligated to clarity as an ideal. The esoteric character of Pico's thought widens the gulf between his philosophy and the discipline as practiced since the Cartesian revolution. But the same alien quality is a valuable object of historical understanding, specifically of the historical understanding of philosophy's past.

Midwest Studies in Philosophy, XXVI (2002)

Between Republic and Monarchy? Liberty, Security, and the Kingdom of France in Machiavelli

CARY J. NEDERMAN AND TATIANA V. GÓMEZ*

In the Machiavelli scholarship of earlier generations, the fundamental problem of interpretation was centered on a strict dichotomy between his "republican" and his "monarchist" dimensions, as represented by his two major works, *Discourses on the First Ten Books of Titus Livy* and *The Prince*. The title of Hans Baron's germinal 1961 essay—"Machiavelli the Republican Citizen and the Author of *The Prince*"—captures perfectly the tension that characterized the scholarly literature.[1] Was the "authentic" Machiavelli the "teacher of evil" who counseled princes in the wiles of deception and treachery?[2] Or was Machiavelli "genuinely" a devoted republican who, whether out of personal desperation or political irony, sought to expose the real basis of successful monarchic rule?[3] Regardless of the response a given scholar provided, the key exercise became the reconciliation of one's interpretation with the apparently conflicting evidence to the contrary. The only alternative was to declare the body of Machiavelli's writings internally "inconsistent" and incoherent—a view that, while superficially

* The authors wish to thank Professor Tim Duvall and Ms. Allison Hinson for help in the initial conceptualization of this essay. A version of this essay was presented to the International Society for Intellectual History Conference on "Quarrels, Polemics, Controversies" at Trinity College, Cambridge, July 2001.

1. Originally published in 1961 and republished in revised form in Hans Baron, *In Search of Florentine Civic Humanism: Essays on the Transition from Medieval to Modern Thought*, 2 vols. (Princeton: Princeton University Press, 1988), I, pp. 101–151.

2. The position famously advanced by Leo Strauss, *Thoughts on Machiavelli* (Glencoe, IL: Free Press, 1958).

3. Quentin Skinner, *The Foundations of Modern Political Thought*, 2 vols. (Cambridge: Cambridge University Press, 1978), I, pp. 113–189 passim; Skinner, *Machiavelli* (Oxford: Oxford University Press, 1981); and J. G. A. Pocock, *The Machiavellian Moment* (Princeton, NJ: Princeton University Press, 1975), pp. 156–218.

accurate, seems satisfying neither intellectually nor in light of the manifest linguistic continuities across his corpus.[4]

In recent times, however, the dichotomous approach within Machiavelli scholarship has increasingly been eroded and replaced with a line of interpretation that identifies a middle ground as his starting point—a kind of "broad band" framework that can embrace both monarchic and republican institutions and systems of rule. One version of this thesis, associated with Friedrich Meinecke and lately propounded by Harvey Mansfield and Nathan Tarcov, holds that Machiavelli's "republicanism was of a rather special sort" (in the words of Maurizio Viroli), able to endorse monarchism as conducive to the republican cause.[5] Along similar lines, Nicholai Rubinstein has argued that Machiavelli's conception of *vivere politico* or *vivere civile* designates a generic "constitutional order," indifferent to institutional arrangements.[6] Developing Rubinstein's case, Janet Coleman has asserted that Machiavelli's supposed indifference to regime type—"un vivere politico can be either a republic or a monarchy"—reflects his extension of a quintessentially medieval belief "about the liberty that . . . was natural to political men and which the 'state,' monarchy or republic, was meant to acknowledge and secure."[7] For these scholars, therefore, the alleged tension between Machiavelli-the-republican and Machiavelli-the-monarchist is illusory and perhaps a product of anachronism.

One of the main pieces of evidence supporting this attempt to locate Machiavelli's political thought on a middle ground between monarchy and republic is his repeated and effusive praise for the political arrangements of France, alongside those of Sparta, Venice, and Rome. The French state in the early sixteenth century was already well on its way toward the structures that would yield the classic absolutist regime one hundred years later. Throughout his writings, but especially in the *Discourses*, Machiavelli lauds the contemporary French monarchy for its law-abiding character, its constitutionality, and its success at calming the feudal chaos of earlier centuries. In this—perhaps surprising—commendation of France, Rubinstein finds confirmation that "Machiavelli's *vivere politico* encompasses both republics and monarchies . . . He firmly believed that a constitutional

---

4. The charge of inconsistency is leveled, for instance, by Felix Gilbert, *Machiavelli and Guicciardini* (New York: Norton, 1984), pp. 166–167. One recent attempt to refute this view is Marcus Fischer, *Well-Ordered License: On the Unity of Machiavelli's Thought* (Lanham, MD: Lexington Books, 2000).

5. Maurizio Viroli, *Machiavelli* (Oxford: Oxford University Press, 1998), p. 115.

6. Nicolai Rubinstein, "The History of the Word *Politicus* in Early-Modern Europe," in Anthony Pagden, ed., *The Languages of Political Theory in Early-Modern Europe* (Cambridge: Cambridge University Press, 1987), pp. 52–53. Also see Rubinstein's "Italian Political Thought, 1450–1530," in J. H. Burns and Mark Goldie, ed., *The Cambridge History of Political Thought, 1450–1700* (Cambridge: Cambridge University Press, 1991), pp. 41–58.

7. Janet Coleman, "Structural Realities of Power: The Theory and Practice of Monarchies and Republics in Relation to Personal and Collective Liberty," in Martin Gosman, Arjo Vanderjagt, and Jan Veenstra, eds., *The Propagation of Power in the Medieval West* (Gronigen: Egbert Forsten, 1998), pp. 218, 230. Coleman has more recently reiterated this interpretation in her *A History of Political Thought: From the Middle Ages to the Renaissance* (Oxford: Blackwell, 2000), pp. 266–271.

order could be achieved by either. The one contemporary monarchy which represented such an order was, according to him, that of France."[8] Likewise, Coleman asserts, "Machiavelli firmly believed that a constitutional order could be achieved by either a monarchy or a republic and he thought that in his own time, the French monarchy had achieved it."[9] Machiavelli's remarks about France, then, highlight the possibility that he was less committed to a fixed set of political institutions than to a general principle of good political order.

The intent of the present paper is to challenge this "generic" constitutionalist reading of Machiavelli and to help restore to him the status of a profoundly republican thinker.[10] Our central claim is that Machiavelli consistently and clearly distinguishes between a minimal and a full conception of "political" or "civil" order, and thus constructs a hierarchy of ends within his general account of communal life. A minimal constitutional order is one in which subjects live securely (*vivere sicuro*), ruled by a strong government that holds in check the aspirations of both nobility and people, but is in turn balanced by other legal and institutional mechanisms. Such is the character of monarchic government in France. In a fully constitutional regime, however, the goal of the political order is the freedom of the community (*vivere libero*), created by the active participation of, and contention between, the nobility and the people. Only in a republic, for which Machiavelli expresses a well-known preference, may this goal be attained. Hence, our conclusion is that the significance of Machiavelli's commendation of France, as evidence for his supposed indifference to regime type, has been seriously misunderstood and even distorted by some recent scholarship.

MACHIAVELLI'S FRANCE

During his career as a secretary and diplomat in the Florentine republic, Machiavelli came to acquire vast experience of the inner workings of French government. He was intimately involved in negotiations between Florence and the French crown in order to maintain the traditional alliance between the two.[11] Moreover, he wrote several short treatises on topics related to the cultural and social traditions, as well as political structure, of France.[12] And, as mentioned previously, the French monarchy receives substantial treatment in the more theoretical and scholarly tomes composed by Machiavelli. Yet many major contributions to Machiavelli scholarship in English have largely overlooked his remarks about the governance of France,[13] or (on rare occasions) have explicitly dismissed their

8. Rubinstein, "The History of the Word *Politicus* in Early-Modern Europe," p. 53.

9. Coleman, "Structural Realities of Power," p. 219.

10. In this general project, we concur with Viroli, *Machiavelli*, pp. 115–116.

11. The details of the relations between Florence and France are discussed by Gilbert, *Machiavelli and Guiccardini*, pp. 30–34; and Giorgio Cadoni, *Machiavelli: Regno di Francia e "Principato Civile"* (Rome: Bulzoni, 1974), pp. 13–29.

12. These are collected in Sergio Bertelli, ed., *Arte Della Guerra e Scritti Politici Minori* (Milan: Feltrinelli, 1961).

13. See Hanna Pitkin, *Fortune Is a Woman* (Berkeley: University of California Press, 1984); Harvey Mansfield, *Machiavelli's Virtue* (Chicago: University of Chicago Press, 1996); Skinner, *Machiavelli*; Viroli, *Machiavelli*; Fischer, *Well-Ordered License*.

importance.[14] Only a few Italian scholars, to our knowledge, have endeavored to examine Machiavelli's views on French politics in any detail or depth.[15]

Perhaps the most distinctive feature of Machiavelli's analysis of France is his insistence, throughout his corpus, upon examining the relationship between the socioeconomic and political factors shaping French society. Initially, Machiavelli constructs this bridge in a wholly empirical manner, devoid of any theoretical implications. In his *Ritratto di cose di Francia*, probably completed while still in the service of Florence in 1510 or 1511,[16] Machiavelli correlates the status of the French "crown and king"—which he calls the "strongest, richest and most power-ful" monarchy of the time—with the circumstances of both the nobility and popular segment of society.[17] He recognizes that the conditions obtaining in France resulted from a unique confluence of historical events: the dynastic failure, and consequent elimination at the end of the Middle Ages, of most of the indepen-dent, fragmented baronies that had long prevented establishment of the hegemony of the crown. As the reversion of land and rights occurred,[18] French kings wisely assigned baronial titles to members of their own blood line, thus cementing the loyalty of a previously unruly, uncooperative, and disruptive nobility. In particu-lar, Machiavelli remarks, even the most distant members of the royal family, estab-lished in their own fiefdoms, were motivated to obey the king in the hope (however dim) that they or their progeny might someday inherit the throne.[19]

The barons, in turn, directly aid the king in maintaining his authority over the people; what he ordains, the magnates execute.[20] The French subjects have, in any case, developed habits of deference, obedience, and humility toward the crown and the nobles.[21] Despite the fact that France enjoys a great abundance of natural resources, Machiavelli observes, the people remain poor, yet they do not threaten to revolt against the crown or bear a grudge against the monarchy.[22] Nor is the nobility especially wealthy by more cosmopolitan standards, but the great men of the realm appear satisfied with their incomes, permitting the king to accumulate the largest share of the riches in the nation.[23] While these socioeconomic condi-tions are conducive for a tranquil kingdom, Machiavelli does not think they bode well for a successful army. Although praising the valor of the nobility, whose lesser sons diligently prepare to fight, he points out that the people are unfit to man the infantry. The king dare not arm them, lest they be given a chance to act upon their

---

14. Mark Hulliung, *Citizen Machiavelli* (Princeton, NJ: Princeton University Press, 1983), p. 149.

15. See Cadoni, *Machiavelli*; Nicola Matteucci, "Machiavelli Politologo," in Myron Gilmore, ed., *Studies on Machiavelli* (Florence: Sansoni, 1972), pp. 209–248.

16. Bertelli, ed., *Arte Della Guerra e Scritti Politici Minori*, pp. 146–147.

17. Ibid., p. 164. An English translation of this tract has never been published, to our knowl-edge; we have completed one that we plan to publish in the near future.

18. On the legal and political history behind this process, see Charles T. Wood, *The French Apanages and the Capetian Monarchy 1224–1328* (Cambridge, MA: Harvard University Press, 1966).

19. Bertelli, ed., *Arte Della Guerra e Scritti Politici Minori*, p. 165.

20. Ibid., p. 169.

21. Ibid., pp. 172–174.

22. Ibid., pp. 166, 168, 173.

23. Ibid., pp. 169, 173.

resentment toward the nobles who directly govern the populace. Since the king cannot depend upon his own subjects to fight in his army, he must turn to mercenaries, who are costly and unreliable.[24] On Machiavelli's account, the military is the only significant weakness of the French kingdom.

The *Ritratto* seems to provide the source material for the appraisal of French government and society that appears in Machiavelli's later work. Many of its observations recur, although now placed in a developed and sophisticated theoretical framework. Interestingly, Machiavelli makes relatively little comment about the French monarchy in *The Prince*, instead incorporating most of his analysis of the topic into his great work of republican thought, the *Discourses*.[25] (There are also some references to the circumstances of France in several other writings, such as *A Discourse on Remodelling the Government of Florence* and *The Art of War*.) The discussion in *The Prince*, however, summarizes Machiavelli's mature attitude toward the strengths of the French regime. He recognizes that the strength of the king of France derives from his relationship with the barons, over whom he exercises effective control (despite their apparent independence) and who in turn assist him in governing the subjects.[26] Indeed, Machiavelli contends that this general means of arranging political rule is so successful that "it is impossible to hold without difficulty states organized like France."[27] In France, then, the unity of the ruling elite is the source of royal strength.

Such strength is explicitly praised in chapter 19 of *The Prince*. In the context of substantiating the claim that the wise prince strives neither to harass the magnates nor to disturb the contentment of the people, Machiavelli states, "Among the best well-ordered and well-governed kingdoms of our time is that of France." He thereby returns to the observation of the *Ritratto* concerning the social foundations of French rule, this time pointing to the role of the Parlement in deflecting the resentment of both the nobility and the people toward the crown. In France, he says,

> are found infinite good institutions on which the liberty and security of the king depend. Of those, the first is Parlement and its authority. Because the orderer of that kingdom, knowing the ambition of the powerful and their insolence, and judging that it was necessary to rein (*correggere*) them in with a bridle, and, on the other hand, knowing the hatred of the masses against the great, founded on fear, and wanting to secure (*assicurare*) them, he did not want their care to be the king's particular duty, in order to take away the burden that he could incur from the great by favoring the people, and from the people by favoring the great . . .

24. Bertelli, ed., *Arte Della Guerra e Scritti Politici Minori*, p. 166.

25. References to Machiavelli's major works will be to Francesco Flora and Carlo Cordià, eds., *Tutte le Opere di Niccolò Machiavelli*, 2 vols. (Milan: Arnoldo Mandadori, 1949–1950). Translations are our own. Citations will be given to the chapter numbers from these works, followed parenthetically by the volume and page number from the Italian edition.

26. Machiavelli, *Il Principe*, 3, 4 (I, pp. 7, 14–15).

27. Ibid., 4 (I, p. 15).

Parlement functions as an intermediary institution, defending the masses against the nobility, without direct royal involvement. "Nothing could be better or more prudent, or a greater cause of security (*securità*) for the king and kingdom."[28] The genius of the French political system stems from the ability of the king to rule effectively by keeping both people and nobility in check and arousing the hostility of neither.

Beyond the novelty of his observation about Parlement, which receives no substantial attention in the *Ritratto*, the passage in *The Prince* constructs a clear link between the kingdom of France and the goal of security. Security (as a matter of domestic, rather than foreign, concern) is a theme that is not widely addressed among scholars of Machiavelli.[29] But security—that of the prince, but also of his subjects—is a central topic of concern for Machiavelli. It is clear from his many remarks in *The Prince* that monarchic government—whether that of a hereditary ruler or a "new" prince—must place security at the top of its priorities in order to achieve glory. An insecure royal regime—one in which either the nobility or the people or both have the capacity and desire to strike out against one another or their prince—will quickly and inevitably fail. "A wise prince must think of ways through which his citizens always and in every type of weather have need of the state and of him," Machiavelli declares, "and they will be forever loyal."[30] Only that ruler who discovers and employs the appropriate methods of controlling his subjects—dampening down their passions and ambitions, or at any rate, directing them toward the interests of the state—stands a chance of overcoming the vicissitudes of *fortuna*. This is the heart of security, as Machiavelli understands it. And clearly, he believes in *The Prince* that the French monarchy had, in his own day, succeeded beyond any other regime in achieving this goal.

VIVERE SICURO

At first glance, the presence of Machiavelli's most extensive remarks about the French king and kingdom in the *Discourses* rather than *The Prince* might seem odd, if we uphold the image of him as a dedicated republican. Why would Machiavelli effusively praise (let alone even analyze) a hereditary monarchy in a work supposedly designed to promote the superiority of republics? The answer, we think, stems from Machiavelli's aim to contrast the best case scenario of a monarchic regime with the institutions and organization of a republic. Even the most excellent monarchy, in Machiavelli's view, lacks certain salient qualities that are endemic to well-ordered republican government and that make the latter constitution more desirable than the former.

While Machiavelli's treatment of France in the *Discourses* echoes some of the themes touched upon in the *Ritratto* and *The Prince*, he also introduces important new elements into the analysis. In particular, he asserts that the greatest virtue

28. Ibid., 19 (I, p. 69).

29. Among recent commentators, only Fischer comments on the topic at all in *Well-Ordered License*, pp. 64, 88.

30. Machiavelli, *Il Principe*, 9 (I, p. 34).

of the French kingdom and its king is the dedication to law. "The kingdom of France is moderated more by laws than any other kingdom of which at our time we have knowledge," Machiavelli declares.[31] In explaining this situation, Machiavelli refers to the function of the Parlement. "The kingdom of France," he states, lives under more laws and orders than any other kingdom. "These laws and orders are maintained by Parlements, notably that of Paris: by it they are renewed any time it acts against a prince of the kingdom or in its sentences condemns the king. And up to now it has maintained itself by having been a persistent executor against that nobility."[32] These passages of the *Discourses* seem to suggest that Machiavelli has great admiration for the institutional arrangements that obtain in France. Specifically, the French king and the nobles, whose power is such that they would be able to oppress the populace, are checked by the laws of the realm that are enforced by the independent authority of the Parlement. Thus, opportunities for unbridled tyrannical conduct are largely eliminated, rendering the monarchy temperate and "civil."

Yet such a regime, no matter how well ordered and law abiding, remains incompatible with *vivere libero*. Discussing the ability of a monarch to meet the people's wish for liberty, Machiavelli comments that "as far as the . . . popular desire of recovering their liberty, the prince, not being able to satisfy them, must examine what the reasons are that make them desire being free." He concludes that a few individuals want freedom simply in order to command others; these, he believes, are of sufficiently small number that they can either be eradicated or bought off with honors. By contrast, the vast majority of people confuse liberty with security, imagining that the former is identical to the latter: "But all the others, who are infinite, desire liberty in order to live securely (*vivere sicuro*)." Although the king cannot give such liberty to the masses, he can provide the security that they crave:

> As for the rest, for whom it is enough to live securely (*vivere sicuro*), they are easily satisfied by making orders and laws that, along with the power of the king, comprehend everyone's security. And once a prince does this, and the people see that he never breaks such laws, they will shortly begin to live securely (*vivere sicuro*) and contentedly.

Machiavelli then applies this general principle directly to the case of France, remarking that "the people live securely (*vivere sicuro*) for no other reason than that its kings are bound to infinite laws in which the security of all their people is comprehended."[33] This is not to say that the French king lacks absolute authority in certain matters, such as the military and public finance; but his power is not, as Matteucci notes, "arbitrary."[34] Machiavelli's larger point here is that the law-abiding character of the French regime ensures security, but that security, while

31. Machiavelli, *Discorsi* 1.58 (I, pp. 217–218).
32. Ibid., 3.1 (I, p. 331).
33. Ibid., 1.16 (I, pp. 139–140).
34. Matteuci, "Machiavelli Politicologo," pp. 223–224.

desirable, ought never to be confused with liberty. This is the limit of monarchic rule: even the best kingdom can do no better than to guarantee to its people tranquil and orderly government.

Machiavelli holds that one of the consequences of such *vivere sicuro* is the disarmament of the people. Reiterating the observation he makes in the *Ritratto*, he comments that regardless of "how great his kingdom is," the king of France "lives as a tributary" to foreign mercenaries.

> This all comes from having disarmed his people and having preferred . . . to enjoy the immediate profit of being able to plunder the people and of avoiding an imaginary rather than a real danger, instead of doing things that would assure them and make their states perpetually happy. This disorder, if it produces some quiet times, is in time the cause of straitened circumstances, damage and irreparable ruin.[35]

A state that makes security a priority cannot afford to arm its populace, for fear that the masses will employ their weapons against the nobility (or perhaps the crown). Yet at the same time, such a regime is weakened irredeemably, since it must depend upon foreigners to fight on its behalf. In this sense, any government that takes *vivere sicuro* as its goal generates a passive and impotent populace as a inescapable result. By definition, such a society can never be free in Machiavelli's sense of *vivere libero*, and hence is only minimally, rather than completely, political or civil.

VIVERE LIBERO OR *VIVERE SICURO*?

Confirmation of this interpretation of the limits of monarchy for Machiavelli may be found in his further discussion of the disarmament of the people, and its effects, in *The Art of War*. Addressing the question of whether a citizen army is to be preferred to a mercenary one, he insists that the liberty of a state is contingent upon the military preparedness of its subjects. Acknowledging that "the king [of France] has disarmed his people in order to be able to command them more easily," Machiavelli still concludes "that such a policy is . . . a defect in that kingdom, for failure to attend to this matter is the one thing that makes her weak."[36] In his view, whatever benefits may accrue to a state by denying a military role to the people are of less importance than the absence of liberty that necessarily accompanies such disarmament. The problem is not merely that the ruler of a disarmed nation is in thrall to the military prowess of foreigners. More crucially, Machiavelli believes, a weapons-bearing citizen militia remains the ultimate assurance that neither the government nor some usurper will tyrannize the populace. "So Rome was free four hundred years and was armed; Sparta, eight hundred; many other cities have been unarmed and free less than forty years."[37] Machiavelli is confident

---

35. Machiavelli, *Discorsi*, 2.30 (I, p. 317).
36. Machiavelli, *Arte Della Guerra*, 1 (I, pp. 466, 468–469).
37. Ibid., 1 (I, p. 467).

that citizens will always fight for their liberty—against internal as well as external oppressors. Indeed, this is precisely why successive French monarchs have left their people disarmed: they sought to maintain public security and order, which for them meant the elimination of any opportunities for their subjects to wield arms. The French regime, because it seeks security above all else (for the people as well as for their rulers), cannot permit what Machiavelli takes to be a primary means of promoting liberty.

The case of disarmament is an illustration of a larger difference between minimally constitutional systems such as France and fully political communities such as the Roman republic, namely, the status of the classes within the society. In France, as we have seen, the people are entirely passive and the nobility is largely dependent upon the king, according to Machiavelli's own observations. By contrast, in a republic, where the realization of liberty is paramount, both the people and the nobility must take an active (and sometimes clashing) role in self-government.[38] The liberty of the whole, for Machiavelli, depends upon the liberty of its component parts. In his famous discussion of this subject in the *Discourses*, he remarks,

> To me those who condemn the tumults between the Nobles and the Plebs seem to be caviling at the very thing that was the primary cause of Rome's retention of liberty . . . And they do not realize that in every republic there are two different dispositions, that of the people and that of the great men, and that all legislation favoring liberty is brought about by their dissension.[39]

Machiavelli knows that he is adopting an unusual perspective here, since customarily the blame for the collapse of the Roman republic has been assigned to warring factions that eventually ripped it apart. But Machiavelli holds that precisely the same conflicts generated a "creative tension" that was the source of Roman liberty. For "those very tumults that so many inconsiderately condemn" directly generated the good laws of Rome and the virtuous conduct of its citizens.[40] Hence, "Enmities between the people and the Senate should, therefore, be looked upon as an inconvenience which it is necessary to put up with in order to arrive at the greatness of Rome."[41] Machiavelli thinks that other republican models (such as those adopted by Sparta or Venice) will produce weaker and less successful political systems, ones that are either stagnant or prone to decay when circumstances change.

It will hardly come as a surprise to readers of Machiavelli that he expresses particular confidence in the capacity of the people to contribute to the promotion

---

38. A point underscored by Neal Wood, "The Value of Asocial Sociability: The Contributions of Machiavelli, Sidney and Montesquieu," in Martin Fleischer, eds., *Machiavelli and the Nature of Political Thought* (New York: Atheneum, 1972), pp. 287–291. Also see Benedetto Fontana, "Machiavelli and the Rhetoric of Republican Liberty," presented at the 2000 Meeting of the American Political Science Association, Washington, D.C.

39. Machiavelli, *Discorsi*, 1.4 (I, p. 104).

40. Ibid., 1.4 (I, p. 104).

41. Ibid., 1.6 (I, p. 112).

of communal liberty. In the *Discourses*, he ascribes to the masses a quite extensive competence to judge and act for the public good in various settings, explicitly
contrasting the "prudence and stability" of ordinary citizens with the unsound dis-
cretion of the prince. Simply stated, "Government by the people is better than government by princes."[42] This is not an arbitrary expression of personal preference
on Machiavelli's part. He maintains that the people are more concerned about,
and more willing to defend, liberty than either princes or nobles.[43] Where the latter
tend to confuse their liberty with their ability to dominate and control their fellows,
the masses are more concerned with protecting themselves against oppression and
consider themselves "free" when they are not abused by the more powerful or
threatened with such abuse.[44] In turn, when they fear the onset of such oppression, ordinary citizens are more inclined to object and to defend the common
liberty. Such an active role for the people, while necessary for the maintenance of
vital public liberty, is fundamentally antithetical to the hierarchical structure of
subordination-and-rule on which monarchic *vivere sicuro* rests. The preconditions
of *vivere libero* simply do not favor the security that is the aim of constitutional
monarchy.

One of the main reasons that security and liberty remain, in the end, incompatible for Machiavelli—and that the latter is to be preferred—may surely be
traced to the "rhetorical" character of his republicanism.[45] Machiavelli clearly
views speech as the method most appropriate to the resolution of conflict in the
republican public sphere; throughout the *Discourses*, debate is elevated as the best
means for the people to determine the wisest course of action and the most qualified leaders. The tradition of classical rhetoric, with which he was evidently familiar, directly associated public speaking with contention: the proper application of
speech in the realms of forensic and deliberative genres of rhetoric is an adver-
sarial setting, with each speaker seeking to convince his audience of the validity
of his own position and the unworthiness of his opponents'. This theme was taken
up, in turn, by late medieval Italian practitioners and theorists of rhetoric, who
emphasized that the subject matter of the art was *lite* (conflict).[46] Thus,
Machiavelli's insistence upon contention as a prerequisite of liberty also reflects
his rhetorical predilections. By contrast, monarchic regimes—even the most secure
constitutional monarchies such as France—exclude or limit public discourse,
thereby placing themselves at a distinct disadvantage. Machiavelli points out that
it is far easier to convince a single ruler to undertake a disastrous or ill-conceived
course of action than a multitude of people.[47] The apparent "tumult" induced by
the uncertain liberty of public discussion eventually renders more likely a decision

42. Ibid., 1.58 (I, p. 220).
43. Ibid., 1.5 (I, p. 106).
44. Ibid., 1.4 (I, p. 105).
45. See Viroli, *Machiavelli*, pp. 73–113 and passim; Cary J. Nederman, "Rhetoric, Reason, and
Republic: Republicanisms—Classical, Medieval, and Modern," in *Renaissance Civic Humanism*,
ed. James Hankins (Cambridge: Cambridge University Press, 2000), pp. 247–269.
46. See Virginia Cox, "Ciceronian Rhetoric in Italy, 1260–1350," *Rhetorica* 17 (Summer 1999),
pp. 239–288.
47. See Nederman, "Rhetoric, Reason, and Republic," p. 265.

conducive to the common good than does the closed conversation of the royal court.

CONCLUSION

Ultimately, Machiavelli's argument for the superiority of tumultuous republics of the Roman variety over either French-style monarchy or even other republican models stems from his belief that they are better equipped to deal with the vicissitudes of fortune and to succeed in expansion and conquest.[48] France and Sparta may have lasted longer, but neither enjoys the glory and honor that redound to Rome. Of course, one may object that Machiavelli's reasoning has troubling militaristic or even imperialistic overtones. Despite Viroli's recent efforts to rescue Machiavelli from such a charge,[49] we are inclined to agree with this objection. Consequently, we may properly debate whether, for ourselves, Machiavellian *vivere libero* is to be preferred to the *vivere sicuro* offered by constitutional monarchy. But this is a different question than that of what Machiavelli himself valued most highly. For him, a free regime constituted the pinnacle of human political achievement. And such a system of self-government distinguished itself most obviously by its ability to expand its boundaries and to include larger territories under its rule.

Machiavelli's distinction between *vivere libero* and *vivere sicuro* also highlights an important feature of his vexed relation to antecedent political philosophy. The general question of Machiavelli's "originality" has been widely, but inconclusively, debated.[50] Perhaps the most plausible conclusion is that Machiavelli's thought rests on a cusp between "classical" or "medieval" and "modern" world views, an altogether representative figure of the intellectual transitions of the Quattrocento.[51] In the case of *vivere sicuro*, the unconventional character of Machiavelli's teaching is revealed. From Plato and Aristotle through the late Middle Ages and Renaissance, political theory had commonly placed a premium on order, peace, and tranquility as counting among the highest goods of public life. By contrast, Machiavelli's preference for tumultuous *vivero libero* over *vivere sicuro* suggests a profound reorientation of fundamental political priorities. As Antony Black has emphasized, "Machiavelli took the crucial step of identify-

48. For some other aspects of the superiority of republics over principalities, see Cary J. Nederman, "Machiavelli and Moral Character: Principality, Republic, and the Psychology of *Virtù*," *History of Political Thought* 21 (Summer 2000), pp. 349–364.

49. Maurizio Viroli, *For Love of Country* (Oxford: Clarendon Press, 1995). We tend to agree with the view espoused by Jean Bethke Elshtain: "The citizen = the self-sufficient, armed warrior = the armed militia = armed civic virtue/the popular state: this is the Machiavellian recipe for civic autonomy" (*Women and War* [New York: Basic Books, 1987], p. 57); she follows a position pioneered by John Pocock.

50. See Cary J. Nederman, "Amazing France: Fortune, God, and Free Will in Machiavelli's Thought," *Journal of the History of Ideas* 60 (1999), pp. 619–620 and note 12.

51. A position defended, for example, by Roger D. Masters, *Machiavelli, Leonardo, and the Science of Power* (Notre Dame: University of Notre Dame Press, 1996), p. 338; and Nederman, "Machiavelli and Moral Character," pp. 363–364.

ing factional class conflict as an actual source of benefits," hence surpassing a salient feature of ancient and medieval political thought that his own contemporaries continued largely to embrace.[52] An Aristotle or a Marsiglio of Padua would probably have preferred the French monarchy as described by Machiavelli to the Roman Republic just because the aim of the former was a secure existence. In reversing this judgment, Machiavelli demonstrates just how great a distance his republicanism has traveled from the preceding tradition of political theory and thus defines precisely his contribution to the foundations of modern political thought.

---

52. Antony Black, "Harmony and Strife in Political Thought c. 1300–1500," in *Sozialer Wandel im Mittelalter*, ed. Jürgen Miethke and Klaus Schreiner (Sigmaringen: Jan Thorbecke Verlag, 1994), pp. 361–362.

Midwest Studies in Philosophy, XXVI (2002)

Montaigne, *An Apology for Raymond Sebond*: Happiness and the Poverty of Reason

BRUCE SILVER

To be a philosophical sceptic is, in a man of letters, the first and most essential step toward being a sound, believing Christian.

—David Hume[1]

Perhaps as a consequence of Richard Popkin's searching analysis, Michel de Montaigne's *An Apology for Raymond Sebond* (1575–80) has emerged as the most philosophically rich of all his *Essays* (1571–88).[2] Despite Popkin's insistence that Montaigne be recognized as a thinker whose contributions to the history of skepticism cannot be exaggerated, interpreters sometimes miss what is important about the *Apology* and what sets it apart from other expressions of classical Pyrrhonism.[3]

In what follows, therefore, I wish to identify specific elements in the *Apology* that make it an especially rich document for skeptics, theists, and historians of philosophy. To do this, I will first summarize the principal arguments of the *Apology* and, secondly, I will examine the specific ties between the *Apology* and Sextus's *Outlines of Pyrrhonism*, first published in Latin by Henri Estienne (1562).[4] Next, I will turn briefly to the *paradox of inquiry* in Plato's *Meno*, 80d–e, and to its bearing on the view that there is an essential connection between knowledge and

---

1. *Dialogues Concerning Natural Religion* (1779), Part XII.

2. *The History of Scepticism from Erasmus to Descartes*, revised edition (New York, 1964), 44–66.

3. Benson Mates is one of those who neither miss nor underestimate Montaigne's importance as a skeptic or his debts to Sextus Empiricus (c. 2nd century C.E.). *The Skeptic Way: Sextus Empiricus's Outlines of Pyrrhonism* (Oxford, 1995), 4–6.

4. Popkin, *The History of Skepticism*, 18, 34. Mates says that Estienne's translation was published in 1572 (*The Skeptic Way*, 221), but this is not the date given by other sources.

happiness. Finally, I must examine the foundations for Montaigne's view, implied in *Of Experience* (1587–88) and certified in the *Apology*, that for human beings happiness is unattainable.

I

In his introduction to his translation of *An Apology for Raymond Sebond*, M. A. Screech reviews two of the principal objections to Sebond's (Raymond Sibidua's) *Natural Theology or Book of Creatures*.[5] Against the first charge Sebond's critics make, that he errs in trying to support Christian beliefs with human reason, Montaigne replies that Sebond's understanding of Catholicism, as well as the relation of faith to reason, surpasses that of his critics: "I do not believe that purely human means are in the least able (to support religious beliefs through reason alone). If they were capable, so many rare and excellent minds that were equipped with natural powers in antiquity would not have failed to arrive at this knowledge through their reason. Faith alone grasps vigorously and certainly the high mysteries of our religion."[6]

This quotation looks like a conventional statement of medieval fideism, but by adding a qualification Montaigne also echoes some rationalist elements that one can find in Aquinas's *Summae*.[7] We must accompany "our faith with all the reason we possess, but always with the reservation that we neither assume that our faith depends upon us nor that attempts at arguments are powerful enough to arrive at a supernatural and divine science" (484).[8] The error of natural theologians, Sebond excepted, is the hubristic presumption that reason, unaided by faith, is enough to validate the belief that God exists and has the properties traditionally attributed to him (491–2).

One who scans only the first ten pages of the *Apology* might believe Montaigne is cut from the same cloth as rational theologians such as Anselm, Albertus Magnus, and Aquinas. But few serious readers will put down the *Apology* before they review all its arguments. After a thorough reading, their temptation to think of Montaigne even as a marginal rationalist should disappear. In this context, Montaigne's extended answer to a second charge against Sebond, viz., that the arguments of his *Natural Theology* are weak, dominates the *Apology*.[9]

Montaigne's replies, against critics who maintain that Sebond provides only weak arguments for natural religion, vary from serious to frivolous. Sebond's book

---

5. Michel de Montaigne, *An Apology for Raymond Sebond*, trans. and intro. M. A. Screech (London, 1993), xvi–xxx. For some biographical details on Sibidua's work and on how Montaigne developed an interest in it, see Popkin's *The History of Scepticism*, 44–6, and B. C. Copenhaver and C. B. Schmitt, *A History of Renaissance Philosophy* (Oxford, 1992), 250–2.

6. *Essais de Montaigne*, ed. A. Thibaudet (Bruges, 1950), 484. Subsequent citations and quotations from this edition are in parentheses in my text. Unless otherwise noted, translations from French and Latin are my own.

7. See Screech's introduction to *An Apology for Raymond Sebond*, xvii.

8. See *Classical Statements on Faith and Reason*, ed. E. L. Miller (New York, 1970), 38.

9. For an abbreviated summary and discussion of these two charges against Sebond, see Terence Penelhum, *God and Skepticism* (Dordrecht, 1983), 22–3.

is his inspiration, but Montaigne's own declarations and arguments go far beyond it. Screech, without referring to Sebond, summarizes the overriding point of Montaigne's skeptical arguments: *Pride is the sin of sins*: intellectually it leads to Man's arrogantly taking mere opinion for knowledge. In terms that were common to many Renaissance writers, Montaigne emphasized that 'there is a plague (a *'peste'*) on Man: *the opinion that he knows something'*."[10]

The last two hundred pages of the *Apology* are aimed at documenting and deriding the baseless pride of human beings, pride that is accentuated by men's convictions that, *qua* rational, they are the zenith of God's handiwork. To document "the presumption that pride is our natural and original illness" (497), Montaigne describes man just as he is: isolated, unarmed, lacking the grace and knowledge of God that give him whatever dignity and power he is thought to have (494).[11]

Evidence abounds that man is pathetic. He is the pawn of outside influences like the stars (496). He thinks he is superior to the animals, but his evidence is inconclusive. In probably the most familiar passage from the *Apology*, Montaigne wonders, "When I play with my cat, who knows whether she passes her time with me more than I pass my time with her?" (498).

If we try to say what sets human beings apart from animals, we are pressed to answer. We communicate; so do animals (498, 504–5). We are social and skillful beings, but birds and insects manifest society and craftsmanship that equal ours (500–1). We raise to the skies our own rational capacities even as we ignore the "reasoning" of an unremarkable dog that disjoins, conjoins, and enumerates propositions to determine which of three paths will take him home. Whether the decision of the dog arises from reasoning or from another principle, we are not able to make a firm distinction between human rationality and the natural capacities of animals (510–11).

Here the similarity between Montaigne and Hume is familiar. Whether one wishes to praise animals because they reason or criticize human beings for not seeing that what passes for reasoning is nothing more than habitual behavior, these two skeptics meet at a common center: "Nothing shews more the force of habit in reconciling us to any phaenomenon, than this, that men are not astonish'd at the operations of their own reason, at the same time that they admire the *instinct* of animals . . . To consider the matter aright, reason is nothing but a wonderful and unintelligible instinct in our souls, which carries us along a certain train of ideas."[12]

Even if it is true that men reason and that animals do not, Montaigne believes that reason unsettles us. Indeed, it is often the chief cause of the troubles

---

10. *An Apology for Raymond Sebond*, xxii; emphasis added. Sincere concerns about man's prideful nature need not lead to an indictment of reason. The closing pages of Thomas More's *Utopia* (1516) describe pride as the worst of the seven deadly sins, although the strength of More's Utopians is their rationality. See *Utopia*, tr. and ed. R. M. Adams, 2nd edition (New York, 1992), 84.

11. Screech notes that from this point until its closing page, "revealed wisdom is left aside" in the *Apology*, 13, note 37.

12. David Hume, *A Treatise of Human Nature* (1739–40), ed. L. A. Selby-Bigge, rev. P. H. Nidditch (Oxford, 1978), 178–9.

that seize us, e.g., sin, illness, irresolution, confusion, and despair (506). One need only recall the Renaissance humanist tradition, especially its celebration of human nature and intelligence, to see how far Montaigne is from the "official" version of what sets human beings apart from all other earthly beings. He presses his sentiments in passages that show the distance between him and humanists like Marsilio Ficino, Giovanni Pico della Mirandola, Pietro Pomponazzi, and Juan Luis Vives. For Montaigne, but not for humanists who are rhapsodic about human dignity, man obeys the same laws of nature and is subject to identical vagaries of fortune that govern all other animals beneath the stars (506).[13]

But the poverty of reason takes numerous forms; hence, Montaigne, revealing in the *Apology* the primitivism that is conspicuous in his essay *Of Cannibals* (1578–80), writes that our "civilized" excesses have extinguished what is natural and sufficient for our brief stay on the surface of this planet. Inventing needs that are not needs is a mark of human foolishness, not of rationality (520–1).[14] We deviate from nature's counsel and finally corrupt ourselves trying to satisfy desires that are antagonistic to our welfare (521).

Rehearsing a strain of thought familiar from Erasmus' *Praise of Folly* (1508), Montaigne also affirms that reason (actively realized as a desire to know) frustrates happiness and cannot be its source: "In my time I have seen a hundred artisans and another hundred laborers who are also wiser and happier than university rectors, and I wish I were more like them" (540). Montaigne covets simple contentment more than the specious wisdom of scholars, even as Erasmus speaks with nostalgia of the Golden Age in which "simple men flourished, without all that armor-plate of the sciences, under the leadership of nature and natural instincts alone."[15]

"The plague on Man is the opinion that he knows something. That is why ignorance is so highly recommended by our religion as a quality proper to belief and obedience" (541).[16] Following something close to the Epicurean position, Montaigne insists that given our limitations, the best we can attain in this life is an existence unencumbered by pain: "I hold that if ignorance and simplicity can bring us to the *absence of pain*, then it brings us to a very happy state *given the human condition*" (547).[17] To provide "evidence" for this claim, Montaigne reminds us how many times and ways philosophy has been forced to concede its failure to provide the happiness we desire (548–53). In the final analysis, then, if we are going to be happy, happier than those who live a pain-free life, we must look beyond our own meager capacities since, "In truth we are nothing" (554).

13. For a discussion of the humanist glorification of man, see P. O. Kristeller, *Renaissance Thought II: Papers on Humanism and the Arts*, 107–10.

14. Compare a similar expression of primitivism in Rousseau's *Discourse on the Origins of Inequality among Men* (1755), Part I.

15. Desiderius Erasmus, *The Praise of Folly and Other Writings*, tr. and ed. R. M. Adams (New York, 1989), 33.

16. For Montaigne's disapproval of ancient authors who prize learning and human knowledge beyond its worth, see pages 541–3.

17. Emphasis added. Epicurus takes precedence over Aristotle for Montaigne. See *Hellenistic Philosophy: Introductory Readings*, tr. B. Inwood and L. P. Gerson (Indianapolis, 1988), 24, 26.

Having set the stage for a sustained assault on reason and its protean manifestations, Montaigne turns directly to Sextus Empiricus. Sextus believed that all of philosophy could be divided into three categories. *Dogmatists* claim they have found what they seek, while *Academics* say what they seek cannot be found. *Skeptics* continue to search. Each, paradoxically, has in common, "*the design to obtain truth, science and certainty*" (558; emphasis added).[18] Montaigne understands, borrowing not only from Sextus but also from Lucretius's *De Rerum Natura* (c. 60 B.C.E.), the approach of the Pyrrhonian skeptics: "to shake convictions, to doubt, to inquire and neither to affirm nor to respond to anything," and thereby to arrive at "*ataraxia* . . . which is a condition of life that is calm, peaceful, and free from agitation" (559). Montaigne also understands how the Pyrrhonian skeptics use reason in their searching and how their suspension of judgment ("*epochē*") serves their aims: "They employ their reason for inquiry and debate but not to make choices or decisions. One who imagines an endless confession of ignorance and judgment without any tendency or inclination . . . conceives what Pyrrhonism is" (562).

Finally, Montaigne adds that Pyrrhonists, having suspended all judgments, live in terms of the customs and laws of their own time and setting. Living this way is a source of comfort, not an investment in any conviction. Pyrrhonists do not have to make a dogmatic or intellectual surrender to laws and conventions in order to obey and honor them (562–3).

Grasping the message and tactics of the Pyrrhonians is not enough. Montaigne wishes to serve his own end, the triumph of Counter-Reformation Catholicism over the incursions of the Protestant Reformation. One of the pillars of Reformed Catholicism, Terence Penelhum notes, is a respect for customs and modes of conduct that had served long and well to preserve the Universal Church: "Man, placed individually in history, and unable to rise above the relativities that derive from this, must recognize his inability to do so, and should submit to the religious forms and teachings that surround him, rather than try arrogantly to assert or deny them from an objective standpoint that is impossible for him . . . This position is almost purely Pyrrhonistic."[19]

Montaigne approves the neo-Pyrrhonian revival because none of its competitors has "greater utility nor a greater appearance of truth which exhibits man naked, empty and aware of his natural shortcomings, suited to receive outside power from on high, bereft of human learning and thus better able to lodge his faith. Thus stripped of all human understanding and so better able to lodge faith in the divine within him, man destroys his intellect to make room for his faith" (563).[20]

Montaigne is most obviously at odds with philosophers who pretend to have found the truth or who are invigorated by (hopelessly) seeking it. Almost no one, from Socrates and Plato to the later Dogmatists, is spared. And in a touch of prag-

---

18. See *Outlines of Pyrrhonism*, Part I, chapter 1.

19. *God and Skepticism*, 23. For a discussion of the defining features of the Counter-Reformation, see Owen Chadwick, *The Reformation*, rev. ed. (Harmondsworth, 1972), 251–362.

20. Emphasis added. This is an obvious reminder of Kant's famous declaration "I have therefore found it necessary to deny *knowledge* in order to make room for *faith*," in the *Critique of Pure Reason* (1781), tr. N. K. Smith (New York, 1929), 29.

matism, he stresses the emptiness of our expectations: "It is the misery of our condition that often presents as truth what we imagine and what has least use for the purposes of life" (571).

To address specifically the bankruptcy of competing philosophies, Montaigne rehearses in detail the endlessly opposed views that ancient philosophies and pagan religions promote with respect to God's nature, attitudes toward death and the afterlife, the union of the soul and body, the origin of the soul, the transmigration of the soul, and the creation of bodies (573–624). The details of these views are less important to Montaigne than what they tell us about reason: if philosophers "have anything to advance, reason is their touchstone, but certainly it is a touchstone full of falsity, errors, faults and foibles . . . When we cannot rely on reason when we talk about it, can we appropriately use reason to judge anything outside it?" (607).

Having addressed barren reason, the reason of animals, and the poverty of nearly every philosophy known to the Renaissance, in the last quarter of the *Apology* Montaigne produces arguments for the limits of reason and sense. His examples are familiar to anyone who has read Plato and Sextus.

In case Montaigne needs to remind us of our frailty, he offers a pejorative characterization of "Reason" as the faculty that is supposed to elevate us over those beings that lack it: "I always call *reason* that appearance of rationality which each of us forges for himself . . . It can be stretched, bent or adjusted to every size and bias" (635; emphasis added). Clever men and women can shape reason to suit various needs, but it cannot take them to knowledge and thus not to what is supposed to make them happy. Their reasoning is swayed by passions, health and feelings. What they know today is what they doubt tomorrow. We all want certainty, but what do we get? "What certainty can we take from what is so restless and unstable as the soul, subject to the dominance of perturbations and never moveable except under force . . . Can we anticipate security from it?" (639).

Even a judge eager to render a just verdict is no different from the rest of us. He too is moved by inclinations, relatives and friends, or the desire for revenge. Like anyone else, he can be swayed by a fleeting impulse that induces him to choose in light of his sympathies or hostilities (635–6).

The weather, our moods, and the appeal of conflicting hypotheses (641–2) make reason a pawn, not an arbiter of truth.[21] The Pyrrhonists used their reason to reveal that we have no justification for beliefs based upon experience, even when experience seems to render them likely. Reason, far from serving a constructive role, expands doubts about the convictions we take from experience (643).

Reason fails to illuminate our highest good (650–1). We often pursue what we desire as an end but are puzzled about what satisfies our quest. The problems of philosophy and of reason's search for truth are compounded by what we learn through exploration, anthropology, and geography. What passes for truth varies from place to place and from culture to culture. Some argue that natural laws are

---

21. And the discovery of the New World casts doubt on ancient attitudes about the Antipodes (643).

universal, yet between cultures there is wide disagreement about these laws and about what they demand from us (151–8).[22]

As an empiricist no less than a skeptic, Montaigne insists, "the senses are our masters . . . Knowledge begins through them and is reduced to them" (663). In this respect he looks back to Aquinas and ahead to Gassendi or Locke. They all agree that at birth the human intellect is a kind of blank tablet on which nothing is written. We know, of course, from reading skeptically inclined empiricists like Locke and Hume, that Montaigne can be an empiricist and not defend the truth-securing credentials of his empiricism. After all, as Cicero noted in antiquity, if during our unreflective moments we feel certain that what the senses convey to us is so, in our philosophical moments we discover that our senses are inherently fallible (663–4).

What are the problems that our senses generate and leave unresolved? First, how do we know that we have senses enough to take in the facts that serve as the basis for knowledge? How can we know whether we lack other senses, since no sense discovers another sense and reason cannot promise that we have all the possible senses (664)? Second, a man born blind can never know the visible world. Perhaps those of us with the five working senses stand in relation to other animals as a blind man stands to us: "How can one know that the difficulties we have in discovering many of the works of Nature do not arise from defective or insufficient senses? *How many of the actions of animals exceed our capacities and are produced by a sense-faculty which we lack? Perhaps some of them, through such a sense or means, have a fuller life and more complete life than ours*" (665–6).[23]

Beyond declaring the fallibility of our senses, Montaigne also rehearses arguments familiar to students of modern philosophy. Echoes make us believe that sounds come from sources that do not produce them. Sight, overpowering reflection, causes us to fear heights that we have no reason to fear (671). "For a man in pain and affliction, the clear light of day seems dark and obscure. Our senses are not only altered; they are often dazed altogether by the passions of the soul" (673). And Montaigne, before Descartes, thinks there are more than enough reasons to confuse vigorous dreams with wakefulness: "Why should we not doubt whether our thinking, our acting, are not another dream and our waking up another species of sleeping?" (674).

Similar problems of sense arise even if the "dreaming argument" is not an issue. To those suffering from inflamed eyes objects look red, and there is a good chance that animals, whose eyes are often different from ours, do not see what we see even though we look at the same thing. To human beings with jaundice, everything appears to be yellow (675).[24] Montaigne misunderstood the nature and

22. Compare Locke's similar grounds for criticizing innate ideas in *An Essay Concerning Human Understanding* (1690), Book I, chapter iii, sections 10–13.

23. Emphasis added. This is at least partly a knife in the back of Aristotle and Aristotelians for denying that animals can lead a happy life. *Nicomachean Ethics*, 1178b, 24–8.

24. Berkeley presses the differences between human and animal vision, as well as the supposed effects of jaundice, as he argues for the mind-dependence of all colors. *Principles, Dialogues, and Philosophical Correspondence*, ed. and intro. C. M. Turbayne (Indianapolis, 1965), "Dialogue I," 124.

effects of jaundice, but whether there is any way to certify as veridical the perceptions of those who have *normal* vision is a perennial question that does not allow one to dismiss Montaigne as naïve or out of his depth (675).

The same arguments apply to the perceptions of children, adults, and very old people whose grip on the world is infirm. At different ages, we see and taste things differently (676–7). But do we have a way to identify a particular age and *its* perceptions as definitive when the issue is perceiving objects as they are, not as they appear?

We encounter objects *as-sensed*. We can neither evade standing in a lockstep with our senses nor can we, as a consequence, be certain that **p** is in *itself* as **p** *appears* to us when it is filtered through our senses: "Our imagination is not in immediate contact with any external objects, which are perceived solely by the intervention of the senses, and the senses do not embrace outside objects themselves but only their impressions of them . . . So whoever judges from appearances judges from something different from the object itself" (679).

Furthermore, there is no way that we can appeal to some privileged standard to determine the actual qualities a thing possesses. We have already conceded that the senses cannot get beyond themselves to the thing as it is *in itself*, and reason cannot infer from sensory experience to that which, in fact and in principle, neither reason nor sense apprehends.[25] Moreover, any effort to appeal to some nonsensuous standard miscarries. If we turn to reason to decide a dispute about the true nature of things, we will have to validate our reasoning, but in reasoning, we must appeal to reasons, which sets the table for an infinite regress (679).[26]

Montaigne concludes *An Apology for Raymond Sebond* with what Popkin characterizes as a "symphony of doubt." This is precisely what we should expect from a follower of Sextus Empiricus: "There is not any constancy either in our existence or in that of objects. We, our judgment and all mortal things flow and move endlessly. There is no establishing anything certain about us or the objects we seek to know, since what is judged and judging continuously shift and change" (679).

If there were no need to interpret this catalog of doubts and limitations, Montaigne could simply take his place on a long list of skeptics. But because skepticism in the *Apology* actually reaches beyond the grounds we have for doubting our reason and senses, we need to turn next to other issues to which my discussion points.

II

More than the sum of its arguments and references to authority make Montainge's *Apology* a classic. Montaigne uses Sextus Empiricus explicitly to establish that the

---

25. See, for example, Berkeley's *Principles of Human Knowledge* (1710), section 18. Berkeley's reference is to Locke's efforts to defend knowledge of an external world of bodies (*Essay*, IV, xi). Hume is probably indebted to Locke and to Berkeley in *A Treatise of Human Nature* (1739–40), Book I, part ii, section 6; iv, 2.

26. See Popkin's discussion of this and other aspects of Montaigne's arguments against the solvency of reason, in *The History of Scepticism from Erasmus to Descartes*, 51–3, and Copenhaver and Schmitt, *Renaissance Philosophy*, 257–8.

Socratic, Platonic, and Aristotelian identification of happiness with the excellent employment of reason generates a futile quest for happiness.

In a sense, but with a crucial difference, Montaigne voices in prose what Dante sings in *terza rima*: pagan knowledge cannot possibly deliver the happiness that all of us seek. To whatever degree, therefore, that our happiness depends upon reasoning well and upon natural means to satisfy our natural desire to know, we are not happy.

The reference to Dante is not a digression. Dante meets Beatrice in the Earthly Paradise, and she chides him, very far through Purgatory, for looking still to Virgil as his guide to happiness. Is Dante unaware that happiness is available only to the redeemed Christian? Reason, properly directed, reveals the soul's vices, but this for Dante, which is far more than for Montaigne, is all it can do. "Sweet reason" can never allow Dante the ineffable happiness that he experiences in the ephemeral vision of God with which the *Comedy* closes.

Even when reason has done everything it can do, it cannot, since happiness is the end for which we act, do enough. This is Dante's message in *The Purgatorio*, XXVII, 127–43, and XXX, 50–63. It is the same message that John Ciardi summarizes when he introduces *The Inferno*. As Dante is lost in the Dark Wood of worldly excess, the figure of Virgil appears and "explains that he has been sent to lead Dante from error . . . Virgil offers to guide Dante, but only as far as Human Reason can go. Another guide (*Beatrice*, symbol of Divine *Love*) must take over for the final ascent, for Human Reason is self-limited."[27]

Dante's poetry, not his commitment to orthodoxy, is exceptional. A wayward Christian, under the direction of reason, does what he can in an effort at self-discovery and purification, but this is never enough for salvation and for the authentic happiness that comes from divine election. Reason enables Dante to advance toward a divine love that is the conduit to happiness, but Beatrice must first summon Virgil—faith has to wake reason—for the process to begin.[28]

Still, Dante is a late Thomist, and even his brief for the limited role of reason in becoming happy sets him apart from Montaigne. To make a case that no human being can be happy—that is, as Socrates, Plato, and Aristotle conceive happiness as rational contemplation—Montaigne appeals to Sextus. In reading the *Outlines of Pyrrhonism*, Montaigne does not doubt the claim, "all men wish for happiness is a fundamental assumption of the Socratic, as well as Platonic and Aristotelian moral psychology,"[29] but he doubts that "all men," as men, get what they want.

By reviving the arguments and tropes in *Outlines of Pyrrhonism*, Montaigne has an arsenal to show that whether a person appeals to the senses (with the empiricists) or to reason (with the rationalists), he will never know anything.[30] The

---

27. *The Inferno*, tr. John Ciardi (New York, 1952), 27.
28. Ibid., 34.
29. *The Symposium*, tr. and analysis R. E. Allen (New Haven, 1991), 54.
30. The model for knowing emerges in the *Theaetetus*, *Meno*, *Republic* and *Posterior Analytics*. But even if one settles for a more dilute view of knowledge, probability, or right opinion, Montaigne (following Sextus) argues that the case is hopeless.

problem is insurmountable. If happiness consists in knowing and is the yield of productive inquiry, one must abandon prospects for happiness and settle for something else, as Sextus does. Even if he entertains the claim that knowing and being happy are inseparable, finding no reason to think that we can know he settles for *ataraxia*.[31]

Benson Mates makes the Pyrrhonian point in discussing Sextus's attitude toward *ataraxia*: "The goal . . . of the Skeptic is *ataraxia* (. . . 'imperturbability'); as regards things that are forced upon him, it is to have moderate *pathē* ['affects']. *Ataraxia* is not to be pursued directly; instead it arises as a byproduct of *epochē* ['suspension of judgment'], which in turn follows upon the state of *aporia* that results from the Skeptics' attempts to resolve the anomaly (*anōmalia*) of phenomena and noumena by discovering what *is* the case, as contrasted with what merely *appears* to be the case."[32]

Insofar as *ataraxia* is freedom from perturbation, Sextus insists that we err if we think about it as we think of happiness, as a "panacea for life's troubles, such as might be held out by religion or perhaps by a Seneca-style stoicism. Instead, the Skeptic's *ataraxia* is . . . only a relief from whatever unpleasant puzzlement one might have about what is really the case in a supposedly mind-independent external world."[33]

The Pyrrhonists find that no assertion is safe or secure in the sense that it is indubitable. They can never say to a level of certainty or even to justified true belief that any proposition **p** is true or false, and *ataraxia* provides a respite from trying to decide what is undecidable. Still, they need not retreat from living simply because they live without beliefs. Pyrrhonists will yield to some emotions. They will honor the traditions and customs of the city in which they reside, and they will do what they can to earn a living.[34] No Pyrrhonist will mistake his own choices for dogma; hence, at the outset of *Outlines of Pyrrhonism* Sextus says, "As regards none of the things that we are about to say do we firmly maintain that matters are absolutely as stated, but in each instance we are simply reporting, like a chronicler, *what now appears to us to be the case*."[35]

Obviously, then, if Pyrrhonists are skeptical of all assertions, they must resist every temptation to believe, and they must avoid dogmatism.[36] What, then, is Pyrrhonism? What does it amount to? It is a way of living and of thinking about which Sextus writes:

> The Skeptic Way is a disposition to oppose phenomena and noumena to one another in any way whatever, with the result that, owing to the equipollence among the things and statements thus opposed, we are brought first to *epochē* and then to *ataraxia* . . . By "equipollence" we mean equality as

---

31. Indeed, Pyrrhonists are pleased to reach *ataraxia* as an epiphenomenon of *aporia* and *epochē*.
32. *The Skeptic Way*, 45.
33. Ibid.
34. Ibid., 9.
35. Ibid., 89; emphasis added.
36. Ibid., 601.

regards credibility and lack of it, that is, that no one of the inconsistent statements takes precedence over any other as being more credible. *Epochē* is a
state of the intellect on account of which we neither deny nor affirm anything. *Ataraxia* is an untroubled and tranquil condition of the soul.[37]

One might wonder why, if Pyrrhonism promotes a life that evades stress and confusion, Sextus's Pyrrhonists "continue to search" for the truth?[38]

Mates addresses this question by saying that the Pyrrhonist's "*aporia*, leading
through *epochē* to *ataraxia*, is . . . consistent with his 'continuing to search' . . . , for
the 'searching' that the Skeptic does turns out to be, in most cases, nothing more
than the raising of questions about the meaning and seeming implications of
Dogmatic assertions purporting to be true."[39] I agree but make the point a bit differently. Dogmatists, insisting that they know the truth, have no reason to search.
This is what makes them dogmatic in the first place. Academics are just as certain
that neither they nor anyone else can ever know the truth; hence, they regard
searching for it as useless.

What about the Pyrrhonists? They search in the most passive sense of
"search," i.e., remain barely open, not optimistic, to the possibility of knowledge.
Indeed, as a practical philosophy Pyrrhonism seems to have developed more by
accident than by design: "the Skeptics were hoping to achieve *ataraxia* by resolving the phenomena and noumena, and, being unable to do this, they suspended
judgment. But then, *by chance as it were*, when they were suspending judgment the
ataraxia followed, as a shadow follows the body."[40] The search for knowledge bears
no fruit, but the willingness to suspend one's judgment leads to imperturbability.

Pyrrhonists do not satisfy their desire to know, but unlike the Academics and
Dogmatists, they find calm in failure. Frustration, not tranquility, might *seem* the
more likely consequence of failure; however, a product of suspending judgment
when knowledge or resolution does not follow inquiry is *ataraxia*. On Sextus's sympathetic account, then, the consistent Pyrrhonist can find contentment even when
he cannot find knowledge.[41]

Throughout the *Outlines of Pyrrhonism*, Sextus emphasizes *ataraxia*, that
elusive "untroubled and tranquil condition of the soul," not *eudaimonia* or happiness, as the likely result of a Pyrrhonist's behavior.[42] One could claim that other
Hellenistic philosophies such as Epicureanism and Stoicism also stress contentment, tranquility, or pleasure but are themselves relatively mute about happiness;
however, understanding the position of the Pyrrhonists, not that of Epicureans and
Stoics, is vital for getting at the marrow of Montaigne's *Apology*.

Unless I have misinterpreted an argument in *Outlines of Pyrrhonism*, Sextus
does *not* claim that *ataraxia* is one's highest conceivable good. His claim is more

37. Ibid., 89–90.
38. Ibid., 89.
39. Ibid., 32.
40. Ibid., 93.
41. Ibid.
42. Ibid., 90.

modest and defensive: given the restrictions imposed upon us by the limits of reason, by our few and defective senses, by the intrusive character of our passions, and by other impediments to thinking and knowing, we can at best surrender to our limitations and attain *ataraxia*. This does not imply that being calm and being happy are identical.

We can suggest that Sextus could well have shared the Socratic, Platonic, and Aristotelian notion that knowing and being happy are inseparably linked, but suggesting and securing an interpretation are different. The searching that Sextus defends might, were it successful, beget the happiness we desire and not merely the calm with which we can live.[43] Nonetheless, and this is too important to neglect, the hypothesis that knowledge leads to—or amounts to—happiness cannot be tested unless we not only desire knowledge but actually acquire it. An untested hypothesis is nothing more than empty speculation (605), but for Sextus and Montaigne the assertion "Knowledge makes us happy" is that kind of hypothesis.[44] No less serious, each philosopher believes that the insuperable limitations on our capacity to *know* **p** or justifiably to *believe* **p** militate against our ever being in a position to verify or to disconfirm the claim "Knowledge makes us happy."

One can more safely claim, then, that Sextus and Montaigne are far from assuming knowledge leads to happiness or **S** is happy if and only if **S** is a member of the set of those who know. When, therefore, Aristotle declares at the close of the *Nicomachean Ethics*, Book X, that philosophers, second only to the gods whose activity they imitate, are the happiest beings insofar as they know and contemplate, he obviously does not speak for skeptics like Sextus or for neo-Skeptics like Montaigne. For Aristotle, in the *Nicomachean Ethics*, X, viii, "Happiness extends . . . just so far as contemplation does, and those to whom contemplation more fully belongs are more truly happy, not accidentally, but in virtue of the contemplation; for this is itself precious. Happiness, therefore, must be some form of contemplation."[45]

But for Sextus and Montaigne, the choice looks disappointing where happiness is our concern: (a) one can seek knowledge with the hope of attaining happiness, *or* (b) one can claim that happiness is independent of knowledge.[46] I find no clinching evidence in *Outlines of Pyrrhonism* or *An Apology for Raymond Sebond* that (b) "happiness" is independent of knowledge, and (a) is out of the question insofar as both philosophers argue that looking for happiness in knowl-

43. Ibid., 32.

44. For Hume on barren speculative hypotheses, see *A Treatise of Human Nature*, 82–3.

45. *Nicomachean Ethics*, 1178b, 28–32, tr. W. D. Ross, rev. J. O. Urmson, in *The Complete Works of Aristotle*, ed. Jonathan Barnes (2 vols., Princeton, 1984), II, 1863. Whether Aristotle is consistent in his picture of happiness, even within the limits of the *Nicomachean Ethics*, is a matter of sustained debate. Some interpreters find a tension between what Aristotle says about the complete, happy life in I, vii, and what he says about the contemplative life in X, viii. For a recent discussion of this issue, see Jonathan Lear, *Happiness, Death, and the Remainder of Life* (Cambridge, Mass., 2000), 35–60. For a more traditional effort at an Aristotelian reconciliation of the happy lives of moral and contemplative human beings, see J. L. Ackrill, *Aristotle the Philosopher* (Oxford, 1981), 135–41.

46. One can profitably look at Plato's *Apology*, 29d–30b, and *Republic*, 353d–354b, for hints at the connective tissues between Socrates, Plato, and Aristotle on happiness and the good life.

edge ends neither in knowledge nor in the happiness that is supposed to depend upon knowing.

Perhaps there is another choice (c), viz., the admonition to find happiness in the *quest* for knowledge even if the quest is bound to fail. This is a choice that Augustine mentions in the *Contra Academicos* (c. 386 C.E.),[47] but neither Sextus nor Montaigne endorses *seeking* truth when happiness is what we are after. The searching they describe reveals the grounds for doubting our senses, our reason, and our conventional beliefs about the world.[48] Moreover, Augustine himself rejects (c) and promotes a position that points to Montaigne's but that is somewhat more hospitable to reason: "philosophy is not wisdom itself but is called the study of wisdom. If you give yourself to philosophy, you will not . . . be wise here, during this life, for wisdom is found only with God and man cannot attain it, but when you have studied and have purified yourself, *you will certainly enjoy wisdom after life, when you are no longer mortal.*"[49]

This is a claim that skeptics could, with an obvious modification, accept. Augustine's spokesman says this life affords no happiness because it offers no knowledge. Whether someone can be happy in a life to come is unanswerable because believing there is a life after death and believing one actually *knows* anything in a life after death far exceed what Sextus would ever affirm.

III

One can make even shorter work of the futile search for truth than what (c) above describes. Consider the famous *paradox of inquiry* in the *Meno*, 80d–e. Montaigne knew the *Meno* and quoted it in *Of Experience* (1200), but even if he had never read it, the problem of the paradox is a salient feature of *An Apology for Raymond Sebond*.

The nominal concern of the *Meno* is how virtuous men come by their virtue; its deeper concern is how anyone *knows* what "virtue" (*aretē*) is. Socrates states the paradox when Meno, frustrated by all his failed attempts, doubts that he can ever find a definition for "virtue": "I know what you mean to say, Meno. Do you realize what a debater's argument you are bringing up, that a man cannot search either for what he knows or for what he does not know? He cannot search for what he knows—since he knows it, there is no need to search—nor for what he does not know, for he knows not what to seek for" (80e).[50]

Plato defuses the paradox by introducing the metaphysical and epistemological equipment with which all subsequent Platonists are familiar—the eternally knowing soul in which necessary truths (*objects of knowledge*) are eternally stored (81a–d) and the method of "recollection" (*anamnesis*) that enables anyone, with direction and diligence, to recall these truths (85c–e).[51] But Plato's solution is

---

47. *Contra Academicos*, I, iii, in *Corpus Augustinianum*, ed. C. Mayer (Makrolog, 2000).
48. *The Skeptic Way*, 30–2.
49. *Contra Academicos*, III, xx; emphasis added.
50. Plato, *Meno*, 2nd ed., tr. G. M. A. Grube (Indianapolis, 1981), 13.
51. For what characterizes an object of Platonic knowledge, see the *Cratylus*, 439d–440b.

unavailable to Montaigne. If Montaigne had been friendly to Plato's epistemological nativism, rather than to empiricism, the skepticism at the center of the *Apology* would not have been an issue in the first place.

What, then, is the point? Granting the force of Plato's paradox—a paradox that Plato himself treats as insoluble without introducing into the *Meno* metaphysical and epistemological elements that belong to the middle dialogues—successful inquiry is impossible; hence, so too is the acquisition of knowledge. Where Plato is willing to craft an extravagant metaphysics and a doctrine of innate ideas to rescue knowledge and inquiry, Montaigne is not. Where Plato finds only deficiencies in empiricist theories of knowledge, Montaigne insists (without discounting these deficiencies) that non-empiricist theories of knowledge are too extravagant to entertain.[52] The message is simple and is one we have already seen in Sextus's arguments. A philosophy that insists upon a necessary connection between knowledge and happiness, but denies the possibility of knowledge, must deny the possibility of happiness. That this is obvious does not make it less true, and I think that Montaigne seized and appreciated the consequences of this connection.

IV

Where does what I have said in I through III leave Montaigne's treatment of happiness? Here too I think the answer is transparent. Although, as I have noted throughout my discussion, Montaigne talks about degrees of contentment and about the question whether a sage is more fully at peace than an untutored Brazilian, he does not quite go so far as to make the *absolute* claim that there is no connection between knowing and being happy or, for that matter, between reasoning with excellence and being happy (545). The problem for Montaigne is that men and women are, as we have seen over and over, fallen and imperfect. One of the many consequences of that fall, as well as of the inherent imperfections of being a creature, is that human beings cannot know anything to a level of certainty nor can they sense beyond the phenomena of experience. This means, unless I have misread the *Apology*, that *human* beings (with an emphasis on "*human*") cannot be happy, if to be happy is to know. Sextus, his predecessors and epigones are correct: the best we can manage on our own, in this life, is something close to *ataraxia*. This is because knowledge, that is, strict knowledge that the ancients praised as contemplation and called "*theoria*," is unattainable. Even Aristotle, without any notion of Christian doctrine or grace, hinted that human beings could at most approximate, not experience, happiness at its highest registers.[53]

We try to understand the world, and inevitably we come up short of the mark (600). This is not news; it is inevitable. We are as far from knowing the things we

---

52. One might read the subtext of the *Meno* as Plato's effort to explain how we know truths that are necessary, universal, and eternal, even though we live in a world of contingent particulars.

53. *Nicomachean Ethics*, 1178b, 20–3.

hold in our hands as we are from knowing the remotest stars (602). Where does all this take us?

In a sense, but without stretching a claim beyond its tolerances, Montaigne speaks—as some think Aristotle might have—for two different roads to happiness.[54] This binary approach may lead some commentators of the first rank, such as Popkin and Stephen Toulmin, to describe Montaigne as "mildly religious" or as a man of his times who "did not find it indispensable, either to be forever invoking the name of God, or to voice a continual anxiety about . . . personal salvation."[55] I believe, however, to characterize Montaigne in religiously tepid terms, even if such a characterization turns out to be accurate, is not very helpful in getting at Montaigne's attitude toward happiness.

Those who celebrate *Of Experience* and read it as Montaigne's last word because it is his last essay may themselves emphasize the secular man who finds contentment in following nature and perhaps in detecting, through self-examination, limitations of the human condition.[56] They too will celebrate Montaigne for embracing as his motto the question "*Que sçay-je?*"—"What do I know?" (589), and they will praise him insofar as he chides all those who cannot find value in living the life of a human being:

> We are great fools: He has spent his life in idleness. We say, "I have done nothing today." Really, have you not lived? This is not only the most fundamental but the most illustrious of your occupations . . . Have you been able to think about and manage your life? You have managed the greatest burden of all . . . To compose our nature is our responsibility, not to write books. To gain order and tranquility, not to win battles and provinces, is our goal. *Our grand and glorious masterpiece is to live suitably* (1,247; emphasis added).

This passage is Montaigne's picture of the self-made man or woman. It is the epitome of a person who, within the perimeter of what is *humanly* possible, lives as well as life can be lived (1,250).

But none of this is an answer to the question of whether living well as a human being is the same as being a happy human being. I think that for Montaigne the answer is clear, but perhaps clarity depends upon how one puts the question. If one wishes to know for Montaigne whether a human being can be happy, the answer is different from the answer to the question of whether a *transformed* human being can be happy. To put the matter briefly and directly, Montaigne's position, which is no different from that of Aquinas, Dante, or Erasmus, is that "happy" and "human" are incompatible. More directly still, the answer to the

---

54. Lear, *Happiness, Death, and the Remainder of Life*, 45–55.

55. See, respectively, *The History of Skepticism*, 56, and Toulmin's *Cosmopolis* (Chicago, 1990), 37.

56. These are the interpreters who also find much to admire in *Of Moderation* (1572–80) and *Of Cannibals* (1578–80). For Harold Bloom on *Of Experience*, see *The Western Canon: The Books and School of the Ages* (New York, 1994), 154–7.

question "Can a human being be happy?" is for Montaigne "no." But the answer to the question "Can a transformed human being be happy?" is, of course, "yes."

There is nothing surprising about these answers, nor is there anything surprising about Montaigne's position: happiness comes only to those to whom God offers it. Something less comes to those who make the most of what their limited humanity allows. Montaigne agrees with his classical and medieval antecedents that human beings desire happiness as an end in itself, and he agrees with many of them that no one can satisfy this desire through some rational quest for certainty: "Men who have assayed and probed everything, within those masses of learning and many diverse things, have found nothing solid or firm—nothing but vanity. *Then they have renounced their arrogance and realized their natural condition*" (556; emphasis added).

Recognizing one's ignorance and abandoning a futile search for knowledge will not alone make one happy. Resignation is not enough. The recipe for happiness requires faith and election. True believers offer their faith, but God makes them eligible for happiness: "The things that come from Heaven alone have the right and the authority to persuade us. They alone come with the mark of the truth; *but we cannot see them with our eyes, nor do we acquire them through our means. So great and holy an image cannot reside in such a puny domicile if God does not prepare it for that use, if God does not reform and fortify it by his particular grace and supernatural favor*" (634; emphasis added).[57]

At the end of the *Apology*, Montaigne states unmistakably his view that no one can make himself happy. He approves Seneca's declaration, "Oh, man, a vile and abject thing . . . *if he does not rise above his humanity*" (682; emphasis added). The pagan Seneca was actually writing of a need to extend ourselves as far as is "humanly" possible. Montaigne has something different in mind. No human being can reach beyond his or her humanity. Because this is the case, no one can make himself happy or change herself into the sort of being for whom happiness is possible. Human beings will rise to become something more than men or women if and only if God, by extraordinary means, offers his hand. "*He will rise by abandoning and renouncing his own means, allowing himself to be raised and lifted by purely heavenly means.*" Finally, therefore, "It is our Christian faith, not Stoic virtue, to aspire to this divine and *miraculous metamorphosis*" (683; emphasis added).

If this quotation is radical, then so is Catholic orthodoxy. Montaigne here says nothing very different from what Aquinas defends in the *Summa Contra Gentiles*. For Aquinas *consummate* happiness is not possible in this life because knowledge akin to that of the angels, as well as knowledge of God, exists only in a deified being, and a deified being is no longer human.[58] The transformation, which

---

57. See similar texts in 555–6, 622.

58. In the introduction to his translation of Aquinas's *Treatise on Happiness* (Notre Dame, 1983), xiii, John A. Oesterle says that Aquinas admits a diminished level of happiness is possible for human beings in their natural condition, but "The determination of what natural happiness is and in what it consists is difficult to make," and "in his theological work St. Thomas can put this question aside."

Aquinas labors to explain in Book III, chapters XL–XLIII, is paradoxical, not metaphorical. According to him, and after him Montaigne, a human being satisfies the ultimate desire for happiness only by being turned into something that is super-human, namely, into a being that has more than opinions, "sacred science" (theology) and faith, but also unmediated knowledge of God: "Because it is necessary to place our ultimate happiness in some type of knowledge of God, *it is impossible that man's happiness should be in this life*."[59]

Striving to become happy, like trying in this life to know to a level of certainty or to perceive things *as they are* and not *as they appear*, offers no more promise than a serious search for knowledge in *Outlines of Pyrrhonism*. Happiness comes to pious Christians who, through God's intervention, are made into much more than extraordinary men and women. Sextus, unwilling to admit even the possibility of "true opinions," would have been among the last to condone metaphysical speculation about a "miraculous metamorphosis."

Montaigne, using everything he could from Sextus's skeptical modes, argues that satisfying the universal desire for happiness occurs only if God saves us from the poverty of our nature.[60] This means that reasoning, our characteristic human talent, is unsuited to satisfying our characteristically human desire.[61] One can, accordingly, draw a moral from *An Apology for Raymond Sebond* that makes it darkly philosophical and consistently orthodox: *one cannot be happy and human*. This is Montaigne's answer to the question, "*Que sçay-je?*"[62]

59. *Summa contra Gentiles*, III, xlviii, in Thomas Aquinas, *Opera Omnia* (25 vols., New York, 1948–50), XII; emphasis added. Erasmus' "fool for Christ," like the pilgrim Dante, enjoys a glimpse of God in this life, but this supreme happiness that the Christian fool experiences does not last and "is just the tiniest taste of the bliss to come." *The Praise of Folly*, 87. For Jonathan Edwards, Calvinist saints, who are among the few "elect," behold directly God's loveliness and holiness through the "spiritual light" or "sense of the heart." But Edwards is clear that this faculty has nothing in common with ordinary reason and that what it discerns is never revealed to unsanctified humans. *A Jonathan Edwards Reader*, 121–2, 136–49.

60. For Screech's discussion of Montaigne's on human nature and its ties to religion, see *Montaigne and Melancholy: The Wisdom of the Essays*, 2nd ed. (London, 1991), 46–51, 95–9, 138–45.

61. In this respect, Montaigne anticipates his brooding, deeply religious countryman Pascal. Charles Taylor, *Sources of the Self* (Cambridge, Mass., 1989), 177–84.

62. I am grateful to my graduate students—especially to Chad Hale—for searching comments on the first draft of this paper.

Midwest Studies in Philosophy, XXVI (2002)

The Natural Philosophy of Giordano Bruno

HILARY GATTI

E ver since Bruno began to be studied seriously as a key figure in the European philosophical tradition, there has been uncertainty as to what kind of philosopher he was. John Toland proposed him to the more radical components of the Enlightenment culture of his time as a fundamentally anti-hierarchical thinker, drawing out all the most subversive implications of his post-Copernican, infinite cosmology, with its relativization of values, not only spatial but also social, political, historical, and religious.[1] But when Friedrich Heinrich Jacobi included some pregnant passages from one of Bruno's major philosophical dialogues in Italian, *De la causa, principio et uno*, in the second edition of his critique of the pantheism of Spinoza, *Über die Lehre des Spinoza in Briefen an Herrn Moses Mendelssohn*, published in 1789, it was Bruno's metaphysical enquiry that was being brought to the reader's attention, and that, in defiance of Jacobi's disapproval of its pantheistic tendencies, would become a strong influence in the following half century on the post-Kantian idealists, not only in Germany.[2]

In the opening years of the nineteenth century, when in Germany Shelling was writing his dialogue entitled *Bruno: or a Discourse on the Divine and Natural Principles of Things*, Samuel Taylor Coleridge, in England, started what would become a lifelong reading of Bruno's philosophy, which is remarkable both for its conceptual subtlety and for its depth of vision.[3] For, on one side, Coleridge admired

---

1. For Toland's relationship to Bruno, see Margaret C. Jacob, *The Radical Enlightenment: Pantheists, Freemasons and Republicans* (London, 1981), and Saverio Ricci, *La fortuna del pensiero di Giordano Bruno 1600–1750* (Florence, 1990), 239–330.

2. See Saverio Ricci, "La recezione del pensiero di Giordano Bruno in Francia e Germania. Da Diderot a Schelling," *Giornale critico della filosofia italiana* 70 (1991), 431–465.

3. Hilary Gatti, "Coleridge's Reading of Giordano Bruno," *The Wordsworth Circle* 27: 3 (1996), 136–145.

the studies of electricity of Joseph Priestly whose *Disquisitions on Matter and Spirit* of 1777 refers to "the famous Jordano Bruno" as a precursor of Locke and Andrew Baxter in the conviction that all the vital powers of matter should be considered the direct work of God, thus making Bruno the first exponent of a dynamic philosophy in the physical sciences. And it is in these terms, as one of the first thinkers to develop a fully dynamic idea of the processes of both being and thought, that Coleridge refers to Bruno in his most famous work, the *Biographia Literaria* of 1816, in a chapter entitled "Philosophy as Science." On the other hand, Coleridge linked Bruno closely to the Christian mysticism of Jacob Böehme, and to an idea of the Divinity as an absolute synthesis of a cosmic struggle between contraries. Indeed, Coleridge would go so far as to write in his marginal notes to Böehme's works, read in the English translation by William Law: "Plato in *Parmenides* and Giordano Bruno passim have spoken many things well on this aweful Mystery/the latter more clearly."

Throughout the nineteenth century, comment on Bruno ran along this double track.[4] His works regularly found a dignified niche in the most qualified histories of science of the period, such as the section on the diffusion of the Copernican theory in William Whewell's *History of the Inductive Sciences from the Earliest to the Present Times* of 1837, or John Tyndall's widely read *Fragments of Science for Unscientific People* of 1879. There was also much discussion throughout the century of the influence that Bruno's vitalistic theory of matter had exercised on the major scientific debate of the period, the theory of evolution, which culminated in the substantial reference to his natural philosophy by Henry F. Osborn in *From the Greeks to Darwin, an Outline of the Development of the Evolution Idea*, published in New York in 1894. It was Bruno's intrepid enquiry into the new scientific theories of the late Renaissance, such as the implications of the Copernican revolution or the newly revived atomism, heedless of the protests being raised by the European theologians on both sides of the religious divide, which was celebrated by American figures of note, such as Thomas Davidson during a memorable evening dedicated to *Giordano Bruno: Philosopher and Martyr* by the Philadelphia Contemporary Club in 1890. But the other side of the picture was always present, if often in a subdued form. Emerson, for example, was reading Bruno as one of "the waiting lovers of the primal philosophy," or "that fragmentary highest teaching which comes from the half (poetic) fabulous personages Heraclitus and Hermes Trismegistus," although he kept such thoughts to his private notebooks and journals. In the same mid-century years, the militantly Catholic and anti-Hegelian philosopher Franz Jakob Clemens, in Germany, made an important comparison between the theory of the coincidence of opposites in Cusanus and in Bruno.[5] Although unfavorable to the Italian, accused of illegitimately transposing an absolute identity from God to the infinite universe, thus

---

4. Hilary Gatti, "Bruno nella cultura inglese dell'Ottocento," in *'Brunus redivivus': Momenti della fortuna di Giordano Bruno nel XIX secolo*, ed. Eugenio Canone (Pisa-Rome, 1998), 19–66.

5. Paul Richard Blum, "Franz Jakob Clemens e la lettura ultramontistica di Bruno," in *'Brunus redivivus'*, op. cit., 67–103.

confusing the identity that characterizes the substance of God with that of the substance of His effects, Clemens was the first to study Cusanus as a major source of Bruno's metaphysics: a theme that continues to lie at the center of comment on his philosophy today.[6] Toward the end of the nineteenth century and the beginning of the twentieth, with the revival of spiritualistic, esoteric themes, often of Oriental inspiration, which aimed at polemicizing with the dominant scientific positivism of the age, Bruno can be found permeating the ardently undisciplined thought of the theosophical societies of the period. For Annie Besant, he was *Theosophy's Apostle in the Sixteenth Century*, according to whom "man's true and primitive form is divinity; if he has the consciousness of his own divinity, if he realizes it, he may regain his primitive form, and raise himself to the highest heaven."[7]

The nineteenth-century commentators of Bruno's philosophy had no apparent difficulty in reconciling these two dimensions of his thought. Hegel in his lectures on the history of philosophy paid as much attention to Bruno's dialectical logic of contraries (or what Coleridge before him had called Bruno's "polar logic") as he did to his resolution of those contraries in an absolute monad or the identity of an indeterminate One.[8] Influenced undoubtedly by Hegel's reading of Bruno, Isabel Frith-Oppenheim, in the excellently researched first book-length study of Bruno to appear in English, published in 1887, was as eager to claim Bruno as a pioneer of the early stages of the so-called "scientific revolution" as she was to underline the modernity of his idealism.[9] But with the beginning of the new century, a polarization of interpretations of Bruno's philosophy becomes clearly evident against a cultural background dominated by the reasons of an increasingly scientific and technological society, with anti-metaphysical and neo-positivist philosophical foundations. The book on Bruno by J. Lewis McIntyre, published in 1903, follows the positivist and neo-rationalist readings of the major Italian commentators of the second part of the nineteenth century, such as Felice Tocco and Domenico Berti, for whom the magical and spiritualistic elements in Bruno's thought appeared as fastidious frills or leftovers from a previous age.[10] Appreciated in Italy by the early twentieth-century editor of Bruno's Italian dialogues, Giovanni Gentile, McIntyre's volume is clearly concerned to present Bruno as primarily a precursor of Francis Bacon's scientific method, just as Gentile himself, in

6. See, for example, Sandro Mancini, *La sfera infinita. Identità e differenza nel pensiero di Giordano Bruno* (Milan, 2000), 245–274.

7. Annie Besant, *Giordano Bruno, Theosophy's Apostle in the Sixteenth Century: A Lecture Delivered in the Sorbonne at Paris on June 15, 1911* (Madras, India, 1913).

8. F. Hegel, *Vorlesungen über die Geschichte der Philosophie* (Berlin, 1833–36), vol. 3. For a critical appreciation of Hegel's comment on Bruno's philosophy, see Eugenio Canone, *Introduzione* to '*Brunus redivivus*', op. cit., xxiv–xxix.

9. I. Frith, *Life of Giordano Bruno the Nolan* (London, 1887). Frith's book was published under a decidedly German influence by the London publisher of German origin, Nicolas Trübner. The book was controlled and revised by the German-born Moriz Carrière, a Hegelian as well as a Bruno scholar.

10. J. Lewis McIntyre, *Giordano Bruno* (London, 1903).

his essays on Bruno's thought as the culminating moment of the philosophy of the Renaissance, will place him just before his chapter on Galileo.[11] When, in the central years of the twentieth century, a number of distinguished French commentators dedicate their attention to Bruno, it is the scientific components of his thought that are at the center of their attention.

Paul Henri Michel's seminal essay on Bruno's atomism of 1957, followed by his book on the cosmology of 1962, together with the extensive treatment of Bruno's thought by Alexandre Koyré, both in his *From the Closed World to the Infinite Universe* (1957) and in his *Etudes Galiléennes* (1966), represent authentic milestones in the study of Bruno's works in the context of the natural philosophy of the late Renaissance.[12] And if it is true that Koyré considered what he thought of as Bruno's "residual animism," deriving from an earlier phase of medieval and Renaissance neo-platonism, as excluding him from the modern world, he was nevertheless of the opinion that Bruno's cosmological picture, at once prophetic, rational, and poetic, had profoundly influenced both the philosophy and the science of the centuries to come: a conviction whose enduring importance has been underlined by Eugenio Garin in his volume of 1975 on *Renaissances and Revolutions: Cultural Movements from the Fourteenth to the Eighteenth Centuries.*[13] This is the Bruno we find in the major publications in English of the middle years of the century, such as Dorothea Singer's translation of and comment on the *De l'infinito universo et mondi* of 1950, as well as Paul Oscar Kristeller's section dedicated to Bruno in his *Eight Philosophers of the Renaissance* (1964). It is also the Bruno of Hélène Vedrine's major philosophical study entitled *La conception de la nature chez Giordano Bruno*, published in 1967, which remains an important point of reference for scholars concerned with Bruno's natural philosophy and science today.[14]

For the first sixty years or more of the twentieth century, then, it seemed as if the die had been cast finally in favor of a Bruno whose philosophy found its historical collocation as a prelude and prophecy of the scientific revolution of the later Renaissance, which was thought of as the origin of the modern world. It was precisely this interpretation of both Bruno and of the modern world that was questioned by the studies of Frances Yates, and particularly by her influential book, *Giordano Bruno and the Hermetic Tradition* of 1964.[15] It is worth noticing that Yates herself made no mention, and indeed seemed quite unaware, of the nineteenth-century anticipations of her Hermetic reading of Bruno: rather, she

11. See Gentile's frequent references to McIntyre's book in his notes to his edition of Bruno's *Dialoghi italiani*, 2 vols. (Bari, 1925, 1927).

12. P. H. Michel, "L'atomisme de Giordano Bruno," in *La science au siezième siècle* (Paris, 1957) and *The Cosmology of Giordano Bruno* [1962] (Ithaca, N. Y., 1973). A. Koyré, *From the Closed World to the Infinite Universe* (Baltimore, 1957), and *Etudes Galiéennes* (Paris, 1966).

13. E. Garin, *Rinascite e rivoluzioni: movimenti culturali dal XIV al XVIII secolo* (Bari-Rome, 1975).

14. D. Singer, *Giordano Bruno. His Life and Thought* (New York, 1950), P. O. Kristeller, "Giordano Bruno," in *Eight Philosophers of the Italian Renaissance* (Stanford, 1964) and H. Vedrine, *La conception de la nature chez Giordano Bruno* (Paris, 1967).

15. Frances A. Yates, *Giordano Bruno and the Hermetic Tradition* (London, 1964).

interpreted that century entirely in the light of the scientific positivism, which was its dominant, if not only, outcome. In this conviction, it became for her the reign of error itself, which had given rise to what she began to define as the "old" reading of Bruno, which had enclosed him within the scientific-technological organization of existence while disregarding the magical and hermetic dimension of his thought expressed in his search for the divinity as the ineffable unity of being.

Undoubtedly the influence of the studies of Aby Warburg and his successors with their alternative reading of Renaissance culture in the light of its search for primitive origins, or a *prisca theologia*, cannot be overvalued in a consideration of the Bruno proposed by Frances Yates, a distinguished member of the Warburg Institute in London with which she had begun an association as far back as 1936. Clearly the book by her Warburg colleague D. P. Walker on *Spiritual and Demonic Magic from Ficino to Campanella*, published in 1958, is present in the background.[16] The immediate source of this radically overturned reading of Bruno, however, as Yates explicitly indicates in the introduction to her book, was the contemporary study of the Renaissance in the light of the presence of the Hermetic texts translated from Greek into Latin by Marsilio Ficino at the request of Cosimo dei Medici in 1463: a previously unsuspected presence demonstrated in a seminal paper by Paul Oscar Kristeller of 1938, which had become the basis of a new study of the period in the light of its magical and hermetic doctrine proposed by Eugenio Garin and his school of scholars in Florence.[17] Garin himself had not extended this reading of the Renaissance to Bruno, and indeed has repeatedly insisted, despite his admiration of Yates's work, on the necessity of making distinctions between the different ways in which the Hermetic texts permeated different periods and areas of Renaissance culture.[18] However, the Yates thesis itself, both in the original book on Bruno and in her later works, belies such distinctions. If Bruno is differentiated from Ficino and his neo-platonist reading of the Hermetic texts, it is only in the sense of a less cautious and more radical assumption on Bruno's part of the Hermetic doctrines, made even more anti-rationalistic and anti-scientific by the Cabalistic and magical strands that were later introduced by Pico della Mirandola and Cornelius Agrippa. From this perspective, it is Bruno's science that becomes for Yates a leftover from a previous century, which had, in her view, insisted on dressing him in clothes that were theirs rather than his. And if it was difficult to deny that he had been reading Copernicus in a cosmological context and Lucretius in an atomistic one, and that such readings had been the subject of serious attention both by Bruno's contemporaries and in the following centuries, Yates thought she could explain away, in a few sentences or even in a footnote,

16. D. P. Walker, *Spiritual and Demonic Magic from Ficino to Campanella* (London, 1958).

17. Kristeller first noted the remarkable circulation of Hermetic texts during the Renaissance in the paper "Marsilio Ficino e Ludovico Lazzarelli: contributo alla diffusione delle idee ermetiche nel rinascimento," *Annali della R. Scuola Normale Superiore di Pisa*, Lettere, Storia e Filosofia, 2° series, 7 (1938), 237–262, republished in *Studies in Renaissance Thought and Letters* (Rome, 1956), 221–247. Garin's studies of the Renaissance in terms of its magical and hermetic doctrines can be found above all in *Medioevo e rinascimento* (Florence, 1954) and *La cultura filosofica del Rinascimento italiano* (Florence, 1961).

18. See on this subject Garin's more recent *Ermetismo del Rinascimento* (Rome, 1988).

both the infinite universe and the atomistic theory of matter as emblematic images of the mysterious secrets of being.[19]

It is not necessary here to trace in detail the long and complicated *querelle* that followed the publication of Yates's book of 1964. Some general comments on how the field of Bruno studies adapted itself to the dramatic swing of the pendulum that led from the scientific Bruno of the first half of the twentieth century to the Hermetic Bruno of the last decades are, however, desirable in order to define the sense in which his natural philosophy will be considered in this paper. For there can be no doubt that Yates raised a valid point in claiming that large areas of Bruno's works, such as his many texts devoted to Lullian and mnemotechnical themes, which Yates herself would look into in more detail in her volume on *The Art of Memory* of 1966, had been ignored or even despised by previous commentators.[20] These texts are today considered by many to be more closely connected to logic or to rhetoric than to the magical arts that Yates so insistently underlined.[21] Nevertheless, Bruno's detailed knowledge of ancient, medieval, and Renaissance magic, which depended conceptually on the ubiquitous presence at the heart of matter itself of a vital spirit or universal soul, is nowadays considered, largely thanks to Yates's studies, to be present as a major aspect of his works.[22] It is a concept that Bruno tends to radicalize rather than reject, incorporating it into his matter theory as a substitute for the traditional idea of form, which thus acts from inside the universal material substance as a kind of creative force, or yeast. At other times, Bruno posits a boundary line between the world of things or becoming and the eternal envelope of indeterminate being, which is seen as the magic or indefinable moment at which the logic of contrary forces begins. There seems no reason why such speculative definitions of magic, which appear again and again in Bruno's published works, should necessarily invalidate the scientific endeavor, or the attempt to penetrate, and appropriate for the use of civilized society, the forces at work within the world of becoming. And in fact, many of the most valid studies of Bruno in the post-Yatesian era have been concerned with an attempt to understand in what ways his natural philosophy, unwaveringly emphasized by scholars, such as Giovanni Aquilecchia, Hélène Vedrine, Ramon G. Mendoza, or Leen Spruit, among others, can be reconciled with his magic, his reading of the Cabala, and his frequent references to the Hermetic texts.[23] So that what appears

---

19. See, for example, the famous page in which Bruno's Copernicanism is dismissed as "a Hermetic seal hiding potent divine mysteries of which he has penetrated the secret," in *G. B. and the Hermetic Tradition*, op. cit., 241, or footnote 1 on p. 265, which contains all that Yates has to say on Bruno's neo-Lucretian atomism.

20. Frances A. Yates, *The Art of Memory* (London, 1966), in particular, chapters 11–14.

21. This alternative reading of Bruno's art of memory goes back to the study by Paolo Rossi, *Clavis universalis* (Milan, 1960), recently published in English translation by the University of Chicago Press.

22. See, for example, Hilary Gatti, "Tra magia e magnetismo: la cosmologia di Giordano Bruno ad Oxford," *Paradigmi* 53 (2000), 237–260.

23. See, in particular, G. Aquilecchia, *Le opere italiane di Giordano Bruno: critica testuale e oltre* (Naples, 1991) and *Schede bruniane (1950–1991)* (Manziana, 1993), H. Vedrine, *La conception de la nature chez Giordano Bruno*, op. cit., Ramon G. Mendoza, *The Acentric Labyrinth: Giordano Bruno's Prelude to Contemporary Cosmology,* (Shaftesbury, 1995), and L. Spruit, *Il problema della conoscenza in Giordano Bruno* (Naples, 1988).

to be the agenda for the coming century is a reading of Bruno's works in their completion that accounts both for his science and for his magic, without becoming shipwrecked in the shallows of the either/or attitude that dominated the twentieth-century debate.

A development of the critical discussion along such lines is made even more necessary by the recent publication of the first volume to present in integral form, surrounded by a dense apparatus of comment and notes, the unpublished manuscripts that Bruno left unfinished at his death.[24] Entitled *Opere magiche*, this large and well-produced volume gives the confusing impression that all the manuscripts published in it are concerned with Bruno's thoughts on the magical arts, although this is not in fact the case. By far the longest, and undoubtedly the major work that Bruno himself never published, the *Lampas triginta statuarum* actually contains few if any references to magic, as the editors of the new volume admit in their notes to the text.[25] It is rather an elaboration of Bruno's ontological considerations, already developed in his philosophical dialogue in Italian *De la causa, principio et uno*, written and published in London in 1584, on the relation of the apparently fragmented world of becoming and of things to the original principle of unified being: one of Bruno's most constant and characteristic themes, as Coleridge rightly claimed. Other works, such as the *Theses de magia* or the *Medicina Lulliana* appear to be little more than compendiums of notes of reading on those subjects, as the detailed quotations from Bruno's sources, which are one of the major characteristics of this valuable volume, make clear. This leaves the four brief works on magic, *De magia mathematica*, *De magia naturali*, *De vinculis in genere*, and *De rerum principiis*, which Yates already knew, although only in the reduced form in which they were published in the nineteenth century in the third volume of Bruno's collected Latin works. Curiously, however, as Michele Ciliberto notes in his introduction to the new volume, she made little use of these final, unpublished texts on magic, despite the fact that they indicate a definite interest on Bruno's part, in the final months before his arrest and imprisonment on the part of the Roman Catholic Inquisition, in the possible uses of magical techniques as a means of achieving a new dominion within the world of time and nature.

As we have already seen, the technical details of Bruno's natural philosophy have been the subject of a number of major studies during the twentieth century, and, therefore, are too well known to need repeating here. Rather there is a need to re-state the relationship he establishes between the two distinct philosophical poles between which his ontology constantly moves—of being and becoming, of permanence and time—and the sense in which he contemplates a new scientific activity in the context of a constant reference to eternal principles, or divine truths. This appears, indeed, in a general way, to be more and more clearly understood as the major characteristic of the so-called "scientific revolution" of the late European Renaissance, which today, after the discussion that has in the

---

24. Giordano Bruno, *Opere magiche*, eds. M. Ciliberto, S. Bassi, E. Scapparone, and N. Tirinnanzi (Milan, 2001).
25. "Nella *Lampas* non emergono prove di un marcato interesse per la magia." G. Bruno, *Opere magiche*, op. cit., 1491.

last decades involved the science of Isaac Newton with relation to his recently discovered papers on alchemy and his massive Biblical studies, can no longer be discussed in terms of a science *versus* religion interpretative scheme. In the case of
Newton, this new realization has given rise to numerous differing emphases on the
relative importance of his religion with respect to his science, or to the traditional
inquiries in which he was still deeply involved, such as alchemy, with its cult of
secrecy and its recognition of magical or occult qualities, and the modern scientific undertaking, based on shared and repeatable experiments, projected into the
public domain. But despite some extreme positions to the contrary, such as that
expressed by Betty Jo Teeter Dobbs in a much discussed paper of 1993, the consensus of the most qualified Newton scholars appears to be determined by their
desire to preserve his position as the major figure of the early modern scientific
experience, while at the same time recognizing the deeply felt need that his private
papers—largely unpublished at his death, and for centuries ignored by Newton
scholars—clearly express to relate his science to a dimension beyond logic and
reason, which clearly involves an element of faith.[26]

The reference to Newton is not to be considered irrelevant here, as the
purpose of this paper is to propose just such a synthesis as the basis of a new discussion of Bruno's philosophical endeavor. Indeed, it is Bruno himself who spells
out the meaning of his philosophy in these terms in the work that will be proposed
here for comment and analysis: the work entitled *Lampas triginta statuarum*, or
The Torch of the Thirty Statues, which Bruno also left unpublished at his death. As
we have seen, this work, first published in the third volume of the nineteenth-
century edition of Bruno's Latin works, has recently appeared in the new volume
of the posthumous manuscripts, together with an excellent Italian translation and
detailed comment and notes. Bruno is concerned here with precisely that
relationship between eternal truths and the world of becoming that appears to
have been a constant preoccupation of the new scientists up to and including
Newton himself. Indeed, in a section of this work entitled *The Field of Minerva,
or Knowledge*, Bruno spells out with particular clarity his thought on such a
relationship.

The *Lampas* shows a marked desire on Bruno's part to contain his very
complex ontology within a coherent system of discourse. The statues, although they
can be considered as magically endowed with their original light, should be seen
primarily as the files in which Bruno stores his distinctions relating to the various
grades of being. Each statue is itself divided into thirty subfiles, the *Field of*

---

26. Dobbs's paper was delivered at the Annual Meeting of the History of Science Society
and has been published as "Newton as Final Cause and First Mover" in *Rethinking the Scientific
Revolution*, ed. Margaret Osler (Cambridge, 2000), 25–39. It was at once contested, above all by
Newton's biographer Richard S. Westfall, in the paper "The Scientific Revolution Reasserted"
published in the same volume at 43–55. Also of much interest on the theological outlook that
underlies the structure of Newton's *Principia* is the paper by J. E. McGuire, "The Fate of the Date:
The Theology of Newton's *Principia* Revisited," published in the same volume at 271–295. For a
more general treatment of the relation of the new science to its theological premises, see Brian
P. Copenhaver, "Natural Magic, Hermeticism, and Occultism" in *Reappraisals of the Scientific
Revolution*, eds. D. C. Lindberg and R. S. Westman (Cambridge, 1990), 261–301.

Minerva being no exception to this rule.[27] Knowledge, according to Bruno in these thirty sections, derives from an inner light in the mind that illuminates us as to the conclusions which we may draw from the first principles. These principles, or eternal truths, are not themselves the domain of reason but rather of intuition or of faith. This is of two sorts: what Bruno calls a "well regulated" faith, characterized as a simple recognition of the necessity of the first principles themselves, and what he considers an over-excited or perverse faith, based on the superstition of false prophets. This last remark clearly refers to revealed religions and includes a reference to Bruno's long-standing anti-Christian polemic. The first principles themselves are not known by the mind, except insofar as it reasons a number of conclusions from them. These conclusions constitute what Bruno calls "science," or knowledge, which he defines in a later paragraph in suggestive terms that, although based on ancient sources among which Aristotle's *Analitics* are specially mentioned, clearly project his idea of science into the modern world.[28]

Science is related to our powers of judgement, and it involves both sense experience and a process of reasoning. The results of the logic of such science must be articulated in some sort of discourse, which becomes a shared experience. The logical process defined must be repeatable: it requires a second examination that controls and verifies its exactitude. Only this process of verification guards the new scientific truth against the lies of imposters. Bruno thinks of geometry as an essential example of such a science. But another kind of science derives from the necessity of matter as much as from the necessity of form, and these two elements can concur together to constitute the "garment" of a new form of knowledge. This is knowledge as form, or the knowledge of knowledge, or the matter of intellectual truth.

These sections dedicated to Minerva, which also include references to far more traditional forms of knowledge, precede a long final section of the work dedicated to Venus and Cupid, who are seen as the forces of concord or harmony, which bring sense and meaning into an otherwise confusing world.[29] Confusion, for Bruno, has to be clearly distinguished from Chaos, which, on the contrary, together with the abyss and privation, constitutes—in Anaxagorean terms together with what appears to be a clear reference to the *Liber chaos* of Ramon Lull—the first of the first principles themselves.[30] Chaos, the Abyss and privation, which Bruno calls Ancient Night, are nothing or everything—substance in a state of com-

---

27. The thirty sections relating to the *Field of Minerva* are in *Opere magiche*, op. cit., 1227–1239.

28. See sections XXIV and XXV of the thirty considerations dedicated to *Minerva's Ladder, or the Disposition towards Knowledge*, which immediately follows the *Field of Minerva*. In *Opere magiche*, op. cit., 1246–1247.

29. For the sections dedicated first to Venus and then to Cupid, see *Opere magiche*, op. cit., 1248–1277.

30. For Lull's *Liber chaos* (circa 1275), see Frances Yates, "Essays on the Art of Ramon Lull: Ramon Lull and John Scotus Erigena," now in *Lull and Bruno: Collected Essays vol. I* (London, 1982), 95–98. It is significant that Yates, in the introduction to her essays on Lull, states quite unambiguously that "The Lullian artist is not a magus," and that his arts are logical not magical. She underlines how Lull traces the passage from Chaos, through Bonitas, to the elements of the natural world.

plete indetermination—and as such "they are so far from being accidents of things that they are, on the contrary, the principles according to which the accidents come into being, are related to one another, and enter into relation with substance."[31] For this to be the case, however, there must be a "superior" triad, which Bruno denominates the Universal Apollo, or a universal spirit or light, which brings the state of indeterminate privation into an ordered whole as a universe of individual entities. These are perceived by the mind as realities through the senses, but their order is "modelled by the artifice of fantasy and imagination," which, as the ancient philosophers understood, was in its proper function not a faculty designed to confuse the truths of reason, but rather to illustrate them, to explicate their order and maintain such order in the memory. The imagination is thus, for Bruno, an intimate part of the scientific activity.[32]

It is only in what Bruno calls this "universal perspective" that the world of nature can be understood as a third order of things, which, precisely because it is illuminated by the light of the one Apollo, or divine Monad, can also be considered as the good: "id est bonitate naturali."[33] Science, therefore, for Bruno, is closely related to ethics: an understanding of the correct order of things in the natural world leads to a correct perception of what is virtue and what is vice. The essence of the scientific endeavor itself, however, is founded on the notion of quantity, and as such Bruno presents it as the field of Ocean.[34] Here we find the attributes of magnitude in all its characteristics, which lead to a perception of the universe as a physical entity founded on the concepts of multiplicity and number. Within these concepts, Bruno emphasizes in particular the notion of addition, for it is through ideas such as increase, expansion, aggregation, and completion that the mind is able to conceive of a universe that is not susceptible to any further increment of any kind. That is to say, it is precisely the post-Copernican universe that is eternal in time and infinite in space: the universe that Bruno had presented to his readers in his Italian philosophical dialogues written and published in London in 1584 and that, probably at the same time as he was writing the *Thirty Statues*, he defined for the last time in his Latin masterpiece *De immenso et infigurabili*, published as the last work of his so-called Frankfurt trilogy in 1591.

The section of *Thirty Statues* dedicated to "The Field of Ocean" thus reaches its conclusion with a paragraph entitled "The Universe: The World," which is the way in which magnitude becomes quantitative and corporeal in its explication as physical reality.[35] And the physical universe is founded for Bruno on one specific

---

31. See the twenty-sixth consideration on Chaos in *Opere magiche*, op. cit., 956–957.

32. These considerations on the imagination close a section of the *Lampas* dedicated to *The Multiple Forms of Investigation* in *Opere magiche*, op. cit., 940–941. The relation between Bruno's science and the imagination has been treated at length by Luciana de Bernart in the volume *Immaginazione e scienza in Giordano Bruno* (Pisa, 1986).

33. For the investigation into nature as the third order of being in *Thirty Statues*, see *Opere magiche*, op. cit., 1164–1295. The remaining part of the work is dedicated to technical instructions as to how to develop the mnemonic techniques, which will allow the statues to be used as a mental filing system.

34. *Opere magiche*, op. cit., 1180–1183.

35. Ibid., 1184–1187.

quality, which is heat: a clear reference to that "giudiciosissimo Telesio" whom Bruno had already praised with unusual vigor in the second of his Italian philosophical dialogues written and published in London in 1584, *Cause, Principle and One*. Telesius, in his major work *De rerum natura*, first published in two books in Naples in 1570, had cautiously attempted to replace the Aristotelian physics by a new physical dualism based on a universal dialectical contrast between heat and cold: a contrast that Bruno had incorporated as a fundamental one within his own far more radically post-Copernican, infinite cosmology, using it as an explanation of the movements of the stars and planets of his infinite number of solar systems around their central suns.[36] In *Thirty Statues*, moreover, heat is not only considered as a universal, life-giving quality, but also as one that can be subjected to measurement as a quantity: a fact that guarantees for Bruno the possibility of a rational inquiry into natural things. For the concept of size is to be considered "absolute" among all other physical realities. Size defines perfectly the particular and individual entities, but at the same time it creates a similitude with that which is beyond size, or the infinite. The nature of the universe in its totality as infinite is thus confirmed by the mind as true.

A later section, which is dedicated to motion within the universe or the physical world and is entitled *The Field of the Earth, or of Potency*, appears at first sight to be founded on an Aristotelian concept of potentiality and to lead back to the traditional idea of matter as the passive element subjected to the potentiality of its specific form, which contains within it the impetus toward a motion defined by its individual nature and ends.[37] However, such an impression is mistaken, as Bruno reaffirms here his complete reversal of the Aristotelian equation, making matter into the active substance that underlies an infinite world of finite objects and contains within it the total potentiality of all forms: a potentiality that precedes the single form with its acts of motion, and on which all motion logically depends. Conceptually, this reversal of the Aristotelian relationship between matter and form, in the context of motion, can be considered as supplying the speculative foundation of a quantitative, universal law of motion, such as will eventually be formulated by Newton's law of gravity. However, Bruno here draws back well before defining such a possibility with any clarity, apparently resolving the question of motion in the more traditional terms of impetus theory. Thus, he can still write that the impetus which leads to the motion of an individual thing derives from the internal principle of that thing's propensity toward a certain end, even if for Bruno such a propensity depends only in a secondary sense on the potential present in what is for him the accidental and impermanent nature of the individual form. Even Aristotle's substantial forms, which are the forms of a species rather than an individual of that species, partake in what is, for Bruno, a universal mutability. For they

---

36. For Bruno's praise of Telesius, see *De la causa, principio et uno*, ed. M. Ciliberto, in *Giordano Bruno: Oeuvres complètes*, eds. Y. Hersant and N. Ordine (Paris, 1995), pp. 166–167. For a critical comment on Bruno's important relationship with the work of Telesius, see Giovanni Aquilecchia, "Ramo, Patrizi e Telesio nella prospettiva di Giordano Bruno" and "Ancora su Bruno e Telesio," in *Schede bruniane*, op. cit., 293–310.

37. See *Opere magiche*, op. cit., 1192–1199.

also ultimately depend on the universal potentiality present throughout the infinite substance, which precedes the single form and the single act of motion. It is on this infinite, universal potentiality that the single motion ultimately depends.

This line of reasoning reaches its logical conclusion in the following section entitled "The Field of Juno," who is considered the mediator between the individual things of which the infinite universe is composed.[38] Here the idea of universal laws of physics is explicitly defined. Bruno sees the concept of laws in physics as intimately linked to the idea of civil laws, which are generally binding, such as treaties or oaths "or other things of that kind." The field of physics also contemplates a situation in which superior principles exercise their influence on inferior ones according to some law or prescription. These natural laws constitute the necessary intermediary principles without which nothing can happen in the world of things. Bruno thinks of them as knots, or chains, or even forms of glue which guarantee that all things are linked together in some universal formulation, which, like an oath, is repeatable and generally respected: a public and not a private or secret act. Here it is Plato rather than Aristotle who is called in as witness, insofar as his idea of a universal *spiritus* or world soul, which reflects throughout the physical universe the divine light of Apollo, is more agreeable to the idea of universal physical laws than Aristotle's concept of individual souls or forms, or even of substantial forms, whose motions are laws only unto themselves or, at the most, unto their species. Universal physical laws, moreover, are, according to Bruno, an assurance of the central role of humankind within the universe, for they are part of the human intellectual horizon. The eternal truths, or first principles, are explicated within the infinite world of things in terms of universally intelligible laws of physics capable of comprehension within the intellectual horizon of the human mind.

This scheme of natural philosophy extracted from *Thirty Statues* represents an aspect only of that work, which is concerned primarily with defining the complex structure of first principles on which the world or universe depends. Even when Bruno does reach the final part of his work dedicated to the universe itself and the laws on which its movements depend, he has as much to say on the civic and ethical implications of a scientific inquiry into the natural world as he does on the more specifically logical or intellectual character of such an exercise. Nor can it be claimed that his thought on the inquiry into the natural world is always as clearly projected toward an endeavor that would rapidly become the modern scientific enterprise as the pages presented and commented on here would suggest. At times he is evidently concerned with more traditional philosophical concepts and inquiries, for which he found available an already established vocabulary. For example, the concept of links between every aspect of being in the universe, which in *Thirty Statues* is seen as the necessary rational idea justifying the possibility of universal, natural laws, could be seen from the quite different perspective of the unknowable nature of the links themselves. In their occult essential nature, the links, or *vinculi*, will later become the center of the magical techniques of persuasion and dominion investigated in the work *De vinculis in genere*, also left unpub-

---

38. Ibid., 1198–1209.

lished at his death, where Bruno is attempting to inquire into areas of psychological tension that defeat the understanding of the conscious mind.[39] In many other parts of his *oeuvre*, however, both in *Thirty Statues* and in a large number of his major published works, Bruno insists rather, in terms which Francis Bacon must surely have appreciated, on the necessity of turning the attention of the active, inquiring intellect toward physical realities too long ignored; attempts to comprehend the first principles that underlie the physical world are necessarily arduous and may finish up by engaging with phantasms whose truth remains in question. So it is Thetis, standing for the natural causes of things, the lover of the universal laws of matter that dictate the multiple and ever-changing forms of the natural world, who turns into the new "tiger" whose forces the human mind must now attempt to know and tame.

Bruno's considerations on Thetis as the material substance that underlies all the specific formations composing the natural world are of particular interest in indicating at the same time both the possibility and the inevitable limits of an inquiry into natural causes. They may thus be used as the conclusive remarks to this paper. For Thetis, who is associated with the ocean in its infinite Protean capacity for metamorphosis, is by no means easy to "catch" or to define in definite and certain terms. Indeed, Bruno sees her as the wife of many husbands, none of whom can truly be said to possess her. Although her forms can be pursued by reason (*"subiectum ratione formabile"*), she resists all attempts at such dominion and renders the hunt for her secrets difficult and problematic. Bruno portrays her as riding on a dolphin, whose back only at times appears as well defined above the moving waters of becoming. Thetis, after all, is the daughter of both the sky and the earth, and so should not be seen as crude or lowly matter, but rather as divinely inspired. Insofar as she represents nature, she is the object of natural philosophy, but insofar as she represents God, she is the object of theology, or metaphysics, or a philosophy of religion. The natural philosopher would be unwise to think that it is possible to penetrate her essence. All that can be hoped for is to understand something "around and about" her ways and habits. When she assumes specific forms, such as a horse or a tree, then investigation through the senses, reason, and intellect into and about them (*"circa quod"*) is in order and to be encouraged. But it should not be assumed that the knowledge gained will ever reveal the ultimate secrets of the thing in itself. For this reason Bruno, in this section, pictures the human intellect as a sunflower, unwearily turned toward the ultimate truth of things, but destined to find joy mixed always with suffering, without ever reaching the final goal.[40] As I have already pointed out elsewhere, this crisis epistemology renders Bruno's inquiry into natural things more consonant with modern, post-relativity science than with the rational optimism of the mechanical sciences of the seventeenth and eighteenth centuries.[41]

---

39. *De vinculis in genere* is published in *Opere magiche*, op. cit., 413–584.

40. For the long and beautiful section of the *Lampas* entitled *The Statue of Thetis, or Substance*, see *Opere magiche*, op. cit., 1122–1143.

41. See Hilary Gatti, *Giordano Bruno and Renaissance Science* (Ithaca, 1999).

Midwest Studies in Philosophy, XXVI (2002)

Francis Bacon and the Humanistic Aspects of Modernity

ROSE-MARY SARGENT

Francis Bacon was a complex thinker who combined the universal and practical concerns of Renaissance Humanism with a thoroughly modern emphasis on a progressive break with traditional learning. His writings covered a broad spectrum of styles, from detailed analyses and commentaries to aphorisms, tables, histories, essays, and fables, specifically designed to serve his general project for advancing all areas of learning. Although there has been an occasional resurgence of interest in Bacon's thought, the last in the mid-twentieth century by literary scholars, philosophers have most often settled for an overly simplistic account of his work bordering on caricature. This unfortunate neglect of Bacon has adversely affected our ability to understand his influence on the next generation of English philosophers, despite the fact that they were quite explicit about their debt to him. Instead, numerous studies have been generated claiming to have found the social, political, or continental influences on the philosophers of Restoration England. More importantly, however, by dismissing Bacon's significance, philosophers have deprived themselves of an opportunity to study the subtle ways in which Bacon displayed and sought to reconcile the tensions between traditional values and progressive learning that became an inherent part of modernity.

Superficial readings of Bacon's individual works in isolation from his project or his context have led to some familiar criticisms. Indeed, at one time or another he has been accused of being responsible for generating most of the problems associated with the modern world. Literary and social studies have included discussions of his supposed advocacy of industrial capitalism, colonialism, imperialism, gender inequality, and other forms of political power struggle. The philosophical literature, on the other hand, tends to be preoccupied with a popular account of his call for an unthinking domination of nature to be pursued by a hopelessly naïve inductive and anti-hypothetical methodology.[1] The social criticisms of Bacon focus on the *New Atlantis*, early manuscript material, and selected passages from the *New Organon* and *De Augmentis*, while the philosophical criticisms are often based solely on isolated aphorisms from the *New Organon*. Little attention has been paid to how these works relate to each other and to his other works, particularly to his natural histories.

Bacon would be better seen as a situated philosopher. He believed that his method could be applied in a general way to all areas of learning, but he was careful to note that "the nature of things" would have to be taken into account when applied. This is why he gave "many and diverse precepts in the doctrine of Interpretation, which in some measure may modify the method of invention according to the quality and condition of the subject of the inquiry" (vol. 4, 112, I: 127).[2] Bacon engaged in some speculative philosophical systematizing early on, remnants of which can be seen in his discussion of the forms and latent processes of bodies in Book II of the *New Organon*. He evidently abandoned this type of project, however, in order to work out the details of his method for directly investigating the particular natures of things.[3] Unlike Descartes' works that can in large part be studied in isolation from his context because of the internal coherence of his system, Bacon's works lack such coherence. Thus, when compared with the Cartesian ideal in Western philosophy, his works appear to be confused and unsophisticated.[4] Bacon was quite methodical in his approach, however, and he actually had a sophisticated plan for the advancement of learning, but he believed that it would be premature to construct systems of knowledge. It is, therefore, a mistake to compare his work with that of Descartes.

Spanning the divide between the Renaissance and Modernity, Bacon agreed with the Humanists' emphasis on the need for practical experience of all kinds. The experience he thus acquired uniquely informed his vision for a new philosophy. He learned in what areas knowledge was lacking and how difficult it would be to establish any truth with finality. Yet he also saw that the more truth one could find, even if it were local or tentative, the more ability one would have to aid humanity by regaining dominion over nature. There is a developmental transition in Bacon's thought. The more he worked on plans for a great instauration, the more he came to see the dynamic and progressive aspects of his project. After

1. See, e.g., Farrington (1979), Martin (1992), Merchant (1980), Weinberger (1986), and Whitney (1990) for some of the social and political theses. Popper (1968) is, of course, the best known proponent of the twentieth-century philosophical critique of Bacon's inductive method.

2. See as well *De Augmentis*, Bk. 6: "the method used should be according to the subject-matter which is handled" (vol. 4, 451–2) All references to Bacon are given in the text to volume and page number of the Spedding, Ellis, Heath edition of his works. When a reference is from the *New Organon*, Book and Aphorism number are also provided.

3. For Bacon's early speculative philosophy, see Rees (1996). On Bacon's forms and processes, see Hesse (1968) and McMullin (1990).

4. Not all philosophical studies are critical of course. Horton (1973) and Urbach (1987), e.g., have attempted to show Bacon's method as more in line with the twentieth century ideal of the hypothetico-deductive method. Perez-Ramos (1988) and Vickers (1987, 1996) have also written favorably of Bacon's philosophy but have tried to place it more within the concerns and practices of the late Renaissance.

twelve years of writing the *New Organon*, for example, he found it necessary to publish it in an incomplete form, because, although he thought that his method was relatively "easy to explain," he had learned that it is "hard to practice" (vol. 4, 40). Most of Bacon's works were published in an incomplete and tentative form. He experimented with learning, with what methods would work in what areas, and how best to communicate such information to his readers. His modernity, which consisted in the call for a revolution in learning, was tempered not only by an emphasis on practical experience, but also by the humanistic themes of charity and fallibilism. The following discussion will focus primarily on how these humanistic elements make questionable the numerous criticisms of his philosophy. The charitable intent of Bacon's project, for example, contrasts with the social utilitarian characterization of Bacon as a prophet of the industrial revolution of Western capitalism. In a like manner, Bacon's fallible approach contrasts with the philosophical portrayal of his method as a mechanical means that leads unproblematically to certain knowledge.

BACON'S HUMANISTIC PROJECT

Bacon's parents were both accomplished Tudor humanists who ensured that their sons, Francis and Anthony, were well educated in the classics, history, and rhetoric. In Bacon's early manuscripts and in parts of his later works, such as Book 1 of the *Advancement of Learning*, one can find traces of his humanist education in his discussion of the wisdom of the ancients. In passages in the *New Organon* (I: 71–73) and the *New Atlantis*, one can also see his belief in the possible existence of intellectually advanced, lost civilizations. As a lawyer and a statesman, Bacon was deeply immersed in the political and social life of Tudor and Stuart England and, as had the humanists before him, he appreciated the importance of knowledge in these realms.[5] He used his position to seek patronage first from Elizabeth I and then from James I, arguing that the search for knowledge is not an activity to be kept separate from the moral sphere. All of these elements came together when Bacon compared James to Hermes Trimegistus, the legendary writer of alchemical and magical texts. In his dedication of the *Advancement of Learning*, he wrote that James had "the power and fortune of a king, the knowledge and illumination of a priest, and the learning and universality of a philosopher" (vol. 3, 263). In a similar manner, in the Epistle Dedicatory to *The Great Instauration*, Bacon combined his search for patronage with an appeal to ancient wisdom when he there compared James to King Solomon and suggested that he should "follow his example in taking order for the collecting and perfecting of a natural and experimental history." It was only by this means, Bacon maintained, that "philosophy

---

5. For Bacon's life, see Coquillette (1992), Jardine and Stewart (1998), Peltonen (1996), and Pinnick (1998). The Humanist themes discussed in this section are based on those identified by Toulmin (1990), Shapiro (1991), and Vickers (1968b, 1996). Shapiro, however, regards these Humanist sentiments as being more influential during the generation after Bacon.

and the sciences may no longer float in air, but rest on the solid foundation of experience of every kind" (vol. 4, 12).

Bacon devoted part of his time to a defense of learning in general and contributed to the attempted compilation of all known learning that was part of the encyclopedic project begun by the Renaissance humanists. In Book I of the *Advancement of Learning*, he argued first for its excellence in response to criticisms primarily of humanistic learning from the political, social, and religious spheres. Within his defense he provided numerous examples drawn from history that displayed the broad range and depth of his own learning. After a lengthy dedication to James I, Book II began with Bacon's more practical advice about how to advance learning, on which he would elaborate in much more detail in Books II–IX of *De Augmentis*. Bacon sought to "make a general and faithful perambulation and survey of learning" by cataloguing what he called its "particular acts and works" (vol. 4, 290). In addition, however, he expanded the humanistic project to include as well a discussion of "what defects and undervalues I find in such particular acts" (vol. 3, 264). As Bacon saw it, "the works or acts which pertain to the advancement of learning are conversant about three objects; the places of learning, the books of learning, and the persons of the learned" (vol. 4, 284). Among the defects he noted that there was not "any public designation of fit men either to write or to make inquiry concerning such parts of knowledge as have not been sufficiently labored." Therefore, a review ought to be "made of the sciences, and account be taken what parts of them are right and well advanced, and what poor and destitute" (vol. 4, 290). In the preface to *The Great Instauration* he echoed these sentiments in his discussion of the first part of his six-part plan designed to lay out the "divisions of the sciences" concerning "not only things already invented and known, but likewise things omitted which ought to be there" (vol. 4, 22–23).

Given discussions in the secondary literature about Bacon's rejection of metaphorical language in the sciences, it might be surprising to some that he approved of rhetoric and poetry as legitimate parts of knowledge in both the *Advancement of Learning* and *De Augmentis*. In Book II, Bacon described "poesy" as the "joining at pleasure things which in nature would never have come together" and noted that this "is the work of the imagination" (vol. 4, 292). He was not speaking of poetry as a particular style of speech (that he covered in Book VI), but as any style that had "feigned history" as its subject matter (vol. 4, 315). In this sense, poetry could be divided into Narrative, Dramatic, and Parabolical forms all of which composed for Bacon the "second principal part of learning" (vol. 4, 314). Narrative poetry was that which employed "mere imitation," whereas Dramatic "made visible" actions as if they were present, and Parabolical was that with "sacred" or allegorical content (vol. 4, 316). At the end of his discussion of these types, Bacon provided the reader with three lengthy examples of the Parabolical, as "philosophy according to the Fables of the Ancients," using the Fable of Pan for natural philosophy, the story of Perseus for politics, and the fable of Dionysus for moral philosophy (vol. 4, 318–335). Poetry could be an effective way to excite curiosity about questions concerning nature or to instill moral precepts and social norms. Because poetry is an area of "feigned" history, however, it clearly would not be appropriate for the construction of natural histories. But then neither was the traditional logic taught at the schools.[6]

Bacon shared the humanist's critical attitude toward the scholastic focus on logical and dialectical manipulation. In the preface to *The Great Instauration*, he argued that syllogisms only served "to overcome an opponent in argument." His new logic was designed instead "to command nature in action" (vol. 4, 24). Bacon argued that the "subtlety of nature is greater many times over than the subtlety of the senses and understanding; so that all those specious meditations, speculations, and glosses in which men indulge are quite from the purpose." The "logic which we now have" is no help to us "in finding out new sciences," because it "serves rather to fix and give stability to the errors which have their foundation in commonly received notions than to help the search after truth." Thus, the syllogism is "no match for the subtlety of nature." Although it "commands assent" to the proposition, it "does not take hold of the thing" (vol. 4, 48–49, I: 10–13). Syllogisms are made "of propositions, propositions consist of words, words are symbols of notions. Therefore if the notions themselves (which is the root of the matter) are confused and over-hastily abstracted from the facts, there can be no firmness in the superstructure" (vol. 4, 49, I: 14). Because the logic of his day depended upon such notions, Bacon maintained that "vicious demonstrations are as the strongholds and defences of Idols; and those we have in logic do little else than make the world the bond-slave of human thought, and human thought the bond-slave of words" (vol. 4, 70, I: 69).

Syllogisms also yield propositions that are "barren of works, remote from practice, and altogether unavailable for the active department of the sciences" (vol. 4, 24).[7] As Bacon noted, "logical invention does not discover principles and chief axioms, of which arts are composed, but only such things as appear to be consistent with them" (vol. 4, 80–81, I: 82). In a highly critical statement he declared, "if the truth must be spoken, when the rational and dogmatical sciences began the discovery of useful works came to an end" (vol. 4, 83, I: 85). In the preface to *The Great Instauration*, he wrote of his hope to "establish forever" the "true and lawful marriage" of the rational and the empirical faculty, the "separation of which has thrown into confusion all the affairs of the human family." To accomplish this, he "fervently" prayed to "God the Father, God the Son, and God the Holy Ghost, that they will vouchsafe through my hand to endow the human family with new mercies." It was the duty of natural philosophers to "cultivate truth in charity" (vol. 4, 20).

The "power" or "utility" of which Bacon spoke is often interpreted as modern utilitarianism, but Bacon's notion was much closer to the Humanist ideal of the improvement of the moral and social worlds. Bacon criticized scholasticism

---

6. In opposition to the emphasis upon dialectic presented by Jardine (1974), Vickers (1996) argues that Bacon saw the rationality of rhetoric as well. See also Briggs (1989) on Bacon's use of rhetoric and his "innovative traditionalism."

7. See Perez-Ramos (1988), Sargent (1999), and Vickers (1987) for Bacon's emphasis on Christian charity and ethical responsibility.

because he saw it as a useless and barren philosophy full of abstract terms that had no bearing on the moral life of the individual or the conduct of society. Just as Bacon appropriated the encyclopedic impulse and used it for new purposes, so he sought to extend the concerns of morality and the promotion of an active life into the sphere of natural philosophy. He urged his readers to "join in consultation for the common good" (vol. 4, 21). At the end of his preface to *The Great Instauration*, Bacon added a "general admonition to all; that they consider what are the true ends of knowledge, and that they seek it not either for pleasure of the mind, or for contention, or for superiority to others, or for profit, or fame, or power, or any of these inferior things; but for the benefit and use of life; and that they perfect and govern it in charity" (vol. 4, 20–21).

Bacon's desire to produce charitable works through advancements in natural philosophy went far beyond the merely expedient. He opposed the mechanics who sought the "empirical and operative" only, and he criticized previous "industry in experimenting" that had "begun with proposing to itself certain definite works to be accomplished" and then "pursued them with premature and unseasonable eagerness" (vol. 4, 17). Rather, one should begin with "experiments of light" and "first endeavour to discover true causes and axioms . . . for axioms rightly discovered and established supply practice with its instruments, not one by one, but in clusters and draw after them trains and troops of works" (vol. 4, 110, I: 70). As Bacon explained, "Human knowledge and human power meet in one, for where the cause is not known the effect cannot be produced. Nature to be commanded must be obeyed, and that which in contemplation is as the cause is in operation as the rule" (vol. 4, 47, I: 3). It was a sign that one had truly discovered the causes operative in a particular process if one were able to manipulate them to produce a desired effect. Therefore, in addition to the charitable intent of utility, it also had an epistemic aspect: "works themselves are of greater value as pledges of truth than as contributing to the comforts of life" (vol. 4, 110, I: 124).

Works, as tests of knowledge, are required because of the fallible nature of human reason. As Bacon often reminded his readers, the "human understanding is no dry light, but receives an infusion from the will and affections" (vol. 4, 57, I: 49). Indeed, "the universe to the eye of human understanding is framed like a labyrinth; presenting as it does on every side so many ambiguities of way, such deceitful resemblances of objects and signs, natures so irregular in their lines and so knotted and entangled" (vol. 4, 18). Bacon would later maintain that "by far the greatest hindrance and aberrations of the human understanding proceeds from the dullness, incompetency, and deceptions of the senses" (vol. 4, 58, I: 50). Reason and the senses may both fail us and thus experiments are needed as "sponsors and sureties for the truth of philosophies" (vol. 4, 73, I: 73). The "fruits and works" that Bacon sought can provide the necessary constraints on our senses and reason. With the production of works, "the sense decides touching the experiment only, and the experiment decides touching the point in nature and the thing itself" (vol. 4, 58, I: 50). Bacon began with the goal of certainty. As late as *The Great Instauration*, he would sometimes write of induction as a process that could lead to an "inevitable conclusion" (vol. 4, 25). He was cautious, however, about how soon one could expect the completion of the project.

Bacon's fallibilism, derived partly from Humanist influences and partly from his own experience, led him to a probabilistic stance toward knowledge.[8] Inquiry was in a constant state of development and thus knowledge acquisition would require a dynamic and tentative process. In the preface to the *New Organon*, Bacon proposed "to establish progressive stages of certainty" (vol. 4, 40). At the end of Book I, he noted that it was now "time for me to propound the art itself of interpreting nature; in which, although I conceive that I have given true and most useful precepts, yet I do not say either that it is absolutely necessary (as if nothing could be done without it) or that it is perfect." Then, he added, "It is true however that by my precepts everything will be in more readiness and much more sure" (vol. 4, 115, I: 130). He did not pretend to provide a final theory. He was only "sowing . . . for future ages the seeds of a purer truth and performing my part towards the commencement of the great undertaking" (vol. 4, 104, I: 116). The Organon could do the work, it was the right method, but it had to be applied differently to different cases. Even the method itself was not immune to amendment. It could require future alteration because "the art of discovery may advance as discoveries advance" (vol. 4, 115, I: 130).

The *New Organon* was only part two of a six-part plan for *The Great Instauration*. After the encyclopedic compilation of part one and the method of part two, came part three that was intended to provide the natural histories to serve as the material upon which the method would work. As Bacon described this part, "the object of the natural history which I propose is not so much to delight with variety of matter or to help with present use of experiments, as to give light to the discovery of causes and supply a suckling philosophy with its first food" (vol. 4, 28–29). The fourth part, the "Ladder of the Intellect," was to provide examples of the application of the principles of the new method that could be used as models for those who followed (vol. 4, 31). The fifth part, concerning "Anticipations," was to provide "speculations" before "certain conclusions," in order to establish "provisionally certain degrees of assurance, for use and relief until the mind shall arrive at a knowledge of causes in which it can rest" (vol. 4, 32). Finally, the sixth part was to be devoted to the "new philosophy." Bacon noted that "the completion, however, of this part is a thing both above my strength and beyond my hopes" (vol. 4, 32). After his retirement from public life, Bacon spent his time composing natural histories on particular subjects and compiling masses of observations in his *Sylva Sylvarum* to contribute to the third and fourth parts of his great instauration. It was his experience with this project that led him to see even more clearly the tremendous amount of effort that his project would require.

At the end of his life, he wrote the incomplete and curious fable of *New Atlantis* about a utopian society governed by a scientific elite that was somewhat

---

8. Shapiro (1991) recognized that practical experience and probabilism are humanistic themes, but she traced the development of these at mid-seventeenth century England to the influence of Continental thinkers, such as Gassendi and Mersenne. See Briggs (1989), Gilbert (1960), Perez-Ramos (1988), Sargent (1989, 1999), and Vickers (1968a) for how Bacon had earlier incorporated these elements within his philosophy.

at odds with his earlier call for a more "democratic" process of investigation. Bacon introduced the readers to details about the island's scientific institution, Solomon's House, by telling of the elaborate arrival of one of the fathers of the house to the city in which the shipwrecked sailors were staying. The father agreed to a meeting with the narrator of the story and explained to him the purpose for which they worked: "The End of our Foundation is the knowledge of Causes, and secret motions of things; and the enlarging of the bounds of Human Empire, to the effecting of all things possible" (vol. 3, 156). The remainder of the father's narration is devoted to detailed descriptions of the laboratories, gardens, instruments, and workers who were actively engaged in the continuing process of the discovery and application of new knowledge. He told, for example, of parks of animals kept "for dissections and trials that thereby we may take light what may be wrought upon the body of man" (vol. 3, 159). Among the workers he described were "Merchants of Light" who traveled in secret to other lands to gather information about their current states of learning (vol. 3, 164). Among the other fellows of Solomon's House were experimenters, compilers, and interpreters, such as the "Miners" who "try new experiments of their own devising" (vol. 3, 164). Bacon's description of this society mirrors well his vision for a continuous process of discovery and invention designed for charitable goals. The islanders had many innovations and seemingly miraculous discoveries, but this was not a closed society where everything had been accomplished.[9]

BACON AND MODERNITY

Although Bacon was heavily influenced by the Humanists, he was involved in more than the rebirth of letters that marked the Renaissance. To all of the elements discussed above, from the encyclopedic and charitable projects to the recognition of the fallibility of human reason and the need for practical experience, Bacon gave a distinctive twist by extending the range of their application. In a modern manner, he sought not merely to advance but to revolutionize the process of learning by turning away from the traditions of antiquity. "Party zeal and emulation are at an end," he proclaimed (vol. 4, 41). In their place was to be the progressive compilation of new discoveries.

Bacon knew the ancient texts well, but he rejected appeals to their authority because he saw this as anti-progressive. "Men have been kept back as by a kind of enchantment from progress in the sciences by reverence for antiquity, by the authority of men accounted great in philosophy, and then by general consent" (vol. 4, 81–82, I: 84). He maintained that his thoughts and suggestions were "quite new; totally new in their very kind: and yet they are copied from a very ancient model;

9. Whitney (1990), e.g., sees the merchants of light as indicative of imperialistic and colonizing elements within the story. But these explorers were employed only for the discovery of knowledge from less advanced civilizations and were not charged with plundering or in any way altering the countries that they visited. There is also an implicit criticism of imperialism in the story. The island of Bensalem was described as the only ancient civilization to survive because it was a peaceful realm, unlike the other more warlike lost civilizations of the ancient Americas.

even the world itself and the nature of things and of the mind" (vol. 4, 11). Like others of the early modern era, Bacon was most impressed by the discovery of new worlds and the benefits that society had derived from such technical inventions as the compass, printing press, gunpowder, and the manufacture of silk (vol. 4, 18, 99–100, I: 109, 110). As indicated most perspicuously by the titles that he chose for his works, he sought to employ new methods for new ends in order that humanity would be endowed with even more "new discoveries and powers" (vol. 4, 79, I: 81).

Bacon was clearly modern in his desire for progress, yet he was opposed to the strain in modernity that Toulmin has called the "narrowing of rationality"— the idea that all rationality is reducible to deductive logic and that it can be applied in all areas indiscriminately.[10] The modernity expressed in the systematic style of Descartes' philosophy, for example, would be more akin to what Bacon in his day saw as "the most ordinary method" by which a person to discover something "first seeks out and sets before him all that has been said about it by others; then he begins to meditate for himself; so by much agitation and working of the wit solicits and as it were evokes his own spirit to give him oracles" (vol. 4, 80, I: 82). Bacon's criticisms of philosophical systematizing were mainly aimed at the Aristotelians, although his criticisms would apply to the style that Descartes would later develop. In particular Bacon argued "that method of discovery and proof according to which the most general principles are first established and then intermediate axioms are tried and proved by them, is the parent of error and the curse of all science" (vol. 4, 70, I: 69). As he wrote: "the Rational School of philosophers snatches from experience a variety of common instances, neither duly ascertained nor diligently examined and weighed, and leaves all the rest to meditation and agitation of wit" (vol. 4, 63–64, I: 62).

Bacon had "no entire or universal theory to propound" and he was opposed to those who did (vol. 4, 104, I: 116). Systems were as "stage plays" (vol. 4, 55, I: 44). These "play books of philosophical systems" (vol. 4, 62, I: 61) were nothing more than Idols of the mind, specifically Idols of the Theatre, because they were like the "stories invented for the stage" that "are more compact and elegant, and more as one would wish them to be, than true stories out of history" (vol. 4, 63, I: 62). Systems inhibit the progress of learning because their creators "set them forth with such ambition and parade, and bring them into the view of the world so fashioned and masked, as if they were complete in all parts and finished" (vol. 4, 85, I: 86). Bacon chose instead to follow more "ancient seekers after truth" who put what they had learned "into aphorisms, that is, into short and scattered sentences, not linked together by an artificial method, and did not pretend or profess to embrace the entire art" (I: 86). In *De Augmentis*, Bacon returned to this theme stating his opposition to "methods" as a means of transmission. "Methodical delivery is fit to win consent or belief, but of little use to give directions for practice" (vol. 4, 451). Instead, he favored aphorisms that as "only portions and as it were

---

10. Toulmin (1990), p. 20. Others have either tried to make Bacon fit this mold or have criticized him for failing to do so. See, e.g., Campbell (1986), Hattaway (1978), Jardine (1990), and Whitney (1986).

fragments of knowledge, invite others to contribute and add something in their turn; whereas methodical delivery carrying the show of a total makes men careless, as if they were already at the end" (vol. 4, 451).

Most of the works discussed above were programmatic works wherein Bacon set out his method for pursuing his project and his hopes about the benefits that would accrue from the results achieved. As mentioned briefly, however, he also produced detailed natural histories in order to provide models for his method and the material upon which his method would work. His natural histories were not to be compiled simply as a repertoire of an empirical knowledge of particulars for curiosity or entertainment value. Rather they were to be carefully compiled in such a way as to aid in the discovery of causes. Ever mindful of the dynamic and progressive nature of his enterprise, however, Bacon tried to leave his histories open-ended so that others could make additions or corrections to them. In a preliminary manner in Book II of the *New Organon*, he gave some examples of compiling tables where one would ask questions of nature in a particular manner. He also included there a lengthy discussion of twenty-seven prerogative instances that provided numerous examples of how to construct testing situations when pursuing inquiry (see, e.g., the Instance of the Fingerpost, II: 36).

In the *Parasceve* or *Preparative towards a Natural and Experimental History*, appended to the *New Organon*, Bacon gave more practical advice concerning part three of his great plan. In ten aphorisms on how to compose natural history, he maintained that materials should be collected that are useful for philosophy, that sources should be provided for the information, and that all observations should be set down as completely and quantitatively as possible. But this was not meant to be the rather mindless "objective" collection of singular facts that has often been described. Bacon noted in his rules for writing that one should include "five things that will make the history fitter and more convenient for the work of the interpreter" (vol. 4, 261). He began by suggesting that "questions (I do not mean as to the causes but as to the fact) should be added, in order to provoke and stimulate further inquiry" (vol. 4, 261). Secondly, he noted that "in any new and more subtle experiment the manner in which the experiment was conducted should be added, that men may be free to judge for themselves whether the information obtained from that experiment be trustworthy or fallacious, and also that men's industry may be roused to discover, if possible, methods more exact" (vol. 4, 261). Thirdly, he noted that it would be useful to include remarks on whether there is "anything doubtful or questionable in the reports" (vol. 4, 261). Fourthly, "it would not be amiss to intersperse observations occasionally" (vol. 4, 261). Finally, one should give "a brief review" of currently received opinions "that they may touch and rouse the intellect, and no more" (vol. 4, 262).

In 1622, after he retired from public life, Bacon published his first full-scale natural history, *The History of the Winds*, that would fulfill a portion of part four of the great instauration, "the ladder of the intellect," by serving as a model for others to follow. In the preface to this work, he admonished his readers to put aside reverence for the authority of philosophers and instead to have reverence for the works of the creator and to seek useful knowledge by direct investigations of nature. He acknowledged that although there was much left to be perfected in the *New Organon*, he had turned his attention to natural histories because they provide the material on which his logic is to work and he thought it best to make a start so that others may know how to make a contribution to this part of his project (vol. 5, 133). As he said, even if the Organon "were complete," it "would not without the Natural History much advance the Instauration of the Sciences" (vol. 5, 134). Therefore, he "thought it better and wiser by all means and above all things to apply myself to this work" (vol. 5, 134).

Between the preface and the history proper, Bacon inserted a Rule "more exact and more succinct" than that of the *Parasceve* on how to write such histories (vol. 5, 135–36).[11] Bacon suggested that writers of natural histories first need to pose questions concerning the subject matter handled and then provide a detailed account of the experiments performed. Interspersed throughout the histories, Bacon noted that one should include injunctions, methodological explanations, admonitions and cautions, observations, speculations, and reminders concerning practice. He explained that the methods followed had to be carefully described "for there may be a mistake, and it may stimulate others to devise better and more exact methods" (vol. 5, 136). The "admonitions and cautions concerning the fallacies of things, and the errors and scruples which may occur in inquiry and discovery" were also required so as to "exorcise as much as possible all delusions and false appearances" (vol. 5, 136). Speculations that are "rudiments of interpretation concerning causes" were to be "introduced sparingly, and rather as suggesting what the cause may be than defining what it is" as things "useful, if not altogether true" (vol. 5, 136).

Bacon followed this rule in the histories that he wrote. In *The History of Dense and Rare*, for example, he began with an introduction that contained a discussion about the importance of studying the quantity and proportions of matter and how they are distributed in bodies. He acknowledged the general principle that "the sum total of matter remains always the same" but added "that this sum of matter is variously distributed among different bodies cannot be doubted" (vol. 5, 339–40). The history itself began with a table of the comparative weights of various bodies enclosed within the same space followed by a discussion of how he set up the experimental situation for collecting the data provided in the table (vol. 5, 341–43). He then provided four admonitions concerning the experimental set up. Among these were his remarks on how the "smallness of the vessel employed" for weighing the materials was "not favorable for verifying the exact proportions" and that he had only been able to include weights for "such bodies as could conveniently be made to fill up the space or measure" (vol. 5, 343). This discussion was followed by seven observations on the experiment that explored its significance, such that it provided information that contradicted the opinion of Aristotle (vol. 5, 344–47). Interspersed within these observations were "injunctions" such as suggestions for future areas of inquiry, and "Reminders concerning Practice" including his conclusion from the data that the "transmutation of metals into gold, is to be much doubted of" (vol. 5, 346).

---

11. See Sargent (1999) for discussions of, and selections from, these historical works.

The most popular work by Bacon during the seventeenth century was his *Sylva Sylvarum*, a massive compilation of observations, published shortly after his death by his chaplain William Rawley (vol. 2, 339–680). Composed of ten "centuries," Bacon grouped together according to topic a total of 1,000 observations, a number of which were taken from the works of others such as Aristotle, Pliny, and Porta. Although the *Sylva Sylvarum* in this respect resembles the compilations of learning that Bacon put together in Books II–IX of *De Augmentis*, it was intended as a model for how to write natural histories and thus was also a contribution to part four of *The Great Instauration*. In addition, the observations of others that were included here were stripped of what Bacon found to be the speculative and erroneous explanations of the original authors and supplied with his own alternative interpretations. He also included methodological comments concerning problems with interpreting experiments and advocated the idea of reporting "experiments in consort"—grouping together experiments that have similar import so that they might shed light on each other.

As he had hoped, Bacon's two types of histories, as well as the methodological advice of his *New Organon*, served as a model for the next generation of natural philosophers in England. His influence can be seen in the work of one of his most famous followers, Robert Boyle. Among Boyle's early manuscripts are many loose sheets and notebooks filled with observations compiled for the purpose of continuing Bacon's *Sylva Sylvarum*.[12] Boyle also frequently followed Bacon's example by grouping experiments together under the explicit heading of "experiments in consort" in published works, such as his *History of Colours* and *Experimenta et observationes physicae*.[13] Most significantly, in Boyle's first major scientific work, his *New Experiments Physico-Mechanical Touching the Spring of the Air*, he followed Bacon's pattern for a natural and experimental history almost to the letter. He began with a brief discussion of the importance of studying the air. He followed this with a detailed description of the air pump together with experiments that concerned its construction and the phenomena that it exhibited. He then proceeded in an orderly progression to those experiments performed in order to prove the weight of the air. In his well-known, but frequently misunderstood, "digressions," Boyle provided numerous observations and admonitions concerning the functioning of his air pump and tentative speculations concerning the causes responsible for the effects produced in order to excite the curiosity of his readers and thus involve them in the experimental project.[14]

12. Boyle (1772/1965), vol. 1, 305. See Sargent (1995), ch. 6 for more detailed discussion of this manuscript material. See Sargent (1986, 1989) for more information on Bacon's influence on Boyle.

13. Ibid., vol. 1. Part 2 of *Colours* (pp. 708–24) has fifteen experiments in consort on black and white that were designed to show how the texture of bodies is responsible for the different capacities that they have for absorbing or reflecting light. Part 3 (pp. 724–88) contains fifty numbered experiments along with numerous annotations concerning the production of all other colors. In Boyle's last work, *Experimenta et observationes physicae*, he explicitly discussed the role of experiments in consort once again and described them as those "wherein divers experiments and observations, all of them relating to the same subject or purpose, are set down together" (vol. 5, 567).

14. Ibid., vol. 1, pp. 1–117. See Sargent (1995), ch. 7–8, for more detail on Boyle's practices of experimenting and writing up experimental reports.

CONCLUSION

Having a more nuanced and sophisticated understanding of Bacon's philosophy can help us understand the next generation of English philosophers. Of course, the works of other natural philosophers, such as Galileo, Pascal, and Descartes, were influential by then as well, but Bacon was considered by some as their primary source and model for natural philosophy. Yet instead of taking Boyle at his word when he wrote about continuing Bacon's project, for example, historians have often gone to great lengths to deny Bacon's import. This is unfortunate for a number of reasons. First, it hampers our understanding of how the themes of charity, morality, social obligation, political responsibility, and modesty all played a role in the rhetorical approach taken by natural philosophers of Restoration England and how these themes were not unique to this time but were tied, via Bacon, to the humanist tradition. Secondly, when looking for continental counterparts, the ones normally seen as influential are those that followed a strict empiricist epistemology that then tends to be attributed to philosophers like Boyle despite the fact that he speculated freely concerning unobservable causal processes. This flawed epistemological picture is often then read further back into Bacon's philosophy as well and subsequently gives rise to the erroneous idea of a generalized program of English empiricism. Finally, the failure to recognize Bacon's influence leads to a lack of appreciation for the import of Boyle's diffidence and his many theoretical and methodological digressions. The experimental method and its so-called "literary technology" can be better understood not as addressing particular concerns of Restoration England but as part of Bacon's project for knowledge acquisition through a dynamic process of discovery.[15]

Bacon was a revolutionary and progressive thinker who made significant contributions to the development of modern experimental science and its philosophy. Indeed, writing in 1733, Voltaire went so far as to describe Bacon as "the father of experimental philosophy." He went on to maintain that "In a word, nobody before Chancellor Bacon had understood experimental philosophy; and of all the physical experiments that have been made since his time, hardly one was not suggested in his book." However, he also noted that Bacon's *New Organon*, which was the "best of his works," had also become "the most useless." It was "the scaffolding by which the new philosophy has been built; and when that edifice had been erected at least in part, the scaffolding was no longer of any use."[16] Bacon's experimental works were to be eclipsed by later generations. There was a renewed interest in his philosophical and methodological works in the nineteenth century,

---

15. Shapin and Schaffer (1985) discuss the notion of literary technology as being fashioned by Boyle in order to enhance "virtual witnessing" and thus lend legitimacy to the experimental program. They maintain that "Although Boyle's inspiration may, plausibly, have been Baconian, the 'influence' of Bacon is sometimes exaggerated . . . It is useful to remember that it was Boyle, not Bacon, who developed the literary forms for an actual programme of systematic experimentation; it is hard to imagine two more different forms than Bacon's aphorisms and Boyle's experimental narratives" (p. 63, n. 85). I would respond that it is useful to know that Bacon wrote more works than the *New Organon*.

16. Voltaire (1773/1961), pp. 47–9.

but in that post-Humean context Bacon came to be seen by philosophers such as Mill and Reid as little more than a strict empiricist and anti-hypothetical inductivist. Such interpretation would in turn lead to Popper's severe criticisms of Bacon's naiveté in the twentieth century and Bacon's subsequent frequent dismissal by philosophers in general.[17]

In addition to a more nuanced understanding of historical development, however, Bacon's works can provide a valuable philosophical resource for issues today. Because of Bacon's myriad interests and his attempt to design a progressive approach to learning in all areas, there are numerous tensions in the complete body of his works.[18] He sought the dual goals of knowledge and power, for example, but often these goals appear to be in conflict. He called for a rather democratic approach to inquiry, yet he recognized that as knowledge progressed, a hierarchical division of labor would also be required. In a similar manner, while he advocated the free communication of information among all investigators in all countries, he also acknowledged that in some cases secrecy would be appropriate. In part, these and other tensions are the result of Bacon's eschewal of philosophical systematizing that, in turn, reflects the humanistic influence on his thought. As modern science and its narrative developed in the nineteenth and twentieth centuries, the earlier humanistic elements were lost and forgotten. By the end of the twentieth century, modern science and modern philosophy were severely criticized from a number of perspectives for their presumed autonomy from the influences of the social world. Paradoxically, perhaps, one way to respond to such challenges is through a more careful study of Bacon's modernity. Because of the mitigating influence of humanism seen, for example, in his charitable impulse and fallible approach, a retrieval of his works can help to point to ways in which to reconcile, without necessarily resolving, the tensions inherent in modernity.

REFERENCES

Bacon, F. 1857–74. *The Works of Francis Bacon.* 14 vols. James Spedding, Robert L. Ellis, and Douglas D. Heath, eds. London: Longman and Co.

Boyle, R. 1772/1965. *The Works of the Honourable Robert Boyle.* 6 vols. Thomas Birch, ed. Reprint: Hildesheim, Germany: Georg Olms.

Briggs, J. C. 1989. *Francis Bacon and the Rhetoric of Nature.* Cambridge, MA: Harvard University Press.

Campbell, J. A. 1986. "Scientific Revolution and the Grammar of Culture: The Case of Darwin's Origin." *The Quarterly Journal of Speech* 72:351–76.

Coquillette, D. R. 1992. *Francis Bacon.* Stanford, CA: Stanford University Press.

Farrington, B. 1979. *Francis Bacon: Philosopher of Industrial Science.* New York: Henry Schuman.

Gilbert, N. 1960. *Renaissance Concepts of Method.* New York: Columbia University Press.

17. See Sargent (1999) for more detail on the historical reception of Bacon's philosophy in the nineteenth century. The nineteenth-century interpretations became a part of the lore of the twentieth century. See, e.g., Campbell (1986) who describes how Reid "out-Baconed Bacon in his polemic against hypotheses" (p. 356). It would be closer to the mark to say that Reid transformed Bacon's precepts to fit his own purposes.

18. These and similar tensions are discussed more fully in McMullin (1985), Peltonen (1992), Sargent (1996), and Whitney (1986).

Hattaway, M. 1978. "Bacon and 'Knowledge Broken': Limits for Scientific Method." *Journal of the History of Ideas* 39:183–97.

Hesse, M. 1968. "Francis Bacon's Philosophy of Science." In *Essential Articles for the Study of Francis Bacon*. Brian Vickers, ed. Hamden, CT: Archon Press, pp. 115–39.

Horton, M. 1973. "In Defence of Francis Bacon." *Studies in History and Philosophy of Science* 4:241–78.

Jardine, L. 1974. *Francis Bacon: Discovery and the Art of Discourse*. Cambridge: Cambridge University Press.

Jardine, L. 1990. "*Experientia Literata* or *Novum Organum*? The Dilemma of Bacon's Scientific Method." In *Francis Bacon's Legacy of Texts*. William A. Sessions, ed. New York: AMS Press, pp. 47–67.

Jardine, L. and A. Stewart. 1998. *Hostage to Fortune: The Troubled Life of Francis Bacon*. London: Gollancz.

Martin, J. 1992. *Francis Bacon, the State and the Reform of Natural Philosophy*. Cambridge: Cambridge University Press.

McMullin, E. 1985. "Openness and Secrecy in Science: Some Notes on Early History." *Science, Technology, and Human Values* 10:14–23.

McMullin, E. 1990. "Conceptions of Science in the Scientific Revolution." In *Reappraisals of the Scientific Revolution*. David C. Lindberg and Robert S. Westman, eds. Cambridge: Cambridge University Press, pp. 27–92.

Merchant, C. 1980. *The Death of Nature*. New York: Harper and Row.

Peltonen, M. 1992. "Politics and Science: Francis Bacon and the True Greatness of States." *The Historical Journal* 35:279–305.

Peltonen, M., ed. 1996. *The Cambridge Companion to Bacon*. Cambridge: Cambridge University Press.

Perez-Ramos, A. 1988. *Francis Bacon's Idea of Science and the Maker's Knowledge Tradition*. Oxford: Clarendon Press.

Pinnick, C. L. 1998. "Francis Bacon: A Sure Plan." *Metascience* 7:515–23.

Popper, K. R. 1968. *The Logic of Scientific Discovery*. New York: Harper and Row.

Rees, G. 1996. "Bacon's Speculative Philosophy." In *The Cambridge Companion to Bacon*. Markku Peltonen, ed. Cambridge: Cambridge University Press, pp. 121–45.

Sargent, R.-M. 1986. "Robert Boyle's Baconian Inheritance: A Response to Laudan's Cartesian Thesis." *Studies in History and Philosophy of Science* 17:469–86.

Sargent, R.-M. 1989. "Scientific Experiment and Legal Expertise: The Way of Experience in Seventeenth-Century England." *Studies in History and Philosophy of Science* 20:19–45.

Sargent, R.-M. 1995. *The Diffident Naturalist: Robert Boyle and the Philosophy of Experiment*. Chicago: University of Chicago Press.

Sargent, R.-M. 1996. "Bacon as an Advocate for Cooperative Scientific Research." In *The Cambridge Companion to Bacon*. Markku Peltonen, ed. Cambridge: Cambridge University Press, pp. 146–71.

Sargent, R.-M. 1999. "General Introduction." In Francis Bacon, *Selected Philosophical Works*. Indianapolis: Hackett Publishing, pp. vi–xxxvi.

Shapin, S. and S. Schaffer. 1985. *Leviathan and the Air-Pump*. Princeton: Princeton University Press.

Shapiro, B. 1991. "Early Modern Intellectual Life: Humanism, Religion and Science in Seventeenth-Century England." *History of Science* 29:45–71.

Toulmin, S. 1990. *Cosmopolis: The Hidden Agenda of Modernity*. Chicago: University of Chicago Press.

Urbach, P. 1987. *Francis Bacon's Philosophy of Science: An Account and a Reappraisal*. LaSalle, IL: Open Court.

Vickers, B., ed. 1968a. *Essential Articles for the Study of Francis Bacon*. Hamden, CT: Archon Books.

Vickers, B. 1968b. *Francis Bacon and Renaissance Prose*. Cambridge: Cambridge University Press.

Vickers, B. 1987. *English Science, Bacon to Newton*. Cambridge: Cambridge University Press.

Vickers, B. 1996. "Bacon and Rhetoric." In *The Cambridge Companion to Bacon*. Markku Peltonen, ed. Cambridge: Cambridge University Press, pp. 200–31.

Voltaire. 1733/1961. *Philosophical Letters*. Ernest Delworth, trans. Indianapolis: Bobbs-Merrill.

Weinberger, J. 1986. "Science and Rule in Bacon's Utopia: An Introduction to the Reading of the *New Atlantis*." *American Political Science Review* 70:865–85.

Whitney, C. 1986. *Francis Bacon and Modernity*. New Haven, CT: Yale University Press.

Whitney, C. 1990. "Merchants of Light: Science as Colonization in the *New Atlantis*." In *Francis Bacon's Legacy of Texts*. William A. Sessions, ed. New York: AMS Press, pp. 255–68.

Midwest Studies in Philosophy, XXVI (2002)

Hobbes's Atheism[1]

DOUGLAS M. JESSEPH

Thomas Hobbes was an atheist, which is to say that he did not believe in the existence of gods. Few would challenge the conclusion that Hobbes disbelieved in such deities as those of classical antiquity, but I hold that he was equally unwilling to acknowledge the existence of the God of traditional Judeo-Christian monotheism—the all-powerful, personal creator who supposedly brought the world into existence and rules over it. I maintain this interpretation despite the fact that Hobbes never publicly announced his disbelief in a deity. Indeed, he filled many pages of his published works with seemingly sincere references to God, even to the point of appearing to offer arguments for the existence of a supreme being. If I am right, the sincerity of these professions of faith is only apparent, and Hobbes was really a sly and ironic atheist who concealed his disbelief behind a screen of disingenuous theological verbiage while constructing a philosophical system that makes the concept of God inadmissible. The nature of the case rules out certainty on this issue, but I claim that the preponderance of the evidence makes it quite likely that Hobbes was not a believer. This reading of Hobbes and his philosophy

---

1. Earlier versions of this paper were presented to the NEH Seminar "Descartes and His Contemporaries" at Virginia Tech and Macalester College. I thank participants in both venues for helpful comments. I also thank Prof. Karl Schumann for constructive criticisms of an earlier version. My references to *De Corpore* (Hobbes 1655) use the abbreviation "*DCo*" followed by part, chapter, and section numbers separated by periods; references to *Leviathan* (Hobbes 1651) use the abbreviation "*L*" followed by part, chapter, and page numbers (in the 1651 edition) separated by periods; references to the *Answer to Bramhall* (Hobbes 1682) use the abbreviation "*AB*" followed by page number. In all cases, citations to the *Opera Latina* (Hobbes [1839–45] 1966a) or *English Works* (Hobbes [1839–45] 1966b) follow, using the abbreviations *EW* and *OL*. For Hobbes's works other than *DCo*, *L*, and *AB*, citations are to page number in the original edition as well as volume and page of *EW* or *OL*.

is nothing new, but it has become a decidedly minority view among scholars in recent decades.[2]

For all that such an interpretation may be a disputed issue among scholars of our era, it was a commonplace in Hobbes's own day. In fact, nearly all of Hobbes's opponents claimed to detect atheism lurking, so to speak, in the shadows of his system.[3] My purpose here is to argue that Hobbes's contemporary critics were essentially correct, and to do that I will first concentrate on what I take to be the implied case for atheism that can be readily constructed from principles central to Hobbes's philosophy. Others have held that Hobbes's materialism makes it unlikely that he could have embraced traditional conceptions of a deity, but I intend to show that Hobbes explicitly and repeatedly endorsed principles that render the concept of God an absurdity to be banished from the true philosophy. Having done this, I will then take up Hobbes's supposed arguments for the existence of a deity and show that there are good reasons to think that he could not have intended them seriously. I will then attempt to make a broader case and adduce grounds for thinking that all of Hobbes's professions of religious sentiment are ironic. The final section contains some reflections on the consequences that an atheistic reading of Hobbes's thought has for his metaphysics, natural philosophy, and political theory.

Before undertaking this task, a few comments on matters of broad interpretive method are in order. Three salient questions concerning Hobbes and God can usefully be distinguished. First, did Hobbes himself believe in the existence of God? Second, what role (if any) does the concept of God play in Hobbes's philosophy? Third, what is the status of religion (and, more specifically, Christianity) in Hobbes's thought? I hold that there are adequate grounds for answering the first question in the negative, assuming (as I do) that Hobbes's pronouncements on matters of general philosophical principle were intended seriously and should be taken as definitive when they conflict with professions of theistic belief.[4] This

2. Taylor ([1938] 1965) is very influential in promoting a reading of Hobbes as a believer, and specifically one with a deontological moral theory that requires sincere theological commitment. Warrender (1957) and Hood (1964) advance a similar interpretation. More recently, Arp (1999), Geach (1981), Lloyd (1992), Martinich (1992), and Zarka (1996) have held that Hobbes must be understood as a sincere theist, although the content of his theistic beliefs is a matter about which they disagree. Berman (1988), Curley (1992, 1998), and Skinner (1969, 1996) stand out as contemporary scholars who take Hobbes to have been an atheist; Polin (1981, chapter 1) offers an interpretation that is consistent with mine, while Strauss (1952) looms large in the secondary literature as proposing the kind of ironic reading of Hobbes's professions of religious belief that I pursue.

3. Mintz sums up the seventeenth-century reading of Hobbes on religion when he describes atheism as the central issue around which Hobbes's otherwise diverse opponents could unite: "[i]t was atheism then which was at the heart of the controversy about Hobbes, the source of all the fears and seething indignation which Hobbes's thought inspired, the single charge which is most persistently made, and to which all other differences between Hobbes and his contemporaries can be reduced" (Mintz 1962, 45).

4. The way is open, of course, for an alternative interpretive principle, namely that Hobbes's many repeated professions of belief in God should be taken as definitive, while his statements of metaphysical principles should be disregarded whenever they contradict his pronouncements on the nature of God. As I hope will become evident in what follows, there is little to be said for this sort of interpretive stance.

determines an answer to the second question, namely that the proper interpretation of Hobbes's philosophy should assign no role to God, either in his metaphysics or in his political theory. On the third question, I hold that Hobbes viewed religion as an inescapable part of the human condition which must be rigorously controlled by the sovereign. Hobbes took religion to consist in outward forms of observance that are to be regulated by law in order to ensure civil peace; it is irrelevant that the propositions expressed in religious language turn out to be false, just as it is irrelevant whether any citizen actually believes these propositions. From the standpoint of Hobbes's political theory, what matters is that citizens obey the sovereign's dictates concerning external practices of worship: any citizen's internal state of mind is beyond the sovereign's control and not a matter for politics. Keeping these three questions separate can help obviate confusion that otherwise threatens to obscure the issues involved here.

THE INCOHERENCE OF HOBBESIAN THEISM

The principal reason for reading Hobbes as an atheist comes from a consideration of his materialistic metaphysics, together with his pronouncements on the nature of God. Hobbes embraced a decidedly materialistic ontology according to which the only substance is body; in his words: "that which is not Body, is no part of the Universe: And because the Universe is All, that which is no part of it, is *Nothing*; and consequently *no where*" (*L* 4.46.371; *EW* 3: 672). He further held that all phenomena of the natural world arise from the motion and impact of material bodes and notoriously insisted that the expression "immaterial substance" is insignificant because it combines "two Names, whose significations are contradictory and inconsistent" (*L* 1.4.17; *EW* 3: 33). Such expressions of materialism led many of Hobbes's contemporaries to conclude that his equation of substance with body was tantamount to the open denial of God's existence. The traditional Christian concept of God is that of an essentially immaterial being, and Hobbes's metaphysics clearly rules out any deity of the traditional sort.

However, materialism does not lead to atheism all by itself, since it is consistent to hold that God is a material being. In fact, Hobbes made precisely this point and cited the authority of the Church Father Tertullian to defend himself against the charge of atheism. Responding to John Wallis's allegation that materialism implies atheism, Hobbes insisted "whatsoever can be inferr'd from the denying of *Incorporeal Substances*, makes *Tertullian*, one of the ancientest of the Fathers, and most of the Doctors of the Greek Church, as much Atheists as [me]: For *Tertullian*, in his treatise *De Carne Christi*, says plainly, *Omne quod est, corpus est sui generis. Nihil est incorporale, nisi quod non est.* That is to say, *Whatsoever is any thing, is a body of its kind. Nothing is Incorporeal, but that which has no Being*" (Hobbes 1662, 37; *EW* 4: 429). Elsewhere, in reply to Bishop Bramhall's complaint that "by taking away all incorporeal substance, [Hobbes] taketh away God himself" (Bramhall 1676, 3: 873), Hobbes characterized God as "an infinitely fine Spirit" (*AB* 36; *EW* 4: 310) or "a most pure, simple, invisible Spirit Corporeal" (*AB* 40; *EW* 4: 313). In explicating the notion of a "Spirit Corporeal" Hobbes explained that he used the term 'spirit' to denote a "Thin, Fluid, Transparent

Invisible Body" (*AB* 36; *EW* 4: 309). Although the concept of a material God is not incoherent in itself and may even have an orthodox pedigree, it cannot be consistently combined with other things Hobbes claimed about the Deity. Indeed, when we inquire into the principal features of such a Hobbesian God and His relationship to the world, it becomes impossible to take Hobbes's supposed theology seriously or to think that he ever intended it seriously.

To begin with, we should try to determine what sort of material body a Hobbesian deity might be. We have seen that Hobbes characterized God as some sort of thin invisible "Spirit Corporeal"; a further specification of this concept of a deity comes from Hobbes's declaration that God is to be understood as "eternal, ingenerable, and incomprehensible" (*DCo* 1.1.8; *OL* 1: 9). We can conclude that any Hobbesian God must be an everlasting, uncreated, incomprehensible, invisible, thin, fluid body. Hobbes understood God's incomprehensibility to mean that "we understand nothing of *what he is*, but only *that he is*; and therefore the Attributes we give him, are not to tell one another, *what he is*, nor to signifie our opinion of his Nature, but our desire to honor him with such names as we conceive most honorable amongst our selves" (*L* 3.34.208; *EW* 3: 383). Furthermore, such a God would owe much of His incomprehensibility to the fact that He is infinite. Hobbes's epistemology has it that all ideas must ultimately derive from sensation, but this leaves us without an idea of anything infinite, except insofar as we have a conception of our own limitations. In Hobbes's words:

> Whatsoever we imagine, is *Finite*. Therefore there can be no Idea, or conception of anything we call *Infinite*. No man can have in his mind an Image of infinite magnitude; nor conceive infinite swiftness, infinite time, or infinite force, or infinite power. When we say any thing is infinite, we signifie onely, that we are not able to conceive the ends, and bounds of the thing named; having no Conception of the thing, but of our own inability. And therefore the Name of *God* is used, not to make us conceive him; (for he is *Incomprehensible*; and his greatnesse, and power are unconceivable;) but that we may honour him. (*L* 1.3.11; *EW* 3:17)

Thus, in addition to being an eternal and incomprehensible body, any God Hobbes was prepared to acknowledge must also be an infinite body, that is, one without conceivable limits.

The issue of God's incomprehensibility is the source of insuperable problems for any view of Hobbes as a believer. I should stress that the simple fact that Hobbes endorsed the thesis of God's incomprehensibility does not commit him to atheism straightaway. The incomprehensibility of the Divine nature is, after all, a perfectly orthodox doctrine and there were plenty of seventeenth-century figures who were clearly believers but insisted that humans could have no adequate idea of God.[5] Nevertheless, on closer examination it becomes clear that the conception

---

5. Martinich makes this point when he observes that "[t]he reason Hobbes thinks that humans can have no idea of God is that all human ideas are analyzable or reducible to sensations and that God cannot be sensed. There is nothing radical in this view" (Martinich 1992, 186).

of God as an incomprehensible, infinite *body* makes no sense, on Hobbes's principles or anybody else's. Therefore, a God of this sort is very unlikely to be something in which Hobbes could have believed. Indeed, there is already something odd in Hobbes's insistence that, notwithstanding the incomprehensibility of the Divine nature, we can know with certainty that God must be a material body. Yet when we consider just what follows from the concept of a material God, the notion is quickly burdened with a variety of contradictions.

In the first place, we can ask whether Hobbes's epistemology and metaphysics even allow for the concept of an incomprehensible, infinite body. Hobbes defines body as "that, which having no dependence on our thought, is coincident with some part of space" (*DCo* 1.8.1; *OL* 1: 91), or "that which filleth, or occupyeth some certain room, or imagined place; and dependeth not on the imagination, but is a real part of that we call the *Universe*" (*L* 3.34.207; *EW* 3: 381). Hobbes certainly held that there are bodies so complex that we cannot understand the means by which they produce their characteristic effects. Furthermore, he recognized that our knowledge of how bodies act upon one another is radically incomplete and conjectural; so, for instance, we must rely upon fallible hypotheses to explain why water dissolves sugar and not gold.[6] Notwithstanding this incompleteness in our scientific knowledge of how nature works, it is impossible to see how Hobbes's definition of body might allow for there to be an infinite and incomprehensible body. To put the matter bluntly, Hobbes's ontology admits only bodies, each of which is coincident with some bounded, determinate part of space; God, however, is infinite and incomprehensible, and this rules out the possibility that God could be a body in the sense defined by Hobbes.[7] Thus, no Hobbesian God exists.

The incoherence of this notion can be made more evident by asking where God might be located. An infinite body, in Hobbes's sense of the term 'infinite', has no conceivable limits: it cannot be comprehended, both in the sense that it cannot be contained in some determinate part of space and in the sense that it cannot be the object of our understanding. On the other hand, Hobbes held that "No man . . . can conceive any thing, but he must conceive it in some place" (*L* 1.3.11; *EW* 3: 17). However, there is literally no conceivable place for an incom-

---

6. As Hobbes puts it, the "Principles of naturall Science . . . are so farre from teaching us any thing of Gods nature, as they cannot teach us our own nature, nor the nature of the smallest creature living" (*L* 2.31.191; *EW* 3: 354). See Jesseph (1996) for an account of Hobbes's philosophy of science.

7. Yves-Charles Zarka has noticed the problems inherent in this conception of God as incomprehensible body, but he does not conclude that Hobbes was an atheist. He asks, "After all, doesn't Hobbes define God as a body? Doesn't this call into question any suggestion of a theology of absolute transcendence? Or, in other words, isn't what I am calling a divided foundation in fact a doubtfully coherent basis for the rest of Hobbes's system, doubtfully coherent because it tries to reconcile the two conflicting claims that God is unknowable and that God is a body?" He concludes only that "Hobbes did not think through the idea of a theologically divided foundation, and the quest for foundations remains to some extent open and uncertain" (Zarka 1996, 79–80). A more plausible conclusion is that Hobbes was fully aware of the incoherence of the concept of God as an incomprehensible body and held that no such thing could exist. This will become more evident shortly.

prehensible, infinite God in Hobbes's system. Hobbes insisted that no body could occupy multiple locations at once, and he admitted that the traditional notion of God's omnipresence was something he could neither "comprehend nor conceive" (*AB* 18; *EW* 4: 296). One might therefore be tempted to think that a pantheistic notion of God (which does not distinguish between God and the universe) could be made consistent with Hobbes's conception of God as an infinite body lacking spatial location. But I take it that pantheism differs only verbally from outright atheism, and Hobbes expressed the same view: "those Philosophers, who sayd the World, or the Soule of the World was God, spake unworthily of him; and denyed his Existence: For by God, is understood the cause of the World; and to say the World is God, is to say there is no cause of it, that is, no God" (*L* 2.31. 190; *EW* 3: 350). Hobbes declared that "I mean by the Universe, the Aggregate of all things that have being in themselves, and so do all men else. And because God has a being, it follows that he is either the whole Universe, or a part of it" (*AB* 86; *EW* 4: 349). This, however, requires that God be identified with a (proper) part of the universe because the pantheistic identification of God with the universe has been ruled out. Therefore, a Hobbesian God must be an infinite, boundless part of the universe, notwithstanding the fact Hobbes requires that that every part of the universe must be determinate, bounded, and finite.

Theologians in the tradition of St. Thomas had taken up the question of divine location and offered a distinction between *circumscriptive* and *definitive* place in order to avoid pantheism while upholding the doctrine that God is wholly present throughout the universe.[8] Roughly put, the distinction is this: a body has circumscriptive place insofar as it is bounded by a region of space, but an immaterial substance (such as a soul or form) can have definitive location when it is wholly located in every portion of a space through the exercise of its actualizing capacity in that space. Thus, the soul is definitively located in the body because it exercises its spiritual activity over the body. This sort of distinction allows one to claim that God is everywhere present definitively without requiring Him to be identified with space itself by being everywhere circumscriptively. Hobbes, however, heaped contempt on this distinction with the remark that "the Circumscription of a thing, is nothing else but the Determination, or defining of its Place; and so both the terms in the Distinction are the same" (*L* 4.46.373; *EW* 3: 675).[9]

---

8. See Thomas Aquinas, *Summa Theologica*, Part I, Question 52, Article 2: "From what has been said it is clear that to be in place is attributed to bodies, to angels, and to God in quite different ways. A body is in place as *circumscribed*, for it is commensurate with the place it is in. An angel is not commensurate with any place, and therefore is not in place as circumscribed; but he is in place *determinately*, for his being *here* means that he is not *there*. God, however, is in place in neither of these ways; he is simply everywhere" (Aquinas 1964, 9: 49).

9. A similar sentiment is expressed in his *Six Lessons to the Professors of Mathematics*: "[T]his *determination* is the same things with *circumscription*; and whatsoever is any where (*UBIcunq*;) *definitivè* is there also *circumscriptivè*; and by this means, the distinction is lost, by which Theologers, when they deny God to be in any place, save themselves from being accused of saying he is no where; for that which is no where is nothing" (Hobbes 1656, 6; *EW*: 7: 204–5). Elsewhere (*AB* 19–20; *EW* 4: 297–8) Hobbes engages in a long and detailed attack on the distinction as "Canting" and "Fraud."

As a result, he had no means to avoid the consequence that God's omnipresence means that the Deity must be identified with space itself—but this is a consequence he explicitly rejects.

The result of these reflections is that the Hobbesian concept of God does not simply surpass our understanding—it is flatly unintelligible because although God is a material body there is no content to the claim that He occupies any determinate place, and yet the very concept of body is defined in terms of the occupation of a determinate part of space.[10] In his account of the various "Attributes of Divine Honour" in chapter 31 of *Leviathan*, Hobbes embraced this consequence with his declaration that "to attribute *Figure* to [God], is not Honour; for all Figure is Finite . . . Nor to attribute to him *Parts*, or *Totality*; which are the Attributes onely of things Finite: Nor to say he is in this, or that *Place*: for whatsoever is in Place, is bounded, and Finite" (*L* 2.31.190; *EW* 3: 351–2). So any Hobbesian God would have to be a locationless, partless body without shape or figure.[11] This, simply put, is utter nonsense.

Might Hobbes have thought that God exists somewhere inconceivable (to us), say in some extra dimension to which we lack epistemic access or in some remote, infinite region of which we have no conception? This is impossible because Hobbes defined space as "the phantasm of an existing thing, insofar as it exists," or "the phantasm of a thing existing without the mind simply" (*DCo* 1.7.2; *OL* 1: 83; *EW* 1: 94). There is consequently no space of which we can have no "phantasm," even including Hobbes's concept of "imaginary" space, or the representation of exteriority without a representation of objects.[12] Thus, because we can neither perceive nor imagine a location for the incomprehensible body that is God, Hobbes's basic ontological principles commit him to the conclusion that if God existed, He would have to be a body that lacks spatial location, which is equivalent to God's being a body that is not in space. All this is a very obvious contradiction.

The upshot here is that we cannot read Hobbes as some sort of theological innovator who attempted to reconcile the traditional Christian notion of God with a materialistic ontology and a mechanistic natural philosophy. Hobbes's principles entail that God cannot be identified with space itself, characterized as some sort of mysterious immaterial spiritual body, or taken as the over-arching spiritual sub-

10. This incoherence becomes apparent in Hobbes's objection to Bramhall's contention that God is omnipresent, where he declared "I cannot comprehend nor conceive this. For methinks it implies also that the whole World is also in the whole God, and in every part of God, nor can I conceive how any thing can be called *Whole*, which has no parts" (*AB* 18; *EW* 4: 296). But if Hobbes's corporeal deity is to be infinite and omnipresent, such a God must be a body of a very strange kind; and if the usual theological notion of God's essential unity is upheld, then the fluid body that is God would have to be indivisible.

11. Hobbes's contemporary critic Seth Ward took up this point when he cited the passage at *L* 2.31.190 and complained that "Now if God cannot be a body (because all corporeal affections are removed from Him) . . . nor can there be any incorporeal substance because these terms are mutually contradictory, I do not understand how in Hobbes's view there can be a God" (1656, 340).

12. On Hobbes's conception of space, including his doctrine of imaginary space, see Leijenhorst (1998, Ch. 3).

stance in which corporeal distinction is made possible. Further, it is no use to object that the concept of body as defined by Hobbes concerns finite, physical bodies, while the notion of God is a limit-concept rather than a concept to be applied only within natural philosophy. If this were the case, an infinite, incomprehensible, corporeal God would not be *a* body, but rather body itself. Hobbes insisted that "*Body* [*Lat.*] *Corpus* [*Græc.*] σῶμα, is that substance which hath magnitude indeterminate, and is the same with Corporeal Substance; but *A Body* is that which hath Magnitude determinate, and consequently is understood to be the *totum* or *integrum aliquid*" (*AB* 35; *EW* 4: 309). Therefore, to say that God is indefinite or infinite corporeal substance is to deny that there is a specific body that is God and instead to make God into body quite generally. But this is a sort of pantheism that Hobbes explicitly denied and it cannot be reconciled with his characterization of God as a "most pure, and most simple Corporeal Spirit" distinct from other bodies perceivable by sense (*AB* 31; *EW* 4: 306).

A further question to ponder is that of how the Hobbesian God might act in the world. Hobbes held that is metaphysically impossible for a body to initiate its own motion, and that the only way one body could act upon another is by motion and contact.[13] Thus, if God were to bring about anything, He would have to act by moving and coming into contact with other bodies. Yet because He is a material body, God cannot be the source of His own motion; this implies either that there is something outside of God which has put Him in motion or that He has been in motion throughout all eternity and this motion is simply uncaused. The first alternative is inconsistent with any theism worth considering, while the second yields the odd consequence that, rather than being an "unmoved mover," God is the perpetually moving mover.[14] Even worse, Hobbes defines motion as "the continual relinquishing of one place and acquisition of another" (*DCo* 2.8.10; *OL* 1: 97), but because God has no location it is metaphysically impossible for Him to move and therefore impossible for him to act. As Hobbes put the issue, it is improper to say that God "is *Moved*, or *Resteth*; for both these Attributes ascribe to him Place" (*L* 2.31.190; *EW* 3: 352). In consequence, the Hobbesian God would have to combine the inconsistent attributes of being a locationless body neither in

13. The principle that all action is by local motion and contact finds its most succinct expression in *DeC* 2.9.7. "There can be no cause of motion in a body, except in a body contiguous and moved" (*OL* 1: 110). He also argues that "it is necessary that mutation can be nothing else but motion of the parts of that body which is changed . . . And to this it is consequent, that rest cannot be the cause of anything, nor can anything *act* by rest; since neither motion nor mutation can be caused by it" (*OL* 1: 121–2). Hobbes declares the impossibility of a body initiating its own motion in these terms: "Whatever is at rest is understood always to be at rest, unless there is some other body outside of it, by whose action it is supposed that it can no longer remain at rest" (*DCo* 2.8.19; *OL* 1: 102).

14. Hobbes actually embraced this consequence at *DCo* 4.26.1: "Besides, from the fact that nothing can move itself, it may rightly be inferred that there was some first moving thing, which is eternal, but it cannot be inferred what some have been accustomed to infer, namely that there is an eternally unmoved mover, but rather that it is eternally moved; for as it is true that nothing is moved by itself, so it is also true that nothing is moved except by something moved" (*OL* 1: 336). I will have more to say about this sort of inference when I consider Hobbes's arguments for the existence of God.

motion nor at rest which nevertheless causes effects in the world by coming into contact with bodies and imparting motion to them.[15]

Finally, the notion that a material God should be the creator of the material world is problematic; if God is an everlasting, uncreated material body, then matter itself must be eternal and uncreated, and God is part of the material world. We are thus left to wonder how God might properly be deemed the creator of the material world and how postulating a God can explain anything about the current state of the universe. I conclude that, even in the highly unlikely event that Hobbes believed in the existence of God, he was firmly committed to the thesis that there is no intelligible sense in which God could do anything to affect the world. At best, then, Hobbes's philosophy makes the concept of God explanatorily otiose.

Hobbes's definition of religion as "*Feare* of power invisible, feigned by the mind, or imagined from tales, publiquely allowed" (*L* 1.6.26; *EW* 3: 45) has been taken as a "superbly condensed statement of unbelief" (Berman 1987, 65). The atheistic overtones of this definition are particularly strong because Hobbes's contrast between religion and superstition is drawn purely in terms of whether the tales "publiquely told" are permitted by the sovereign: religion consists of approved tales, superstition of disapproved tales. But, as Edwin M. Curley puts the matter, "it surely does not bespeak much genuine religiosity to suggest that the distinction between religion and superstition depends on whether the state has authorized the tales causing . . . fear" (1992, 524). This issue was pointedly raised by Hobbes's contemporary critic Alexander Ross, who objected that

> It seems then both Religion and Superstition are grounded upon tales and imagination, onely they differ in this, that publickly allowed beget Religion, not allowed Superstition: but what will he say of the Gentiles, among them tales were publickly allowed, were they therefore religious and not superstitious; and is Religion grounded upon fiction or imagination, even true Religion? (Ross 1653, 10)

David Berman has made the additional point that when Hobbes defined true religion to be that "where the power imagined, is truly such as we imagine" (*L* 1.6.26; *EW* 3: 45), true religion is made impossible because Hobbes's God is literally unimaginable (Berman 1987, 66). These points admittedly concern the nature of religion rather than the existence of God, but they underscore the extent to which Hobbes forecloses the possibility that religious belief could ever be true.

Additional grounds for reading Hobbes's philosophy as atheistic can be found by considering his treatment of scripture, prophecy, and revelation. One strategy for justifying belief in an incomprehensible God is to appeal to the authority of revealed scripture, since supernatural evidence in the form of revealed truths

---

15. Lupoli (1999) considers Hobbes's conception of God in the context of his natural philosophy, and particularly with the development of his attempts to construct a plenist physics in which an all-pervasive etherial medium is the fundamental explanatory principle. He interprets Hobbes's talk of a corporeal God in terms of this fluid medium but does not address what I take to be the essential incoherence of the notion.

might warrant belief where ordinary epistemic procedures fail to justify it. But Hobbes poured scorn on the idea that claims of supernatural revelation might yield anything like a reliable means for justifying belief. As he put it "How God speaketh to a man immediately, may be understood by those well enough, to whom he hath so spoken; but how the same should be understood by another, is hard, if not impossible to know. For if a man pretend to me, that God hath spoken to him supernaturally, and immediately, and I make doubt of it, I cannot easily perceive what argument he can produce, to oblige me to beleeve it" (*L* 3.32, 196; *EW* 3: 361). He also dismissed the reliability of any prophetic tradition with the conclusion "though God Almighty can speak to a man, by Dreams, Visions, Voice, and Inspiration; yet he obliges no man to beleeve he that so done to him that pretends it; who (being a man) may erre, and (which is more) may lie" (*L* 3.32, 196; *EW* 3: 367).

Although Hobbes did not explicitly deny that there could be true prophets who reliably report revelations, he was evidently skeptical of any prophetic claims. The Earl of Clarendon, in his 1676 denunciation of Hobbes's "Dangerous and pernicious Errors," complained that "if those marks, and conditions which he makes necessary to a true Prophet, and without which he ought not to be beleeved, were necessary, *Moses* was no true Prophet, nor had the Children of *Israel* any reason to believe, and follow him" (Clarendon 1676, 196). Clarendon was right: Hobbes's doctrines cannot be consistently maintained by anyone who regards supernatural revelation as a source for the justification of theistic belief. Hobbes explicitly argued that dreams, visions, and inspiration cannot be reliable indicators of divine intentions, and he also held that it was difficult to make sense of the notion that God might literally speak to man. Thus, Hobbes's principles imply that there is never sufficient evidence to support another's claim to supernatural contact with God. Likewise, they demand that the extraordinary claims made by the Old Testament prophets, Moses, and Jesus should not be regarded as true today, nor should these claims have been so regarded when they were first propounded centuries ago.

If we attend to what Hobbes wrote about the "insignificant speech" of the Scholastics, it becomes clear that, on his account of meaning, the term "God" cannot signify anything. Hobbes held that the "generall use of Speech, is to transferre our Mentall Discourse, into Verbal; or the Trayne of our Thoughts, into a Trayne of Words" (*L* 1.4.12; *EW* 3: 20). Insignificant speech is one of the principal sources of absurdity, and one way for error and absurdity to arise is by the use of "names that signifie nothing; but are taken up and learned by rote from the Schooles, as *hypostatical*, *transubstantiate*, *consubstantiate*, *eternal-Now*, and the like canting of Schoole-men" (*L* 1.5.20–21; *EW* 3: 35). But the term 'God' is insignificant in very much the same way as these Scholastic terms: like them, it is used in the Schools and it is taken up and learned by rote to signify something we cannot understand. But in point of fact it cannot signify anything—for no mental discourse answers to the inconsistent expression 'infinite, incomprehensible, locationless thin fluid body'.

Indeed, when he insisted that we can have no idea of God, or that God is utterly unlike anything we can understand or reason about, Hobbes might not have been expressing pious opinions, but rather inviting the reader to conclude that the concept of God is another senseless notion to be purged from the true philosophy. Thus, I suspect that Hobbes intentionally left something out of the list of explanatorily useless concepts he put at the end of *De Corpore* when he complained that "those who say that anything is moved or produced by itself, by species, by power, by substantial form, by incorporeal substance, by instinct, by antiperistasis, by antipathy, by sympathy, by occult quality, and the other inane words of the scholastics, these are all said to no purpose" (*DCo* 4.30.15; *OL* 1: 431). I hold that, were it not for a well-founded fear of persecution, Hobbes would have added 'by God' to this catalog of words "said to no purpose."

HOBBES'S ARGUMENT FOR A DEITY CONSIDERED

One obvious objection to the foregoing line of reasoning is to point out that Hobbes explicitly argued for the existence of God. Since philosophers rarely try to establish the existence of things they do not believe in, this seems quite solid evidence for Hobbes's sincere commitment to theism. Moreover, the reasoning he offered certainly *looks* like an attempt to show that one can be justified in believing in God even if there can be no idea answering to God's nature. The sort of argument Hobbes seems to have favored is the familiar "cosmological" argument, which involves reasoning from the causal dependence of events in the universe back to a "first cause" of the universe itself.[16] Hobbes claimed that individuals infer the existence of such a cause because the investigation of causes "must come to this thought at last, that there is some cause, whereof there is no former cause, but is eternall; which is it men call God" (*L* 1.11.51; *EW* 3: 93). Furthermore, Hobbes appears to think that this conclusion can be justified even if we lack an idea of God:

> For as a man that is born blind, hearing men talk of warming themselves by the fire, may easily conceive, and assure himselfe, there is somewhat there, which men call Fire, and is the cause of the heat he feeles; but cannot imagine what it is like; nor have an Idea of it in his mind, such as they have that see it: so also, by the visible things of the world, and their admirable order, a man may conceive there is a cause of them, which men call God; and yet not have an Idea, or Image of him in his mind. (*L* 1.11.51; *EW* 3: 93)

A preliminary point to make is that Hobbes's claims can be read as a simple description of the process by which people come to postulate the existence of God,

---

16. K. C. Brown (1962) interprets Hobbes as having sct most store by a version of the design argument that reasons teleologically from the order and purposiveness of parts of nature to the existence of a divine designer. I agree with Ronald Hepburn (1972, 91) that "[w]hile Hobbes certainly alludes . . . to teleological argumentation, and presents such an argument in *outline*, his allusions are much too perfunctory and incidental to provide a philosophical foundation for theism." I will therefore concentrate on Hobbes's presentation of the cosmological argument. For lack of space, I also ignore other presentations of the argument to be found in Hobbes's *Elements of Law* and *De Homine*; considering these other presentations of the argument would not alter the essential line of argument pursued here.

without actually endorsing the validity of such reasoning. In other words, Hobbes's language in the relevant passages is loose enough that this alleged argument need not be taken as an argument at all. Although this is a reading that the texts in question bear, I will proceed on the assumption that these comments are most plausibly read, not merely as describing the causal genesis of the concept of God, but as justifying belief in such a God. A second point worth stressing is that even if Hobbes intended to offer an argument for the existence of God, he could take it as probable at best rather than demonstrative. In Hobbesian methodology, all true demonstrations must proceed "synthetically" from causes to the literal construction of the conclusion; however, in the case of God we must move "analytically" from effects to causes, and in Hobbes's estimation such arguments must be conjectural and will generally not confer certainty.[17] As we have already seen, there are insuperable difficulties involved in the idea that an infinite, incomprehensible, locationless body (i.e., God) can impart motion to the world, so any such argument is bound to be problematic.

Nonetheless, the very fact that Hobbes appears to have undertaken an argument for the existence of God is *prima facie* evidence against the interpretation I favor. How, it might be asked, can we reconcile these pronouncements of belief with the case for atheism that I claim to find in Hobbes's philosophy? At best, it would be urged, I could show only that Hobbes embraced principles leading to atheism, but not that he consciously embraced the atheistic consequences of his principles.[18] The result is that my atheistic reading of Hobbesian philosophy can be correct only if there are good grounds for thinking that Hobbes was not serious when he set out this argument for the existence of God. But I think there are plausible grounds to think that Hobbes was ironic rather than serious, not only in his argument for God's existence but in his treatment of essentially all theological issues.

The first salient fact about cosmological argument in *Leviathan* is that it is contradicted by what Hobbes claimed in other of his writings. In *De Corpore* (published some four years after *Leviathan*, but the object of Hobbes's efforts for at least a decade), Hobbes rehearsed the argument for God as a first cause but concluded that only "weariness" of seeking further causes leads to the postulation of a first cause.[19] More significantly, he claimed in *De Corpore* that there is no way to determine whether the universe has a beginning. Instead, Hobbes announced that those "lawfully responsible for regulating the worship of God" should settle

---

17. See Hanson (1990) for an account of Hobbes's theory of demonstration.

18. Hobbes characterized a person who did not see the atheistic implications of his principles as an "atheist by consequence" (*AB* 130–31; *EW* 4: 385). On my interpretation, however, Hobbes was fully aware of, and accepted, the atheistic consequences of his metaphysics.

19. Hobbes reasons: "Whatever we men know we take from our phantasms; but there is no phantasm of an infinite, whether of magnitude or time; nor can a man or any other thing have any conception of the infinite, beyond that it is infinite; nor if someone should ascend by right reasoning from any effect to its immediate cause, and thence to a further cause, and so on perpetually, yet he will not be able to proceed eternally, but wearied will at some point give up, not knowing whether he could have gone further. Nor will anything absurd follow, whether the world is agreed to be finite or infinite" (*DCo* 4.26.1; *OL* 1: 336).

the matter by declaring what their subjects are to believe (*DCo* 4.26.1; *OL* 1: 336). Since Hobbes claimed in *Leviathan* that "to say the World was not Created, but Eternall, . . . is to deny there is a God" (*L* 2.31.190; *EW* 3: 350), his declarations in *De Corpore* amount to skepticism of God's existence. A further difficulty for taking *Leviathan* seriously on this point is the fact that in his critique of Thomas White's *De Mundo* (probably written in 1642–1643), Hobbes insisted that "those who declare that they will show that God exists . . . act unphilosophically" (Hobbes 1976, 305).[20]

At the very least these facts show a serious diachronic inconsistency in Hobbes's attitude toward the cosmological argument—in the early 1640s he rejected the possibility of an argument he seems to have attempted in the early 1650s, but by 1655 he expressed skepticism about the whole project. Of course, one might hold that the argument in *Leviathan* is Hobbes's considered position on the issue, but such an interpretation requires justification, and it is far from clear what could justify it.[21] On the other hand, we could read the arguments in *Leviathan* and *De Corpore* as ironic parodies of the traditional grounds for theistic belief.[22] In fact, Hobbes's enemy Wallis read them in precisely this way when he insinuated that *Leviathan* had failed to win the approval of the reading public "Unless with such, as thought it *a piece of Wit* to pretend to *Atheism* . . . for one while they find him affirming, That, beside the Creation of the World, there is no Argument to prove a Deity; Another while, That it cannot be evinced by any Argument, that the World had a beginning; and, That, whether it had or no, is to be decided not by Argument, but by the Magistrates Authority" (Wallis 1662, 6).

Another important point to keep in mind is that Hobbes had ample reason to profess belief in a deity, whether or not such professions were sincere. Hobbes never lived under a sovereign who permitted the expression of atheistic opinions, and his own political theory stresses the subject's duty of conformity to the sovereign's dictates concerning pronouncements on religion, irrespective of any privately held beliefs. Consequently, Hobbes would never have openly professed

20. See Pacchi (1988) for a more detailed investigation into the theological and philosophical problems raised by Hobbes's critique of White.

21. Robert Arp has observed some of the difficulties involved here and remarks "there is an apparent contradiction that arises when placing the *Leviathan* and *De Corpore* passages together. We could throw our hands up and simply agree that such answers should be left to those entrusted with temporal/religious power." He declines this option and holds that "On Hobbes's own terms, we can argue that he, too, would acknowledge the possibility of an unmoved mover outside of time. If reason cannot discern this, maybe faith can" (1999, 378). This leads him to reconcile the contradiction between *Leviathan* and *De Corpore* by attributing to Hobbes the preposterous doctrine that God is a body outside of space and time who nevertheless exercises causal power in the world. Given Hobbes's metaphysical and epistemological commitments, a much more reasonable conclusion is that he was not serious in his employment of the cosmological argument.

22. Hepburn (1972, 95) admits that "Hobbes' natural religious arguments for God's existence are not well presented or well defended," but he holds "there is no strong case for seeing them as consistently ironic and obliquely sceptical—though the *De Corpore* passage does make it hard to see him as caring whether his reader retains belief in arguments from the world to God." I hope to show that Hepburn underestimates the case for reading Hobbes's argumentation as ironic.

atheism. The punishments for profession of atheism were typically severe in Hobbes's day, ranging from fines and imprisonment to mutilation or execution, depending on the severity of the offense and the laws in force at the time.[23] Hobbes himself faced the prospect of capital punishment for his alleged atheism in October of 1666, when a Parliamentary committee was "impowered to receive Informacion toucheing such bookes as tend to Atheisme Blasphemy or Prophanenesse or against the Essence or Attributes of God. And in perticular . . . the booke of Mr Hobbes called the Leviathan, and to report the Matter with their Opinion to the House."[24] According to John Aubrey, Hobbes felt sufficiently threatened by these events that he destroyed a large number of his papers (1898 1: 339). It would be foolish to conclude that Hobbes was an atheist simply from the fact that members of Parliament were prepared to have him punished for the crime of atheism; yet these events reinforce the idea that Hobbes had compelling reasons to avoid any open declaration of atheism, and they strongly suggest he had something to hide.

Because the public profession of atheistic opinion was forbidden, it is difficult to tell how many atheists there might have been in Hobbes's day and whether Hobbes numbered among them.[25] The matter is further complicated by the fact that 'atheist' was a general term of abuse in the seventeenth century and could be applied to anyone whose religious views were regarded as suspect, whether or not such views included the nonexistence of God.[26] There is, however, circumstantial evidence for atheistic tendencies in seventeenth-century intellectual circles. One tantalizing example comes from the deathbed confession and conversion of the Earl of Rochester in 1680.[27] In his sermon at Rochester's funeral, the Rev. Robert Parsons repeated a report of the late Earl: "*One day at an Atheistical Meeting, at a person of Qualitie's, I undertook to manage the Cause, and was the principal Disputant against God and Piety, and for my performances received the applause of the whole company*" (Parsons 1680, 23). Parsons also reports Rochester as claiming that "*that absurd and foolish Philosophy, which the world so much admired, propagated by the late Mr. Hobbs, and others, had undone him, and many more, of the best parts in the Nation*" (Parsons 1680, 26).

Secondhand reports of deathbed repentance and confession are admittedly not the strongest evidence, but the image of an "atheistic underground" devoted to the philosophy of Hobbes cannot be dismissed out of hand. Berman has argued that

23. See Berman (1988, 48–9) for a discussion of the various blasphemy acts in seventeenth-century England. A more complete treatment can be found in Nokes (1928).

24. British Library, MS. Harl. 7257 (Journal of the House of Commons), f.220^r. On the Parliamentary investigation of Hobbes, see Milton (1993).

25. Aylmer (1978) tries to gauge the extent of atheistic belief in seventeenth-century England. Although there are numerous published attacks on atheism during the century, the actual identification of atheists is difficult. As he notes, "From the 1580s onwards, there were numerous attacks on atheism and on alleged, but normally unnamed unbelievers. Indeed, until the time of Hobbes and Spinoza (the 1650s or 1660s) they are seldom if ever identified" (1978, 22).

26. Martinich (1992, 19–22) has drawn attention to this fact and cautioned against inferring the atheism of Hobbes from the mere fact that he was frequently called an atheist.

27. On Rochester's "apostate atheism," see Berman (1988, 52–6).

[t]here was, particularly in the Restoration period, an explosion of atheism, largely confined to the upper classes and based primarily on the thought of Hobbes. This upper-class Hobbesian atheism was not published or publicly avowed in any straightforward manner; hence it is difficult to identify. But it existed, and the failure to recognise it must distort any intellectual history of the seventeenth century in Britain. (Berman 1988, 48)

If indeed there were circles of "upper-class Hobbesian atheism," we must surely suspect Hobbes himself to be a member of such a circle. We can therefore take it as at least a plausible conjecture that Hobbes was a closet atheist.

Some anecdotes concerning Hobbes and the scholar-jurist John Selden are very suggestive in this context. Aubrey reports that Selden "kept a plentiful table, and was never without learned company" (Aubrey 1898; 2: 221), so it appears that his household must have been the scene of numerous discussions of meetings among educated men. In Aubrey's account of Selden's last days, "the minister (Mr. [Richard] Johnson) was comeing to him to [absolve] him: Mr. Hobbes happened then to be there; sayd he, 'What, will you that have wrote like a man, now dye like a woman?'" (Aubrey 1898; 2: 221). It is not clear what writings might have led Hobbes to judge that Selden had written "like a man," but one candidate is his *Historie of Tythes* (1618). In this work Selden concluded that the institution of tithes was not justified *jure divino* and he thereby "drew a great deale of envy upon him from the clergie" (Aubrey 1898, 2: 220). The book was suppressed and Selden was force to recant, but thereafter "he would never forgive the bishops, but did still in his writings levell them with the presbyterie" (Aubrey 1898, 2: 220). Another incident involving Hobbes and the final days of Selden is recorded in a letter from Wallis to Thomas Tenison (later Archbishop of Canterbury and an author of a 1670 anti-Hobbesian tract, *The Creed of Mr. Hobbes Examined*). Wallis's letter repeats a story from Selden's last illness, when "Mʳ Hobbs then coming to give Mʳ Selden a visit; Mʳ Selden would not admitt him; but answered No Hobbes, No Atheist. Of whom, I hear, Mʳ Hobbs censure was, that he (Mʳ Selden) had lived like a wise man, & dyed like a Fool" (Bodleian Library, Ms. Add. D.105, f.71r). These reports should obviously be treated with some caution and are perhaps garbled versions of the same (possibly apocryphal) story. They are nevertheless consistent with what we know about Hobbes and Selden, and we can read them in the light of the remark from Selden's *Table Talk* that nobody can tell "what impious atheisticall thoughts I may have about me when I am approaching to the very table" (Selden 1856, 146). We thus have circumstantial evidence that both men were part of an intellectual circle which saw the expression of anticlerical and perhaps atheistic opinion, although such opinions were never made public.

Of course, one need not suppose that seventeenth-century atheism was confined to Britain, and there is good reason to think that Hobbes must have encountered expressions of atheistic opinion during his extended stays on the continent, and particularly in Paris.[28] A pivotal development in Hobbes's intellectual career

---

28. On irreligion in France during the first half of the seventeenth century, see Pintard (1983), esp. part 1.

was his exposure to the mechanistic "new philosophy" during his tour of the continent in 1634–1636. Hobbes met Marin Mersenne during this period and was introduced to Parisian intellectual circles in which Mersenne played a prominent role. When he returned to Paris in 1640, Hobbes immediately became involved in the intellectual life of the city and remained an active participant in it until he returned to England in 1651. Mersenne was a devout believer who was convinced that Paris was practically overrun with atheists. In his 1623 *Quæstiones in Genesim*, he fulminated against atheists and claimed that 50,000 of them could be found in the city.[29] Although such an atheistic census is wildly implausible, it is obvious that atheism was not unknown in Mersenne's circles. There is consequently no great interpretive leap in thinking that Hobbes found the opportunity to discuss the grounds of religious belief with skeptics and atheists in Paris. Given the huge impact that Parisian intellectual life had on the shaping of Hobbes's philosophy, such contacts may very well have made him a convinced atheist.[30]

Turning from the intellectual climate in which Hobbes wrote to recent interpretations of his philosophy, we can find additional grounds for seeing his claims about God as insincere or evasive. This evidence lies in the astonishing lack of consensus about the content of Hobbes's religious beliefs among scholars who take him to have been a believer. Such lack of agreement shows that we are dealing with texts that are at least ambiguous and perhaps intentionally deceptive. Some examples drawn from the current state of scholarly opinion should make this point abundantly clear. On the basis of what he takes to be numerous points of agreement between Hobbesian and Socinian teachings, Peter Geach concludes that "Hobbes was a believing and professed Socinian" (Geach 1981, 556). In contrast, A. P. Martinich holds that "Hobbes was a sincere, and relatively orthodox Christian," who held "a strong intellectual commitment to the Calvinist Christianity of Jacobean England" (Martinich 1992, 1). Opposed to both of these readings is that of Robert Arp, who sees Hobbes as pursuing the project of natural theology in the tradition of St. Thomas Aquinas (Arp, 1999). S. A. Lloyd thinks that "Hobbes believed in the truth of the basic doctrines of the Judaeo-Christian tradition"

---

29. On Mersenne and atheism, see Lenoble (1943, 171–5). The figure of 50,000 was included in the original version of column 671 of *Quæstiones in Genesim*, which was part of a vituperative anti-atheistic colophon covering columns 669–74. This was later toned down, but Mersenne always maintained that avowed atheists could be found among the intellectuals of Paris.

30. One might object that Hobbes's friendship with Mersenne should count against the suspicion that he disbelieved in God. Nobody questions Mersenne's piety, and it might be thought improbable that Hobbes could have been on good terms with a man who had attacked atheism so vigorously. Mersenne, however, was a Catholic, and whatever his religious opinions may have been, Hobbes was no Catholic. In fact, if this objection had any force it should conclude that a friendship between a staunch Catholic and a true-believer Protestant is more difficult to conceive than one between a Catholic and an atheist—the atheist holds that the Catholic is deluded and his worship is a waste of time, but the Protestant regards him as a hell-bound minion of the Prince of Darkness himself. More likely, then, is the thought that Mersenne and Hobbes followed the usual polite practice of seventeenth-century intellectuals in the face of religious differences: they probably avoided detailed discussion of religion altogether. This assumption is still consistent with Hobbes having had the opportunity to discuss religious matters with other of his Parisian acquaintances.

(1992, 272), but assigns him no specific denominational commitments. On her interpretation he seems to have embraced some kind of vanilla-flavored Christianity, although she elsewhere describes his religious views as "extremely unorthodox and inflammatory" (1992, 17). Faced with such a multiplicity of interpretations, we can at least conclude that Hobbes did not go out of his way to make his religious beliefs unambiguous. It is therefore worth asking whether Hobbes's pronouncements in favor of theism should be taken at face value. I claim they are best read as ironic, and the time has come for me to make a more sustained case for the "ironist" reading of Hobbesian discussions of God.

HOBBES AS A RELIGIOUS IRONIST

There is nothing new in the suggestion that Hobbes's professions of belief in a deity can and should be read as exercises in irony. Leo Strauss held that "to hide the dangerous nature of [his] skepticism, to keep up an appearance that he attacked only scholastic theology and not the religion of the Scripture itself, Hobbes fought his battle against natural theology in the name of strict belief in the Scriptures and at the same time undermines that belief by his historical and philosophical criticism of the authority of the Scriptures" (Strauss 1952, 76). Similarly, Skinner has proposed that a proper understanding of Hobbes's theories must recognize that he "intended to deal both ironically and destructively with prevailing theological orthodoxies," and was constrained by circumstances to avoid a literal statement of his views (Skinner 1969, 34). I am convinced that such an approach to Hobbes is correct and will attempt to defend it against the view that Hobbes's pronouncements on the existence of God should be taken at face value.

The central question to be faced when propounding an ironist reading is an epistemological one: how can we tell whether the author intended his words to be taken ironically? In general, the trope of irony involves saying (or writing) one thing and intending another; as defined by Cicero, irony arises "when the whole drift of your oration shows that you are joking in a solemn way, speaking in a manner contrary to your thoughts" (1942, 1: 263). Spoken irony can be readily indicated by tone of voice, but detecting irony in a written work is a more delicate matter. One factor that eases the task in the present case is that seventeenth-century English writers were well-acquainted with a complex system of rhetorical tropes and figures derived from classical authors, so that in Hobbes's day "the deployment of these techniques had become a matter of second nature to the educated" (Skinner 1996, 211). There is no doubt that Hobbes himself understood these conventions, so there is reason to think that his ironic intentions can be detected in an attentive examination of his writings.

When a writer treats a subject ironically, there is an incongruity between his professed principle and his actual practice, as when a supposedly solemn issue is presented humorously or a trifling matter is described in terms appropriate to tragedy. Therefore, if Hobbes's treatment of God involves him consistently *claiming* to pursue one course but actually *following* another, and if the incongruity between his principle and practice has a humorous or derisive element, we should read his pronouncements in favor of the existence of God as ironic. Skinner has made the point that when writing "about the veracity of the Bible and the mysteries of the Christian faith. . . . Hobbes makes systematic use of the various devices specifically recommended by the theorists of eloquence for contriving a tone of irony and ridicule" (1996, 14). I propose to illustrate Hobbes's use of ironic modes of expression by two examples from *Leviathan*. The first is his account of the respective roles of faith and reason and the second is his investigation of the puzzle of the divine voice. These are admittedly only two of many theological subjects taken up in that work, but I think my reading can be generalized to cover essentially everything Hobbes has to say about the grounds for religious belief.

Hobbes's treatment of faith and reason opens with the declaration that "we are not to renounce our senses, and Experience; nor (that which is the undoubted Word of God) our naturall Reason," so that these rational faculties are "not to be folded up in the Napkin of an Implicite Faith." Yet in the case of theological mysteries above reason

> wee are bidden to captivate our understanding to the Words; and not to labour in sifting out a Philosophicall truth by Logick, of such mysteries as are not comprehensible, nor fall under any rule of naturall science. For it is with the mysteries of our Religion, as with wholsome pills for the sick, which swallowed whole, have the vertue to cure, but chewed, are for the most part cast up again without effect. (*L* 3.32.195; *EW* 3:360)

This is admittedly an expression of traditional doctrine, but the image of mysteries being "swallowed whole" can readily be construed as carrying the ironic implication that gullibility is a precondition of orthodoxy.[31]

More to the point, Hobbes himself approached problematic passages in the Scriptures with precisely the kind of critical "sifting out of Philosophicall truth by Logick" that he had claimed to be inappropriate. His detailed and closely reasoned investigations into prophecy, miracles, the nature of the holy spirit, the trinity, the incarnation, and other difficult points of theology are patently at variance with his recommendation that the faithful simply swallow such things without question. Clarendon, in observing the huge difference between Hobbes's declared exegetical principle and his theological practice, opined that

> it is a great pitty that [Hobbes] had not rather rested under that sober consideration [of swallowing mysteries whole], then embark'd himself, in the two next Chapters, in a Sea of new and extravagant interpretations of several

31. The *Oxford English Dictionary* reports usages of "swallow" as early as 1594 with the meaning "to accept mentally without question or suspicion; to believe unquestioningly," and carrying the negative connotation that to swallow something involves credulity. One interesting usage from 1643 has it that "So many, especially of the younger sort, do swallow down almost any error that is offered them."

texts of Scripture, without any other authority then of his own ungovern'd fancy, which can only amuse men with the novelty into impertinent enquiries, or dispose them to believe, that he hath not that reverence to the Scripture, or adoration of the Author of it, that would become him to have. (Clarendon 1676, 202)

This criticism amounts to the charge that Hobbes's approach is ironic and intended both to amuse readers and to lessen their reverence for the Scriptures. When we turn to some of *Leviathan*'s treatment of prophecy and revelation, and particularly the question of how God might communicate to His prophets, there is ample confirmation of Clarendon's judgement that Hobbes's "light and comical interpretations" expose the Word of God "to the mirth of those who are too much inclin'd to be merry with Scripture" (1676, 199).

In treating some of the difficulties that arise in interpreting prophetic claims, Hobbes asked how we are to understand scriptural accounts of God literally speaking to His prophets. He then offered an approach to the notion of a divine voice that is at once amusing, scatological, and pretty obviously ironic:

And hereupon a question may be asked, in what manner God speaketh to such a Prophet. Can it (may some say) be properly said, that God hath voice and language, when it cannot be properly said, he hath a tongue, or other organs as a man? The Prophet David argueth thus, *Shall he that made the eye, not see? or he that made the ear, not hear?* But this may be spoken, not (as usually) to signifie Gods nature, but to signifie our intention to honour him. For to *see* and *hear* are Honorable Attributes, and may be given to God, to declare (as far as our capacity can conceive) his Almighty power. But if it were to be taken in the strict, and proper sense, one might argue from his making of all other parts of mans body, that he had also the same use of them which we have; which would be many of them so uncomely, as it would be the greatest contumely in the world to ascribe them to him. (*L* 3.36.226; *EW* 3: 415)

Here again, the doctrine set out is strictly orthodox—a long tradition holds that terms cannot apply univocally to God and finite creatures—but Hobbes's way of expressing it is mocking and utterly lacking in the sort of reverence normally associated with the topic. Hobbes proclaimed his intention to honor God by eschewing rational inquiry in favor of "admiring, and adoring the Divine and Incomprehensible Nature; whose Attributes cannot signifie what he is, but ought to signifie our desire to honour him, with the best Appellations we can think on" (*L* 4.46.374; *EW* 3: 677). But his efforts resulted in a series of detailed readings of Scripture that provoke laughter. The hypothesis of ironic intent is the best (and perhaps the only) way to make sense of this incongruity, and I conclude there are strong grounds for seeing Hobbes's excursions into theology as exercises in irony.

A somewhat different case for Hobbes's ironic treatment of religion has been mounted by Curley, who argues from a comparison between Hobbes and

Spinoza.[32] Curley holds that Spinoza's approach to questions of theology and scriptural interpretation is consistently more bold than that set out by Hobbes. There is also the episode recorded by Aubrey, who reported that upon reading Spinoza's *Tractatus Theologico-Politicus*, Hobbes declared Spinoza "had outthrown him a bar's length, for he durst not write so boldly" (Aubrey 1898, 1: 357).[33] In light of this, Curley concludes that we should seek a reading of Hobbes that presumes he was constrained to express his opinions with less "boldness" than he might have preferred.

A crucial piece of his approach is Curley's claim that Hobbes's uses a rhetorical device he calls "suggestion by disavowal," wherein an author marshals evidence or argument that tends toward a particular conclusion but then disavows the seemingly obvious consequence. The purpose of suggestion by disavowal is clear enough: it provides a kind of cover in case one is later charged with expressing unsavory opinions, while at the same time it indicates the author's real intention. I find Curley's case compelling and think it greatly strengthens the general case for Hobbesian irony that I have been building. There are numerous instances where Hobbes's treatment of specific theological or scriptural issues leads ineluctably to skeptical or atheistic conclusions, but Hobbes refuses to endorse such conclusions and instead serves up bland declarations of orthodox opinion. I showed above, for instance, that Hobbes's materialism pretty easily yields the result that there can be no God, but Hobbes never announces this conclusion and instead claims to be a devout believer. This sort of thing makes perfect sense if we think of Hobbes as an ironic atheist, but it is difficult to reconcile with his being a sincere theist.

The principal objection to any sort of ironist interpretation of Hobbes's religious writings is that it is presumptuous to think that Hobbes would write so extensively on a subject without intending his words to be taken seriously. Martinich, for example, holds that Hobbes generally meant what he said and should be taken literally; he concludes that "the vast amount of what Hobbes wrote about religion is on the face of it favorable to religion or presupposes it. Given this general appearance of approval, a few allegedly dubious passages cannot be used to drive an interpretation" (Martinich 1992, 351). Peter Geach takes a similar approach and concludes that even Descartes's theological writings are more amenable to an ironist reading than Hobbes's because "Descartes might impress some people as a shifty character, whereas this is a ludicrously inept epithet for Hobbes" (1981, 556). I accept that the hypothesis of disingenuity is an interpretive last resort, and I have already gone into reasons why it is appropriate in this instance to read Hobbes as dissembling when he takes up the topic of religion. Nevertheless, it is important to try to come to some resolution of the question of Hobbes's sincerity.

32. See Curley (1992) for the extensive treatment of Hobbes and Spinoza. Curley (1998) makes the case for irony from a somewhat different comparison, involving Machiavelli in addition to Spinoza.

33. The version of Aubrey's *Brief Lives* edited by Andrew Clarke renders this passage "he had cut through me a bar's length," but this reading has been corrected by more recent scholarship. See Curley (1992, 497, n. 2).

The best way to resolve the question of how to take Hobbes's religious writings is to pay attention to the interpretations offered by his contemporary readers. They were aware of the rhetorical conventions in play, and there is every reason to believe that they would more readily detect irony, if it is indeed there to be detected. In point of fact, Hobbes's seventeenth-century critics were all but unanimous in their complaint that he used irony in his writings on religious issues (Skinner 1996, 394–5). We have seen the example of Clarendon, who objected to Hobbes's ironic tone, complained of his "naughty and impious discourse" concerning religion, and concluded that he "handles [Scripture] as imperiously as he doth a Text of *Aristotle*, putting such unnatural interpretations on the words, as hath not before fallen into the thoughts of any other man, and drawing very unnatural inferences from them; insomuch as no man can think he is really earnest" (1676, 72–3). Clarendon was hardly alone, as we can see from the judgement rendered by Wallis, who challenged the sincerity of Hobbes's professions of belief:

> You take it to be ridiculous, and what could never be conceived by any imagination, that anything should ever exist that is not a body; and you also hold . . . that all "incorporeal substances" are to be dismissed as the "inane words of the scholastics." Who does not see that thereby you not only deny (and not just in words) angels and immortal souls, but the great and good God himself; and if you were not wary of the laws . . . you would profess this openly. And however much you may mention God and the sacred scriptures now and again . . . it is nevertheless to be doubted whether you do this ironically and for the sake of appearance rather than seriously and from conviction. (Wallis 1655, 90)

Examples could be multiplied, but the point should be clear enough: Hobbes's readership took his treatment of religion as ironic, and this is *prima facie* evidence that we should, too. In consequence, I conclude that Hobbes was in all likelihood an atheist.

Geach's judgement that Hobbes was too forthright to engage in deception is demonstrably false, as can be easily seen in the dealings between Hobbes and Henry Stubbe. Stubbe was a fellow of Christ Church and a friend of Hobbes who undertook a Latin translation of *Leviathan* (a task that remained unfinished). He was also reputed to be a closet atheist, which is a fact that makes him especially interesting in this context.[34] Hobbes enlisted Stubbe's philological skills in the course of his long-running battle with Wallis in order to rebut charges of inelegant Latin usage. In his 1657 *Stigmai*, Hobbes printed a letter from Stubbe on the philological points in dispute, pretending that an unnamed friend "shewed me a letter written to himself from a learned man," whom Hobbes claimed to be an anonymous scholar "who had better ornaments then to be willing to go clad abroad in the habit of a Grammarian" (Hobbes 1657, 16; *EW* 7: 393). This pretense was a

---

34. Aylmer reports the judgement of Andrew Marvell, who wrote of "[Stubbe] physician atheist found dead I mean drowned . . . suppost drunk. *es magne Deus*" (Aylmer 1978, 45).

sham because the letter was in fact solicited by Hobbes from Stubbe.[35] The evidence therefore shows that Hobbes was not above subterfuge and dissimulation, and we have no reason to think he would not resort to such devices to camouflage any atheistic opinions he may have held.

A related objection raised against my sort of ironist reading is that removing God from Hobbes's philosophy makes nonsense of his political theory. Following the lead of Taylor, who claimed that "a certain kind of theism is absolutely necessary to make [Hobbes's] theory work"([1938] 1965, 50), many interpreters claim that Hobbes's theory of obligation requires an all-powerful deity (as well as some sort of afterlife).[36] Such interpretations hold that, absent a deity, there is no supernatural enforcer to compel humans to obey such laws of nature as "seek peace" or "keep covenants." If violation of such laws could go unpunished, people in the state of nature would not have adequate incentive to observe them, and the Hobbesian political project founders. I do not dispute that Hobbes's politics can consistently be read as requiring a deity to ground obligations. After all, Hobbes had good reason for presenting his theories in a theological dress, and the mention of God is prominent in his formulation of his political principles. By the same token, however, "secularist" interpreters of Hobbes's philosophy have shown that the basic line of argument can be construed in a way that makes the role of God inessential.[37] This is not the place to resolve the question of how we should read Hobbes's political philosophy, but I think that the strength of the case for Hobbes's atheism gives some additional weight in favor of the secularist interpretation. At the very least, we need not conclude that anything in Hobbes's political philosophy makes it unreasonable to interpret his system as not requiring a God.

Lloyd has advanced somewhat different grounds for thinking that Hobbes's political theory requires his sincere commitment to theism. She objects to a thoroughly secular interpretation of *Leviathan* because i makes the second half of that work an utterly mysterious digression into religion. She finds it highly implausible that "the half of the book concerned with religion is intended to, as it were, cover Hobbes's atheistic tracks" (1992, 17) and concludes that Hobbes should be taken at his word in his professions of belief. I am very sympathetic to the idea that parts three and four of *Leviathan* should be taken seriously, but there is a difference between taking them seriously and taking them literally.

---

35. This is evident from Stubbe's letter to Hobbes of 26 November/6 December 1656, where Stubbe writes of an enclosure, "I here send yo^u a long letter; I doubt not but you can forgiue such faults . . . as are occasioned by excesse of zeale to serue yo^u . . . I leaue ye busynesse wholly to yor management" (Hobbes 1994, 1: 378).

36. Principal examples of this sort of interpretation are Hood (1964), Martinich (1992), and Warrender (1957).

37. Gauthier (1969) is the most influential of the "secularist" interpretations, which can be supplemented by Gauthier (1977). Gauthier does not question the sincerity of Hobbes's pronouncements of belief, but he thinks that the fundamental argument can be made to work without assuming the existence of God. Curley (1998, section 10) is a succinct summary of a secularist approach to Hobbesian moral theory.

The sort of objection Lloyd has in mind seems to confuse God with religion, apparently on the principle that an author who writes extensively about scriptural interpretation or church history must accept the Scriptures or church doctrines as true. But this is a highly suspect way of reading *Leviathan*. Although the truth of religion requires the existence of God, the existence of religion obviously does not. Hobbes held that religion was a natural consequence of human curiosity and anxiety about the future, which together lead people to postulate invisible forces behind events (*L* 1.12.52–4; *EW* 3: 94–100). These "seeds" of religion are part of the human condition, and there is little prospect that humans will simply give up religion or outgrow the habit of invoking "invisible Agents" to account for events. Nevertheless, just as the philosopher must disregard commonly held opinions about the nature of the cosmos, he or she need not think that the entities postulated by religion actually exist. Hobbes held that one of the main goals of the true philosophy is to overcome our ignorance of the world's workings—a process that involves discarding many of the entities invoked by earlier generations to explain the phenomena of nature. Consequently, there is nothing in Hobbes's methodology to guarantee that ancient stories about God and His messengers on Earth will withstand philosophical scrutiny.

Furthermore, religion can be made to work either for social stability or disruption—a fact that was all too obvious in Hobbes's day. As a result, Hobbes had every reason to present his political philosophy in a way that reconciles religious belief to the institution of a supreme civil sovereign. Lloyd rightly stresses the fact that one of Hobbes's central projects in *Leviathan* is to redescribe religious obligation in such a way that a subject's religious beliefs, properly understood, can never authorize disobedience to the civil sovereign. The whole point of Hobbes's extensive forays into scriptural exegesis and his lengthy rebuttal to Bellarmine's theory of papal supremacy is to show his reader that there is nothing in the content of Christian belief that should undermine a subject's loyalty to the sovereign. Indeed, Hobbes was convinced that in a properly ordered commonwealth the impulse toward religious belief could function as a powerful source of social stability.[38] But all of this can be true without supposing that Hobbes personally embraced the Christianity whose disruptive potential he was trying to minimize, and I think the evidence indicates that he did not embrace it.

CONCLUSIONS: THE ROLE OF GOD IN HOBBES'S PHILOSOPHY

Having made the case for reading Hobbes as an atheist, I would like to close by remarking on some of the consequences this reading has for his philosophy as a whole. In particular, since I deny that Hobbes believed in God, I want to indicate briefly how this fact should influence our interpretation of his metaphysics, natural philosophy, and political theory. This is obviously a topic too large to be discussed in detail, but three significant points emerge.

---

38. Sutherland (1974, 379–80), although not endorsing an atheistic reading of Hobbes, nevertheless sums up this point with the remark that "[f]or all his irony and attack on religion, Hobbes did see some positive values deriving from religious belief."

First, Hobbes is quite systematic in excluding any mention of God from his epistemology and metaphysics, especially when he presents it in its canonical formulation in *De Corpore*. Hobbes conceived of philosophy as an enterprise that begins with quite general definitions and proceeds *more geometrico* through demonstrative syllogisms to establish irrefutable truths. The definitions that lie at the heart of Hobbes's first philosophy are stipulative truths about the meanings of words ratified by human agreement: they do not explicate the essences of things and need not be underwritten by some sort of divine warrant. Likewise, the syllogisms in which Hobbesian philosophy is to be cast require no supernatural guarantee. Hobbes regarded the basic concepts at the heart of his first philosophy as transparently unproblematic, and the fundamental truths about them as necessary and binding on everything. The contrast with Descartes is illuminating. Where Descartes' metaphysical program requires a nondeceiving God to guarantee the veracity of its central concepts and the reliability of the most basic inferences, Hobbes makes a point of excluding theological considerations from philosophy altogether.

Second, at the level of natural philosophy a Hobbesian God would literally have nothing to do: He is not needed in the justification of the basic laws of physics, and the phenomena of the natural world are all to be explained purely in terms of the motion and impact of material bodies. Hobbes's principles ultimately demand that if God existed, He would have to be a material body subject to the same metaphysically necessary laws of motion governing every other body, which is to say that God cannot move Himself or act except by motion and contact. So much for the traditional notion of divine omnipotence. Again, the contrast with Descartes is instructive. Descartes held that the basic laws of motion and impact must be derived from the immutability of the divine nature, and Hobbes's refusal to engage in such reasoning underlines the extent to which his philosophical system requires no supernatural foundation.

Finally, in the area of political theory, I propose that we read Hobbes's account of the state of nature and the institution of sovereignty in a manner analogous to his natural philosophy. Just as the laws of motion require no reference to God in their formulation, derivation, or application, so we should see Hobbes's "laws of nature" in the state of nature not as divine commands, but as counsels of prudence telling rational agents how best to serve their long-term interests. The strategy of keeping one's covenants is one that is most likely to serve your interests, not because some supernatural lawmaker will punish you if you disobey, but because your fellow humans will make your life miserable and short if you should cross them. In short, the "mortal God" which is Hobbes's humanly instituted sovereign is the only God we need postulate in order to interpret *Leviathan*.

In the end, Hobbes's mechanistic materialism comports poorly with his declarations of pious orthodoxy, and any interpreter is faced with trying to make sense out of the Hobbesian philosophical *corpus*. One could abandon the hope of finding a consistent body of doctrine in Hobbes, but this would make him a much less interesting figure. I read Hobbes as having an unshakable intellectual commitment to a theory of the world in which matter and motion account for all the phenomena of nature and there is quite literally no place for God. As a result, I find his proclamations of theistic belief insincere and highly ironic. On the other hand, an interpreter who takes Hobbes to have been a committed theist will ultimately have to regard his materialism as a concession to intellectual fashion or a half-serious and ill-considered embrace of a doctrine he did not really understand. In either case, something has to go, and I think it makes more sense to read Hobbes as a sly, ironic, and interesting atheist rather than a confused, bizarre, and ultimately incoherent Christian.

REFERENCES

Aquinas, Saint Thomas. 1964. *Summa theologica: Latin text and English translation, introduction, notes, and appendices.* 60 vols. Cambridge: Blackfriars; New York: Macmillan.

Arp, Robert. 1999. The *Quinque Viae* of Thomas Hobbes. *History of Philosophy Quarterly* 16:367–94.

Aubrey, John. 1898. *"Brief Lives," chiefly of Contemporaries, set down by John Aubrey, between the Years 1669 & 1696.* 2 vols. Ed. Andrew Clark. Oxford: Oxford University Press.

Aylmer, G. E. 1978. "Unbelief in Seventeenth-Century England." In *Puritans and Revolutionaries: Essays in Seventeenth-Century History presented to Christopher Hill,* ed. Donald Pennington and Keith Thomas, 22–46. Oxford: Oxford University Press.

Berman, David. 1988. *A History of Atheism in Britain: From Hobbes to Russell.* London: Croom Helm.

Bramhall, John. 1676. *Works.* 3 vols. Dublin.

Brown, K. C. 1962. "Hobbes's Grounds for Belief in a Deity." *Philosophy* 37:336–44.

Cicero. 1942. *De Oratore.* Ed. and trans. E. W. Sutton and H. Rackham. 2 vols. Loeb Classical Library. Cambridge, MA: Harvard University Press.

Clarendon, Edward, Earl of. 1676. *A Brief View and Survey of the Dangerous and pernicious Errors to Church and State, in Mr. Hobbes's Book, Entitled "Leviathan."* Oxford.

Curley, Edwin M. 1992. "'I Durst Not Write So Boldly' or, How to Read Hobbes's Theological-Political Treatise." In *Hobbes e Spinoza, Atti del Convegno Internazionale, Urbino 14–17 ottobre, 1988,* ed. Daniela Bostrengi, 497–593. Naples: Bibliopolis.

Curley, Edwin M. 1998. "Religion and Morality in Hobbes." In *Rational Commitment and Social Justice: Essays for Gregory Kavka,* ed. Jules L. Coleman and Christopher W. Morris, 90–111. Cambridge and New York: Cambridge University Press.

Gauthier, David. 1969. *The Logic of "Leviathan."* Oxford: Oxford University Press.

Gauthier, David. 1977. "Why Should One Obey God?" *Canadian Journal of Philosophy* 7: 212–33.

Geach, Peter. 1981. "The Religion of Thomas Hobbes." *Religious Studies* 17: 549–58.

Hanson, Donald W. 1990. "The Meaning of 'Demonstration' in Hobbes's Science." *History of Political Thought* 9: 587–626.

Hepburn, Ronald. 1972. "Hobbes on the Knowledge of God." In *Hobbes and Rousseau: A Collection of Critical Essays,* ed. Maurice Cranston and Richard Peters, 85–108. New York: Anchor.

Hobbes, Thomas. 1651. *Leviathan, Or The Matter, Forme, & Power of a Common-Wealth Ecclesiasticall and Civill.* London.

Hobbes, Thomas. 1655. *Elementorum Philosophiæ Section Prima De Corpore.* London.

Hobbes, Thomas. 1656. *Six Lessons to the Professors of the Mathematiques, one of Geometry, the other of Astronomy: In the Chaires set up by the Noble and Learned Sir Henrey Savile, in the University of Oxford.* London.

Hobbes, Thomas. 1657. *Stigmai . . . ; or, Markes of the Absurd Geometry. Rural Language. Scottish Church-Politicks. And Barbarismes of John Wallis Professor of Geometry and Doctor of Divinity.* London.

Hobbes, Thomas. 1662. *Mr Hobbes Considered in his Loyalty, Religion, Reputation, and Manners. By way of Letter to Dr. Wallis.* London.

Hobbes, Thomas. 1682. *An Answer to a Book Published by Dr. Bramhall, late Bishop of Derry; called "The Catching of the Leviathan."* London.

Hobbes, Thomas. [1839–45] 1966a. *Thomæ Hobbes Malmesburiensis Opera Philosophica Quæ Latine Scripsit Omnia in Unum Corpus Nunc Primum Collecta.* Edited by William Molesworth. 5 vols. Reprint. Aalen, Germany: Scientia Verlag.

Hobbes, Thomas. [1839–45] 1966b. *The English Works of Thomas Hobbes of Malmesbury, now First Collected and Edited by Sir William Molesworth.* Edited by William Molesworth. 11 vols. Reprint. Aalen, Germany: Scientia Verlag.

Hobbes, Thomas. 1976. *Thomas White's "De Mundo" Examined.* Ed. and trans. Harold Whitmore Jones. London: Bradford University Press.

Hobbes, Thomas. 1994. *The Correspondence.* Edited by Noel Malcom. 2 vols. *The Clarendon Edition of the Works of Thomas Hobbes,* vols. 6–7. Oxford: Oxford University Press.

Hood, F. C. 1964. *The Divine Politics of Thomas Hobbes: An Interpretation of "Leviathan."* Oxford: Oxford University Press.

Jesseph, Douglas M. 1996. "Hobbes's Philosophy of Natural Science." In *The Cambridge Companion to Hobbes,* ed. Tom Sorell, 86–107. Cambridge and New York: Cambridge University Press.

Leijenhorst, Cornelis H. 1998. *Hobbes and the Aristotelians: The Aristotelian Setting of Thomas Hobbes's Natural Philosophy.* Quæstiones Infinitæ vol. 25. Utrecht: Zeno Institute for Philosophy.

Lenoble, Robert. 1943. *Mersenne, ou La Naissance du Mécanisme.* Paris: Vrin.

Lloyd, S. A. 1992. *Ideals as Interests in Hobbes's "Leviathan": The Power of Mind over Matter.* Cambridge and New York: Cambridge University Press.

Lupoli, Agostino. 1999. "Fluidismo e Corporeal Deity nella filosofia naturale di Thomas Hobbes." *Rivista di storia della filosofia* 54:573–609.

Martinich, A. P. 1992. *The Two Gods of "Leviathan": Thomas Hobbes on Religion and Politics.* Cambridge and New York: Cambridge University Press.

Mersenne, Marin. 1623. *Quæstiones celeberrimæ in Genesim.* Paris.

Milton, Philip. 1993. "Hobbes, Heresy and Lord Arlington." *History of Political Thought* 14:501–46.

Mintz, Samuel I. 1962. *The Hunting of Leviathan: Seventeenth-Century Reactions to the Materialism and Moral Philosophy of Thomas Hobbes.* Cambridge and New York: Cambridge University Press.

Nokes, Gerald D. 1928. *A History of the Crime of Blasphemy.* London: Sweek & Maxwell.

Pacchi, Arrigo. 1988. "Hobbes and the Problem of God." In *Perspectives on Thomas Hobbes,* ed. G. A. J. Rogers and Alan Ryan, 171–188. Oxford and New York: Oxford University Press.

Pintard, René. 1983. *Le Libertinage Érudit dans la première moitié du XVIIe siècle,* 2nd ed. Paris and Geneva: Slatkine.

Polin, Raymond. 1981. *Hobbes, Dieu et les hommes.* Paris: Presses Universitaires de France.

Ross, Alexander. 1653. *Leviathan Drawn out with a Hook: or Animadversions upon Mr. Hobbs His Leviathan.* London.

Selden, John. 1618. *The Historie of Tythes.* London.

Selden, John. 1856. *The Table-Talk of John Selden.* Ed. S. W. Singer. 2nd ed. London: John Russell Smith.

Skinner, Quentin. 1966. "The Ideological Context of Hobbes's Political Theory." *Historical Journal* 9:286–317.

Skinner, Quentin. 1969. "Meaning and Understanding in the History of Ideas." *History and Theory* 8:3–53.

Skinner, Quentin. 1996. *Reason and Rhetoric in the Philosophy of Thomas Hobbes.* Cambridge and New York: Cambridge University Press.

Strauss, Leo. 1952. *The Political Philosophy of Thomas Hobbes: Its Basis and Genesis.* Trans. Elsa M. Sinclair. Chicago: University of Chicago Press.

Sutherland, Stewart R. 1974. "God and Religion in *Leviathan.*" *Journal of Theological Studies.* New Series. 25:373–80.

Taylor, A. E. [1938] 1965. "The Ethical Doctrine of Hobbes." In *Hobbes Studies,* ed. Keith Brown, 35–56. Oxford and New York: Oxford University Press.

Wallis, John. 1655. *Elenchus Geometriæ Hobbianæ, sive, Geometricorum, quæ in "Elementis Philosophiæ," à Thoma Hobbes Malmesburiensi proferuntur, Refutatio.* Oxford.

Wallis, John. 1662. *Hobbius Heauton-timorumenos; or a Consideration of Mr. Hobbes his Dialogues in an Epistolary Discourse Addressed to the Honourable Robert Boyle, Esq.* Oxford.

Ward, Seth. 1656. *In Thomæ Hobbi Philosophiam Exercitatio Epistolica.* Oxford.

Warrender, Howard. 1957. *The Political Philosophy of Hobbes: His Theory of Obligation.* Oxford and New York: Oxford University Press.

Zarka, Yves-Charles. 1996. "First Philosophy and the Foundation of Knowledge." In *The Cambridge Companion to Hobbes*, ed. Tom Sorell, 62–85. Cambridge and New York: Cambridge University Press.

Midwest Studies in Philosophy, XXVI (2002)

New Wine in Old Bottles: Gassendi and the Aristotelian Origin of Physics

MARGARET J. OSLER[1]

The demise of Aristotelianism is the main theme of many accounts of the Scientific Revolution.[2] Accordingly, the rise of modern science is said to have coincided with and depended upon the rejection of Aristotelian physics. Examination of physics texts from the early modern period, however, calls for a more complicated understanding of the relationship between Aristotelian physics and early modern natural philosophy. In this paper I argue that although much of the *content* of early modern physics resulted from profound intellectual changes that involved the replacement of Aristotelian concepts with those associated with Galileo's new science of motion and the mechanization of nature, the *framework* in which natural philosophers wrote about physics continued to follow the Aristotelian model. This continuity of form was reflected in the definition of physics, certain methodological tenets, and the order in which topics were treated.

Pierre Gassendi's (1592–1655) book on physics is a telling example of this phenomenon. Gassendi, a French Catholic priest, is best known for his recovery of the philosophy of Epicurus, which he modified in an attempt to make it acceptable to Christian thinkers.[3] An outspoken critic of Aristotelian philosophy,

1. Conversations with Sachiko Kusukawa helped me formulate the theme of this paper. I am grateful to Margaret G. Cook and Edward Grant for careful readings and thoughtful comments on an earlier version of this paper.

2. For example, E. A. Burtt, *The Metaphysical Foundations of Modern Science* (Garden City, NY: Doubleday, 1954; first published 1924); Alexandre Koyré, *Metaphysics and Measurement: Essays in the Scientific Revolution* (London: Chapman and Hall, 1968); Richard S. Westfall, *The Construction of Modern Science: Mechanisms and Mechanics* (New York: John Wiley, 1971); and Steven Shapin, *The Scientific Revolution* (Chicago: University of Chicago Press, 1996).

3. See Margaret J. Osler, *Divine Will and the Mechanical Philosophy: Gassendi and Descartes on Contingency and Necessity in the Created World* (Cambridge: Cambridge University Press, 1994), Chaps. 2–4.

Gassendi pursued his Epicurean project throughout his life.[4] He wrote about the new astronomy;[5] he advocated Galileo's new science of motion;[6] and he developed one of the most influential versions of the mechanical philosophy.[7] Despite his vehement criticism of Aristotelianism in his first published work, *Exercitationes paradoxicae adversus Aristoteleos* (1624), in which he used skeptical arguments to criticize the content, method, and utility of Aristotelianism for natural philosophy and for philosophy more generally, Gassendi's own natural philosophy continued to reflect Aristotle's approach to physics.

Gassendi gave his most systematic and sustained treatment of natural philosophy in "The Physics," the second and by far the longest of the three main sections of his compendious *Syntagma philosophicum* (1658), the posthumously published culmination of his Epicurean project. The other two sections, "The Logic" and "The Ethics," complete his philosophy, forming a Christianized version of Epicureanism that he explicitly designed to serve as a replacement for Aristotelianism. An analysis of the structure of "The Physics" discloses its close similarities to Aristotle's *libri naturales*, the books that formed the intellectual and textual basis of natural philosophy through the Middle Ages and Renaissance.[8]

In this paper I first summarize the salient features of Aristotle's natural philosophy as presented in *The Physics*, *On the Heavens*, *On Generation and Corruption*, and *On the Soul*, as well as his books on animals. Following a brief account of Scholastic textbooks on natural philosophy, I show how the format of Gassendi's "Physics" reflects this Aristotelian tradition, despite the fact that the content of his natural philosophy in many respects differs profoundly from that of Aristotle and the Aristotelians.

4. His first published book is vehemently anti-Aristotelian. See Pierre Gassendi, *Exercitationes paradoxicae adversus Aristoteleos* (Grenoble, 1624). On the development of his Epicurean project, see Bernard Rochot, *Les travaux de Gassendi sur Épicure et sur l'atomisme, 1619–1658* (Paris: J. Vrin, 1944).

5. Pierre Gassendi, *Instituto astronomica iuxta hypotheseis tam veterum quam Copernici et Tchonis Brahei* (Paris, 1647).

6. Pierre Gassendi, *De motu impresso a motore translato epistolae duae, in quibus aliquot praecipue, tum de motu universe, tum speciatim de motu terrae attributa, difficultates explicantur* (Paris, 1642).

7. Pierre Gassendi, *Syntagma philosophicum*, in *Opera omnia*, 6 vols. (Lyon, 1658; a facsimile reprint, F. Fromann, Stuttgart-Bad Cannstatt, 1964), vols. 1 and 2. On Gassendi's influence, see Robert H. Kargon, *Atomism in England from Hariot to Newton* (Oxford: Oxford University Press, 1966) and Richard S. Westfall, *Never at Rest: A Biography of Isaac Newton* (Cambridge: Cambridge University Press, 1980), p. 303. See also Margaret J. Osler, "The Intellectual Sources of Robert Boyle's Philosophy of Nature: Gassendi's Voluntarism and Boyle's Physico-Theological Project," in *Philosophy, Science, and Religion in England, 1640–1700*, edited by Richard Kroll, Richard Ashcraft, and Perez Zagorin (Cambridge: Cambridge University Press, 1992), pp. 178–198.

8. William A. Wallace, "Traditional Natural Philosophy," in *The Cambridge History of Renaissance Philosophy*, edited by Charles B. Schmitt, Quentin Skinner, and Eckhard Kessler (Cambridge: Cambridge University Press, 1988), pp. 201–235. See also Charles B. Schmitt, *Aristotle and the Renaissance* (Cambridge, Mass.: Harvard University Press, 1983).

THE ORDER OF TOPICS IN ARISTOTLE'S *LIBRI NATURALES*

Aristotle distinguished physics from mathematics and theology on the basis of its subject matter, substance that is perishable and sensible:

> There are three kinds of substance—one that is sensible (of which one sub-division is eternal and another is perishable, and which all recognize, as comprising e.g. plants and animals), of this we must grasp the elements, whether one or many; and another that is immovable, and this certain thinkers assert to be capable of existing apart, some dividing it into two, others combining the Forms and the objects of mathematics into one class, and others believing only in the mathematical part of this class. The former two kinds of substance are the subject of natural science (for they imply movement); but the third kind belongs to another science, if there is no principle common to it and to the other kinds.[9]

Aristotle opened *The Physics* with a general discussion of the topics to be considered. "When the objects of an inquiry, in any department, have principles, causes, or elements, it is through acquaintance with these that knowledge and understanding is attained."[10] In the case of physics, he sought the principles, causes, and elements, the study of substances that are sensible and movable. His treatment of these topics comprised the subject matter of *libri naturales*—the treatises on physics, the heavens, generation and corruption, the soul, and animals. In the opening passage of *The Meteorology*, he stated his reasons for the order in which he treated these topics.

> We have already discussed the first causes of nature, and all natural motion, also the stars ordered in the motion of the heavens, and the corporeal elements—enumerating and specifying them and showing how they change into one another—and becoming and perishing in general. There remains for consideration a part of this inquiry which all our predecessors called meteorology. It is concerned with events that are natural, though their order is less perfect than that of the first of the elements of bodies. They take place in the region nearest to the motion of the stars . . . When the inquiry into these matters is concluded let us consider what account we can give, in accordance with the method we have followed, of animals and plants, both generally and in detail. When that has been done we may say that the whole of our original undertaking will have been carried out.[11]

9. Aristotle, *Metaphysics*, translated by W. D. Ross, in *The Complete Works of Aristotle*, edited by Jonathan Barnes, 2 vols. (Princeton: Princeton University Press, 1984), 1069a30–1069b2, vol. 2, p. 1689.

10. Aristotle, *Physics*, translated by R. P. Hardie and R. K Gaye, in *The Complete Works of Aristotle*, 184a10–12, vol. 1, p. 315.

11. Aristotle, *Meteorology*, translated by E. W. Webster, in *The Complete Works of Aristotle*, 338a20–339a9, vol. 1, p. 555. Although "we owe both the arrangement of the treatises and the text

This order of decreasing perfection became the framework for subsequent texts on natural philosophy through the Middle Ages, Renaissance, and the seventeenth century.

Aristotle began with a consideration of the most general questions. In the eight books of *The Physics*, he spelled out the basic terms in which he couched his entire philosophy of nature. After summarizing the views of earlier philosophers, he stated,

> We will now give our own account, approaching the question first with reference to becoming in its widest sense; for we shall be following the natural order of inquiry if we speak first of common characteristics, and then investigate the characteristics of special cases.[12]

He began in Book I by establishing that the basic principles according to which he would explain things in the world, namely matter, form, and privation. Following this enumeration of the principles that constituted the world, he turned to the nature of causality. In Book II, he described the four-fold nature of causality, the concepts of potentiality and actuality, and the causal characteristics of chance, spontaneity, and necessity. Having answered the general questions of what the world consists of and how the constituent entities interact, he proceeded, in the remaining books, to discuss the nature of motion, place, void, infinity, and time. Thus, by the end of *The Physics*, Aristotle had outlined the ultimate terms of explanation for his philosophy of nature.

In further books on natural subjects, which read as a direct continuation of *The Physics*, Aristotle incorporated the entire range of natural phenomena into his conceptual framework.[13] In *On the Heavens*, he dealt with cosmology, using his concepts of matter, motion, and cause to describe the celestial region and to contrast it with the terrestrial. In *On Generation and Corruption*, he addressed questions about matter and change and presented his theory of the four elements. In *The Meteorology*, Aristotle set out to explain various phenomena that he believed occur in the Earth's atmosphere, including shooting stars, comets, the Milky Way, various kinds of precipitation, and weather, as well as the saltiness of the sea, earthquakes, thunder and lightning, rainbows, and a host of other things. Included among these natural books is *On the Soul*, which opens with the following statement:

> The knowledge of the soul admittedly contributes greatly to the advance of truth in general, and, above all, to our understanding of Nature, for the soul is in some sense the principle of animal life. Our aim is to grasp and understand, first its essential nature, and secondly its properties; of these some are

itself to the first editor of Aristotle, Andronicus of Rhodes [1st century B.C.]," there are many clues embedded in the texts as to what order Aristotle intended for many of his writings. See G. E. R. Lloyd, *Aristotle: The Growth and Structure of His Thought* (Cambridge: Cambridge University Press, 1968), pp. 13–18.

   12. Aristotle, *Physics*, in *The Complete Works of Aristotle*, 189b30–34, vol. 1, p. 324.

   13. I borrow the term "conceptual framework" from R. Harré, *Matter and Method* (London: Macmillan, 1964).

thought to be affections proper to the soul itself, while others are considered to attach to the animal owing to the presence of soul.[14]

In addition to his account of the soul, there are several books on animals, based on his empirical researches, including *The History of Animals*, *The Parts of Animals*, *The Movement of Animals*, and *The Generation of Animals*.

Taken collectively, Aristotle's *libri naturales* bring the entire natural world under the rubric of his philosophy of nature. He applied the terms of matter, form, privation, and the four causes to explain all natural phenomena. The books begin with the consideration of general principles in *The Physics* and proceed to explain particular phenomena, proceeding from the cosmic to the terrestrial, from the inanimate to the animate. Aristotle frequently referred to the ideas of his predecessors, usually with the aim of demonstrating the superiority of his own ideas and valuing his forebears to the extent that they anticipated his own theories and explanations. It is these general features of Aristotle's works that continued to characterize subsequent works on natural philosophy.

NATURAL PHILOSOPHY TEXTS IN THE MIDDLE AGES AND RENAISSANCE

Natural philosophy developed in the medieval universities in the wake of the translation of Aristotle's works from Arabic to Latin during the late eleventh century and through the twelfth. Aristotelian natural philosophy provided the world view of the Latin Middle Ages, and his "natural books were the best available guides for the study of the universe, which is why they served as the fundamental texts for natural philosophy in the universities of the Middle Ages."[15] Aristotle's *libri naturales* were incorporated into the curriculum of the Arts Faculty at the University of Paris by the middle of the thirteenth century.[16] These books thus defined the subject of natural philosophy, or physics, for medieval academic culture. A decree issued to the Faculty of Arts at the University of Paris in 1254 stated that

all and single masters of our faculty . . . shall be required to finish the texts which they have begun on the feast of St. Remy at the times below noted, and not before. . . . The *Physics* of Aristotle, *Metaphysics*, and *De animalibus* on the feast of St. John the Baptist; *De caelo et mundo*, first book of *Meteorology*, with the fourth, on Ascension Day; *De anima*, if read with the books of nature, on the feast of the Ascension . . . ; *De causis* in seven weeks; *De sensu et sensato* in six weeks; *De sompno* [sic] *et vigilia* in five weeks; *De*

14. Aristotle, *On the Soul*, translated by E. S. Forster, in *The Complete Works of Aristotle*, 402a5–9, vol. 1, p. 641.

15. Edward Grant, *The Foundations of Modern Science in the Middle Ages: Their Religious, Institutional, and Intellectual Contexts* (Cambridge: Cambridge University Press, 1996), p. 127. See also Roger French and Andrew Cunningham, *Before Science: The Invention of the Friars' Natural Philosophy* (Aldershot: Scolar, 1996).

16. Gordon Leff, *Paris and Oxford Universities in the Thirteenth and Fourteenth Centuries: An Institutional and Intellectual History* (New York: John Wiley, 1968), p. 140.

plantis in five weeks; *De memoria et reminiscentia* in two weeks; *De differentia spiritus et animae* in two weeks; *De morte et vita* in one week.[17]

Although this list does not exactly coincide with what we think of as Aristotle's natural books and although some of them—such as *De causis* and *De differentia spiritus et animae*—are now known to be wrongly attributed to Aristotle, the list comprises what medieval thinkers considered to be his *libri naturales*.[18]

During the Middle Ages, texts on natural philosophy were written in three different genres. In commentaries on the *Sentences* of Peter Lombard, scholars addressed questions about the creation, the structure of the heavens, and light. Another genre was the commentary on specific books of Aristotle. In these commentaries, Scholastic writers followed Aristotle's order and discussed questions about particular points in his books. In addition to commentaries on the *Questions* and on Aristotelian books, scholars wrote treatises (called *tractatus* or *compendia*) in which they presented Aristotle's opinions in a systematic way.[19] Although these genres persisted among scholastic writers, non-Scholastic writers in the early modern period abandoned the commentary form but continued to write treatises.[20]

The study of natural philosophy continued to be centered upon Aristotle's *libri naturales* for the next four centuries. Although Renaissance humanists produced new editions of Aristotelian texts more faithful to the originals than those that had been available during the Middle Ages, the use of these improved texts did not alter the Aristotelian structure of the study of natural philosophy.[21] Despite reorganization of the curriculum in both the universities and the Jesuit colleges, the inclusion of post-Renaissance scholarly apparatus, and considerable disagreement on a host of substantive issues, natural philosophy textbooks continued to follow the structure and order of Aristotle's *libri naturales*.[22] For example, Eustachius a Sancto Paulo (1573–1640), whose textbook on natural philosophy Descartes particularly esteemed as a typical Scholastic textbook,[23] wrote accord-

17. Edward Grant, editor, *A Sourcebook in Medieval Science* (Cambridge, Mass.: Harvard University Press, 1974), pp. 43–44. For bibliographical details about the works cited, see Grant's annotations.

18. Ibid. In the early thirteenth century, the *Liber de causis*, really a treatise by the Greek Neoplatonic philosopher Proclus (411–485), was mistakenly thought to be the third book of Aristotle's *Metaphysics*. See Leff, *Paris and Oxford Universities*, pp. 182 and 194–195.

19. Grant, *Foundations*, pp. 131–133.

20. Edward Grant, private communication.

21. Wallace, "Traditional Natural Philosophy," pp. 202–203. See also Sister Patricia Reif, "The Textbook Tradition in Natural Philosophy, 1600–1650," *Journal of the History of Ideas*, 1969, 30: 17–32.

22. Roger Ariew, "Aristotelianism in the Seventeenth Century," in *The Routledge Encyclopedia of Philosophy*, edited by Edward Craig, 10 vols. (London and New York: Routledge, 1998), vol. 1, p. 387. For a detailed account of the concepts and subject matter of these books, see Dennis Des Chene, *Physiologia: Natural Philosophy in Late Aristotelian and Cartesian Thought* (Ithaca: Cornell University Press, 1996) and Dennis Des Chene, *Life's Form: Late Aristotelian Concepts of the Soul* (Ithaca: Cornell University Press, 2000).

23. Roger Ariew, *Descartes and the Last Scholastics* (Ithaca: Cornell University Press, 1999), pp. 26–27.

ing to the order of topics that he believed Aristotle to have followed. This order consisted of three parts:

(1) natural bodies in general, from the principles of natural things to their causes and common properties, from matter and form, to causes, to place, infinity, void, time and motion; (2) inanimate natural bodies, from the world to the heavens and from elements to heterogeneous bodies; (3) animate natural bodies, from soul in general to vegetative, sensible and rational soul.[24]

This order, reflecting Aristotle's, continued to characterize natural philosophy textbooks, even when their content began to depart from his metaphysical, physical, and cosmological theories.

Two textbooks from the first half of the seventeenth century illustrate this point. The first, a textbook in the Scholastic tradition written in French, is Scipion Dupleix's (1569–1661(?)) *La Physique* (Paris, 1603). This work was part of a larger *Corps de Philosophie* that also included *La Logique*, *La Métaphysique*, and *L'Ethique*. This text, which contains a healthy dose of Christian theology that is obviously absent from its Aristotelian prototype and differs in many details from Aristotle's views, nevertheless contains the Aristotelian framework of topics, albeit in a slightly modified order. After asserting God's creation of the world and the views of earlier philosophers about the principles of natural things, Dupleix discusses the "three principles of natural things, Matter, Form, and Privation."[25] He proceeded to a discussion of the four causes and of Aristotle's opinions about chance and fortune, reinterpreting them in terms of divine providence.[26] There follows a lengthy discussion of motion, which leads Dupleix into a discussion of generation and corruption, growth and decay,[27] and then of space, void, infinity, and time.[28] He then turned to cosmology, the nature of the heavens, then the elements and qualities, the composition of mixed bodies, meteorological phenomena (in the Aristotelian sense), and finally the soul, the senses, and the understanding.[29] In other words, this seventeenth-century scholastic textbook in physics follows the framework laid out in Aristotle's *libri naturales*.

The second example is Johannes Magirus' *Physiologiae Peripateticae* (1642), the textbook from which Newton learned Aristotelian physics at Cambridge.[30] Not surprisingly, Magirus' Aristotelian textbook, written in the genre of the commentary, follows the order of the *Libri naturales*. (See Appendix A.) Written as a commentary on the Aristotelian texts, the *Physiologiae Peripateticae* opens with a consideration of the principles of natural things, the causes, and then turns to motion, rest, the finite and infinite, light, void, and time. Magirus discussed the

24. Ariew, "Aristotelianism in the Seventeenth Century," p. 388.
25. Scipion Dupleix, *La Physique*, revised edition (Rouen, 1640; reprinted Paris: Fayard, 1990), pp. 13–14. This reference and the ones that follow refer to the detailed table of contents in the book.
26. Ibid., pp. 16–18.
27. Ibid., pp. 23–25.
28. Ibid., pp. 25–30.
29. Ibid., pp. 31–61.
30. Westfall, *Never at Rest*, p. 84.

nature of the world in general, its causes and accidents, before turning to the heavens. His treatment of cosmology is followed by an account of the elements, then meteorological phenomena, then inanimate bodies (such as metals and stones), then plants and animals. In the final section of the book, he considered the soul, perception, the intellect, and the will.[31] Although Magirus referred to a variety of medieval and Renaissance writers in his commentaries and even discussed (and rejected) the possibility of the Earth's motion,[32] his overarching conception of the nature of physics and the proper order for treating its topics remained true to the model of Aristotle's *libri naturales*.

THE STRUCTURE OF GASSENDI'S "PHYSICS"

Gassendi's "Physics" is the second part of his tripartite *Syntagma Philosophicum* (1658). Although "The Physics" is clearly a product of new, non-Aristotelian developments in natural philosophy, it is a treatise that follows the traditional Aristotelian model.

Gassendi opened "The Physics" with a definition of the subject that is entirely compatible with Aristotle's:

Physics can be defined as natural science, contemplatrix of things [*Scientia natura rerum contemplatrix*], because through it we now explore the complex of all things by inquiring into anything especially the thing itself, how much there is, and how it is made from first principles and from what principles it is made; by what causes it is produced and to which end it is made; and with which forces and properties it is endowed and what actions and effects it has, and other things of this kind, which, if they are fully known, then the nature of the thing or things is understood.[33]

Like Aristotle, Gassendi believed that it was the task of physics to explore the first principles and causes of things. And like Aristotle, he considered the aim of "Physics"—a synonym for "natural philosophy"—to be a study of the principles and causes of things: Physics is a name for a kind of philosophy "qualified in Latin by '*Naturalis*', that is to say, Natural Philosophy. 'Nature' is used to designate both the generative principle and the thing that is born and thus embraces everything which gives or receives birth, and further, everything which is understood by the entirety of things."[34]

Like Aristotle, Gassendi considered the subject matter of physics to be things that are generable and perishable. "The entirety of things" [*Universitas*] consists

---

31. Johannes Magirus, *Physiologiae Peripateticae libri sex cum commentariis Additis insuper notis quibisdam marginalibus, in posteribus editionibus ommissis: una cum Definitionibus, Divisionibus, Axiomatis, Graece, ex Aristotele petitis* (Cambridge, 1642), "Index capitum," np.

32. Ibid., p. 110.

33. Gassendi, *Syntagma Philosophicum*, in *Opera Omnia*, vol. 1, p. 125. For a French translation of the "Prooemium" to "Physics," see Sylvia Murr, "Pierre Gassendi—Préliminaires à la Physique Syntagma Philosophicum," *XVIIe siècle* (1993) 45: 353–485.

34. Gassendi, *Syntagma Philosophicum*, in *Opera Omnia*, vol. 1, p. 125.

of the entire creation, including the human soul[35] and the ubiquitous evidences of divine design and providence. He considered the study of incorporeal things, like the soul, to be part of physics because they are part of the causal nexus and because they have natures that can be explored by the methods of physics.[36] His inclusion of the study of the soul in physics follows Aristotle who considered the soul to be part of the natural world. Gassendi's physics included a significant theological dimension not present in Aristotle. Gassendi also added a typically Epicurean aim to physics: the achievement of tranquillity of the soul and freedom from troubles and fears.[37] By including the study of the soul in physics, Gassendi followed Aristotle who considered the soul to be part of the natural world.

In determining the proper order in which the topics are to be presented, Gassendi followed the Aristotelian model, although he no longer shared Aristotle's belief in a cosmological hierarchy of perfection. "Physics can be divided into three general sections; of which one is about the things of nature universally; another about celestial things; and finally about things on the earth."[38] It is necessary to understand the general principles that govern all natural phenomena before considering specific phenomena. To spell out these general principles of physics, it is necessary to consider "space, time, the material principles, active causes; motion, changes, qualities, birth, death; and if there are other things of this kind."[39] Gassendi followed this order in the 1286 dense, double-columned pages that comprise *The Syntagma Philosophicum*. (See Appendix B.) He began with an account "Of the Universe and World which it embraces, or the nature of things." He followed this general discussion of the size and shape of the world, whether it is endowed with a soul, and whether it had a beginning and whether it will have an end, with a discussion of space (including an extensive discussion of the void) and time. He then turned to the material and efficient principles of things, that is, the ultimate terms of explanation for his philosophy of nature. Having established matter—in the form of atoms—as the material principle and motion as the efficient principle in his world, Gassendi concluded Part I of "The Physics" with an account of the qualities of things and of generation and corruption. Thus, Part I provided the conceptual tools for explaining the specific phenomena Gassendi considered in Part II.

Gassendi stated that, following the discussion of general principles, physics should begin with a consideration of the heavens. "It ought to comprehend what can be disputed about the heaven and the substance of the stars, the variety, intervals, distances, and like aspects of these stars; also the various motions of the moon, of eclipses, and of predictions from these."[40] Finally, physics should investigate this world and what it "contains, what can be traced, or what can [be known] about

---

35. Although Gassendi regarded the rational soul, or *animus*, to be immortal and thus not perishable, he considered the *anima*, which has the functions of Aristotle's vegetative and sensitive souls, to be material and mortal. See Osler, *Divine Will*, pp. 59–77.

36. Gassendi, *Syntagma Philosophicum*, in *Opera Omnia*, vol. 1, p. 126.

37. Ibid., p. 128.

38. Ibid., p. 130.

39. Ibid.

40. Ibid.

meteors, inanimate things, plants, animals, of man, and especially the soul."[41] In other words, Gassendi believed that physics should treat the same topics and in the same order that Aristotle had in the *libri naturales*. The remaining sections of "The Physics" reflect this order perfectly: "On Celestial Things," "On Inanimate Terrestrial Things," and "On Living Terrestrial Things, or Animals." The final chapter of "Physics" concerns the immortality of the soul.

THE CONTENT OF GASSENDI'S "PHYSICS"

Within each section, Gassendi considered many of the same topics addressed by Aristotle in the *libri naturales* and then attempted to explain them in terms of his own, non-Aristotelian fundamental principles. It is in the principles and detailed explanations that he differed from Aristotle. Although the shape of the enterprise was entirely within the Aristotelian mold, its contents were markedly different. Where Aristotle asserted that the basic explanatory principles were matter, form, and privation, Gassendi invoked indivisible atoms as the fundamental constituents of the physical world. Where Aristotle believed that a complete explanation must include all four causes, Gassendi thought that efficient causes sufficed.[42] Where Aristotle denied the existence of the void,[43] Gassendi proclaimed it.[44] Like Aristotle, Gassendi opened the discussion of each topic with a lengthy account of the views of his predecessors.[45]

A brief summary of "The Physics" will illustrate these points. Dealing first with the fundamental explanatory principles of his natural philosophy, Gassendi, like Aristotle, considered the nature of space and time, matter, and cause. Within this framework, which follows the Aristotelian *Physics*, Gassendi argued for the existence of the void, in direct contrast to Aristotle who denied it.[46] He used both classical arguments, drawn from Lucretius and others, as well as experimental results from seventeenth-century natural philosophy to defend the existence of the void. He distinguished between three kinds of void: extracosmic, interstitial, and *coacervatum* or void produced by human art. He regarded the extracosmic void as the boundless, incorporeal extended space in which God created the universe. To defend the existence of interstitial void between the atoms, Gassendi appealed to the ancient argument that the existence of void is a necessary condition for motion; for without empty spaces, there would be no place into which particles of

41. Ibid.

42. Gassendi did argue for a role for final causes in physics, but he claimed that final causes are really efficient causes introduced by God into the world. See Margaret J. Osler, "Whose Ends? Teleology in Early Modern Natural Philosophy," *Osiris*, 2001, 16: 151–168.

43. Aristotle, *Physics*, Book IV (213a12–217b27), in *Works of Aristotle*, vol. 1, pp. 362–369.

44. Gassendi, *Syntagma Philosophicum*, in *Opera Omnia*, vol. 1, pp. 185–228.

45. On Gassendi's use of the history of philosophy, see Lynn Sumida Joy, *Gassendi the Atomist* (Cambridge: Cambridge University Press, 1987). See also Margaret J. Osler, "Renaissance Humanism, Lingering Aristotelianism, and The New Natural Philosophy: Gassendi on Final Causes," in *Humanism and Early Modern Philosophy*, edited by Jill Kraye and M. W. F. Stone (London: Routledge, 2000), pp. 193–208.

46. See Edward Grant, *Much Ado about Nothing: Theories of Space and Vacuum from the Middle Ages to the Scientific Revolution* (Cambridge: Cambridge University Press, 1981).

matter could move.[47] Other classical arguments were based on the facts that substances differ in density, that water has the capacity to become saturated with salt, that dyes disperse through water, and that light, heat, and cold, all of which he assumed to be particulate, penetrate air. Empty spaces between the particles composing material bodies seemed necessary to explain these phenomena.[48] Hero of Alexandria (fl. 62 A.D.) was a source of arguments for the void as well. Hero had argued that just as individual grains of sand are separated from each other by air or water, so the material particles composing bodies are separated by small void spaces that could explain why air is compressible.[49] Gassendi supplemented these classical arguments by appealing to experimental evidence from contemporary natural philosophy—especially the barometric experiments of Evangelista Torricelli (1608–1647) and Blaise Pascal (1623–1662). Gassendi explained the suspension of mercury in the barometer as a consequence of atmospheric pressure and thus rejected the Aristotelian explanation that appealed to the paradigmatic occult quality, nature's abhorrence of the vacuum. He also argued that the space in the tube above the mercury is actually devoid of matter.[50] Seeking the fundamental principles of explanation, as Aristotle had recommended, Gassendi inquired about the material principle of things. Another aspect of the Aristotelian framework for early modern natural philosophy was the tendency for natural philosophers to redefine Aristotelian concepts in mechanical terms. In formulating his theory of matter, Gassendi used Aristotelian terms and concepts, although he often gave them new meanings consistent with his modified Epicureanism. For example, he entitled a chapter "The Material Principle, or the First Matter of Things," but he stated that the material principle must be understood as indivisible atoms, endowed with magnitude, figure, and weight, a far cry from Aristotle's notion of prime matter as pure potentiality.[51]

The material principle in Gassendi's world consists of atoms moving in empty space. All atoms are made from the same kind of matter, which are full, solid, and hard.[52] They are indivisible and too small to be perceived directly. Gassendi borrowed arguments directly from Lucretius to establish the existence of these atoms. Just as wind, which is invisible matter, can produce visible physical effects, so invisible atoms can produce invisible effects, such as the gradual wearing away of paving stones and ploughshares, even though single acts of rubbing produce no perceptible changes. Consequently there must exist particles of matter so small that they fall below the threshold of sense. The fact that odors pass through the air can be explained in terms of tiny particles travelling from the source of the odor to the nose. Gassendi appealed to observations using the recently invented microscope, as well as traditional observations, such as the dispersion of pigment in water and the large quantity of smoke emitted by smoul-

47. Gassendi, *Syntagma Philosophicum*, in *Opera Omnia*, vol. 1, pp. 182–183.
48. Ibid., p. 196.
49. Ibid., p. 192.
50. Ibid., pp. 197–216.
51. Ibid., pp. 229–282.
52. Ibid., pp. 229–256.

dering logs, to confirm the existence of tiny particles.[53] He believed that Zeno's paradoxes prove that the idea of the infinite divisibility of matter is absurd, thus providing powerful support for the claim that the smallest particles of matter must be indivisible.[54]

After determining that atoms moving in void space are the material principle, Gassendi investigated the efficient principle or the nature of causality in the world. The first cause is God, who created the world, including the atoms and the laws that govern their motions and imparted his design to the creation.[55] In contrast to both Aristotle and Epicurus, each of whom had argued for the eternity of the world, Gassendi claimed that the world had a beginning when God created it and its constituent atoms—a large, but finite number of them—and that he continues to rule the world providentially. Gassendi maintained that in the beginning God created the motions of atoms. He appealed to an extended argument from design to demonstrate God's providential relationship to the creation. Second causes, the natural causes operating in the physical world, are the collisions among atoms moving in void space. In this way, he interpreted finality in terms of efficient causes. One aspect of his argument from design was his insistence that there is a role for final causes in natural philosophy. Although he agreed with Aristotle on the importance of final causes in physics, he reinterpreted them to be an expression of God's intentions impressed on the creation rather than a finality immanent in nature.[56]

Still conforming to the Aristotelian framework, Gassendi went on to demonstrate how all of the qualities of bodies can be explained in terms of the motions and configurations of their constituent atoms. He enumerated the qualities of bodies—including rarity and density, transparency and opacity, size and shape, smoothness and roughness, heaviness and lightness, fluidity and firmness, moistness and dryness, softness and hardness, flexibility and ductility, flavor and odor, sound, light, and color—and showed how they could all be explained in terms of the configurations, motions, and collisions of atoms.[57] Because there can be no action at a distance in the world, even apparently occult qualities, such as magnetism, the sympathies and antipathies favored by the Renaissance naturalists, and the Paracelsian weapon salve, can be explained in mechanical terms.[58] Although Gassendi's intention was to substitute atomistic explanations for Aristotelian explanations in terms of matter, form, and privation, he often drew on other traditions of early modern natural philosophy when explaining particular phenomena.[59]

53. Ibid., p. 259. See Lucretius, *De rerum natura*, with an English translation by W. H. D. Rouse. Revised with new text, introduction, notes and index by Martin Ferguson Smith, second edition (Cambridge, Mass. and London: Harvard University Press and William Heinemann, 1982), I, 265–328.

54. Gassendi, *Syntagma philosophicum*, in *Opera omnia*, vol. 1., pp. 258 and 263–266. Joy discusses the issue of infinite divisibility at some length. See Joy, *Gassendi the Atomist*, chap. 7.

55. Gassendi, *Syntagma philosophicum*, in *Opera omnia*, vol. 1, pp. 283–337.

56. See Osler, "Whose Ends?"

57. Gassendi, *Syntagma philosophicum*, in *Opera omnia*, vol. 1, pp. 372–457.

58. Ibid. pp. 449–457.

59. See Margaret J. Osler, "How Mechanical Was the Mechanical Philosophy: Non-Epicurean Aspects of Gassendi's Philosophy of Nature," in *Late Medieval and Early Modern Corpuscular*

In the second section of "The Physics," which deals with celestial things, Gassendi considered a number of astronomical and cosmological topics: the substance of the sky and stars; the variety, position, and magnitude of the stars; the motions of the stars; the light of the stars; comets and new stars; and the effects of the stars. Although Gassendi had endorsed the new Copernican astronomy enthusiastically in his youth, the condemnation of Galileo in 1633 dampened his enthusiasm, at least in print. In *The Syntagma Philosophicum*, he expressed skeptical doubts about being able to prove any of the three main world systems—Ptolemaic, Copernican, and Tychonic—conclusively, and he proposed the system of Tycho Brahe as a compromise approved by the Church, but not before having stated that the Copernican theory was "more probable and evident."[60] Such probabilism characterized his approach to all natural philosophy and did not represent a retreat in the face of ecclesiastical oppression.[61]

In a final chapter, Gassendi adamantly opposed astrology as "inane and futile,"[62] denying the possibility that the stars cause terrestrial and human events. The configurations of the heavens may be signs of some events on earth, such as the seasons or the weather, but they do not cause terrestrial events. Only God can know the future. Gassendi considered birth horoscopes ridiculous. Why, he asked, should the heavenly bodies have more influence at the moment of birth than at any other moment in a person's life? He rejected the principles of astrology as being based on insufficient evidence, and he thought that astrologers often resorted to deceit.[63]

Turning to terrestrial phenomena, Gassendi followed the Aristotelian format by starting with inanimate things and then considering animate things. He described the physical geography of the Earth, the distribution of water and land, the tides, subterranean heat, and the saltiness of the sea.[64] He then turned to "meteorological" phenomena, including winds, rain, snow, ice, lightning and thunder, rainbows and parhelia, and the Aurora Borealis.[65] He wrote about stones and metals, particularly noting recent observations of the magnet—particularly those of Nicholas Cabeo (1585–1650) and Athanasius Kircher (1602–1680), and to the transmutation of metals, giving the process an atomistic explanation.[66] Finally, he included plants among inanimate things, following Epicurus who had believed that they lack souls.[67] He described the varieties of plants and their parts and discussed a wide range of topics, including grafting, nutrition, germination, growth, and death.[68]

Matter Theories, edited by Christoph Lüthy, John E. Murdoch, and William R. Newman (Leiden: Brill, 2001), pp. 423–439.

60. Gassendi, *Syntagma philosophicum*, in *Opera omnia*, vol. 1, p. 617.

61. Barry Brundell, *Pierre Gassendi: From Aristotelianism to a New Natural Philosophy* (Dordrecht: Reidel, 1987), Chap. 2.

62. Gassendi, *Syntagma philosophicum*, in *Opera omnia*, vol. 2, p. 854.

63. Ibid., vol. 1, pp. 712–752.

64. Ibid., vol. 2, pp. 1–62.

65. Ibid., pp. 63–111.

66. Ibid., pp. 112–143.

67. Ibid., pp. 144–145.

68. Ibid., pp. 144–192.

In the final section of "The Physics," Gassendi turned to terrestrial living things, or animals. Once again following the Aristotelian agenda, he considered the varieties of animals,[69] the parts of animals, which he described in explicitly finalistic terms,[70] and various physiological topics including generation, nutrition, respiration, motion, and the uses of the parts of animals.[71] His emphasis on final causes, which drew heavily on Aristotle and Galen, was cast as part of his concern with divine providence and the argument from design. Gassendi devoted about half of this lengthy section on animals to the topics of sensation, perception, and the immortality of the human soul.[72]

CONCLUSION

The Aristotelian format of Gassendi's "Physics" was not idiosyncratic. Other early modern texts on natural philosophy similarly reflect the Aristotelian origin of the discipline. Numerous textbooks retained the traditional Aristotelian format, at the same time that their content began to reflect new developments in natural philosophy. Many of the major natural philosophy texts share this characteristic. Kenelm Digby's (1603–1665) *Two Treatises* (1644) deals with the same general set of topics, although their order is somewhat altered.[73] René Descartes (1596–1650) explicitly designed his *Principia philosophiae* (1644) to replace the late Scholastic textbooks used in the Jesuit colleges and thus dealt with the usual sequence of topics, albeit using very different categories of explanation.[74] Robert Boyle's (1627–1691) *Origin of Forms and Qualities* (1666) is a deliberate attempt to provide mechanical and corpuscularian interpretations of the fundamental Aristotelian terms "form," "quality," and "substance."[75]

That the Aristotelian corpus continued to serve as the model for physics should not be surprising. Aristotle defined the discipline. When later thinkers wrote about physics they simply assumed that their subject was the one that he had defined and that medieval scholars had institutionalized. This discipline included the topics and phenomena dealt with in the *libri naturales* but not necessarily the same theories and explanations.

The fact that the structure of natural philosophy remained Aristotelian, even while its content was undergoing major modification, calls into question the traditional interpretation of the Scientific Revolution as a complete break from Aristotle.

69. Ibid., pp. 193–214.

70. Ibid., pp. 215–326.

71. Ibid., pp. 260–327.

72. Ibid., pp. 328–658. See Osler, *Divine Will*, pp. 59–77.

73. Kenelm Digby, *Two Treatises in One of which The Nature of Bodies; in the other The Nature of Mans Soule; is looked into: in Way of Discovering, of the Immortality of Reasonable Soules* (Paris: Gilles Blaizot, 1644; facsimile reprint, New York: Garland, 1978).

74. See Stephen Gaukroger, *Descartes: An Intellectual Biography* (Oxford: Oxford University Press, 1995), pp. 364–383. See also Roger Ariew, *Descartes and the Last Scholastics* and Daniel Garber, *Descartes' Metaphysical Physics* (Chicago: University of Chicago Press, 1992).

75. Robert Boyle, *The Origin of Forms and Qualities*, in *The Works of Robert Boyle*, edited by Michael Hunter and Edward B. Davis, 14 vols. (London: Pickering and Chatto, 1999 and 2000), vol. 5, pp. 281–443.

APPENDIX A

Johannes Magirus, *Physiologiae Peripateicae Libri Sex*
Table of Contents

Liber I. De natura rerum naturalium principiis, affectionibus, & accidentibus.

1. Quid Physiologia? Quid item natura?
2. De prima rerum naturalium principiis intrinsecis.
3. De principiis rerum naturalium extrinsecis, causis scilicet efficiente & fine, fortuna item & casu.
4. De Motu.
5. De Motus speciebus.
6. De Quiete.
7. De finito & infinito.
8. De Loco.
9. De vacuo sive inani.
10. De tempore.

Liber II. De Mundo deque ejus Regione aethera.

1. De mundo in genere, ejusque causis & accidentibus.
2. Quid coelum & quae ejus divisio.
3. De Motu sphaerarum coelestium, recto & transverso.
4. De stellarum natura in genere.
5. De stellis fixis.
6. De planetis.
7. De Eclipsis Solis & Lunae.

Liber III. De Elementis eorumque Qualitatibus, Mistione, & Temperamentis.

1. De Elementorum natura in genere.
2. De Igne.
3. De Aere.
4. De Aqua.
5. De Terra.
6. De primis elementorum qualitatibus.
7. De secundis qualitatibus.
8. De occultis qualitatibus.
9. De agentibus & patientibus, deque contactis.
10. De mixtione.
11. De temperamentis.
12. De simplica generatione, eique opposita putrefactione.

Liber IIII. De Corporibus imperfecte mixtis, vel de Meteorilogica.

1. De Meteororum causis in genere.
2. De Meteoris ignitis puris.
3. De Meteoris ignitis mixtis, & primum de Cometis.

   4. De reliquis igniteis Meteoris mixtis, fulmine, tonitru & fulgure.
   5. De Meteoris apparentibus, quae [Greek] ab Aristotele nuncupantur.
   6. De Meteoris aqueis.
   7. De Meteoris aqueis in terra genitis, & primo fontibus & fluminibus.
   8. De Mari.
   9. De Ventis.
  10. De Terrae-motu.

Liber V. De Corporibus perfecte mixtus, tum inanimis, tum animatis.

   1. De Metallis.
   2. De Lapidibus.
   3. De succis vel terris pretiosis.
   4. De stirpium natura in genere, deq; earum corruptionibus.
   5. De quibusdam stirpium affectionibus.
   6. De Plantarum partibus & summis generibus.
   7. De Partibus corporis animati contentis, & primum de Humoribus.
   8. De Spiritibus.
   9. De partibus similaribus corporis animati.
  10. De partibus dissimilaribus, atque externis.
  11. De partibus organicis internis ventris infimi.
  12. De partibus ventris medii, inservientibus facultati vitali.
  13. De partibus facultatis animalis.
  14. De animalis speciebus, nimirum de bestiis tum perfectioribus, tum imperfectis, insectis scilicet.
  15. De homine, ejusque in utero formatione.
  16. De zoophytia.

Liber VI. De Anima

   1. De erroneis Philosophorum opinionibus, quas de Anima habuerunt.
   2. De animae definitione.
   3. De anima vegetante.
   4. De vita & morte.
   5. De hominis aetate, ejusque incremento ac decremento.
   6. De anima sentiente in genere.
   7. De Visu.
   8. De Auditu.
   9. De Odoratu.
  10. De Gustu.
  11. De Tactu.
  12. De sensibus interioribus.
  13. De sensuum affectionibus, nimurum somno & vigilis.
  14. De somnis.
  15. De divisionibus somniorum, eorumque, significationibus.
  16. De potentia appetitive, deque affectibus.
  17. De locomotiva facultate.

18. De Animae rationalis essentia.
19. De intellectu.
20. De voluntate.

APPENDIX B

Pierre Gassendi, *Syntagma Philosophicum*
Table of Contents of "The Physica"

Syntagmatis Philosophici. Pars Secunda, quae est Physica
Sectio Prima.
De rebus Natura universe.
Physicae Prooemium
Praefatio
Liber I. De Universo & Mundo, qui complexus est, seu natura Rerum.
Liber II. De Loco & Tempore, seu spatio & duratione Rerum.
Liber III. De Materiali Principio, sive Materia Prima Rerum.
Liber IV. De Principio Efficiente, seu de Causis Rerum.
Liber V. De Motu, & Mutatione Rerum.
Liber VI. De Qualitatibus Rerum.
Liber VII. De Ortu & Interitu, seu Generatione & Corruptione Rerum.

Physicae Sectio Secunda
De Rebus Caelestibus
Liber I. De Caeli, Siderumque substantia.
Liber II. De varietate, positu & magnitudine Siderum.
Liber III. De Motibus Siderum.
Liber IV. De Luce Siderum.
Liber V. De Cometu & Novis Sideribus.
Liber VI. De Effectibus Siderum.

Partis Secundae, seu Physicae Sectionis Tertiae
Membrum Prius, De Rebus Terrenis Inanimis.
Liber I. De Globo ipso Telluris.
Liber II. De vocatis vulgo Meteoris.
Liber III. De Lapidibus, ac Metallis.
Liber IV. De Plantis.

Physicae Sectionis III.
Membrum Posterius, De Rebus Terrenis Viventibus, seu de Animalibus.
Liber I. De varietate Animalium.
Liber II. De Partibus Animalium.
Liber III. De Anima.
Liber IV. De Generatione Animalium.
Liber V. De Nutritione, Pulsu & Respiratione Animalium.
Liber VI. De Sensu universe.

Liber VII. De Sensibus speciatim.
Liber VIII. De Phantasia, seu Imaginatione.
Liber IX. De Intellectu seu Mente.
Liber X. De Appetitu & Affectibus Animae.
Liber XI. De Vi Motrice & Motionibus Animalium.
Liber XII. De Temperie & valetudine Animalium.
Liber XIII. De Vita & Morte Animalium.
Liber XIV. De Animorum Immortalitate.

Descartes, Mechanics, and the Mechanical Philosophy

DANIEL GARBER

One of philosophical preoccupations of much recent work in the history of early-modern philosophy is the mechanical philosophy. According to the mechanical philosophy, everything in nature is to be explained in terms of the size, shape, and motion of the small parts that make up a sensible body. In essence, for the mechanical philosophy, the whole world can be treated as if it were a collection of machines. The mechanical philosophy is in explicit contrast with the Aristotelian philosophy of the schools. For an Aristotelian physicist, natural philosophy is ulti-mately grounded in the irreducible tendencies bodies have to behave one way or another, as embodied in their substantial forms. Some bodies naturally fall, and others naturally rise; some are naturally cold, and others are naturally hot; some are naturally dry, and others are naturally wet. Increasingly, historians of the period are grasping that one of the most important questions for the historian of seventeenth-century philosophy is that of understanding how the philosophical programs of the great philosophers of the period are connected with the mechanical philosophy. I completely agree with this trend: the mechanical philosophy was, in a sense, the motor that drove the transformation from Aristotelian scholastic philosophy and the obscurities of Renaissance thought to the figures who are generally acknowl-edged to be the first moderns, including, for example, Descartes, Hobbes, Spinoza, and Leibniz. I do not want to suggest, as some writers assume, that the mechanical philosophy was the *only* important alternative to Aristotelian natural philosophy in its day, and that anyone who was not an Aristotelian must have been a mechanist.[1]

1. When Descartes was writing, there were alchemists, Platonists, and Telesians who believed in hot and cold as basic principles, followers of Gilbert who saw magnetism as basic, and many others not so easily categorizable. For a survey of the scientific world as it was in the generation before Descartes came onto the scene, see chapter 5 of Brian P. Copenhaver and Charles B. Schmitt, *Renaissance Philosophy* (Oxford and New York: Oxford University Press, 1992).

But that understood, it certainly emerged in the course of the seventeenth century as one of the principal alternatives, if not *the* principal alternative to the dominant Aristotelianism.

But despite all of the recent attention to the mechanical philosophy, the mechanical philosophy itself is still relatively little understood. In particular, there has been very little study of the relation between the science of mechanics and the mechanical philosophy. That is the project in this essay. To focus the investigation, I intend to concentrate on one particular figure, René Descartes, one of the founders of the mechanical philosophy properly understood. I shall begin with an overview of mechanics as it was practiced in the years before Descartes came onto the scene.[2] Then I shall turn to Descartes himself and examine the role that mechanics and machines play in his thought. I shall argue that in forging the mechanical philosophy, Descartes profoundly transformed not only natural philosophy but mechanics as well, and that the new mechanical philosophy represented a rupture not only with Aristotelian natural philosophy but, in a way, with the science of mechanics as well. At the same time, I shall argue, it was the connection between mechanics and the new mechanical philosophy that allowed Descartes' new science to remain intelligible to the adherents of the Aristotelian tradition he rejected and intended to replace.

MECHANICS AND NATURAL PHILOSOPHY: THE SIXTEENTH-CENTURY TRADITION(S)

The science of mechanics thrived in sixteenth-century Italy. The major ancient traditions that fed into Renaissance and early modern mechanics were that of pseudo-Aristotle and that of Archimedes. Aristotle's *Physica* was widely edited, commented on, and studied in the schools. But in addition to the *Physica*, there was another widely circulated Aristotelian text, one that dealt with mechanics, the *Mechanica* or *Mechanica Problemata*, attributed to Aristotle in the Renaissance, though now known to be a somewhat later text.[3] In the corpus of Archimedes' surviving works, one is particularly important for mechanics in the sixteenth and seventeenth centuries: *On the Equilibrium of Planes.*[4] These two somewhat different traditions came together when both texts were rediscovered in the Renaissance. Figures such as Benedetti, Tartaglia, Guidobaldo del Monte, and even Galileo combined elements of these two traditions, along with some pieces of others and

2. My interest here is in the relation between Descartes' mechanical philosophy and the learned tradition in mechanics. One might also inquire into the connections between the mechanical philosophy and the traditions of practical mechanics. On this question, see, e.g., J. A. Bennett, "The Mechanics' Philosophy and the Mechanical Philosophy," *History of Science* 24 (1986), pp. 1–28.

3. On the importance of this text for sixteenth-century mechanics, see Paul Rose and Stillman Drake, "The Pseudo-Aristotelian *Questions of Mechanics* in Renaissance Culture," *Studies in the Renaissance*, XVIII (1971), pp. 65–104; and François De Gandt, "Les *Mécaniques* attribuées à Aristote et le renouveau de la science des machines au XVIe siècle," *Les Études Philosophiques* (1986), pp. 391–405.

4. See Archimedes, *The Works of Archimedes with the Method of Archimedes*, ed. T. L. Heath (New York: Dover, n.d.), pp. 189–220.

some original speculations, to produce a genuine renaissance in the science of mechanics.[5]

What was it that united these texts and made them all instances of the same program? One simple answer is that mechanics is concerned with machines: as Guidobaldo put it in his influential *Mechanicorum liber* (1577), "mechanics can no longer be called mechanics when it is abstracted and separated from machines."[6]

Aristotle and Archimedes offer somewhat different treatments of machines. Aristotelian mechanics is, in general, very, very concrete. The author of the *Mechanica* never lost sight of the physical embodiment of the machines and the effect that that has on our understanding of how they work: the science of mechanics treated in the *Mechanica* was a science of real material machines in a real material world, dealing with things made of real materials that have physical properties, things that bend, break, and wiggle. Archimedean mechanics, on the other hand, was much more abstract and mathematical. In *On the Equilibrium of Planes*, Archimedes begins with a number of theorems in what we would call statics, the science of bodies in equilibrium configurations. The problems were reduced to their geometrical bare bones and solved as such. The author of the Aristotelian *Mechanica* dealt with real machines made out of real materials. But the objects Archimedes considered were highly idealized. When talking about the balance, he assumed point weights and balance beams that are mathematical lines. Archimedes gives a theory of machines, perhaps, but the machines that interest him are not of this world.

Even though they differ in important respects, the Aristotelian and Archimedean traditions in mechanics both centered on machines, as did the later tradition to which they give rise. But what does it mean to be a machine? In the traditional accounts of mechanics, a machine was defined in terms of its utility, that is to say, in terms of human ends. It was a science of things useful to us. The Aristotelian author of the *Mechanica* wrote in the very opening of the treatise:

> Nature often operates contrary to human interest; for she always follows the same course without deviation, whereas human interest is always changing. When, therefore, we have to do something contrary to nature, the difficulty of it causes us perplexity and art has to be called to our aid. The kind of art which helps us in such perplexities we call Mechanical Skill.[7]

This was the subject matter of mechanics for pseudo-Aristotle: the study of artificial things, things constructed to do particular tasks for us that nature herself, left

---

5. See Stillman Drake, and I. E. Drabkin, eds., *Mechanics in Sixteenth-Century Italy* (Madison: University of Wisconsin Press, 1969). This volume contains important selections from these authors in English translation, together with an introductory essay that remains an invaluable guide to the subject.

6. "Neque enim amplius mechanica, si à machinis abstrahatur, et seiungatur, mechanica potest appellari." Guidobaldo del Monte, *Mechanicorum liber* (Pisa, 1587), praefatio (unpaginated), translated in Drake and Drabkin, *Mechanics*, p. 245.

7. *Mechanica* 847a14f, translated in *The Complete Works of Aristotle*, ed. Jonathan Barnes (2 vols.) (Princeton: Princeton University Press, 1984), vol. II. p. 1299.

unaided, does not do. The conception of mechanics that focuses on the artificiality and the utility of machines was also important in the sixteenth century. For example, Guidobaldo opens his *Mechanicorum liber* with the following implicit definition of the domain of mechanics:

> For whatever helps manual workers, builders, carriers, farmers, sailors, and many others (in opposition to the laws of nature)—all this is the province of mechanics.[8]

Given human interests, it is not surprising that mechanics as practiced focused on the particular machines it did from early on. The lever, the balance, the inclined plane, and, later, when gunnery became important, the motion of projectiles: they are all tools that enable us to do various things that we want to have done.

Embedded in this conception of the domain of mechanics was a certain conception of the natural world, the distinction between the natural and the artificial, and a certain related conception of the relations between the science of physics (natural philosophy) and the science of mechanics. For sixteenth-century Italian mechanics, as for Aristotle and Archimedes, there was a real division between physics on the one hand, and mechanics on the other. In the terminology of the sixteenth and early seventeenth century, mechanics, together with astronomy, optics, and music, were "middle sciences" (*scientiae mediae*) or branches of "mixed mathematics" (*mathematica mixta*), branches of mathematics that used physical premises but were distinct from the physics from which they borrowed.[9] Natural philosophy (physics) treats natural things as they are in themselves, inquiring into their essences and the true causes of natural (physical) phenomena. But things in nature do not always do what we want them to do. Mechanics, on the other hand, is the science of the artificial, natural things as they are configured into devices for our benefit. In this way, it is a supplement to physics proper: it treats at least certain kinds of things not treated in physics, in particular, artificial things, machines.[10]

---

8. "Quandoquidem quodcunque Fabris, Architectis, Baiulis, Agricolis, Nautis, et quàm plurimus aliis (repugnantibus naturae legibus) optulatur; id omne mechanicum est imperium." Guidobaldo del Monte, *Mechanicorum liber*, praefatio (unpaginated), translated in Drake and Drabkin, *Mechanics*, p. 241. The fact that machines are made for particular purposes is one of the features of machines that Dennis Des Chene emphasizes in chapter 4 of *Spirits and Clocks: Machine and Organism in Descartes* (Ithaca: Cornell University Press, 2000). Des Chene provides a very elegant discussion of the machine analogy in Descartes as it applies to humans and other living creatures. Though my own orientation in this essay is somewhat different from Des Chene's, I have learned a great deal from his work.

9. St. Thomas discusses the term *scientiae mediae* in his commentary on the *De trinitate* of Boethius, q5a3ad6; In II Phys. lect. 3, n. 8; Summa Theol. 2–2.9.2, ad 3. *Mathematica mixta* is used by Rudolph Goclenius in his *Lexicon philosophicum* (Frankfurt: 1613), p. 672b, and Francis Bacon, *The Advancement of Learning* (1605) II.8.2. See also James G. Lennox, "Aristotle, Galileo, and 'Mixed Sciences'" in William A. Wallace, ed., *Reinterpreting Galileo* (Washington, D.C.: Catholic University of America Press, 1986), pp. 29–51; and Gary I. Brown, "The Evolution of the Term 'Mixed Mathematics'," *Journal of the History of Ideas* 52 (1991), pp. 81–102.

10. For a discussion of how the art/nature distinction governed later European Aristotelian science, see Dear, *Experience and Discipline* (Chicago: University of Chicago Press, 1995), pp. 153–161.

And, similarly, physics contributes to mechanics. Machines are, of course, made up of natural materials (wood, metal, ropes, etc.), which have their own natural properties. Mechanics must make use of those properties in explaining the behavior of machines. So, for example, heaviness plays a major role in explaining the simple machines (lever, screw, balance, etc.), all of which use human or animal force to overcome the natural effects of heaviness, and shows the mechanic how to lift weights in different ways. Whether one considers them as Archimedean idealizations or as Aristotelian concreta, treatises on mechanics all assumed that that one was dealing with heavy bodies, bodies that tend to fall to the center of the earth. The question of the cause of heaviness and freefall lay outside of the domain of mechanics, and in the domain of physics. It was one of the premises that the mechanic could borrow from the distinct science of physics.[11]

Now, when you talked about physics in the sixteenth and early seventeenth century, it was very difficult to avoid Aristotle. Especially interesting in this connection is the variety of attitudes toward Aristotle's physics among writers on mechanics in the period. Some practitioners accept Aristotle quite willingly, but others reject him quite completely. In this way, even though mechanics is connected with the science of physics, it is not necessarily connected with one physics or another. Specific approaches to projectile motion, Benedetti's for example, do entail giving up elements of Aristotle's physics of motion, to be sure. But it is fair to say that mechanics as practiced in these figures is often combined with a commitment to elements of an Aristotelian physics, as in the case of Guidobaldo.[12] Though the *mechanical philosophy* will later set itself against Aristotelian natural philosophy, the *science of mechanics*, as practiced in sixteenth-century Italy, is not, in and of itself, anti-Aristotelian. It was by no means clear that doing mechanics entailed one particular natural philosophy over another; in particular, it did not entail being anti-Aristotelian.

DESCARTES AND THE MECHANICAL PHILOSOPHY

At the end of his *Principia*, Descartes told the reader, "I have described this earth and indeed the whole visible universe as if it were a machine: I have considered

11. On the relations between physics and mechanics, see, e.g., Alan Gabbey, "Between *ars* and *philosophia naturalis*: Reflections on the Historiography of Early Modern Mechanics," In *Renaissance and Revolution: Humanists, Scholars, Craftsmen and Natural Philosophers in Early Modern Europe*, eds. J. V. Field and F. A. J. L. James (Cambridge: Cambridge University Press, 1993), pp. 133–145; and W. Roy Laird, "The Scope of Renaissance Mechanics," *Osiris* n.s. 2 (1986), pp. 43–68. Robert Westman treats the parallel question with respect to astronomy, another middle science, in his essay, "The Astronomer's Role in the Sixteenth Century: A Preliminary Study," *History of Science* 18 (1980), pp. 105–147. Much of the evidence he cites pertains as much to mechanics (and the other mixed mathematical sciences) as it does to astronomy.

12. On Benedetti's anti-Aristotelianism, see Alexandre Koyré, "Giambattista Benedetti, Critic of Aristotle," in E. McMullin, ed., *Galileo Man of Science* (New York: Basic Books, 1967), pp. 98–117. On Guidobaldo and Aristotle, see Domenico Bertoloni Meli, "Guidobaldo dal Monte and the Archimedean Revival," *Nuncius* 7 (1992), pp. 3–34.

only the various shapes and movements of its parts" (Pr IV, 188).[13] Later in the *Principia*, he wrote:

> I do not recognize any difference between artifacts and natural bodies except that the operations of artifacts are for the most part performed by mechanisms which are large enough to be easily perceivable by the senses—as indeed must be the case if they are to be capable of being manufactured by human beings. The effects produced in nature, by contrast, almost always depend on structures which are so minute that they completely elude our senses. (Pr IV, 203)

Similarly, Descartes suggested to an unknown correspondent in March 1642, seeking to clarify his position, that "all the causes of motion in material things are the same as in artificial machines" (AT V, 546). In his *Traité de l'homme* of 1633, Descartes even assimilated the *human* body to a machine. In the opening pages of that work, Descartes imagined God to have created a very peculiar machine: "I suppose the body to be nothing but a statue or machine made of earth, which God forms with the explicit intention of making it as much as possible like us" (AT XI, 99). There is no doubt that this machine was supposed to represent the way our bodies actually are, as his account in the later "Description of the Human Body" (1647/8) made explicit (AT XI, 226).

But what role did mechanics, the *science* of machines, play in Descartes' thought? Here I find some confusion and at least two different strains in Descartes' thought. In his celebrated "tree analogy" in the introduction to the French edition of the *Principia*, Descartes wrote:

> The whole of philosophy is like a tree. The roots are metaphysics, the trunk is physics, and the branches emerging from the trunk are all the other sciences, which may be reduced to three principal ones, namely medicine, mechanics and morals. (AT IXB, 14)

Understood in this way, mechanics, the theory of machines, is one of the fruits of physics, a science based on physics that helps us to control nature. Consistent with this view, Descartes sometimes argued that mechanics is a proper part of physics. And, therefore, in the *Principia* he wrote that "mechanics is a division or special case of physics, and all the explanations belonging to the former also belong to the latter; so it is no less natural for a clock constructed with this or that set of wheels

---

13. References to Descartes' writings will be given as much as possible in the text. The standard original-language edition of Descartes' writings is René Descartes, *Oeuvres de Descartes*, ed. Charles Adam and Paul Tannery, new edition (11 vols.) (Paris: CNRS/Vrin, 1964–74). This will be abbreviated "AT," followed by volume (in Roman) and page number (in Arabic). References to Descartes' *Principia Philosophiae* (1644; Fr. trans. 1647) are given by "Pr," followed by the part (in Roman) and the section number (in Arabic). The best current translation is René Descartes, *The Philosophical Writings of Descartes*, ed. and trans. John Cottingham, Robert Stoothoff, Dugald Murdoch, and (for vol. III) Anthony Kenny (3 vols.) (Cambridge: Cambridge University Press, 1984–91). Since the passages quoted can readily be found in that edition, I will not cite the translation separately.

to tell the time than it is for a tree which grew from this or that seed to produce the appropriate fruit" (AT IV, 203).[14] Elsewhere, in a letter from 1637 he noted that "the mechanics now current is nothing but a part of the true physics which, not being welcomed by supporters of the common sort of philosophy [i.e., Aristotelian philosophy], took refuge with the mathematicians."[15] Taken literally, this suggests a view that goes beyond what earlier practitioners of mechanics held, but not by much. Though he identified mechanics as a part of physics, and not as a distinct and subordinate discipline, there is nothing in these statements that implies that in addition to mechanics, physics doesn't contain something more. Calling mechanics a part of physics in this sense would seem to be just a linguistic point, an expansion of the notion of physics and little more.[16]

But elsewhere Descartes treated mechanics in a very different way, as being genuinely foundational. In a number of places, Descartes fully identified the laws of nature with the laws of mechanics. In the *Discourse*, for example, Descartes talked about the "laws [*regles*] of mechanics" as being identical to the laws of nature.[17] Similarly, in the French edition of the *Principles*, Descartes wrote:

> I considered in general all the clear and distinct notions which our understanding can contain with regard to material things. And I found no others except for the notions we have of shapes, sizes and motions, and the rules in accordance with which these three things can be modified by each other—*rules which are the principles of geometry and mechanics*. And I judged as a result that all the knowledge which men have of the natural world must necessarily be derived from these notions. (emphasis added; Pr IV, 203)

And so, Descartes held, both artificial and natural things, both animate and inanimate things must be explained in the same way. Descartes, in fact, goes so far as to say that "my entire physics is nothing but mechanics."[18] And so, to explain anything in Descartes' physics, we must do a kind of reverse engineering. Descartes wrote, again in the *Principia*:

14. Cf. *Regulae ad directionem ingenii*, Rule VI, AT X, 379, where Descartes criticizes "those who study mechanics apart from physics and, without any proper plan, construct new instruments for producing motion."

15. Descartes to Plempius for Fromondus, 3 Oct. 1637, AT I, 420–421. See also Descartes to Huygens, March 1638, AT II, 50 and 662 (note the significant variation between the two versions of this text).

16. This is the conception of mechanics that is most of concern to Alan Gabbey in his essay, "Descartes's Physics and Descartes's Mechanics: Chicken and Egg?" in S. Voss, ed., *Essays on the Philosophy and Science of René Descartes* (Oxford: Oxford University Press, 1993), pp. 311–323. Gabbey does not seem to recognize that there is a second sense of the notion of mechanics in Descartes, which I will argue below.

17. AT VI, 54: ". . . les regles des Mechaniques, qui sont les mesmes que celles de la nature . . ." Cf. also ". . . the laws of my mechanics, that is, of my physics" [". . . Mechanicae meae, hoc est Physicae, leges . . ."] [Descartes to Plempius, 15 Feb. 1638, AT I, 524].

18. Descartes to Debeaune? 30 April 1639, AT II, 542.

Men who are experienced in dealing with machinery can take a particular machine whose function they know and, by looking at some of its parts, easily form a conjecture about the design of the other parts, which they cannot see. In the same way I have attempted to consider the observable effects and parts of natural bodies and track down the imperceptible causes and particles which produce them. (Pr IV, 203)[19]

This sense of mechanics seems rather different than the earlier sense that we examined. On that first sense, mechanics is a part of physics, and is one of the final fruits of philosophical (i.e., scientific) inquiry. Call that sense of the term "non-foundational mechanics." Non-foundational mechanics stands in contrast to this second sense in which Descartes takes himself to be interested in mechanics, the sense in which mechanics is taken to be foundational for his physics. Call this second sense "foundational mechanics."

On the mechanical philosophy,[20] mechanics (or, at least, foundational mechanics) subsumes physics: *everything* in physics now receives a mechanical explanation, that is, everything is explained as if it were a machine. This would seem to be a classic instance of intertheoretic reduction, where one discipline becomes reduced to another, physics to mechanics in this case. But matters are rather more complicated than this would suggest. It is extremely curious that when we look at Descartes' actual physics, in either *Le monde* or the *Principia*, we find nothing that looks even vaguely like a sixteenth-century mechanics text. Descartes begins his physics in chapters 6 and 7 of *Le monde* and in part II of the *Principia* (§§36 ff) with an account of the laws of nature. This is followed by an account of how the different elements he recognizes, differentiated from one another by shape, size, and motion, all arise from an initial chaos, and how the shape, size, and motion of the different corpuscles that make up bodies explain their properties. The *Principia* ends with a real tour de force, first an explanation of magnetism in terms of the motion of corpuscles (Pr IV 145 ff), and then a sketch of an explanation of the senses (Pr IV 189f), again in terms of the corpuscles and their motion.

---

19. This follows the Latin version. The French version makes much the same point, but using the example of a watch of unknown construction in place of the more general "machinery" Descartes alludes to in the Latin. Given the freedom allowed to seventeenth-century translators, it isn't clear whether this is Descartes' alteration or the translator's. For a discussion of some of the epistemological implications of this view, see Larry Laudan, "The Clock Metaphor and Hypotheses: The Impact of Descartes on English Methodological Thought, 1650–1670," in his *Science and Hypothesis* (Dordrecht: Reidel, 1981), pp. 27–58.

20. It should be noted in this connection that I am using the term *mechanical philosophy* somewhat anachronistically here. Descartes himself does not use this term. The term seems first to appear in the writings of Robert Boyle in the early 1660s, roughly ten years after Descartes' death, where it designates a conception of natural philosophy that unites a number of views considered by their originators in competition with one another, particularly those of Descartes and Gassendi. I would further claim that it was Boyle who created the idea of the mechanical philosophy, as it was used later in the century, though I will not argue that here. While recognizing the dangers, I will continue to use the term in connection with Descartes. On the history of the term *mechanical philosophy*, see Sophie Roux, *La philosophie mécanique (1630–1690)*, unpublished doctoral thesis, École des Hautes Études en Sciences Sociales, 1996, pp. 19–26.

But there are no levers, no balances, no pulleys, nothing that looks like the sort of machine that was at the center of the tradition in mechanics in the sixteenth century. In October 1637, at the request of Constantijn Huygens, Descartes did write a short treatise on mechanics understood in what has become the classic sense, a treatise on the simple machines (pulley, lever, etc.), with a few general remarks on the principles behind his accounts.[21] Descartes clearly knew what mechanics is. But, at the same time, nothing of that mechanics seems to appear in his actual physics. What is going on? In what way did Descartes think of his physics as mechanics?

CARTESIAN MECHANICS: A MECHANICS WITHOUT HEAVINESS

The project is, then, to make sense of the foundational mechanics, to understand what Descartes meant by "mechanics" when he said that his whole physics is mechanics.

Mechanics was the science of machines, artificial devices that are built in order to do work for us. Now, in practice, the kind of work that interested writers on mechanics in the sixteenth and early seventeenth centuries involved either lifting heavy bodies or shooting heavy bodies out of guns. The studies of machines designed to produce those effects stood at the center of traditional mechanics. In this context, of course, one deals with bodies that are heavy and fall or tend to fall to the center of the earth; mechanics would borrow premises that involve heaviness and free fall from physics, a separate discipline.

But, of course, if Descartes intended to make mechanics foundational and explain all physical phenomena in mechanistic terms, then these machines cannot be as central as they are to the subject matter of the mechanics of his predecessors. If *everything* in nature is to be explained as if it produced effects like a machine, then gravitation cannot be *assumed*; gravitation *itself* must also be explained, and, within the *mechanical* philosophy, it must be explained *mechanistically*. Or, to put it in another way, when mechanics subsumes physics, we can no longer appeal outside of mechanics to some distinct science to supply necessary premises concerning heaviness: the premises necessary for doing the traditional mechanics of heavy bodies must come from within the mechanical philosophy itself.

Descartes seemed to be aware of this. In his correspondence, Descartes discussed on a number of occasions some problems from traditional mechanics. And when he did so, he also made assumptions about heaviness and free fall. But it

---

21. Descartes to Huygens, 5 Oct. 1637, AT I, 435 ff. Descartes identifies the subject matter of the treatise as mechanics earlier in the letter, AT I, 434. Roger Ariew has suggested to me in a personal communication that it is not impossible that this treatise on mechanics had been originally part of a *Le monde*. He writes: "Huygens keeps asking for 'une piece de votre Monde' (AT I, 604) and when he finally requests just 'trois feuillets de mechanique,' it looks as if he's talking about part of *Le monde* (AT I, 642). Descartes talks about *Le monde* in his reply (AT I, 434)." That is possible, but if so, the mechanics in question is what I have called non-foundational mechanics. Furthermore, it is hard to see where it would have fit into the text. In any case, the mechanics does not appear in the text of *Le monde* that has come down to us.

must be said that he was not very happy about this. On one such occasion Descartes wrote:

> We shall suppose that each particle of a given heavy body always has a given force or tendency to descend, whether it is far from the center of the earth or close to it, and no matter how it is situated. As I have already remarked, this assumption is perhaps not true; yet we ought to make it nevertheless, in order to facilitate the calculation. In a similar way astronomers assume that the average motions of the stars are regular [*égaux*], in order to make it easier to calculate the true motions, which are irregular. (AT II, 227)

Consider also Descartes' discussion of Galileo's famous account of projectile motion. Galileo analyzed projectile motion as a combination of what we now call inertial motion (horizontal) at a constant speed together with free fall (vertical), where the distance fallen is proportional to the square of the time. Putting these two together, Galileo concluded that the path of a projectile is parabolic. Descartes wrote:

> If we assume this, then it is very easy to conclude that the motion of projectiles should follow a parabolic line; but these assumptions being false, his conclusion may also be quite far from the truth. (AT II, 387)

The answer you get, in the end, is only as good as the assumptions that you make in the beginning. Because Descartes didn't think that the assumptions were very good, the final result wasn't either. Descartes did not want to reject the mechanics of the Aristotelian and Archimedean tradition altogether. Once we have established the proper account of heaviness in our mechanist physics, for example, we can then use this (non-foundational) mechanics for helping us to shoot straight and to lift heavy loads.

It is no surprise then that Descartes' mechanist physics didn't look much like earlier treatises on mechanics. Because the assumption of heaviness can no longer be borrowed from physics, a different discipline, the entire body of ancient and sixteenth century mechanics as it was actually practiced becomes unusable in Descartes' foundational enterprise. The theories of levers and pulleys, inclined planes, and projectile motion that formed the central topics in mechanics for Galileo and his predecessors are not what Descartes had in mind when he identified mechanics with physics and made mechanics the foundational science.

This gives us a piece of the answer to the question as to why Descartes' mechanical philosophy looks so different from the traditional mechanics from which it seems to have arisen. But it isn't the whole story. Though we know at least something of what Descartes' mechanics *wasn't*, we do not yet know what it *was*.

To raise the question in a very concrete way, let's continue a bit further down the path that we have been taking, and consider further Descartes' account of heaviness. Descartes' mechanical philosophy, his mechanist physics must establish the true nature of heaviness *before* that notion can be used in the mechanics of heavy bodies. How can this be done? Though the full account is rather complex, in outline, Descartes' account is as follows. Gravity, the tendency to fall toward the center of the earth, for Descartes, is explained in terms of the interaction between a body and the vortex of subtle matter that turns around the earth, he argues. Strictly speaking, bodies are pushed toward the center of the earth by colliding with the particles of subtle matter in the vortex. Descartes summarized his account of heaviness as follows:

> My idea of weight is as follows. All the subtle matter which is between here and the moon rotates rapidly around the earth, and pushes towards it all the bodies which cannot move so fast. It pushes them with greater force when they have not yet begun to fall than when they are already falling; for, after all, if they are falling as fast as it is moving, it will not push them at all, and if they are falling faster, it will actually resist them.[22]

Descartes' bodies, extended and extended alone, have no natural tendencies to move in one way or another. In particular, Cartesian bodies do not, as such, tend to fall toward the center of the earth or toward anything else. The true physics must explain why bodies fall toward the earth, and not just assume this as a premise, the way in which it is generally assumed by mechanics. And the means Descartes gives himself for such an explanation is size, shape, and motion alone: it is in those terms that we must explain why heavy bodies fall toward the center of the earth. Hence the Cartesian account of gravity in terms of the collision between a so-called heavy body and the particles of the subtle matter.

This is supposed to be an example of Descartes' own approach to physics, which he identified with mechanics. But in what sense is the explanation of gravity that Descartes offers here *mechanistic*? In what sense is he explaining gravitation as if it were an aspect of the behavior of a machine, as he claims his physics is supposed to do? More generally, if it is not traditional mechanics that Descartes has in mind here, what exactly is it?

CARTESIAN MECHANICS: MECHANICS WITHOUT TELEOLOGY

To approach an answer to this question, let us go back to some of my earlier comments about machines and the science of mechanics. The machine is an artifact, constructed to do some particular piece of work. Considered as an artifact, it has an end, of course; it is constructed by an agent and for some purpose of interest to that agent. This conception of the machine is reflected in the science of mechanics, which is the science of the artificial, the science whose object is the construction and explanation of artifacts built to do things we need to have done. In pre-Cartesian mechanics, the artificial is contrasted with the natural, and the science of mechanics is contrasted with the science of physics or natural philosophy.

---

22. Descartes to [Debeaune], 30 April 1639, AT II, 544. Descartes' account of gravity is treated at greater length in *Le monde*, chapter 11, and in Pr IV 23f.

If machines are defined in terms of their purposes, and natural things are not normally thought of as having purposes, then how can we talk about natural bodies in terms of machines? One way is this. We can imagine natural things *as if* they were machines, by imagining them *as if* they were artifacts, things constructed for a purpose. To say that a natural object is like a machine is to say that we can consider it as, or as if it had been made by someone for a purpose, God, perhaps, and explain it as such. And so, for example, at the beginning of the *Traité de l'homme*, Descartes imagined God having created the man/machine that is the subject matter of the treatise:

> I suppose the body to be nothing but a statue or machine made of earth, which God forms with the explicit intention of making it as much as possible like us. Thus God not only gives it externally the colors and shapes of all the parts of our bodies, but also places inside it all the parts required to make it walk, eat, breathe, and indeed to imitate all those of our functions which can be imagined to proceed from matter and to depend solely on the disposition of our organs. We see clocks, artificial fountains, mills, and other such machines which, although only man-made, have the power to move of their own accord in many different ways. But I am supposing this machine to be made by the hands of God, and so I think you may reasonably think it capable of a greater variety of movements than I could possibly imagine in it, and of exhibiting more artistry than I could possibly ascribe to it. (AT XI, 120)

In this situation the natural human body is set along side an artifactual human body, a machine/body that God, the artifex maximus, has made. This artifact, this machine has its own purpose: to look and behave as much like a real human body as possible. Since God is the artisan here, of course the resemblance is exact. What is Descartes' point here in positing such a strange object? As Descartes put it in a number of places in the treatise, the machine God creates "represents" what happens in the body.[23] That is, we can conjecture that in our natural bodies, the phenomena in question are produced in the same way in which they are in the body of the machine God built to imitate us.

Elsewhere, Descartes took a somewhat different approach. I return to a passage quoted earlier in the essay:

> Men who are experienced in dealing with machinery can take a particular machine whose function [*usus*] they know and, by looking at some of its parts, easily form a conjecture about the design of the other parts, which they cannot see. In the same way I have attempted to consider the observable effects and parts of natural bodies and track down the imperceptible causes and particles which produce them. (Pr IV, 203)

The idea here seems to be that we can look at nature through the eyes of the mechanic or engineer, and ask how he would build a machine whose purpose it

23. E.g., AT XI, 173.

would be to mimic nature in just the way God's man/machine mimics us. What is the point of this? The point, as I understand it, is to argue that the natural object could be identical to the mechanical substitute that we imagine is being made. For any given natural thing with its particular behaviors, we can substitute a man-made artifact whose purpose it is to mimic nature.

We can talk about natural things as machines by attributing purposes to them; we can imagine them to be machines made for the purpose of producing certain behavior or phenomena. But there is another strategy we can use: we can bracket, or even eliminate, the purposes from machines, and in that way assimilate them to natural objects. In a certain sense, Descartes insisted, the purpose of a machine is something extrinsic to that machine, something that is imposed on the machine by us. And, Descartes argued, this is true not only of things mechanics make, but also of the kind of natural machines treated in his biology. In an important passage in Meditation VI, Descartes wrote:

> [A] clock constructed with wheels and weights observes all the laws of its nature just as closely when it is badly made and tells the wrong time as when it completely fulfils the wishes of the clockmaker. In the same way, I might consider the body of a man as a kind of machine equipped with and made up of bones, nerves, muscles, veins, blood and skin in such a way that, even if there were no mind in it, it would still perform all the same movements as it now does in those cases where movement is not under the control of the will or, consequently, of the mind. I can easily see that if such a body suffers from dropsy, for example, and is affected by the dryness of the throat which normally produces in the mind the sensation of thirst, the resulting condition of the nerves and other parts will dispose the body to take a drink, with the result that the disease will be aggravated. Yet this is just as natural as the body's being stimulated by a similar dryness of the throat to take a drink when there is no such illness and the drink is beneficial. Admittedly, when I consider the purpose of the clock, I may say that it is departing from its nature when it does not tell the right time; and similarly when I consider the mechanism of the human body, I may think that, in relation to the movements which normally occur in it, it too is deviating from its nature if the throat is dry at a time when drinking is not beneficial to its continued health . . . As I have just used it, 'nature' is simply a label which depends on my thought; it is quite extraneous to the things to which it is applied, and depends simply on my comparison between the idea of a sick man and a badly-made clock, and the idea of a healthy man and a well-made clock . . . (AT VII, 84–5)[24]

The telos is something imposed from the outside, imposed by us, both in the case of the artificial machine and in the case of the natural object. In an important sense, it isn't really there.

24. Descartes goes on in this passage to say that considered as a mind/body unity, the human being does have a nature, and it does make sense to say that the person is departing from its nature when ill. However, the case for a body taken alone (or an animal body) is parallel to that of a clock.

When we bracket the purpose of a machine, or, as the Meditation VI passage suggests, eliminate it altogether, what is left to the machine is simply its construction: purpose aside, a machine is just the kind of thing that a mechanic can make with the tools at his disposal, that is, something that works by size, shape, and motion. For traditional mechanics, a machine is an artifact, something made for a particular purpose. For Descartes, I suggest, *a machine has become simply a collection of parts whose states are determined by the size, shape, and motion of those parts, as well as by the collisions among them.* The focus of a Cartesian mechanics, a Cartesian mechanical philosophy, is not on the things that we can do with machines and the purposes for which we might construct them, but on the means at our disposal for constructing them, on the different configurations of size, shape, and motion that produce those effects.

Machines are made with a purpose; natural things are not. But this particular difference between the machine and the natural body to which it corresponds is irrelevant to Descartes' project: his point in establishing a correspondence between the artificial machine and the natural body was that we can now explain everything that happens in the natural body in exactly the same way in which we explain what happens in the artificial machine. That is, we explain things in the natural world as if they had been made by a mechanic who has only parts of different sizes, shapes, and motions to work with when producing his effects. To return to a passage that I cited earlier, Descartes wrote:

> For I do not recognize any difference between artifacts and natural bodies except that the operations of artifacts are for the most part performed by mechanisms which are large enough to be easily perceivable by the senses— as indeed must be the case if they are to be capable of being manufactured by human beings. The effects produced in nature, by contrast, almost always depend on structures which are so minute that they completely elude our senses. (Pr IV, 203)

When we explain how the effect of the machine is accomplished, its purpose doesn't enter in: we explain the behavior of the watch using the kinds of resources available to the watchmaker when he builds such a machine, the wheels and springs and other small parts that work in terms of size, shape, and motion. The purpose of a machine may determine what behavior it is that we are trying to produce, but it does not enter into the way in which the behavior itself is produced. It is in this sense that the theory of gravitation that we briefly discussed above is mechanical: Descartes explains the heaviness of bodies in the terms one uses in explaining the behavior of a machine. In this way the (spring-driven) clock or the planetary system or the magnet (as Descartes understands it) or the rainbow can all be regarded as machines: their behaviors can be explained by Descartes strictly in terms of the size, shape, and motion of their parts.

There is, I suggest, a new sense of what it is to be a machine in Descartes. But with this change, Descartes has changed the subject matter of mechanics. The mechanics practiced before Descartes was the science of the artificial, in contrast with the natural; its focus was on how to do the things we want to do with the means that nature has put at our disposal. And just as the notion of a machine before Descartes was infused with teleology, so was the notion of a science of mechanics: what its objects had in common was a common purpose, doing things that we want to have done. In this sense, the domain of the science of mechanics is defined by us and our needs, not in terms of some natural category of things in nature. But in Descartes, mechanics becomes not the science of machines, artifacts made to help us do things we want done, but the science of things that operate through the physical configuration of their parts. A new sense of mechanics emerges, free of teleology: mechanics becomes the science of complex bodies whose states are determined by the size, shape, and motion of their parts. In 1577 Guidobaldo wrote that "mechanics can no longer be called mechanics when it is abstracted and separated from machines."[25] In essence, this is just what Descartes has done, produced a mechanics without machines in the sense that Guidobaldo and his contemporaries would have understood the term. Mechanics has become in Descartes more like mechanics in the modern (i.e., eighteenth-century) sense, the study of bodies in motion. In 1670, John Wallis published a book entitled *Mechanica, sive de motu* (London, 1670). A hundred years earlier, this title would have been unintelligible; after Descartes it was taken for granted.[26]

It is this conception of the science of mechanics that Descartes wants to identify with physics: the claim is that *everything* in the physical world can be explained using the means at the disposal of the mechanic: the size, shape, and motion of the parts of a body. Once we have established a mechanical philosophy, a mechanical physics, we are, of course, free to study those special machines of particular utility to us, just as we can give special attention to the human body, a body of special interest to us as human beings; hence the sciences of (non-foundational) mechanics and medicine, two of the three ultimate fruits of the tree of philosophy. There, once we reach the branches of our tree of philosophy, we can also talk about machines and human bodies in more traditional teleological ways, about what makes them healthy or functional, as opposed to ill or broken. But insofar as the mechanical philosophy, the mechanics transformed into philosophy, is a natural *philosophy*, its subject matter cannot be defined in the artificial, unnatural, and teleological way that mechanics is traditionally characterized in terms of human interests.

The question of intertheoretical reduction and unification is quite important to recent work in the philosophy of science. The way in which scientists and mathematicians forge links between different scientific disciplines and attempt to subsume one into another is one of the important engines for scientific change. Descartes is well known for his unification of algebra and geometry and for his

25. Guidobaldo del Monte, *Mechanicorum Liber* (Pisa, 1587), praefatio (unpaginated), translated in Drake and Drabkin, *Mechanics*, p. 245.

26. I thank Michael Mahoney for this observation. Mahoney discusses the relations between mechanics and mathematics in the seventeenth century, including the work of Wallis, in his important essay, "The Mathematical Realm of Nature," chapter 22 of D. Garber and M. Ayers, eds., *Cambridge History of Seventeenth-Century Philosophy* (Cambridge: Cambridge University Press, 1998).

reduction of biology to physics. But the mechanical philosophy was probably his most significant such move, expanding mechanics in such a way that it now embodies all physics. What is surprising, though, is that when physics and mechanics merged, the resulting scientific program retained little of either program that preceded it. It certainly did not look very much like the Aristotelian physics that it was intended to replace. And as I have argued, it didn't look very much like the mechanics from which it supposedly had its inspiration. It remained, in a sense, the theory of machines, but machines understood in a way very different from the way in which machines were understood in the tradition of mechanics that preceded Descartes. In that way, the passage from mechanics to the mechanical philosophy was not a smooth transition, but a very surprising rupture. It is ironic, but in understanding the world in terms of machines, Descartes had to set aside the theory of machines as it was then understood.

CONTINUITIES

I have argued that Descartes' mechanical philosophy represented a major shift in the conception of the notion of a machine and the science of mechanics. But even leaving this change aside, the shift from Aristotelian natural philosophy to the new mechanical philosophy in Descartes' thought is generally considered to represent a major shift in the European intellectual tradition, the very paradigm of a Kuhnian paradigm shift, a chasm across which communication would seem to be difficult if not impossible. The further changes in the notion of the mechanical that Descartes' philosophy introduced might be thought to make the situation worse still. But, interestingly enough, this isn't the case. Descartes and his Aristotelian teachers and predecessors certainly disagreed on a great deal. But the idea of the machine and the science of mechanics provided a link between the two worlds.

Now, if we think of the mechanist revolution as the transition between Aristotelian *natural philosophy* taken narrowly and the mechanistic natural philosophy that Descartes introduced, then it does, indeed, look as if we may well be dealing with a gap across which communication would seem to be impossible. What can be more different than the Aristotelian world of souls and forms and innate tendencies, and the Cartesian world of tiny machines? But there is another way of looking at the transition. The Aristotelian world contained more than just natural philosophy taken narrowly: it contained mechanics as well, the science of machines.[27] If we now think of the Aristotelian world as including *both* natural philosophy, strictly considered, *and* mechanics, the science of the artificial that complemented natural philosophy taken narrowly, then the transition from the Aristotelian to the mechanist world looks rather different.

27. Because of this, it is wrong to imagine that there was a radical contrast between mathematical views of the world and Aristotelian, and to see the Scientific Revolution of the seventeenth century as the replacement of the one by the other. For such a view, see, e.g., Alexandre Koyré's classic *Galileo Studies* (Atlantic Highlands: Humanities Press, 1978). For the sixteenth-century savant, there was no tension between the two: Aristotelian natural philosophy could coexist alongside mechanics.

Earlier I emphasized the extent to which Descartes transformed the science of mechanics. But however different it may have been from earlier mechanics, I have no doubt that Descartes' enterprise was fully intelligible to the practitioner of pre-Cartesian mechanics, just as pre-Cartesian mechanics was fully intelligible to Descartes. Though Descartes excised the teleology from machines and the science of mechanics, the conception that he replaced it with was not unfamiliar to the Aristotelian. Even if we give up the characterization of mechanics in terms of artificial machines and their purposes, the idea of things that operate through the size, shape, and motion of their parts is as intelligible to the Aristotelian as it is to the Cartesian. After all, the mechanic built machines that operate through wheels, gears, and pulleys long before Descartes elevated their trade to the level of a natural philosophy. Though he focused on a different aspect of the machine than his predecessors did, the toolbox he had in mind in this connection would have been familiar to any working mechanic, even if Descartes saw more things as machines, oysters and magnets, for example, than did his Aristotelian counterpart.[28]

Descartes, in fact, depended on the fact that his enterprise was intelligible to his Aristotelian reader. In a famous passage in the *Meteors*, for example, he wrote the following:

> . . . to avoid a breach with the philosophers, I have no wish to deny any further items which they may imagine in bodies over and above what I have described [i.e. small corpuscles of different sizes, shapes, and motions], such as 'substantial forms', their 'real qualities', and so on. It simply seems to me that my arguments must be all the more acceptable in so far as I can make them depend on fewer things. (AT VI, 239)

There is, of course, something disingenuous in this passage: Descartes was, indeed, trying to put something past the Aristotelians, as he frankly told his then-disciple, Henricus Regius.[29] Not for a minute did Descartes think that we need to posit forms and qualities. But at the same time the efficacy of the ruse depends on the fact that his mechanical philosophy shares a domain of intelligibility with the science of mechanics as understood by the Aristotelian: it depends on the fact that even the Aristotelian recognizes a domain in which it is possible and, indeed, proper to explain phenomena as the mechanic does, in terms of the size, shape, and motion of the parts of a body, and that that is not at all inconsistent with there

28. Treating living things as machines was not altogether foreign to the Aristotelian tradition in mechanics. In the *Mechanica*, for example, the author uses the tools of mechanics to explain a variety of natural phenomena, such as why pebbles on beaches are rounded (§ 15), or why when people stand from a sitting position they make an acute angle between the thigh and the lower leg (§ 30). Even from the point of view of the Aristotelian, there were some natural phenomena that are to be explained not in terms of forms, qualities, and prime matter, but in terms of the size, shape, and motion of its parts, as if they were machines. Descartes can be seen as just taking this a step (or many steps) further.

29. Descartes to Regius, January 1642, AT III, 492. Descartes also refers to this passage in the *Fourth Replies*, AT VII, 248–249; he seems to have been very proud of it.

being another domain in which explanation in terms of form and matter is appropriate. Descartes' strategy was to argue that phenomena of dioptrics and meteors fall within the domain of the mechanical; he just neglected to say that for him, *everything* falls within this domain. Descartes made a similar observation in his *Principia Philosophiae*:

> *I have used no principles in this treatise which are not accepted by everyone; this philosophy is nothing new but is extremely old and very common.*
>
> I should also like it to be noted that in attempting to explain the general nature of material things I have not employed any principle which was not accepted by Aristotle and all other philosophers of every age. So this philosophy is not new, but the oldest and most common of all. I have considered the shapes, motions, and sizes of bodies and examined the necessary results of their mutual interaction in accordance with the laws of mechanics, which are confirmed by reliable everyday experience. And who has ever doubted that bodies move and have various sizes and shapes, and that their various different motions correspond to these differences in size and shape; or who doubts that when bodies collide bigger bodies are divided into many smaller ones and change their shapes? (Pr IV, 200)

Again, there is something a bit disingenuous here. Though the general mode of explanation in terms of size, shape, and motion was certainly accepted by the followers of Aristotelian mechanics in its appropriate domain, they would certainly deny that *all* natural phenomena can be so explained, just as Descartes would deny that some natural phenomena must be explained in terms of substantial form and prime matter. But again, Descartes was appealing to a common area of intelligibility in order to make his program acceptable to the Aristotelian. Even if the Aristotelian would balk at the claim that *everything* is explicable mechanically, he cannot claim not to understand it.

Descartes was certainly right to assume that his Aristotelian reader could understand what he was up to. Consider, for example, the case of Libertus Fromondus, a professor of theology at the University of Louvain, a defender of the Aristotelian philosophy and a harsh critic of the Epicurean atomism then becoming particularly fashionable. Unsurprisingly, Fromondus was not at all sympathetic to Descartes' project. In a letter from Fromondus to Plempius, 13 September 1637, he made the following remark about Descartes' account of body in the *Meteors*:

> That composition of bodies made up of parts of different shapes . . . by which they reciprocally cohere as by little hooks, seems excessively crass and mechanical. (AT I, 406)[30]

---

30. Fromondus here was complaining specifically about the account of the composition of water, earth, ice, etc. from smaller parts in order to explain their general properties in the *Meteors*, AT VI, 233–234, 237–238.

Descartes immediately took offense at this, and saw it as a general challenge to his mechanical philosophy. In his reply (Descartes to Plempius for Fromondus, 3 Oct. 1637), he wrote:

> If my philosophy seems too "crass" for him, because, like mechanics, it considers shapes and sizes and motions, he is condemning what seems to me its most praiseworthy feature, of which I am particularly proud. I mean that in my kind of philosophy I use no reasoning which is not mathematical and evident, and all my conclusions are confirmed by true observational data ... So if he despises my style of philosophy because it is like mechanics, it is the same to me as if he despised it for being true. (AT I, 420–1)

Fromondus certainly did not approve of what Descartes was proposing, but there is no question but that he understood exactly what Descartes was up to.

In this way, machines and the science of mechanics, common both to Aristotelian thinkers and Cartesian, provided a clear pivot point between the two worlds, a point of common conception that enabled the two to remain intelligible to one another even as they were arguing for radically different ways of understanding the world.[31]

There is a tendency in the literature to think of the rise of the mechanical philosophy as if it were a relatively simple matter, as if the mechanical philosophy rose full blown and fully formed from the head of Zeus sometime in the early 1600s and quickly marched to victory over its outmoded and degenerate Aristotelian opponents. Things weren't that simple. Aristotelian natural philosophy was to maintain its vigor (and its dominance in many circles) for some years to come. Furthermore, Descartes' mechanical philosophy was only one strand among many in the anti-Aristotelian camp in the period; many of that period who we now tend to group with Descartes among the mechanists, such as Galileo, Gassendi, Mersenne, and Hobbes, saw one another as competitors first, and allies against Aristotelianism only second. (We must remember here that not everyone who opposed Aristotle in the early seventeenth century was anywhere near the scientific sensibility of those whom we group among the mechanists.) It will be some years, perhaps not until the 1660s, before we can talk with confidence about *the*

---

31. In this respect the domain of mechanics and the machinist's workroom functioned as a kind of "trading zone" between the Aristotelian and the Cartesian mechanist, to use Peter Galison's extremely fruitful anthropological analogy. See Peter Galison, *Image and Logic: A Material Culture of Microphysics* (Chicago: University of Chicago Press, 1997), chapter 9. Galison writes: "Two groups can agree on rules of exchange even if they ascribe utterly different significance to the objects being exchanged; they may even disagree on the meaning of the exchange process itself. Nevertheless, the trading partners can hammer out a *local* coordination despite vast *global* differences ... [I]n focusing on local coordination, rather than global meaning, one can understand the way engineers, experimenters, and theorists interact" (pp. 783–784). To this one can add Aristotelians and Cartesians. I thank Roger Ariew for pointing out the obvious connection between my concerns in this section and Galison's ideas.

mechanical philosophy, as opposed to a somewhat rag-tag collection of anti-Aristotelian programs that share some features but differ in other important respects.[32] In this essay I have tried to document some aspects of how a mechanical philosophy arose in the case of Descartes, the way in which Descartes transformed the notion of mechanics when he placed it at the center of his own natural philosophy and the way in which machines and mechanics continued to connect Descartes' thought to the intellectual landscape of his predecessors. But this is only part of a larger story.[33]

32. See the remarks above in note 20.

33. This essay started life as two distinct and somewhat contradictory projects, one about the radical distinction between Descartes' program and sixteenth-century mechanics, and the other about the continuity between Descartes and earlier thought, before I realized that the two stories are really complementary. They come together here for the first time. Earlier versions of this material were delivered at Virginia Tech, the University of Wyoming, the University of California, Berkeley, the Centre Alexandre Koyré (Paris), the Keeling Colloquium at University College London (where my presentation received a very useful commentary from Tom Sorrel), Syracuse University, Princeton University, the University of Virginia, and the Eastern Division APA (the memorial session for Margaret Wilson). It also served as the material for some of my seminars at the NEH Summer Seminar I co-directed with Roger Ariew in summer 2000. I would like to thank audiences at all of those presentations for their help, but especially Roger Ariew, my best critic.

Midwest Studies in Philosophy, XXVI (2002)

"Presence" and "Likeness" in Arnauld's Critique of Malebranche

NANCY KENDRICK

The debate between Malebranche and Arnauld concerning the nature of ideas rests on a disagreement about whether representative ideas are modifications of the mind, as they are for Arnauld, or entities distinct from the mind's modifications, as they are for Malebranche. As Malebranche explains in *The Search after Truth*, awareness of sensations, for example, does not require ideas, for "these things are in the soul, or rather . . . they are but the soul itself existing in this or that way."[1] Sensations are, for Malebranche, non-representative modifications of the mind. When we feel pain, see color, or feel sad, these perceptions/sensations do not represent anything external to the mind. Rather, they are modes of the mind, "just as the actual roundness and motion of a body are but that body shaped and moved in this or that way" (ST, 218). Ideas, which are in God, and which are necessary for us to perceive external objects, represent the geometric properties of external objects. These representative ideas are not modifications of the mind, though they do stand in some relation to our minds.[2] They are, in Malebranche's words, "intimately joined" to it.

In contrast, Arnauld holds that both sensations and representative ideas are modifications of the mind.[3] Indeed, ideas can have no other relation to a mind. In

---

1. Nicolas Malebranche, *The Search after Truth*, trans. by Thomas M. Lennon and Paul J. Olscamp (Columbus, OH: Ohio State University Press, 1980), 218. (This work is abbreviated as "ST" hereafter.)

2. Nor are they modifications of God's mind. See ST, 625.

3. In "Arnauld's Alleged Representationalism," *Journal of the History of Philosophy* 12 (1974), Monte Cook claims that "Arnauld admits that some modifications of the soul, namely sensations, are non-representative" (54). Steven Nadler disagrees, arguing in *Arnauld and the Cartesian Philosophy of Ideas* (Manchester, England: Manchester University Press, 1989) that Arnauld points out in the Fourth Set of Replies to Descartes' *Meditations* that "sensations are clearly

short, ideas of external objects are, for Arnauld, essentially representative modalities, while for Malebranche ideas of external objects are representative, but they are not modalities. For this reason, Arnauld charges that Malebranche's ideas are "entities distinct from perception."

Arnauld claims that Malebranche is deceived into positing these "ideas distinct from perception" because he has "blindly accept[ed] . . . two principles . . . : that the soul can perceive bodies only if they are present, and that bodies can only be present to it through certain representative beings, called ideas or species, which are similar to them and take their place, and which are intimately united in their stead with the soul."[4] These principles of "presence" and "likeness" are, respectively, the subject of Arnauld's attack. I discuss these in order to show why Arnauld believes that Malebranche's "ideas distinct from perception" present an answer to what is, in fact, a pseudo-problem.

One of Malebranche's arguments for the necessity of an idea being "present" to the mind occurs in Book III of *The Search after Truth:*

> I think everyone agrees that we do not perceive objects external to us by themselves. We see the sun, the stars, and an infinity of objects external to us; and it is not likely that the soul should leave the body to stroll about the heavens, as it were, in order to behold all these objects. Thus, it does not see them by themselves, and our mind's immediate object when it sees the sun, for example, is not the sun, but something that is intimately joined to our soul, and this is what I call an *idea.* Thus, by the word *idea,* I mean here nothing other than the immediate object, or the object closest to the mind, when it perceives something . . . It should be carefully noted that for the mind to perceive an object, it is absolutely necessary for the idea of that object to be actually present to it—and about this there can be no doubt. (ST, 217)

One type of objection that Arnauld raises in *On True and False Ideas* to the "presence" doctrine focuses on the fact that the way in which ideas are thought to be present to the mind is based on an erroneous analogy with corporeal presence. Consequently, ideas are taken to be spatially or "locally" present to the mind. Arnauld objects that this analogy fails, because, in fact, "the object must be absent from [the eye], since it must be at a distance, and if it were in the eye or too close to the eye, it could not be seen" (TFI, 16). Arnauld's claim is true, but it does not go very far in undermining the view that "present to the mind" is to be understood as spatial or local presence. For if the spatial analogy is itself suspect, it is made no less so by claiming that things need to be at a distance from the eye.

In a second consideration of Malebranche's "strolling mind" argument noted above, Arnauld focuses not on *how* ideas might be present to the mind, but rather

capable of representing, or presenting or displaying a positive content to the mind" (83). My point is simply that representative ideas are modifications of mind for Arnauld. Whether sensations are representative or not, they are also modifications of the mind.

4. Antoine Arnauld, *On True and False Ideas*, trans. by Elmar J. Kremer (Lewiston, NY: The Edwin Mellen Press, 1990), 15. (This work is abbreviated as "TFI" hereafter.)

on Malebranche's reasoning that it is precisely because external objects themselves are spatially distant from us, and thus not present to the mind, that something else must stand in for them that is present to the mind. Arnauld mockingly
describes Malebranche's view in the following way: "In place of the sun, which
would not seem to leave its place so often (that would be too great a difficulty)
we have very cleverly discovered a certain *representative being* to take its place
and to make up for its absence by being intimately united to our souls. We have
given the name of *idea* or *species* to that *being which is representative* of the
sun . . ."(TFI, 36).

Arnauld claims that the principle "our soul cannot see or know or perceive
. . . objects distant from the place where it is, insofar as they remain distant" is "of
the utmost falsity" (TFI, 36), and that it is quite evident that "our soul can know
countless things distant from the place where it is" (TFI, 36). But when Arnauld
gives his evidence for this, he shifts the ground of the debate. He directs us to
Postulate 5 and Definition 9 of Chapter 5, both of which concern our knowledge
of the existence of the external world. The explanation he gives there is not how
we can see, know, or perceive objects at a distance, but how we can know that there
are any objects at all.

First, Arnauld claims that if the senses cannot assure us of the existence of
the external world, reason can. And if reason fails, faith can succeed. (Malebranche
agrees with the latter position.) He concludes "[c]onsequently . . . [since I] have
faith in addition to reason, it is very certain that when I see the earth, the sun, the
stars, and men who converse with me, I do not see imaginary bodies or men, but
works of God and true men whom God has created like me" (TFI, 23). Second,
he claims that although he has to *reason* to the idea of the sun, the stars, the earth,
etc., *as* existing, rather than having this certainty in the *first awareness* of each of
those ideas, "the idea which represents to me the earth, the sun and the stars as
truly existing outside my mind no less merits the name 'idea' than if I had it without
need of reasoning" (TFI, 21). What Arnauld has presented here is not an argument that "our soul can know countless things distant from the place where it is."
Malebranche's (alleged) position—that it is the spatial distance between objects
and a mind that necessitates an idea to make good the absence of the object—
may be false, but it is not equivalent to denying that we can know (by reason or
faith or in whatever way) that external objects exist. Either Arnauld has conflated
the skeptical problem with the problems generated by "ideas distinct from perception," or he thinks Malebranche has.

In any case, it is not entirely clear that Malebranche means the "strolling
mind" argument literally. In the *Réponse*, he says "[i]s it not clear that what I said
was more a kind of jest rather than a principle upon which I establish sentiments
which undermine this same principle?"[5] Even Arnauld presents the motivation for

---

5. Quoted in Steven Nadler, Réponse de l'auteur De la Recherche de la Vérité au livre de
M. Arnauld des vrayes et des fausses idées, in *Malebranche and Ideas* (Oxford: Oxford University Press, 1992), 71. Nadler adds "I see no reason for not taking Malebranche at his word here,
when he denies that the kind of presence he intends as necessary for immediate perception . . . is
local."

Malebranche's representative ideas that stand in for objects spatially distant in something of a jestful way: "But mockery aside, it is certain that our friend has assumed . . . that our soul cannot see . . . objects distant from the place where it is" (TFI, 36).

It would seem, then, that Malebranche does not mean for "presence" to be taken in this simple sense of "locally" or spatially present, and, moreover, that Arnauld is aware of that. Nonetheless, Arnauld does get the last word here. For if spatial distance is not the issue giving rise to the need for ideas distinct from perceptions, then the argument of the "strolling" passage comes to nothing:

> For, if he were now forced to agree that local presence or distance has nothing to do with a body's being able or not being able to be the object of our mind, what he says about the distance of the sun and about the fact that our soul does not leave our body to go look for it would be as unreasonable as if, speaking to a low Breton who had addressed me in his language, which I do not understand, I complained that I was not able to understand anything that he had said to me, because he always spoke too softly. That would be ridiculous since with regard to a language that I do not understand, it is all the same to me whether someone speaks it to me softly or loudly. (TFI, 39)

There is, however, a more subtle interpretation that Arnauld offers of Malebranche's position that presence is to be thought of as local or spatial presence. It will help to clarify Arnauld's position here by looking to his discussion of a position advanced by Gassendi, whose aim is to show, against Descartes, that the soul is extended, and therefore material. Here is Gassendi's argument:

> Our soul has knowledge of bodies only through the ideas that represent them. But those ideas could not represent extended things unless they were material and extended themselves. Hence they are of that kind. But in order to enable the soul to know bodies, they must be present to the soul, i.e., be received in the soul. Therefore, the soul must be extended and consequently corporeal. (TFI, 15)

Gassendi's position has an important implication that bears on the Arnauld-Malebranche debate. Arnauld and Malebranche agree with the first premise of Gassendi's argument, that is, we know bodies by means of ideas that represent them. And at least on the surface, they both disagree with the second premise. However, this premise presupposes that the relation between an idea and that which the idea represents is isomorphic. And Arnauld alleges both that Malebranche accepts this implication of the materialist premise, and that this acceptance leads him to advance presence as a criterion for knowledge of external bodies. Although Malebranche "spiritualizes" Gassendi's material ideas, he does accept the third premise of Gassendi's argument: Ideas must be present to the mind.

The point about isomorphism is made clearer in the following objection Arnauld raises against Malebranche:

> If the object of understanding had to meet the condition of being locally present to our soul in order to be known, it would have to be the case that, just as our will cannot love anything as bad, so our understanding could not conceive anything as locally absent from our soul. But we cannot doubt that our mind conceives countless things as absent from the place where our soul is. When for example, the mother of the young Tobias cried so bitterly because he had not yet returned, her mind certainly conceived of him as absent from her. Thus, local presence is not a necessary condition of an object's being able to be seen by our soul, and consequently, local absence contributes nothing to its not being able to be seen. (TFI, 39–40)

Arnauld is not saying that we can conceive of or perceive objects that are spatially distant from the mind. That is, his concern here is not Malebranche's (alleged) view that the spatial distance of bodies from minds keeps us from perceiving them directly.[6] Rather, his point is that a conception can be *present* to the mind that represents the *absence* of the object conceived. In other words, Arnauld sees Malebranche as unable to account for the fact that we can conceive of something *as* absent. Arnauld's objection is this: if conceiving something *as* present requires the spatial presence of a representative entity, then it would be impos-sible to conceive something as absent, since that would require the spatial absence of a representative entity.

Furthermore, Arnauld sees this position leading to the acceptance of the third premise of Gassendi's argument as well: if these representative entities, understood either as material or mental—are to assist the mind, they must be present to it or received in it. And once they are present to the mind, they must be perceived by it. In yet another objection to Malebranche, Arnauld says:

> I assume that my soul is not thinking of any bodies, but that it is occupied with the thought of itself . . . The question is how it can pass from that thought to the thought of body A. You claim that it can see body A only through a certain *being representative* of it. But I ask you whether it will suffice that the *representative being* . . . be intimately united to my soul, unless a new modification is brought about in my soul, i.e., unless it receives

6. John Laird sees the passage above precisely as a response to Malebranche's (supposed) commitment to the view that the spatial distance of an object (in this case the young Tobias) pro-hibits our knowing it. He says: "[i]f the mind, [Malebranche] says, saw the sun and the stars *par eux-memes* it would have to sally forth and take a walk among them. This is local contact with a vengeance and Arnauld, having to refute a dogma so fantastically put, twists the knife round and round from a variety of angles. His point is that the local absence of things has nothing to do with the possibility of knowing them. A mother may surely weep for her absent child . . ." "The 'Legend' of Arnauld's Realism," *Mind* XXXIII (1924), 12. However, as I show, Arnauld is not objecting that, according to Malebranche, the mother's mind is not where young Tobias is.

a new perception. Obviously not, for that *representative being* can be of no use unless the soul perceives it. (TFI, 45)

Here, Arnauld is pointing out the trouble he has with Malebranche's view that representative ideas are not modifications of the mind. Malebranche's representative entities cannot do any work unless the mind perceives them.

The treatment of "present to the mind" as spatial or local presence may show that Malebranche's position is muddled, but it does not show that his "ideas distinct from perception" are irrelevant, unnecessary, or superfluous. Yet Arnauld claims they are. It is this line of Arnauld's argument to which I now turn.

A second way of understanding Malebranche's claim that bodies cannot be present to or intimately joined to the mind points to the ontological distinction between the material and the mental. Malebranche clearly regards the fact that body is extended and mind unextended as what prohibits bodies from being present to the mind, and it is precisely this ontological gulf that makes it impossible for bodies to be known by the mind directly—that is, without ideas distinct from perception.

But as for things outside the soul, we can perceive them only by means of ideas, given that these things cannot be intimately joined to the soul . . . [H]ere I am speaking mainly about material things, which certainly cannot be joined to our soul in the way necessary for us to perceive them, because with them extended and the soul unextended, there is no relation between them. (ST, 218–9)

Material things, in virtue of their materiality, cannot be intimately joined to the soul. Thus, if they are to be known, something else must both stand in for them and be of the proper ontological sort. Ideas, it would seem, fit the profile.[7]

Now, Arnauld does not reject Malebranche's dualism: the extended and material is ontologically distinct from the unextended and mental. But he does reject Malebranche's view that the ontological gulf between mind and body entails an epistemological gulf. As Arnauld says, "[I]t is the most badly founded fantasy in the world to propose that a body *qua* body is not an object proportioned to the soul in the way it must be to be known by it" (TFI, 46). It is one thing to say that mind and body are too different to causally interact.[8] But it is quite another, at least as Arnauld sees it, to say that mind and body are too different for the latter to be *known by* the former.

Arnauld sees quite clearly that what prevents Malebranche from holding that the soul can know external bodies in precisely the way it knows itself—i.e.,

7. Nadler notes that Malebranche has some trouble here; it is not clear what sort of relation these ideas can have to a mind, since they are not modifications of it. "If ideas are not mental, if they are neither minds nor modifications of mind, then in what sense are they the right ontological type for 'intimate union' with the mind?" *Malebranche and Ideas*, 75.

8. This is a standard Cartesian view, though Descartes casts some doubt on it when he claims that it is a "false supposition . . . that if the soul and the body are two substances whose nature is different, this prevents them from being able to act on each other" (CSM II, 275).

directly, without the need for representative entities distinct from the mind's modifications or perceptions—"is that bodies are too coarse and too dispropor- tionate to the spirituality of the soul to be able to be seen immediately" (TFI, 46). The "disproportionate" distance between minds and bodies here is ontological, not spatial. But Arnauld denies that the ontological "distance" entails that the mate- rial cannot be known by the mind. His view is that to be knowable is "an insepa- rable property of being, just as much as being *one*, being *true*, and being *good*, or rather it is the same as being *true*, since whatever is true is the object of the under- standing . . ." (TFI, 46). Intelligible being is, for Arnauld, a certain manner of being. This is made quite explicit in his use of Descartes' concept of objective existence.

> What is called *being objectively in the mind*, is not only being the object, at which my thought terminates, but it is being in my mind *intelligibly*, in the specific way in which objects are in the mind. The idea of the sun *is the sun, insofar as it is in my mind, not formally as it is in the sky, but objectively*, i.e., in the way that objects are in our thought, which is a way of being much more imperfect than that by which the sun is really existent, but which nevertheless we cannot say is nothing . . . (TFI, 21)

Thus, like Descartes, Arnauld contends that "the same thing can exist in two ways; formally insofar as it is a real (mind-independent) existent; and objectively insofar as it is thought of."[9] The sun existing objectively is a way of being, and it is a distinct way of being from the sun existing formally. That is, the sun's objective existence is is distinct manner of being from the sun's formal existence.

Arnauld agrees with Malebranche, then, that the mental and the material are ontologically distinct, but he denies that the result of this is that the latter cannot be known directly—that is, without ideas distinct from perception—by the former. For Arnauld, Malebranche's insistence that the material cannot be known directly by the mental is equivalent to saying that material being cannot be known by mental being. And as Arnauld sees it, this is to make intelligibility, or "being known," another, in fact, a superfluous relation between the mental and the material, requiring a superfluous entity, viz., ideas.

When Arnauld considers Malebranche's second principle—that the "like- ness" or similarity representations bear to objects permits them to stand in for the objects and be present to the mind—he argues that likeness can be understood only as likeness between ontological types:

> When it is said that our ideas and our perceptions . . . represent to us the things that we conceive, and are the images of them, it is in an entirely dif- ferent sense than when we say that pictures represent their originals and are images of them, or that words . . . are images of our thoughts. With regard to ideas, it means that the things that we conceive are *objectively* in our mind and in our thought. But this *way of being objectively in the mind*, is so

---

9. Thomas M. Lennon, "Philosophical Commentary," in *The Search after Truth*, 799.

peculiar to mind and to thought, being what . . . constitutes their nature, that we would look in vain for anything similar in the realm of what is not mind and thought. As I have already remarked, what confuses this entire matter of *ideas* is that people want to use comparisons with corporeal things to explain the way in which objects are represented by our ideas, even though there can be no true relation here between bodies and minds. (TFI, 20)

Arnauld is again insisting that the same thing can exist in two ways: formally or mind-independently,[10] and objectively, or mind-dependently. The sun existing objectively is a manner of being, and it is a distinct manner of being from the sun existing formally. Furthermore, the sun existing objectively is a kind of existence specific to the mind, so that one could not find anything similar to this outside the mind. Something else may be found outside the mind, viz., the sun existing formally, but that's not *like* the way the sun exists objectively.[11] Similarly, the way the sun exists formally (i.e., as a material object) is a kind of existence specific to material objects, so that one could not find anything similar to this "inside" the mind.

Arnauld is denying that ideas can bear a likeness to extended objects on the grounds that ideas and extended objects are ontologically distinct. Malebranche also subscribes to this view, but he takes it to entail that minds cannot know bodies directly, that is, without ideas distinct from perception. It is in drawing this erroneous conclusion that Arnauld thinks Malebranche has created a problem where there is none. For if ontological dualism commits one at least to the view that some being is mental and some being is material, then the question, How does the intelligible kind of being *know* the material kind of being? is senseless. On Arnauld's interpretation, this question (Malebranche's question) cannot arise. The problem it alleges is, in short, a pseudo-problem. Thus, *any* answer Malebranche gives to it, that is, any entities he might propose as necessary to explain the additional "being known by" relation, would be irrelevant. For Arnauld, "ideas taken in the sense of representative beings, distinct from perceptions, are not needed by our soul in order to see bodies" (TFI, 18). And this is because there is no further knowledge relation to be explained.[12]

---

10. Formal existence is mind-independent existence, but it is not *merely* mind-independent existence. The sun existing formally is not the sun existing merely mind-independently, but existing mind-independently in the specific way in which extended objects exist, viz., materially.

11. Berkeley would later object to this "double existence" theory, but he would approve of the claim that one seeks in vain to find a "likeness" of ideas external to the mind. This is, indeed, Berkeley's "likeness principle," and it becomes the basis for his attack on materialism. See Berkeley's *Treatise Concerning the Principles of Human Knowledge*, especially sections 8 and 90.

12. I thank Tim Griffin for his helpful comments on an earlier draft of this paper.

Pascal's Wagers[1]

JEFF JORDAN

Pascal is best known among philosophers for his wager in support of Christian belief.[2] Since Ian Hacking's classic article on the wager, three versions of the wager have been recognized within the concise paragraphs of the *Pensées*.[3] In what follows I argue that there is a fourth to be found there, a version that in many respects anticipates the argument of William James in his 1896 essay "The Will to Believe."[4] This fourth wager argument, I contend, differs from the better-known three in that it has as a premise the proposition that theistic belief is more rewarding than non-belief in this life, whether God exists or not. As we will see, this proposition provides a way of circumventing the many-gods objection. From the four wagers found in Pascal's *Pensées*, I argue, one can salvage the resources for a version of the wager, Pascalian in nature, even if not in origin, immune to the many-gods objection. A brief comment on the apologetic role Pascal intended for the wagers played is our first task at hand.

THE APOLOGETIC ROLE OF THE WAGERS

While it is impossible to know the role in his projected apologetic work Pascal intended for his wagers, there are hints. Two prominent hints come early in frag-

1. I am grateful to several people who read and offered helpful comments: Steve Davis, Alan Hájek, J. J. MacIntosh, Joel Pust, Paul Saka, David Silver, and Doug Stalker.
2. *Pensées*, translated by Honor Levi (Oxford: Oxford University Press, 1995), 153–6. In the Levi translation, the relevant passage is #680; in the Lafuma edition the passage is #343. All *Pensées* page citations are hereafter cited in the text and are to the Levi edition. *Pensées* numbered passages are cited with the Levi number first, then the Lafuma number.
3. "The Logic of Pascal's Wager," *American Philosophical Quarterly* 9/2 (1972), 186–92.
4. "The Will to Believe" in *The Will to Believe and Other Essays in Popular Philosophy* (New York: Dover, 1956), 1–31.

ment #680.[5] The first is the sentence "Let us now speak according to natural lights" (153); and the second is the use of the indefinite article, "If there is a God, he is infinitely beyond our comprehension" (153). These sentences suggest that Pascal intended the wagers as arguments for the rationality of theistic belief, and not as arguments for the rationality of Christian belief. Theism is the proposition that there exists an all-powerful, all-knowing, morally perfect being. Judaism, Christianity, and Islam are all theistic religions. It is likely that Pascal had in mind a two-step apologetic strategy. The first step consists of arguments in support of theism generally, with the second step being arguments for Christianity in particular.

As an ecumenical argument in support of theism, the wagers were designed to shown that theistic belief of some sort was rational, while appeals to fulfilled prophecy and to miracles were Pascal's favored arguments in support of Christianity. Many of the *Pensées* fragments consist of arguments either that Christianity is the true religion, or that it is superior to Judaism and Islam in significant respects (see #235–76/397–429, for instance). If this speculation is sound, then Pascal's apology was very much in line with the standard seventeenth and eighteenth century apologetic strategy: argue first that there is a god, and then identify which god it is that exists. This is the strategy adopted by Robert Boyle (1627–91) and by Bishop John Tillotson (1630–94), for instance, and by those, like William Paley (1734–1805), who employed the design argument to argue for a divine designer and then used the argument from miracles to identify that designer.[6]

Earlier I mentioned that Pascal is known best for his wager in support of Christian belief. While that may be true, that recognition is misplaced if the argument of this section is correct. Pascal's wagers are arguments in support of theism generally, and not specifically for Christian theism.

THREE WAGERS[7]

About a third of the way into *Pensées* #680, a dialogue commences. Along with most commentators, I assume that Pascal formulates his wager arguments in response to questions and comments from an unnamed interlocutor.

Prior to presenting his wager arguments, Pascal sets the stage with certain observations. The first is that neither the nature nor existence of God admits of rational proof: "Reason cannot decide anything . . . Reason cannot make you

---

5. See Charles M. Natoli, "The Role of the Wager in Pascal's Apologetics," *New Scholasticism* 57 (1983), 98–106.

6. On Boyle, see *Final Causes of Natural Things* (1688); on Tillotson, see "The Wisdom of Being Religious" Sermon I, *Works of Tillotson*, vol. I (London: J. F. Dove, 1820), pp. 317–89; and see Paley's *A View of the Evidences of Christianity* (1795), Part 3, chapter 8.

7. For more detail on the various versions of the wager, see, in addition to Hacking, Edward McClennen, "Pascal's Wager and Finite Decision Theory" in *Gambling on God: Essays on Pascal's Wager* (Lanham, MD: Rowman & Littlefield, 1994), 115–37. And see Alan Hájek, "The Illogic of Pascal's Wager," *Proceedings of the 10th Logica International Symposium*, Liblice, ed. T. Childers et al., 239–49.

choose one way or the other, reason cannot make you defend either of two choices" (153). This should not be taken as asserting that evidence and argument are irrelevant to philosophical theology. Pascal did not think that. Certain kinds of arguments and evidence are irrelevant, while certain kinds are relevant.[8] Pascal clearly thought that his wager arguments were not only relevant but also rationally compelling. The wager presupposes a distinction between (A) a proposition being rational to believe, and (B) inducing a belief in that proposition being the rational thing to do. Although a particular proposition may lack sufficient evidential warrant, it could be, given the distinction between (A) and (B), that forming a belief in the proposition may be the rational thing, all things considered, to do. Pascal probably did not intend, nor should a Pascalian for that matter, to limit the dialectical force of the wager to pragmatic rationality only. The upshot of the wager, if sound, is that belief in God is the rational stance with all things considered. Let's distinguish between something being rationally compelling and something being plausible. An argument is rationally compelling if, upon grasping the argument, one would be irrational in failing to accept its conclusion. On the other hand, an argument is plausible if, upon grasping the argument, one would be reasonable or rational in accepting its conclusion, yet one would not be irrational in failing to accept it. Pascal believed that his wager made theistic belief rationally compelling.

A second observation made by Pascal is that wagering about the existence of God is unavoidable, ". . . you have to wager" (154). Wagering is a forced decision—to refuse to wager is tantamount to wagering against. A forced decision between alternatives occurs whenever deciding nothing is equivalent to one of the alternatives. We can understand wagering on God as taking steps to inculcate theistic belief. For those making a pro-wager, Pascal suggests a regimen of ". . . taking holy water, having masses said . . ." and imitating the faithful (156). Wagering against, then, is deciding not to take steps to bring about belief. It is not anachronistic to note the Jamesian similarities here: wagering about God arises because argument, evidence, and reason are inconclusive. Moreover, wagering is forced, and, clearly, the matter is momentous and involves, for most of Pascal's readers, living options.[9]

Be that as it may, Hacking in his important 1972 paper "The Logic of Pascal's Wager" identifies three versions within the *Pensées* fragments. The first, which Hacking dubs the "Argument from Dominance," is conveyed within the admonition to:

> . . . weigh up the gain and the loss by calling that heads that God exists . . .
> If you win, you win everything; if you lose, you lose nothing. Wager that he exists then, without hesitating. (154)

---

8. See, for instance, Daniel Foukes, "Argument in Pascal's *Pensées*," *History of Philosophy Quarterly* 6/1 (1989), 57–68.

9. One significant difference between Pascal's wagers and James' argument is that the latter is an argument for the permissibility of pro-belief, while the former argues for the rational obligation to believe.

Rational optimization requires adopting a particular alternative among several mutually exclusive and jointly exhaustive options, whenever doing so may render one better-off than by not doing so, and in no case could doing so render one worse-off. According to Pascal, theistic belief dominates.[10] Consider the following:

	God exists	~(God exists)[11]
Believe[12]	F1	F2
~(Believe)	F3	F4

In this matrix, there are two states of the world (possible ways that the world might be), one in which God exists and one in which God does not exist; and two acts (choices available to the agent), whether to bring about belief or not. Given that the outcomes associated with the acts have the following relations: F1 ≫ F3, and F2 is at least as good as F4, belief weakly dominates not believing.[13]

Following Pascal, no great disvalue has been assigned to F3. Nowhere in #680 does Pascal suggest that non-belief results in hell, or an infinite disutility, if God exists. Represented schematically the argument from dominance proceeds:

1. For any person S, if one of the alternatives, α, available to S has an outcome better than the outcomes of the other available alternatives, and never an outcome worse than the others, S should choose α. And,
2. Believing in God is better than not believing if God exists, and is no worse if God does not exist.[14] Therefore,
C. One should believe in God.

This first wager is an example of a decision under uncertainty. Whenever one deliberates with knowledge of the outcomes but no knowledge of the probabilities associated with those outcomes, one faces a decision under uncertainty. On the other hand, if one deliberates armed with knowledge of both the outcomes and the probabilities associated with those outcomes, one faces a decision under risk.

The transition to the second version of the wager is precipitated by the interlocutor's objection to the assumption that theistic wagering does not render one worse-off if God does not exist. In response Pascal introduces probability assignments to the discussion and, more importantly, the idea of an infinite utility:

10. As described, the first version of the wager is an argument from *weak* dominance.
11. Understanding God as the title for that individual, if any, who is omnipotent, omniscient, and morally perfect.
12. While it may be better to understand the acts as bringing about theistic belief, and remaining within non-belief, for convenience, I will formulate the acts as simply *Believe* and ~(*Believe*).
13. The expression $X \gg Y$ should be understood as X *greatly exceeds* Y.
14. Clearly enough, the acts in this case have no propensity to bring about the states.

Since there is an equal chance of gain and loss, if you won only two lives instead of one, you could still put on a bet. But if there were three lives to win, you would have to play . . . and you would be unwise . . . not to chance your life to win three in a game where there is an equal chance of losing and winning. (154)

While probability plays no part in the first argument, it has a prominent role in the second version of the wager, which Hacking calls the "Argument from Expectation." Built upon the concept of maximizing expected utility, the argument from expectation assumes that the probability that God exists is one-half, and that the outcome of right belief if God exists is of infinite utility.[15] With these assumptions, theistic belief easily outdistances not believing, no matter what finite value is found in F2, F3, or F4:

	God exists $\frac{1}{2}$	~(God exists) $\frac{1}{2}$	
Believe	0.5, ∞	0.5, F2	EU = ∞
~(Believe)	0.5, F3	0.5, F4	EU = finite value

Put schematically:

3. For any person S, and alternatives, α and β, available to S, if α has a greater expected utility than does β, S should choose α. And,
4. Given that the existence of God is as likely as not, believing in God carries more expected utility than does not believing. Therefore,
C. One should believe in God.

Hacking asserts that the assumption of equal chance is "monstrous." Perhaps it is. The beautiful thing about infinite utility, though, is that infinity multiplied by any finite value is still infinite.[16] The assumption that the existence of God is just as likely as not is needlessly extravagant, since, as long as the probability of the existence of God is judged to be greater than zero, believing will always carry an expected utility greater than that carried by non-belief. And this is true no matter the value or disvalue associated with the outcomes F2, F3, and F4. This observa-

---

15. One calculates the expected utility of an act φ by (i) multiplying the benefits and probabilities of each outcome associated with φ, (ii) subtracting any respective costs, and (iii) summing the totals from each associated outcome. Therefore, the expected utility of believing in God, given an infinite utility and 0.5 probabilities, is as follows:

$$(\infty \times \tfrac{1}{2}) + (F2 \times \tfrac{1}{2}) = \infty.$$

16. Assuming, plausibly enough, that no sense can be made in this context of infinitesimal probabilities.

tion underlies the third version of the wager, what Hacking titles the "Argument from Dominating Expectation," in which *p* represents a positive probability, with a range greater than zero and less than one-half:

	God exists, p	~(God exists), 1 − p	
Believe	p, ∞	1 − p, F2	EU = ∞
~(Believe)	p, F3	1 − p, F4	EU = finite value

No matter how unlikely it is that God exists, as long as there is some positive non-zero probability that he does, believing is one's best bet:

5. For any person S, and alternatives, α and β, available to S, if α has a greater expected utility than does β, S should choose α. And,
6. Believing in God has a greater expected utility than does not believing. Therefore,
C. One should believe in God.

Because of its ingenious employment of infinite utility, the third version has become what most philosophers think of as Pascal's wager. It is the canonical version. Even so, the argument from dominating expectation is not Pascal's most formidable.

PASCAL'S FOURTH WAGER[17]

The fourth version of the wager found in *Pensées* #680 resides in the concluding remarks that Pascal makes to his interlocutor:

> But what harm will come to you from taking this course? You will be faithful, honest, humble, grateful, doing good, a sincere and true friend. It is, of course, true; you will not take part in corrupt pleasure, in glory, in the pleasures of high living. But will you not have others?
> I tell you that you will win thereby in this life . . . (156).

The fourth version brings us full circle, away from arguments under risk and back to an argument under uncertainty. This version remedies the defect that precluded the first argument from strict dominance.

---

17. Edward McClennen asserts that a fourth version of the wager employing only finite utilities and something like the principle of indifference is also contained in #680. See McClennen, "Pascal's Wager and Finite Decision Theory," pp. 127–9.

	God exists	~(God exists)
Believe	∞	F2
~(Believe)	F3	F4

Like its predecessors, the fourth version implies that the benefits of belief vastly exceed those of non-belief if God exists; but, unlike the others, the fourth implies that F2 > F4. No matter what, belief is one's best bet. Belief strictly dominates non-belief. Let's call this version of the wager the "Argument from Strict Dominance":

7. For any person S, if among the alternatives available to S, the outcomes of one alternative, α, are better in every state than those of the other available alternatives, and the states are causally independent of the available actions, S should choose α. And,

8. Believing in God is better than not believing whether God exists or not. Therefore,

C. One should believe in God.

Premise (8) is true only if one gains simply by believing. Pascal apparently thought that this was obvious. Sincere theistic belief results, he thought, in virtuous living and virtuous living is more rewarding than vicious living. The response of Pascal's interlocutor, we might plausibly imagine, would be that Pascal has made an illicit assumption: why think that virtuous living requires theism? And even if virtuous living requires theism, why think that being morally better is tantamount to being better-off all things considered? Now whether virtue is its own reward only in a theistic context or not, the relevant point is whether theistic belief provides more benefit than not believing, even if God does not exist. If it does, then this is an important point when considering the many-gods objection.

THE MANY-GODS OBJECTION

Like the canonical version, the fourth version seems vulnerable to what is known as the many-gods objection. Notice that in all four Pascalian arguments the wager consists of a 2 × 2 matrix: there are two acts available to the agent, with only two possible states of the world. From Pascal's day to the present, critics have been quick to point out that Pascal's partitioning of the possible states of the world overlooks the obvious—what if some deity other than God exists? What if a deity exists, something like Michael Martin's "perverse master" deity that harbors animus toward theism, such that s/he rewards nonbelief?[18] In effect, the many-gods

18. Michael Martin, *Atheism: A Philosophical Justification* (Philadelphia: Temple University Press, 1990), pp. 232–4.

objection asserts that Pascal's 2×2 matrix is flawed because the states it employs are not jointly exhaustive of the possibilities.[19]

	G	N	D
Believe in G	∞ F1	F2	F3
Believe in Neither	F4	F5	∞ F6
Believe in D	F7	F8	∞ F9

With D representing the existence of a non-standard deity, a "deviant" deity, and N representing the world with no deity of any sort (call this state "naturalism"), theistic belief no longer strictly dominates.[20] With infinite utility residing in both column G and D, and, with the values of F3, F4, and F7, presumably the same, even weak dominance seems lost to theism.[21] Just as the many-gods objection is thought by many to be the bane of the third version, one might think it is fatal to the fourth version of the wager as well.

And so it is. The possibility of an infinite reward presented to nontheists defeats any theistic claim to dominance, weak or strict. Still all is not lost for the Pascalian. With (8) in hand, the Pascalian could salvage from the ruins of the fourth version a wager that circumvents the many-gods objection. Given that the lower two cells of the D column equal the upper cell of the G column, and that F3 = F4 = F7, the Pascalian could employ the N column as a principled way to adjudicate between believing theistically or not. That is, whether one believes theistically, or believes in a deviant deity, or refrains from believing in any deity at all, one is exposed to the same kind of risk (F3 or F4 or F7). The worst outcomes of theistic belief, of deviant belief, and of naturalistic belief are on par. Moreover, whether

19. The number of critics invoking the many-gods objection is legion. Among their number are Paul Saka, "Pascal's Wager and the Many-Gods Objection," *Religious Studies* 37 (2001), 321–41; Graham Priest, *Logic: A Very Short Introduction* (Oxford: Oxford University Press, 2000), 94–8; William Gustason, "Pascal's Wager and Competing Faiths," *International Journal for Philosophy of Religion* 44 (1998), 31–9; Richard Gale, *On the Nature and Existence of God* (New York: Cambridge University Press, 1991), 349–51; Antony Flew, "Is Pascal's Wager the Only Safe Bet?" *God, Freedom and Immortality* (Buffalo, NY: Prometheus, 1984), 61–8; Michael Martin, "Pascal's Wager as an Argument for Not Believing in God," *Religious Studies* 19 (1983), 57–64; J. L. Mackie, *The Miracle of Theism* (Oxford: Clarendon, 1982), 203; Peter Dalton, "Pascal's Wager: The Second Argument," *Southern Journal of Religion* 13 (1975), 31–46; Merle Turner, "Deciding for God—The Bayesian Support of Pascal's Wager" *Philosophy and Phenomenological Research* 29/1 (1968), 84–90; and James Cargile, "Pascal's Wager," *Philosophy* 41 (1966), 250–7.

20. By "non-standard deity," I mean the gerrymandered fictions of philosophers.

21. As before, I exclude infinite disutilities.

one believes theistically, or believes in a deviant deity, or refrains from believing in any deity at all, one enjoys eligibility for the same kind of reward ($\infty = \infty = \infty$). The best outcomes, that is, of theistic belief, of deviant belief, and of naturalistic belief are on par. The Pascalian claim of (8), however, is important. If (8) is well supported, then there is reason to believe that F2 > F5.

Is (8) well supported? Does theistic belief provide more benefit than not believing, even if God does not exist? To answer this, let's adopt something like Bentham's model of utility by stipulating that theistic belief provides more benefit than not believing, even if God does not exist (a better "this-world" outcome), if, on average, believing theistically ranks higher than not believing theistically in at least one of two categories, and is never lower than not believing in either of the two: (i) happiness, and (ii) longevity. To get a handle on the matter, let's assume that happiness correlates with greater life satisfaction. What do the studies show? With regard to (i), one researcher asserts "extensive studies have found the presence of religious beliefs and attitudes to be the best predictors of life satisfaction and a sense of well-being."[22] A study from the University of Minnesota of 3,300 parents of twins found a small but statistically significant correlation (.07) between religious commitment and happiness.[23] More generally, a recent analysis of 100 studies, which examined the association of religious belief and life satisfaction, found that 80% of the studies reported at least one significant positive correlation between the variables.[24] This analysis grouped studies as being either statistically significant in one direction, or in the other direction, or having no statistical significance at all, and then "counted votes." But in the absence of any study that incorporates sample size and magnitude of effect, as well as vote counting, one can remain unmoved by the research with regard to (i).

The effect, if any, of theistic belief on longevity has been an object of study for over a century. In 1872 Francis Galton, a cousin of Darwin, conducted a retrospective study of the life span of royalty, compared with others of similar economic status.[25] Galton hypothesized that royalty have their length of life prayed for more often than do their economic peers, and yet he found no noticeable increase in royal longevity. Galton's study has not, however, survived the test of time. A much more recent (2000) and sophisticated meta-analysis of 29 independent studies, involving data from 125,000 subjects, found that "religious involvement had a significant and substantial association with increased survival."[26] In particular, frequent religious attendance (once a week or more) is associated with

---

22. Quoted in Ralph W. Hood, Jr., Bernard Spilka, Bruce Hunsberger, and Richard Gorsuch, *The Psychology of Religion* (New York: Guilford Press, 1996, 2nd ed.), 384.

23. David Lykken, *Happiness* (New York: St. Martin's Press, 1999), 18–19.

24. Harold Koenig, Michael McCullough, and David Larson, *Handbook of Religion and Health* (Oxford: Oxford University Press, 2001), 117, 215 ff.

25. Francis Galton, "Statistical Enquires into the Efficacy of Prayer," *The Fortnightly Review* 12 (August, 1872), 125–35.

26. Koenig, McCullough, and Larson, *Handbook of Religion and Health*, 328–30. For a detailed discussion of the meta-analysis, see M. E. Cullough, W. T. Hoyt, D. Larsen, H. G. Koenig, and C. E. Thoresen, "Religious Involvement and Mortality: A Meta-analytic Review," *Health Psychology* 19 (2000), 211–22.

a 25%–33% reduction in the rate of dying during follow-up periods ranging from 5 to 28 years. The increased survival rate associated with religious involvement was found to hold independent of possible confounders like age, sex, race, education, and health status. Unlike studies that simply "count votes," a meta-analysis incorporates sample size and magnitude effect. So even though this meta-analysis, like any social science statistical study, establishes a correlation and not causation, that is still reason to think that theism's this-world outcome is better than that of non-belief.

In addition, there is no reason to think there is any deviant analogue of (8). We have no reason, that is, to think that belief in a deviant deity correlates with the kind of positive benefits that correlate with theistic belief. But this absence of evidence to think that belief in a deviant deity correlates with positive benefit, conjoined with the obvious opportunity costs associated with such a belief, is itself reason to think that F2 > F8. Indeed, no matter how we might expand the matrix in order to accommodate the exotica of possible divinity, we would have reason to believe that F2 exceeds any this-world outcome associated with the exotica.[27] So, given that F2 > F5 and that F2 > F8, even if the 2×2 matrix is abandoned in favor of an expanded one, a Pascalian beachhead is established:

9. For any person S making a forced decision under uncertainty, if one of the alternatives, α, available to S has an outcome as good as the best outcomes of the other available alternatives, β and χ, and never an outcome worse than the worst outcomes of β and χ, and, excluding the best outcomes and worse outcomes, has only outcomes better than the outcomes of β and χ, S should choose α. And,
10. Theistic belief has an outcome better than the other available alternatives if naturalism obtains. Therefore,
C. One should believe in God.

Premise (9), which we might dub the "Next Best Thing" principle, is a cousin of the weak dominance principle. The same considerations that support the weak dominance principle also support the Next Best principle. If there is at least one state in which a particular alternative has an outcome better than that of the others and, moreover, that alternative has no outcome worse than the worst outcomes of the other alternatives, then that alternative weakly dominates. Decision-theoretic principles are guides to systematic deliberation, and the Next Best Thing principle advises that decisions should be made in much the same way as dominance principles. Given that the best outcomes and the worst outcomes are on par, one should choose an alternative, if any, whose outcomes are better than those of the other alternatives.

One might object that by returning to a decision under uncertainty, one forgoes the distinctive Pascalian element featured in the canonical version: no matter how unlikely it is that God exists, the infinite payoff guarantees an infinite

---

27. Even though it is possible to imagine any number of deviant gods, any extension beyond a 3×3 matrix is logically redundant given that F2 exceeds the "this world" outcomes of the deviant deities, and given that the best cases and worse cases are on par.

expected utility.[28] But there are good reasons why a Pascalian would be well advised to forego the idea of infinite utility.[29] For one thing, as Anthony Duff has pointed out, deliberating with infinite utilities seems to result in an embarrassment of Pascalian riches.[30] Given a possible infinite utility and any positive non-zero probability, it looks as though any and every action carries an infinite expected utility. This fifth version of the wager saves the Pascalian the effort of trying to limit that embarrassment by returning to Pascal's first version of the wager. Another reason that the Pascalian would be well-advised to forego the infinite is that she can get her conclusion without relying on problematic decision-theoretic concepts. Most people, I suspect, have only naturalism and theism as live options, even if they admit the logical possibility of certain theological exotica, a calculation of expected utilities employing only finite utilities and probabilities, would likely conform to the ranking displayed in the fifth wager.[31]

This fifth version of the wager, unlike its predecessors, is valid and is not obviously unsound: one can reasonably accept both premises. Perhaps the most interesting feature of it is that the contemporary evidence in support of (10), evidence not available to Pascal, provides the wager relief from the many-gods objection. With this fifth wager in hand, we might do no better than to invoke James again, "Pascal's argument, instead of being powerless, then seems a regular clincher, and is the last stroke needed to make our faith . . . complete."[32]

28. Such a complaint is found in J. J. MacIntosh, "Is Pascal's Wager Self-Defeating?" *Sophia* 39/2 (2000), 6–13.

29. For reasons why infinite utilities should be abandoned, see my "Pascal's Wager Revisited," *Religious Studies* 34 (1998), 419–31.

30. "Pascal's Wager and Infinite Utilities," *Analysis* 46 (1986), 107–9.

31. For an argument supporting this assertion, see my "Pascal's Wager Revisited," 427–30.

32. James, op. cit., 11.

Midwest Studies in Philosophy, XXVI (2002)

Eternity and Immortality in Spinoza's *Ethics*

STEVEN NADLER

I

Descartes famously prided himself on the felicitous consequences of his philosophy for religion. In particular, he believed that by so separating the mind from the corruptible body, his radical substance dualism offered the best possible defense of and explanation for the immortality of the soul. "Our natural knowledge tells us that the mind is distinct from the body, and that it is a substance . . . And this entitles us to conclude that the mind, insofar as it can be known by natural philosophy, is immortal."[1] Though he cannot with certainty rule out the possibility that God has miraculously endowed the soul with "such a nature that its duration will come to an end simultaneously with the end of the body," nonetheless, because the soul (unlike the human body, which is merely a collection of material parts) is a substance in its own right, and is not subject to the kind of decomposition to which the body is subject, it is by its nature immortal. When the body dies, the soul—which was only temporarily united with it—is to enjoy a separate existence.

By contrast, Spinoza's views on the immortality of the soul—like his views on many issues—are, at least in the eyes of most readers, notoriously difficult to fathom. One prominent scholar, in what seems to be a cry of frustration after having wrestled with the relevant propositions in Part Five of *Ethics*, claims that this part of the work is an "unmitigated and seemingly unmotivated disaster . . . rubbish that causes others to write rubbish."[2] Another more equaniminous scholar

---

1. "Second Set of Replies," *Oeuvres de Descartes*, 12 vols., eds. Charles Adam and Paul Tannery (Paris: J. Vrin, 1974–83), vol. 7, p. 153.
2. Jonathan Bennett, *A Study of Spinoza's Ethics* (Indianapolis: Hackett, 1984), 357. He goes on to say that "I don't think that the final three doctrines [of Part Five] can be rescued. The only attempts at complete salvage that I have encountered have been unintelligible to me and poorly

confesses that "in spite of many years of study, I still do not feel that I understand this part of *Ethics* at all." He adds, "I feel the freedom to confess that, of course, because I also believe that no one else understands it adequately either."[3] Because of the complexity and opacity of Spinoza's account of the eternity of the mind, which involves some of the most difficult and puzzling propositions of *Ethics*, there has been, since the posthumous publication of his writings, a great deal of debate over whether he defends or allows for personal immortality or rejects it; even today no consensus has emerged.[4]

A number of scholars have thought that what Spinoza is up to, at least in *Ethics*,[5] is a denial of personal immortality, although there is very little agreement on just how he accomplishes this. Thus, Stuart Hampshire notes that, for Spinoza, while there is an eternal aspect of the mind, what survives the death of a person cannot possess any individuality. "The possible eternity of the human mind cannot . . . be intended to mean that I literally survive, as a distinguishable individual, in so far as I attain genuine knowledge; for in so far as I do attain genuine knowledge, my individuality as a particular thing disappears and my mind becomes so far united with God or Nature conceived under the attribute of thought."[6] While he does not necessarily find such an Averroist-type doctrine in *Ethics*, Curley agrees with Hampshire's general point. Despite the difficulty he claims to have in understanding Part Five, he says that "Spinoza does not have a doctrine of personal immortality. What 'remains' after the destruction of the body is not a person . . . whatever the doctrine of the eternity of the mind does mean, it does not mean that *I* can entertain any hope of immortality."[7] James Morrison, too, is of this opinion, although he insists that this is not because, as Hampshire claims, the mind is absorbed into the infinite attribute of thought, but because the essential condition of individuation for Spinoza—that is, the existence of the body—no longer obtains.[8] Although Yirmiyahu Yovel sees yet other reasons for denying that

related to what Spinoza actually wrote . . . After three centuries of failure to profit from it, the time has come to admit that this part of *Ethics* has nothing to teach us and is pretty certainly worthless . . . this material is valueless" (372, 374). Either Bennett is intentionally overstating his case, or he fails to understand the import of the entire work.

3. Edwin Curley, *Behind the Geometrical Method* (Princeton: Princeton University Press, 1988), 84.

4. The leaders of the Amsterdam Portuguese-Jewish congregation, on the other hand, had no trouble understanding what Spinoza had to say on this matter. Among the "heresies" for which he is reported to have received his *cherem*, or ban, from the congregation was the denial of the immortality of the soul; see *Spinoza: A Life* (Cambridge: Cambridge University Press, 1999), chapter 6. I examine the questions surrounding his ban, and especially the importance of the issue of immortality for that community, in *Spinoza's Heresy: Immortality and the Jewish Mind* (Oxford: Oxford University Press, 2002).

5. In this paper, I concentrate only on *Ethics*. The evidence for Spinoza's views on immortality from the earlier, aborted *Short Treatise on God, Man and His Well-Being* is more difficult to interpret. The final chapter of the work is entitled "On Immortality," but the upshot of the brief discussion is not immediately clear; see *Spinoza's Heresy*, chapter 5.

6. Stuart Hampshire, *Spinoza* (London: Penguin, 1951), 175.

7. Curley, *Behind the Geometric Method*, 84–6.

8. James Morrison, "Spinoza on the Self, Personal Identity and Immortality," in Graeme Hunter (ed.), *Spinoza: The Enduring Questions* (Toronto: University of Toronto Press, 1994), 31–47.

Spinoza held a robust doctrine of postmortem survival, he sums up this general line of interpretation nicely: "The transcendent-religious idea of an afterlife, in which our existence will be modified in proportion to what we have done in this life, is foreign to [Spinoza]."[9] There is, in other words, no personal immortality for Spinoza.

Now this is indeed a very tempting reading of Spinoza. It is, in fact, the one I shall argue for (although I shall offer different, more specific reasons as to why there is and can be no personal immortality in Spinoza's system). However, the more popular interpretation of Spinoza seems to be that which somehow finds in his philosophy an account of personal immortality, in one or another of that doctrine's classical senses. Generally speaking, one can hold that the soul is immortal either because as a "substance" (or, so as not to conflict with Spinoza's own metaphysical terminology, "thing") in its own right that is ontologically distinct from the mortal body, the entire soul persists after death (the so-called "Platonic" view); or because there is at least a *part* of the soul—which is in fact not a self-subsisting substance but the inseparable "form" of the body, most of which dies with the body—that remains after death (this is the "Aristotelian" view).[10] On either account, there is a spiritual element of the person—either the whole soul itself or some part of it—that persists, disembodied, after that person's death; an element that is identifiable with that person's self and that bears some relationship to the life he led. Spinoza is usually alleged to have held some version or another of one of these two positions.

Alan Donagan, for example, in much of his work on Spinoza, has adopted this reading. He insists that Spinoza's "affirmation of personal immortality" is not irreconcilable with the rest of his system, and that what remains of a person after his death is a particular, individuated, and personal essence—one, moreover, that bears a strong sense of self. Immortality for Spinoza, he claims, is a "personal and individual affair"; what persists postmortem is "a part of the individuating primary constituent of each mind . . . a part that retains its individuality."[11] I shall return to his arguments for this position below. More recently, Tamar Rudavsky has claimed that "Spinoza's theory of human immortality can in fact be rescued in a way that preserves individuality." Without saying why his views on the mind need such

---

9. Yirmiyahu Yovel, *Spinoza and Other Heretics*, vol. 1, *The Marrano of Reason* (Princeton: Princeton University Press, 1989), 170. Yovel, however, goes too far in limiting the eternity of the mind to what can be experienced in this life. See also Pierre-François Moreau, *Spinoza: L'expérience et l'éternité* (Paris: Presses Universitaires de France, 1994): "Il faut faire violence au texte pour y lire au premier plan une doctrine de l'immortalité de l'âme. Cela n'exlut pas une certaine forme d'immortalité dans le système—celle qui correspondrait à une survie de l'entendement sans imagination; mais elle a une signification limitée et spécifique, et il est impossible qu'elle épuise le sens du mot éternité. En tout cas elle ne concerne pas le totalité de l'âme: elle ne peut donc être assimilée à la conception religieuse traditionelle" (535).

10. This form of the distinction between two views on the immortality of the soul comes from Harry Wolfson, *The Philosophy of Spinoza* (Cambridge, MA: Harvard University Press, 1934), vol. 2, 289–90.

11. Alan Donagan, "Spinoza's Proof of Immortality," in Marjorie Grene (ed.), *Spinoza: A Collection of Critical Essays* (Garden City: Anchor, 1973), 252. See also his *Spinoza* (Chicago: University of Chicago Press, 1988), chapter 10.

rescuing,[12] she insists that "what we call immortality of soul, characterized as eternity of mind, for Spinoza must be personal. Within this unity of mind with God/Substance, there is still something of 'me' that remains."[13]

Perhaps the most extreme version of this reading of Spinoza, however, is also the most prominent one. Harry Wolfson, in his magisterial and justly celebrated study of Spinoza's philosophy, sees in *Ethics* as strong a doctrine of personal immortality as one could hope for. In fact, according to Wolfson, Spinoza is "merely reaffirming an old traditional belief," namely, that "the bliss and happiness of the immortal souls consist in the delight they take in the knowledge of the essence of God."[14] Immortality for Spinoza is, on his account, entirely personal: "the eternal preservation of something that was peculiar to a particular human being during his lifetime . . . the thought element of the mind that survives death bears the particular characteristics of the individual during his lifetime . . . the immortality of the soul, according to Spinoza, is personal and individual."[15] Indeed, Wolfson insists, Spinoza's goal is the entirely conservative project of defending the traditional rabbinic view of immortality against its latter-day critics: "[Spinoza's] main object was to affirm the immortality of the soul against those of his own time who denied it."[16] Spinoza is also concerned to show that there is nothing supernatural about immortality, that it is simply a part of the ordinary course of nature. (In what is the most astounding feature of his interpretation, Wolfson goes so far as to say that Spinoza "retains the traditional vocabulary and speaks of the immortality of the soul."[17] In fact, nothing could be further from the truth: Spinoza obviously goes to great lengths to avoid the traditional vocabulary. The phrase "immortality of the soul [*immortalitas animae*]" does not once appear in Spinoza's own account in *Ethics*. He consistently—and, I am sure, self-consciously—uses instead the phrase "eternity of the mind [*mentis aeternitas*]."[18] Wolfson's constant use of the words "immortality of the soul" to describe Spinoza's view is thus very puzzling indeed.)[19]

12. As I argue in the final section, the desire to "rescue" a "doctrine of immortality" for Spinoza is misguided and represents a fundamental misunderstanding of Spinoza's major project.

13. Tamar Rudavsky, *Time Matters: Time, Creation and Cosmology in Medieval Jewish Philosophy* (Albany: SUNY Press, 2000), 181, 186.

14. Wolfson, *The Philosophy of Spinoza*, vol. 2, 310–1.

15. Wolfson, *The Philosophy of Spinoza*, vol 2, 295.

16. Wolfson, *The Philosophy of Spinoza*, vol. 2, 323. Wolfson has in mind here, in particular, Uriel da Costa. But I believe that it is absolutely clear that Spinoza was, in fact, in agreement with da Costa on the question of immortality.

17. Wolfson, *The Philosophy of Spinoza*, vol. 2, 295.

18. As Moreau notes, "Spinoza distingue très rigoureusement ces deux notions"; see *Spinoza: L'expérience et l'éternité*, 534–6.

19. Numerous other authors attribute to Spinoza, as Wolfson does, an account of personal immortality. Some argue that Spinoza just worked hard to accommodate such a doctrine into his own metaphysical schema and language, to give a Spinozistic spin to it. In his book *The God of Spinoza* (Cambridge: Cambridge University Press, 1997), Richard Mason seems to take just this position (chapter 10). So does Seymour Feldman who, in his work on Gersonides, insists that for Spinoza "immortality is individually differentiated" (see the introduciton to his translation of *The Wars of the Lord* [Philadelphia: The Jewish Publication Society, 1984], vol. 1, p. 76). Other scholars, while noting that Part Five of *Ethics* speaks only of the *eternity* of the mind, insist that far

Despite the vigorous debate around this question, all hands would agree on at least one thing: the question of immortality was of concern to Spinoza from the beginning to the end of his relatively brief philosophical career. It is an issue that is central not only to his metaphysics of the person, but also to his views on religion, morality, and the state. However, it is equally important to see—as a result of both a close reading of his writings and a broader understanding of his philosophy as a whole—that Spinoza *did*, without question, deny the personal immortality of the soul. Given everything he believed about the nature of the soul, and more importantly about true virtue and the happiness of a human being, he *had* to deny that the soul is immortal. And he did so with absolute satisfaction.

II

In *Ethics*, the word *immortality* [*immortalitas*] occurs once and only once. It appears in a context in which Spinoza is describing the foolish beliefs of the multitude, who are often motivated to act virtuously only by their hope for an eternal reward and their fear of an eternal punishment. If they were not convinced that the soul lived on after the body, then morality—difficult as it is—would, in their eyes, not be a burden worth bearing. Such an opinion, he notes,

> seems no less absurd to me than if someone, because he does not believe he can nourish his body with good food to eternity, should prefer to fill himself with poisons and other deadly things, or because he sees that the Mind is not eternal, *or* immortal, should prefer to be mindless, and to live without reason. (Vp41s, G II.307/C 615–16)[20]

The main point of his discussion here is the importance and value of virtue in *this* life; that virtue is, in essence, its own reward. But the passage might also seem important with respect to the question of Spinoza's views on immortality. Spinoza does, as we shall see, argue for the *eternity* of the mind, and this text makes it look as though he is willing to equate the thesis of the eternity of the mind with the

---

from wishing to deny the personal immortality of the soul, Spinoza just wanted to stress its persistence outside of time rather than its mere everlastingness in time (C. Hardin, "Spinoza on Immortality and Time," in *Spinoza: New Perspectives*, eds. Robert W. Shahan and J. I. Biro [Norman: University of Oklahoma Press, 1978], 129–38); while still others, agreeing that for Spinoza there is personal survival after death, argue on the contrary that in fact the eternity of the mind should be understood as a kind of sempiternity (Martha Kneale, "Eternity and Sempiternity," in Grene, op. cit., 227–40; Donagan, "Spinoza's Proof of Immortality"). Finally, there are those who argue that Spinoza did not want to deny the immortality of the personal soul, but only that these immortal souls would be individuated in the same way as they are individuated in this life, that is, by way of their bodies (Erroll Harris, "Spinoza's Theory of Human Immortality," *The Monist* 55 [1971]).

20. All citations of *Ethics* incorporate part number (I–V), proposition (p), definition (d), scholium (s) and corollary (c). References to Spinoza's writings are to *Spinoza Opera*, ed. Carl Gebhardt, 5 vols. (Heidelberg: Carl Winters Universitatsverlag, 1972 [vol. 5, 1987]), abbreviated as "G"; and to the translations by Edwin Curley, *The Collected Works of Spinoza*, vol. 1 (Princeton: Princeton University Press, 1984), abbreviated as "C."

thesis of the immortality of the soul. However, he is here only describing, in a rather derisive way, the naïve and potentially self-destructive opinions of the vulgar who feel that a life of virtue is worth living only if it leads to the alleged eternal rewards in the fictitious afterlife described by manipulative preachers. It is clearly a view that he holds in great contempt.[21]

When Spinoza does get around to discussing the fate of the mind or soul after a person's death, he is obviously very careful to avoid any talk of *immortalitas*, lest his reader—on the lookout for individual immortality—mistake the whole moral of his story. There are parts of the mind that will persist after the demise of the body, Spinoza allows, but it is, as the phrase goes, nothing personal.

Spinoza defines *eternity* simply as that which stands outside of all duration or time. "Eternity can neither be defined by time nor have any relation to time" (Vp23s, G II.96/C 607). Something is not eternal merely if its duration is without beginning or end; this is nothing but sempiternity, or everlastingness in time. True eternity, which Spinoza explicitly contrasts with sempiternity (Id8), stands outside of all temporal categories whatsoever. "Before," "after," "now," "later," and all such ascriptions are completely inapplicable to what is eternal.[22] God, or substance, is eternal; so are the attributes Thought and Extension. In a certain respect, particular finite things are also eternal—not when they are considered in their temporally and spatially bound relationships to other finite things, that is, when what is in question is their actual, durational existence, but rather when they are considered from a more abstract perspective as atemporal essences—what Spinoza calls *sub specie aeternitatis*. This way of looking at things will play a twofold role in Spinoza's account of the eternity of the mind.

The human mind partakes of eternity in two distinct ways.[23] First, there is the eternity that belongs to it because it is the idea—or the expression in the attribute of Thought—of the material essence—in the attribute of Extension—of the human body.

Vp22: Nevertheless, in God there is necessarily an idea that expresses the essence of this or that human body, under a species of eternity [*sub specie aeternitatis*].

Demonstration: God is the cause, not only of the existence of this or that human body, but also of its essence, which therefore must be conceived

---

21. See Moreau, *Spinoza: L'expérience et l'éternité*, 535.

22. Some commentators have argued that the eternity at stake here *is* just a sempiternity, or what Donagan calls "omnitemporality"; see Kneale, "Eternity and Sempiternity," and Donagan, "Spinoza's Proof of Immortality." Most, however, have—correctly, I believe—seen that what Spinoza is talking about is a complete atemporality, or timelessness; see Harris, "Spinoza's Theory of Human Immortality"; Hampshire, *Spinoza*; Moreau, *Spinoza: L'expérience et l'éternité*, 536; and Joachim, *A Study of the Ethics of Spinoza* (Oxford: Clarendon Press, 1901), 298.

23. It is absolutely crucial to see that there are two distinct kinds of eternity; see Moreau, *Spinoza: L'expérience et l'éternité*, 534–9. A failure to distinguish them can lead one into various kinds of misreadings of Spinoza's views on the eternity of the mind (such as is found in Harris, "Spinoza's Theory of Human Immortality;" and Hardin, "Spinoza on Immortality and Time").

through the very essence of God, by a certain eternal necessity, and this concept must be in God. (G II.295/C 607)

Any actually existing human body persists durationally, in time and within the causal nexus of other finite things that affect it and determine it. Toes stub against tables; arms throw balls; snow forts come crashing down on us. This sequence of affairs begins in time, pursues its course in time, and comes to an end in time. The duration of the body as actually existing is limited; so are all the numerous modifications of the body that come about through its interactions with other finite modes. But every human body—in fact, every existing body of any type—also has an aspect *sub specie aeternitatis*, "under a form of eternity." There is an essence of that body in its extensional being, an extended nature abstracted from its temporal duration. Whether it is a case of a table, a baseball, a snow fort, or a human body, its essence would be a type of formulaic mathematical or dimensional mapping of that body that identifies it as the particular parcel of extension that it is. Any body is nothing but a specific ratio of motion and rest among a collection of material parts. Its unity consists only in a relative and structured stability of minute bodies.[24] And this is what is reflected in its essence, its eternal being. At this level, no question whatsoever is raised about whether the body actually exists in nature or not. Because it is outside all duration, making no reference to time, this essence of the body is eternal.

Now the essence of a body as an extended mode is in God (or Substance) under the attribute of Extension. It is "eminently" contained within Extension as one of its infinite potentialities or possible generations. It is, in other words, just one out of an infinitely many ways of being extended. Given Spinoza's general parallelism between the attributes of Extension and Thought—whereby every mode of extension (every body and every state of a body) has a corresponding mode in thought (an idea)—and given the resulting and more particular parallelism in a human being between what is true of the body and what is true of the mind (which is nothing but the idea of the body),[25] there are, then, likewise—and necessarily—two aspects of the human mind. First, there is the aspect of the mind that corresponds to the durational existence of the body. This is the part of the mind that reflects the body's determinate relationships with the other bodies surrounding it. Sensations and feelings—pain, pleasure, desire, revulsion, sadness, fear, and a host of other mental states—are all the expression in the mind of what is concurrently taking place in the body in its temporal interactions with the world. I feel pain when I stub my toe. These passions belong to the mind to the extent that the human being is a part of "the order of nature" and, through his body, subject to being affected by the world around him.[26]

The parallelism also requires, however, that this part of the mind comes to an end when the duration of the body comes to an end, that is, at a person's death.

24. See *Ethics*, Part II, G II.99–100/C 460.
25. IIp11–13.
26. The determinate study of the various affects in a human being is the subject of Part Three.

When the body goes, there are no more pleasures and pains, no more sensory states. All of the affections of the body, of which these sensations, images, and qualia are mental expressions, cease at death; the body is no longer "in the world" responding to its determinations. Thus, their correlative expressions in the mind cease as well. But there is another part of the mind—namely, that aspect of it that corresponds to the eternal aspect of the body. This is the expression in the attribute of Thought of the body's extended essence. Like its correlate in extension, this aspect of the mind is eternal.[27] It is a part of the mind that remains after a person's death.

> Vp23: The human mind cannot be absolutely destroyed with the body, but something of it remains which is eternal.
>
> Demonstration: In God there is necessarily a concept, or idea, which expresses the essence of the human body (by Vp22), an idea, therefore, which is necessarily something that pertains to the essence of the human mind. But we do not attribute to the human mind any duration that can be defined by time, except insofar as it expresses the actual existence of the body, which is explained by duration and can be defined by time, i.e., we do not attribute duration to it except while the body endures. However, since what is conceived, with a certain eternal necessity, through God's essence itself is nevertheless something, this something that pertains to the essence of the mind will necessarily be eternal.
>
> Schol.: There is, then, this idea which expresses the essence of the body under a species of eternity, a certain mode of thinking, which pertains to the essence of the mind, and which is necessarily eternal . . . (G II.295/C 607)

The mind thus includes, as an essential and eternal component, an idea-correlate in Thought of the essence of the body in Extension. This idea-correlate is eternal because it, like the essence of the body it represents, is situated nondurationally within one of God's/Nature's eternal attributes.

Notice, however, that this is a very minimal kind of eternity. It is not something in which human beings can take any pride or comfort, for it is an eternity that belongs to *all* things, human and otherwise. Given Spinoza's metaphysics, and especially the universal scope of the parallelism between Extension and Thought, or bodies and ideas, there is nothing about this eternity of the mind that distinguishes the human being from any other finite being—or, more properly, there is nothing that distinguishes this eternity belonging to the human mind from the eternity belonging to the idea of any other finite body. What Spinoza claims with respect to the general parallelism between modes of extension and modes of thought applies necessarily in this particular case as well: "The things we have shown . . . are completely general and do not pertain more to man than to other individuals . . . and so whatever we have said of the idea of the human body must also be said of the idea of anything" (IIp13s, G II.96/C 458). Human minds are,

---

27. In fact, this aspect of the mind is eternal *because* the mode of extension of which it is an expression is eternal.

naturally, significantly different from the Thought-modes or ideas corresponding
to other, non-human bodies—they have more functions and greater capacities
(including memory and consciousness), because the actually existing bodies of
which they are the ideas are themselves more complex and well-endowed than
other bodies (such as trees).

> In proportion as a body is more capable than others of doing many things
> at once, or being acted on in many ways at once, so its mind is more capable
> than others of perceiving many things at once. And in proportion as the
> actions of a body depend more on itself alone, and as other bodies concur
> with it less in acting, so its mind is more capable of understanding distinctly.
> (IIp13s, G II.97/C 458)

But this means only that what remains in Thought after a person's death is, like
the essence of the body it expresses, more internally complex, so to speak, than
the ideas that remain after the dissolution of some other kinds of bodies.[28] It is not,
however, more eternal.

Nor is it more "personal." It is only the correlate in Thought of a specific
ratio of motion and rest in Extension. It expresses a particularly complex ratio, to
be sure, but it is generically no different from the idea of the essence of any other
body.[29] And there is nothing distinctly personal about this eternal idea of the
body—nothing that would lead me to regard it as my "self," identical to the self I
currently am in this life. I shall return to this below.

III

There is, however, another variety of eternity for the mind in Spinoza's system. It,
too, involves the kind of atemporal being characteristic of ideas of essences. But
it is, in fact, an eternity that is available *only* to human minds, since it is acquired
by rational agents alone.[30]

According to Spinoza, all creatures are essentially (and necessarily)
moved by the pursuit of self-interest; they naturally strive for what will aid their
self-preservation.

---

28. The intrinsic complexity of the body is reflected in the variety and multiplicity of ideas
that make up the human mind; see IIp11–13.

29. See Moreau, *Spinoza: L'expérience et l'éternité*, 537–8.

30. It is his failure to recognize this second variety of eternity for the mind that is responsible for Bennett's failure to make sense of Spinoza's views here. Bennett is troubled by the fact
that Spinoza believes both that the eternal mind is nothing but the (unchanging) idea of the
eternal essense of the body *and* that "how much of my mind is eternal depends upon some facts
about my conduct and my condition"; in other words, that we can *increase* our share of eternity.
Since Bennett recognizes only the eternity of the mind as the idea of the unchanging essence of
the body, there is (he argues) "no provision for my increasing how much of my mind is eternal,
unless I can change my body's essence, whatever that would mean. But now we are told that how
much of my mind is eternal depends on what thinking I do, as though I could work at enlarging
the eternal part of my mind" (*A Study of Spinoza's Ethics*, 361–2). In fact, that is *exactly* what
Spinoza thinks we can do, by increasing our share of adequate ideas, as I show.

IIIp6: Each thing, as far as it can by its own power, strives to persevere in its being.

IIIp7: The striving by which each thing strives to persevere in its being is nothing but the actual essence of the thing. (G II.146/C 498–9)

This, in fact, constitutes (for moral agents, at least) virtue. To act virtuously is to do what will most effectively serve to preserve one's being.

IVp20: The more each one strives, and is able, to seek his own advantage, i.e. to preserve his own being, the more he is endowed with virtue; conversely, insofar as each one neglects his own advantage, i.e. neglects to preserve his being, he lacks power. (G II.224/C 557)

Human beings, when they are acting rationally, strive naturally for knowledge. Since we are, among all creatures, uniquely endowed with reason and the capacity for understanding—that is, with intelligent minds—we recognize that our own proper good, our ultimate perfection and well-being, consists in the pursuit of what benefits this our highest part. But what else could benefit our highest intellectual faculties except knowledge? Thus, if virtue is the pursuit of what is in one's own self-interest, as Spinoza insists; and if the acquisition of knowledge is what is in our own self-interest, then human virtue consists in the pursuit of knowledge.[31]

But Spinoza is concerned here not just with the pursuit of any ordinary kind of knowledge. Rather, what is most beneficial to a rational being is a particular sort of deep understanding that he calls "intuitive knowledge," *scientia intuitiva*, or "the third kind of knowledge." This is an intuitive understanding of individual things in their relations to higher causes, to the infinite and eternal aspects of Nature, and it represents the highest form of knowledge available to us.

The human mind, like God's attribute of Thought, contains ideas. Some of these ideas—sensory images, "feels" (like pains and pleasures), perceptual data—are imprecise qualitative phenomena. They are, as we have seen, nothing but the expression in thought of states of the body as it is affected by the bodies surrounding it. Such ideas do not convey adequate and true knowledge of the world, but only a relative, partial, and subjective picture of how things presently seem to be to the perceiver given the perspectival limitations of his physical place. There is no systematic order to these perceptions, nor any critical oversight by reason. "As long as the human Mind perceives things from the common order of nature, it does not have an adequate, but only a confused and mutilated knowledge of itself, of its own Body, and of external bodies" (IIp29c, G II.114/C 471). Under such circumstances, we are simply determined in our ideas by our fortuitous and haphazard encounter with things in the external world. This superficial acquaintance will never provide us with knowledge of the essences of those things. In fact, it is an invariable source of falsehood and error. This "knowledge from random expe-

---

31. See IVp20–26.

rience" is, for Spinoza, the "first kind of knowledge," and results in the accumulation of what he calls "inadequate ideas."

"Adequate ideas," on the other hand, are formed in a rational and orderly manner. They are necessarily true and reveal certain essential natures. The second kind of knowledge, "Reason," is the apprehension of an essential truth through a discursive, inferential procedure. It is somewhat unclear, however, whether for Spinoza what we apprehend through reason, in knowledge of the second kind, are only *general* truths and principles—"common notions" or "universal notions"—or also truths about *individuals.*

On the one hand, he insists that we can know adequately features that are common to a number of particulars (for example, certain truths about bodies generally, such as the laws governing their motions and the properties that characterize them universally). One way in which we can arrive at such knowledge is through deductive reasoning from other adequate general or common notions, since "whatever ideas follow in the mind from ideas that are adequate in the mind are also adequate" (IIp40, G II.120/C 475). It also seems that we can arrive at common notions inductively, through abstraction from sensory acquaintance with particulars.[32]

On the other hand, it sometimes seems to be the case that in the second kind of knowledge what is apprehended includes truths about individuals. In particular, knowledge of the second kind involves grasping a thing's causal connections not just to other objects but, more importantly, to the attributes of God and the infinite modes (the laws of nature) that follow immediately from them. That is, what one sees in the second kind of knowledge but not in knowledge of the first kind is how the thing is ultimately determined by the nature or essence that it instantiates. In the adequate idea of a particular body, for example, the body will be embedded not only in its mechanistic relations to other bodies, but also within the laws of motion and rest and the nature of matter (extension) itself. (In fact, it is these that render those mechanistic relations lawlike and necessary.) The adequate idea of a thing thus clearly and distinctly situates its object in all of its causal nexuses and shows not just *that* it is, but *how* and *why* it necessarily is. As Yovel puts it, in knowledge of the second kind, we "explicate the object externally, by the intersection of mechanistic causal laws," until we achieve "a point of saturation . . . when a network of lawlike explanations has, so to speak, closed in on the object from all relevant angles."[33] The person who truly knows a thing sees the reasons why the thing was determined to be and could not have been otherwise. "It is of the nature of Reason to regard things as necessary, not as contingent" (IIp44, G II.125/C 480). The belief that something is accidental or spontaneous—that is, causally undetermined—can be based only on an inadequate grasp of the thing's causal explanation, on a partial and "mutilated" familiarity with it. To perceive by way of adequate ideas is to perceive the necessity inherent in Nature. Sense experience alone could never provide the information conveyed by an ade-

32. This reading of what the second kind of knowledge involves is adopted by Margaret Wilson, "Spinoza's Theory of Knowledge," 116–19; and Henry Allison, *Benedict de Spinoza*, 117.
33. Yovel, *Spinoza and Other Heretics*, vol. 1, *The Marrano of Reason*, 156.

quate idea. (At one point, Spinoza suggests that the difference between an adequate idea of a thing and an inadequate one is not unlike the contrast between simply knowing a conclusion versus seeing how the conclusion follows from specific premises.)[34] The senses present things only as they happen to appear from a given perspective at a given moment in time. An adequate idea, on the other hand, by showing how a thing follows necessarily from one or another of God's attributes, ultimately presents it in its "eternal" aspects—*sub specie aeternitatis*—and leads to a conception of the thing without any relation to time or finite and partial perspective. "It is of the nature of Reason to regard things as necessary and not as contingent. And Reason perceives this necessity of things truly, i.e., as it is in itself. But this necessity of things is the very necessity of God's eternal nature. Therefore, it is of the nature of Reason to regard things under this species of eternity."

If knowledge of the second kind does indeed provide this ratiocinative understanding of individuals, then the third kind of knowledge, intuition, takes what is known by Reason and grasps it in a single and comprehensive act of the mind.[35] Where the second kind of knowledge moves discursively through various stages, from the initial starting point (causes) through intermediate steps to its final conclusion (effect), in the third kind of knowledge there is an immediate perception of the necessity of a thing and the way it depends on its ultimate, first causes.

> This kind of knowing proceeds from an adequate idea of the formal essence of certain attributes of God to the adequate knowledge of the formal essences of things. (IIp40s2, G II.122/C 478)

> The third kind of knowledge proceeds from an adequate idea of certain attributes of God to an adequate knowledge of the essences of things. (Vp25, G II.296/C 608)

Intuition synthesizes what Reason knows only discursively. It thereby generates a deep causal understanding of a thing, that is, an "internal" knowledge of its essence (in contrast with what Yovel calls "explicating the object externally"). Such an internal knowledge of the essence situates the thing immediately and timelessly in relation to the eternal principles of Nature that generated and govern it. This conception of ultimate knowledge is already present early in Spinoza's *oeuvre*, in *Treatise on the Emendation of the Intellect* from the late 1650s:

> The essences of singular, changeable things are not to be drawn from their series, or order of existing, since it offers us nothing but extrinsic denominations, relations, or at most, circumstances, all of which are far from the inmost essence of things. That essence is to be sought only from the fixed and eternal things, and at the same time from the laws inscribed in these

---

34. See IIp28.

35. I thus agree with Yovel when he insists that with the third kind of knowledge "nothing new is added to the scientific information already possessed." Both express "the same fundamental information"; see *The Marrano of Reason*, 156, 165–6.

things, as in their true codes, according to which all singular things come to be, and are ordered. Indeed these singular changeable things depend so intimately, and (so to speak) essentially, on the fixed things that they can neither be nor be conceived without them. (G II.37/C 41)

We strive, then, to acquire the third kind of knowledge: an intuitive understanding of the natures of things not merely in their finite, particular and fluctuating causal relations to other finite things, not in their mutable, durational existence, but through their unchanging essences. And to truly understand things essentially in this way is to relate them to their infinite causes: substance (God) and its attributes. What we are after is a knowledge of bodies not through other bodies but through Extension and its laws, and a knowledge of ideas through the nature of Thought and its laws. It is the pursuit of this kind of knowledge that constitutes human virtue and the project that represents our greatest self-interest as rational beings.

> Vp25: The greatest striving of the mind, and its greatest virtue, is understanding things by the third kind of knowledge.
>   Demonstration: The third kind of knowledge proceeds from an adequate idea of certain attributes of God to an adequate knowledge of the essence of things, and the more we understand things in this way, the more we understand God. Therefore, the greatest virtue of the mind, i.e., the mind's power or nature or its greatest striving, is to understand things by the third kind of knowledge. (G II.296/C 608)
>   Vp29scholium: We conceive things as actual in two ways: either insofar as we conceive them to exist in relation to a certain time and place, or insofar as we conceive them to be contained in God and to follow from the necessity of the divine nature. But the things we conceive in this second way as true, or real, we conceive under a species of eternity [*sub specie aeternitatis*], and to that extent they involve the eternal and infinite essence of God. (G II.298–9/C 610)

Sub specie aeternitatis: when we understand things in this way, we see them from the infinite and eternal perspective of God, without any relation to or indication of time and place. When we perceive things in time, they appear in a continuous state of change and becoming; when we perceive them "under a form of eternity," what we apprehend abides permanently. This kind of knowledge, because it is atemporal and because it is basically God's knowledge, is eternal. It is, above all, not connected to the actual existence of any finite, particular thing, least of all the existence in time of the human body.

Now Spinoza suggests, first of all, that the acquisition of true and adequate ideas is beneficial to a person in this lifetime, as the source of an abiding happiness and peace of mind that is immune to the slings and arrows of outrageous fortune. When a person sees the necessity of all things, and especially the fact that the objects that he or she values are, in their comings and goings, not under one's control, that person is less likely to be overwhelmed with emotions at their arrival and passing away. The resulting life will be tranquil, and not given to sudden disturbances of the passions.[36] But there is an additional reason why we should strive to acquire and maintain our store of adequate ideas: they represent for us the closest thing available to what is usually called "immortality."

Because adequate ideas are nothing but an eternal knowledge of things, a body of eternal truths that we can possess or tap into in this lifetime, it follows that the more adequate ideas we acquire as a part of our mental makeup in this life—the more we "participate" in eternity now—the more of us remains after the death of the body and the end of the durational aspect of ourselves. Since the adequate ideas that one comes to possess are eternal, they are not affected by the demise of the body and the end of our (or any) temporal and durational existence. In other words, the more adequate knowledge we have, the greater is the degree of the eternity of the mind.

> Vp38: The more the mind understands things by the second and third kind of knowledge, the less it is acted on by affects which are evil, and the less it fears death.
>
> Demonstration: The mind's essence consists in knowledge; therefore, the more the mind knows things by the second and third kind of knowledge, the greater the part of it that remains, and consequently the greater the part of it that is not touched by affects which are contrary to our nature, i.e., which are evil. (G II.304/C 613)

Now, as we shall see, it is a bit misleading to say, as I have above, that this eternal knowledge is a part of *me* that remains after death. Rather, what remains is something that, while I lived and used my reason, belonged to me and made up a part— the eternal part—of the contents of my mind. The striving to increase my store of adequate ideas is, in this way, a striving to increase my share of eternity. Thus, Spinoza claims, the greater the mind's intellectual achievement in terms of the acquisition of adequate ideas, "the less is death harmful to us." Indeed, he insists, "the human mind can be of such a nature that the part of the mind which we have shown perishes with the body is of no moment in relation to what remains" (Vp38s, G II.304/C 614).

However, if what one is looking for after this temporal existence is a personal immortality in the world-to-come (to use the Jewish phrase that would have been familiar to Spinoza)—a conscious, full-blooded (but, on many accounts, bodyless) life after death in *Gan Eden* or *olam ha-ba* as described by the rabbis of the Talmud and the midrashim—then the eternity of the mind held out by Spinoza will seem a very thin and disappointing recompense for having lived a life of good. It is hard to see Spinoza's account of the eternity of the mind as a doctrine of personal immortality of the soul. Indeed, I believe that he set out to deny, in his own terms, that there is any such thing.

---

36. See Vp6.

IV

The question of "personal immortality" involves two issues. The first concerns the survival of the soul, in whole or in part, as a discrete, individual entity. Any robust theory of personal immortality should hold the soul (or whatever aspect of it persists after death) to be, at the very minimum, quantitatively distinguishable from any other soul-like entity after the demise of the body. Numerical individuality is surely a necessary condition for individuality *tout court*. Without quantitative identity, a person's disembodied, postmortem soul would then have no individuality at all. The second issue concerns the recognizable continuity of specific (and not just generic) identity between the soul in this life and in the afterlife. It must be possible to distinguish *qualitatively* one postmortem soul from another and identify it as the soul that belonged to *this* once-living person and not that one. It must be possible, that is, to take the soul after death and link it up somehow to the life that was a person's durational existence. Only in this way can it be said that it is the soul of *this* person (as opposed to *that* person) that is immortal.

The second question is, in the context of Spinoza's thought, easier to address. One thing is, first of all, perfectly clear. Spinoza will absolutely *not* allow it to be said that a *person* is immortal. For Spinoza, my person or self is an actually existing body together with the mind that is its expression. Or, more precisely, a person is the mode that expresses itself in time as an actually existing body in Extension and as a corresponding mind (or idea) in Thought. A person is not a soul or mind that just happens to be embodied, as many philosophers from Plato onward have pictured it; nor is it the body alone—it is, instead, the unity of the two. "A man consists of a Mind and a Body" (IIp13c, G II.96/C 457).[37] Because, as Spinoza makes clear, the bodily component of a person must be an actually existing human body,[38] there can be no persistence of a *person* after his death. The end of durational existence is the end of the person.

But what about saying that the mind that does persist after one's death, while not the person, can nonetheless be identified as the mind of this or that person? Spinoza makes it very difficult to sustain this claim as well. One solution to this question must be ruled out from the start. It cannot be the case that the eternal mind carries *within itself* any direct reference to what was the person's durational existence—to the existing constituent parts and occuring events that make up a person's lifetime. As we have seen, what is eternal bears no reference to time whatsoever. There will be, in the eternal mind, no traces of durational existence.

Still, might it not be possible to find some way of distinguishing one eternal mind from any other and drawing a connection from it to one particular durational lifetime? The problem with this approach, on Spinoza's terms, is that it is hard to see *how* one eternal mind—or, rather, the body of eternal adequate ideas that once belonged to a person's mind—could be qualitatively differentiated or individuated from another. Or, to put it more precisely, there is no reason why two

---

37. Morrison offers a good defense of this point in "Spinoza on the Self, Personal Identity, and Immortality."
38. IIp13.

eternal minds should *necessarily* be distinguishable from one another. Wolfson, for one, believes that there is no problem here for Spinoza. He argues that one eternal mind is supposed to be distinguished, disembodied, and postmortem, from another eternal mind through its contents, that is, through the quantity and character of the knowledge belonging to each. As different people reach in their lifetimes different levels of intellectual achievement, this will be reflected in their respective stores of adequate ideas. In this way, Wolfson argues, for Spinoza it is the case that "though all souls are immortal and all of them are united with God, there exist certain differences between the individual souls which remain after death . . . Immortality is in a sense personal and individual."[39] But Wolfson does not see that this can be only a *de facto* distinction. These eternal minds are composed only of abstract ideas or knowledge, and there is nothing *in principle* to keep them from having identical contents. The limiting case of such a scenario would be perfect knowledge, whereby a mind, having achieved comprehensive understanding of the entirety of Nature, would mirror God's total and eternal understanding of things— that is, the totality of ideas under the attribute of Thought. Two minds having attained this state would, because their contents are the same, be qualitatively indistinguishable. Of course, no finite mind can achieve such a perfect state of knowledge. But even with lesser degrees of understanding, what is to keep two minds from having acquired in this life exactly the same collection of adequate ideas? Since adequate ideas reflect reality *sub specie aeternitatis*, there would not even be any difference of perspective on the objects so cognized. It may not be a likely event, but it is at least possible. (Spinoza suggests that it may even be a desirable state of affairs. He makes it fairly clear that the more adequate ideas two minds have, the more they "agree with each other."[40] This is the road to social peace and political well-being.) And this means that there is nothing in the nature of an eternal mind that guarantees that it will be qualitatively distinguishable from another.

Individuating a postmortem eternal mind and distinguishing it from others not by its contents, by the knowledge it contains, but by connecting it with a particular durational consciousness in this lifetime, and thus conferring upon it a truly *personal* dimension, is equally problematic. As long as a person lives, the eternal part of his mind—being simply his knowledge of adequate ideas—is a part of that person's consciousness. But it would seem that at the moment of death, the link between that body of knowledge and the consciousness to which it belonged is necessarily broken. For Spinoza, consciousness and memory (the latter, in essence, is nothing but that which gives unity to consciousness) seem to be intimately tied to the (full) person. At one point in *Ethics*, Spinoza suggests that someone who has undergone a radical change in consciousness has, *ipso facto*, undergone a radical change in personhood:

> Sometimes a man undergoes such changes that I should hardly have said he
> was the same man. I have heard stories, for example, of a Spanish Poet who

39. Wolfson, *The Philosophy of Spinoza*, vol. 2, 318.
40. I take this to be the import of IVp35.

suffered an illness; though he recovered, he was left so oblivious to his past life that he did not believe the tales and tragedies he had written were his own. (IVp39s, G II.240/C 569)

It would seem to be the case, as well, that a radical change in personhood through extreme alteration or destruction of the body would, through the parallelism of mind and body, entail a radical change in, or even loss of, consciousness.

Now Spinoza explicitly links self-consciousness to the actual existence of the body, and particularly to the way it interacts with other existing bodies. "The mind does not know itself, except insofar as it perceives the ideas of the affections of the body" (IIp23, G II.110/C 468). This alone is enough to suggest that after death a person's particular and personal consciousness comes to an end.[41] But if, in addition, consciousness and personhood are so closely connected, then it would seem that as personhood goes (which, as we have seen, ends with the body's demise) so goes consciousness. A postmortem mind, then, would no longer be endowed with its living consciousness. Even if it had *a* consciousness—and I see no reason for thinking that it could—it would certainly have no memory of the conscious life it led in its durational term, for memory itself also depends upon the actually existing body: "The mind can neither imagine anything, nor recollect past things, except while the body endures" (Vp21, G II.294/C 607). Spinoza suggests, in fact, that the belief in a conscious immortal soul that is linked via memory to its durational (lived) consciousness is simply to fall prey to a popular misconception of what persists after a person's death, a misconception that involves projecting onto the eternal mind features that properly characterize only a living, embodied consciousness.

If we attend to the common opinion of men, we shall see that they are indeed conscious of the eternity of their mind, but that they confuse it with duration, and attribute it to the imagination, or memory, which they believe remains after death. (Vp34s, G II.301–2/C 611–12)

An eternal mind looks like nothing but a body of knowledge permanently cut off from any kind of consciousness (including access to an earlier consciousness). There will thus be no connection, at least *within* consciousness, between the mind in duration and the mind *sub specie aeternitatis*.

So how can an eternal mind be qualitatively individuated and given a personal dimension, a connection to the life led by a particular person? One final possibility suggests itself, namely, through the body. This is precisely how a mind is individuated in this lifetime—by being the expression in Thought of a particular, actually existing body. So why should not a similar approach work for the mind postmortem? Since the eternal mind is eternal, it cannot bear any direct reference

---

41. It also makes it hard to see how Donagan can sustain his claim that for Spinoza the eternal mind will have a conscious sense of self. Donagan insists, as well, that memory—which, he agrees, ends with the demise of the body—is not essential for this self-identity; see "Spinoza's Argument for Immortality."

either to an actually existing body or (more relevantly) to the historical (temporal) existence that its own body once enjoyed. However, it is important to remember that there are two eternal aspects to the human mind: in addition to the store of adequate ideas that constitute one kind of eternity for the (rational) mind, there is that eternity (common to *all* modes of Thought) that it acquires by being the idea of the eternal essence of the body (defined as a particular ratio of motion and rest between material particles). Therefore, belonging to an eternal mind there is, in addition to its adequate ideas, that ideal component corresponding to the eternal remnant (in Extension) of the particular body that once made up a person. In this way each eternal mind would seem, through its makeup, to pick out a particular body that at one time belonged (durationally) to a person. To put it another way, if a *person* is an actually existing body (as a modal expression within Extension) with its correlative durational mind (as a modal expression within Thought), then, since the eternal mind bears, as one of its constituents, an idea of the eternal essence of that body, is not that mind simply the eternal, ideal expression of the *person*? Will not this suffice to distinguish one eternal mind from another and give it a connection to a human life? If it cannot be done by the adequate ideas the mind contains, surely it can be done by the essence of the once-existing body to which the mind ideally and eternally refers?

This is exactly the approach taken by Donagan. In duration, he insists, human minds "are complex ideas individuated by their primary constituents: ideas of existing human bodies."[42] This is no less true of eternal minds, with the difference being that the body whose idea does the individuating is no longer existing.

> Spinoza's proof that something of the mind remains, which is eternal, confirms Wolfson's emphatic statement that he conceived immortality as "personal and individual." For in it, he set out to show, not that ideas which are common to different minds remain after death, but that a part of the individuating primary constituent of each mind does so, a part that retains its individuality.

That constituent of the eternal mind that accounts for its individuating is "an idea of the formal essence of its body."[43]

42. Donagan, "Spinoza's Argument for Immortality," 251.
43. Donagan, "Spinoza's Argument for Immortality," 252. Rudavsky takes a similar tack. Eternal minds, she insists, are to be individuated by the ideas of the body that constitute them.

> On Spinoza's theory of individuation, part of what makes me who I am is that I am affected by other individuals; individuation on this model turns out to be relational, incorporating both material and formal elements . . . [it] is bodies that are the source of identification of persons: The ideas that make up an individual mind acquire their identity by being ideas of a particular body. This identification with both remains embedded in the mind after the "death of the body." (*Time Matters*, 185)

What Rudavsky does not take note of, however, is the fact that such relational elements—the body's causal relations to external bodies—belong to the body only in duration, in its spatial and temporal relationships to other bodies. They necessarily come to an end with the demise of the body and the termination of its durational existence. Thus, they are not available to individuate (the essences of) bodies postmortem.

However, there is a problem with this approach as well. It is potentially very troublesome, given Spinoza's conception of a body, to individuate bodies outside of duration, that is, outside of their mutual spatial, temporal, and causal relations as actually existing bodies. If a body *sub specie aeternitatis* is nothing but a generic, eternal mathematical formula specifying a parcel of extension—through a relatively stable ratio of motion and rest between material parts—and bearing no reference to time and duration, then, like the collection of adequate ideas that persists after one's death, it, too, need not *in principle* be distinguishable from the mathematical, atemporal formula constituting the essence of another, qualitatively similar body. Two bodies may be precisely alike in all of their "intrinsic" qualities and distinguishable only through the different relations in which they stand to other bodies (relative place and time, causal interactions, etc.) and, thus, only as long as they actually exist.[44] This is a problem that infects the Cartesian account of bodily individuality generally. If, as Descartes claims, a body just *is* extension, then it is nothing but geometrical figure; and, outside of time and physical place, two similar geometrical figures are indistinguishable—one circle looks just like another of the same size; only context allows one to differentiate them. Thus, the abstractness of the eternal essence of a human body might preclude one from being able to distinguish it from the eternal essence of another human body—this could be the case, for example, with ball bearings or (if we concentrate, for the sake of argument, only on external appearance) with perfectly identical twins— and thus from being able to use that component of an eternal mind to distinguish *it* from another.

So much for the question of the *qualitative* individuality of the eternal mind. The first issue raised above, regarding the *quantitative* distinction among eternal minds—or what might be called the mind's ontological *integrity* after death—is more difficult to resolve. Is the postmortem mind even an identifiable *thing*, one that is at least numerically different from other eternal minds? Or, to put the question another way, is there in fact a plurality of eternal minds for Spinoza? The answer to this question is not very clear. Nevertheless, here is a tentative suggestion. The adequate ideas that remain after one's death are not bound together in any way and thus separated from any other "collection" of adequate ideas (say, those that belonged to someone else). Bear in mind that there is no consciousness or memory to unite them, as there was during that person's lifetime; these features of the mind ended with the death of the person. Moroever, all of the evidence points to the mind's integrity as a thing being solely a function of, and thus dependent upon, the actual existence of the body. Proposition Thirteen of Part Two states that "the object of the idea constituting the human mind is the body, or a certain mode of Extension that actually exists, and nothing else" (G II.96/C 457).

My suggestion—and it is, I admit, only a suggestion—is that for Spinoza, after a person's death, what remains of the mind eternally—the adequate ideas, along with the idea of the essence of the body—all disperses and reverts back to the

---

44. This is the problem with Rudavsky's attempted use of the idea of the essence of the body to individuate the eternal mind.

infinite intellect of God (the attribute of Thought), since they are just God's knowledge of things.

> Vp40s: Our mind, in so far as it understands, is an eternal mode of thinking, which is determined by another eternal mode of thinking, and this again by another, and so on, to infinity; so that together, they all constitute God's eternal and infinite intellect (G II.306/C 615).[45]

This passage seems to imply that the eternal mind is a discrete and identifiable mode of Thought, distinguishable from any other eternal mind/mode of Thought. And yet, the adequate ideas themselves all are, always have been, and always will be nothing more than ideas in God's infinite intellect, modes of the attribute Thought. For an all-too-brief span of time they stand in a certain determinate relationship with one another as they enter into the composition of an existing human mind—a mind that, in truth, is nothing but an idea that is a collection of ideas. And for that duration of a person's lifetime, God's knowledge of the objects of those ideas "passes through" the human mind insofar as the ideas form a part of that specific collection. "When we say that the human mind perceives this or that, we are saying nothing but that God, not insofar as he is infinite, but insofar as he is explained through the nature of the human mind, or insofar as he constitutes the essence of the human mind, has this or that idea" (IIp11c, G II.94–5/C 456).

This is, of course, all very vague, and I am genuinely puzzled about how to answer the question of the integrity of the "collection" of adequate ideas constituting an eternal mind. But if my proposed account is right, then there is just one set of eternal, adequate ideas, a body of knowledge that each of us, in this lifetime, is able to tap into. To this extent, we as knowers can "participate" in eternity. In knowing, in the pursuit of a rational understanding of nature and of ourselves, we can transcend our own individuality and temporality. This is, in fact, something that we can be consciously aware of in this life, and it is a source of joy. As he says at one point, "we feel and know by experience that we are eternal" (Vp23s, G II.296/C 607–8).

V

Things do not look good for those who want to find a doctrine of personal immortality in Spinoza's philosophy. In fact, anyone who even tries to do so fails to grasp one of the essential, large-scale aspects of Spinoza's philosophical project. Regardless of what one thinks of my reading of Spinoza's doctrine of the eternity of the mind, and irrespective of the strength or weakness of the arguments that I offer for that reading, there is one very good reason—indeed, to my mind the strongest possible reason—for thinking that Spinoza intended to deny the personal immortality of the soul: such a religiously charged doctrine goes against every grain of

---

45. This seems to be Hampshire's reading, when he notes that "insofar as I do attain genuine knowledge, my individuality as a particular thing disappears and my mind becomes so far united with God or Nature conceived under the attribute of Thought" (*Spinoza*, 175).

his philosophical persuasions. Seeing how this is so requires standing back from a minute analysis of the propositions of *Ethics* a bit to consider his entire philosophical project, particularly its moral and political dimensions.

It is clear from the later books of *Ethics* and *Theological-Political Treatise* that one of the major goals of Spinoza's work is to liberate us from the grip of irrational passions and lead us to an abiding state of *eudaimonia*, of psychological and moral well-being, in the life of reason. And the two passions that he is most concerned about are hope and fear.[46] These are the passions that are most easily manipulated by ecclesiastic authorities seeking to control our lives and command our obedience. These preachers take advantage of our tendency toward superstitious behavior by persuading us that there is an eternal reward to hope for and an eternal punishment to fear after this life. This constitutes the carrot and stick that they wield to move people into submission. What is essential for them to succeed in their appeal to our hope and fear is *our* conviction that there is such an afterlife, that my soul will continue to live after the death of my body and that there is a personal immortality. I believe that Spinoza thought that the best way to free us from a life of hope and fear, a life of superstitious behavior, was to kill it at its roots and eliminate the foundational belief on which such hopes and fears are grounded: the belief in the immortality of the soul. Maybe there is an eternal aspect—or two eternal aspects—of the mind. But, he is saying, it is nothing like the personal immortality perniciously held out to, or *over* us, by the leaders of organized religions.

In this way, the denial of personal immortality is fundamental not only to Spinoza's metaphysics, but also to his moral and political thought. To want to find in Spinoza's philosophy a robust doctrine of personal immortality is deeply to misunderstand Spinoza.

---

46. See, for example, his Preface to the *Theological-Political Treatise*.

Midwest Studies in Philosophy, XXVI (2002)

Occasionalism and Efficacious Laws in Malebranche

NICHOLAS JOLLEY

AccORDING to Malebranche's occasionalism, God is the one true cause; as Malebranche himself says in places, perhaps overdramatically, it is God who does everything (SAT, Elucid. 15, OC 3:213; LO 662).[1] However, there is surprisingly little agreement over how such a claim should be interpreted. It is clear that Malebranche is committed to ruling out any division of genuine causal labor between God and created substances; it is less clear how much causal activity is required on the part of the deity, and what form it takes. Indeed, the proper interpretation of Malebranche's occasionalism has been debated ever since his own time. Thus, when Leibniz charged that Malebranche's God intervenes in the course of nature and resorts to perpetual miracles,[2] Arnauld disagreed sharply with

---

1. Throughout this essay, abbreviations for references are as follows: DM *Dialogues on Metaphysics and on Religion (Entretiens sur la Metaphysique et sur la Religion)*; G C. I. Gcrhardt (ed.), *Die Philosophischen Schriften von G. W. Leibniz*, 7 vols. (Berlin: Weidmann, 1875–90); JS N. Jolley ed., D. Scott trans., *Nicolas Malebranche: Dialogues on Metaphysics and on Religion* (Cambridge: Cambridge University Press, 1997); LO T. M. Lennon and P. J. Olscamp, trans., *Nicolas Malebranche: The Search after Truth and Elucidations* (Cambridge: Cambridge University Press, 1997); OC A. Robinet, dir., *Oeuvres complètes de Malebranche*, 20 vols. (Paris: Vrin, 1958–67); SAT *The Search after Truth (De la Recherche de la Vérité)*.

2. See Leibniz to Arnauld, 14 July 1686, G IV 57–8. For other characteristic statements, see *New System of the Nature and Communication of Substances*, paras. 12–3, G IV 483–4; *Essays in Theodicy*, par. 61, G VI 136. For a partial defense of Leibniz's critique of Malebranche's occasionalism, see Donald Rutherford, "Nature, Laws, and Miracles: The Roots of Leibniz's Critique of Occasionalism," S. Nadler (ed.), *Causation in Early Modern Philosophy* (University Park, Pennsylvania: Pennsylvania State University Press, 1993), pp. 135–58. I am grateful to David Cunning, Tad Schmaltz, and Zoltan Szabo for discussion of the issues, and to Marc Hight for helpful comments on a previous draft.

Leibniz's characterization: "Those who maintain that my will is the occasional cause of the movement of my arm and that God is its real cause," he wrote:

> do not claim that God does this in time by a new act of will each time that I wish to raise my arm, but by that single act of the eternal will by which he has willed to do everything which he has foreseen it will be necessary to do, in order that the universe might be such as he has decided it ought to be.[3]

Arnauld may have been no friend to occasionalism or to Malebranche's philosophy in general, but he did feel the need to defend it against what he regarded as a case of misrepresentation.

On philosophical grounds it seems clear that there are reasons for preferring what we might call a "minimalist" reading of occasionalism in the spirit of Arnauld; that is, if we abstract from the Christian miracles, God's role is limited to willing the initial conditions of the universe and the laws of nature. On this interpretation, occasionalism is a simple and elegant philosophical theory that is far removed from the doctrine, attributed by Leibniz to Malebranche, according to which the occasionalist God is a busybody God. In the first part of this essay, I argue that the minimalist interpretation is not only philosophically superior to its rivals; it is also better supported by the textual evidence, since it is required by Malebranche's claim that laws are efficacious. In the second part of the essay, I address the problem of reconciling Malebranche's doctrine of efficacious laws with his occasionalist thesis that nothing created is causally active. I argue that, despite appearances to the contrary, the doctrine of efficacious laws is consistent with the thesis that laws are divine volitions, and thus are not ontologically distinct from God himself.

I

The central problem in interpreting Malebranche's account of divine causality arises from his repeated claim that God acts by general volitions. Malebranche explains to Arnauld that, for him, to act by general volitions is the same thing as acting according to general laws (*Réponse aux Réflexions*, OC 8:651), but this explanation is perhaps not very enlightening; certainly, it has not settled the problem of interpretation. Steven Nadler has recently argued that to say that God acts by general volitions or according to general laws is simply to say that God's ways are not chaotic and ad hoc, but regular and orderly.[4] As Nadler points out, such a claim plays a central role in Malebranche's whole project of theodicy, that is, the project of reconciling the justice of God with the various kinds of evil in the world.[5] Absolutely speaking, God could intervene to prevent an evil such as a tile's

3. Arnauld to Leibniz, 4 March 1687, G II 84.

4. S. Nadler, "Occasionalism and General Will in Malebranche," *Journal of the History of Philosophy* 31 (1993), 31–47, esp. 42. For some criticism of Nadler's thesis, see D. Clarke, "Malebranche and Occasionalism: A Reply to Steven Nadler," *Journal of the History of Philosophy* 33 (1995), 499–504.

5. Ibid., 35–7.

falling on a person's head, but such an intervention would be inconsistent with the laws of physics that God has established, and God's preference for a world governed by simple, fertile laws is required in order for His work to honor him. But, according to Nadler, the claim that God acts by general volitions or according to general laws is not intended to offer a complete account of divine causality. On this view, Malebranche's occasionalism still requires that God implement or execute the laws for the universe that He has established through his general volitions; that is, He must ensure, through an infinite series of individual volitions, that bodies and created minds behave in conformity to these laws. Thus, on this view, the laws of nature that He has established become no more than a series of notes to Himself, or *aides-mémoire*, on how He will act. According to Nadler, then, God is doubly involved in the management of the universe: not merely must He will the laws but He must implement or execute the laws that He has established through His will. In the words of Nadler, God's activity is "constant and ubiquitous"; Malebranche's God is "personally, directly, and immediately responsible for bringing about effects and causal changes in nature."[6]

This reading seems open to a straightforward refutation; it is in conflict with Malebranche's repeated claim that the laws of nature are efficacious. Such a view is expressed most prominently perhaps in *The Search after Truth*:

> All natural forces are therefore nothing but the will of God, which is always efficacious. God created the world because He willed it: "Dixit, & facta sunt" [Ps. 32:9]; and He moves all things, and thus produces all the effects that we see happening, because He also willed certain laws according to which motion is communicated upon the collision of bodies; and because these laws are efficacious, they act, whereas bodies cannot act. (SAT 6.2.3, OC 2:314; LO 449)

The view is further expressed even in texts that Nadler cites in support of his more Leibnizian reading:

> A body in motion is not at all a true cause [of the motion which it communicates]. It is not a natural cause in the sense of the philosophy of the pagans; it is absolutely only an occasional cause which determines by the collision [*choc*] the efficacy of the general law according to which a general cause must act . . . (*Méditations Chrétiennes*, OC 10:54)

And again, in the First Elucidation of *Treatise of Nature and Grace*, Malebranche speaks of the general and efficacious laws of the union of soul and body and of the communication of motions (OC 5:147). Now as the passage from *The Search* indicates, to say that the laws of nature are efficacious is to say that they (in conjunction with the initial conditions) are sufficient to bring about particular events in the world. In that case, there is no need for another series of individual voli-

---

6. Ibid., 31, 32.

tions by means of which God ensures conformity to the laws that He has established. And if there is no need for such a series, God will not engage in such pointless volitional activity, for as Malebranche says in the Fifteenth Elucidation to *The Search after Truth*, "God does not multiply his volitions without reason; He always acts in the simplest ways" (OC 3:215; LO 663).[7]

The evidence of the doctrine of efficacious laws is, in my view, decisive. But it is only fair to examine the considerations that Nadler advances in favor of his thesis. One source of evidence on which Nadler draws is the lengthy exchange between Malebranche and Arnauld. This exchange is indeed important for our purposes, for as has already been suggested, Arnauld interpreted Malebranche in precisely the way I believe to be correct; that is, in Arnauld's view, Malebranche holds that general volitions are efficacious, and that there is thus no need for further acts of individual volitions. To this doctrine, Arnauld had objected on the ground that it undermines God's paternal care for his creatures.[8] Now, if Malebranche indeed believed that individual acts of volition were needed to execute the laws, it is here, in his reply to Arnauld, that we should expect him to say so; Arnauld's polemic surely offered the ideal opportunity for correcting misapprehension about his true position. In response to Arnauld, Malebranche does indeed speak of God as having further volitions over and above His general ones; He is even prepared to speak of these volitions as particular.[9] But what is striking is that these further volitions are not the individual volitions envisaged by Nadler; they have nothing to do with the execution of the laws of nature:

When a thorn pricks me, God makes me feel pain as a consequence of the general laws of the union of soul and body, according to which he acts in us incessantly. It is not at all that God acts in me by a particular volition. I mean that if the thorn had not pricked me, God would not have made me feel the pain of the prick. I do not claim that God has no particular volitions at all with regard to this pain which I suffer; but [claim] only that it is not at all the effect of a particular volition in this. To have particular volitions is not in God the same thing as acting by particular volitions, or having effective [*pratiques*] particular volitions. God wills in particular that I perform a certain act of charity. But he does not will to act in me to make me do it. God wills in particular everything which is in conformity with Order, everything which perfects his work. But God does not always do it, because the same Order requires that he follows the general laws which he has prescribed to himself so that his conduct may bear the character of his attributes. (OC 8:651)

7. For a similar line of criticism, see A. Black, "Malebranche's Theodicy," *Journal of the History of Philosophy* 35 (1997), 40.

8. *Réflexions philosophiques et theologiques sur le nouveau système de la nature et de la grâce*, *Oeuvres de Messire Antoine Arnauld* (Paris, 1775), vol. 39, pp. 174–5.

9. It should be noted that Malebranche's most characteristic definition of a miracle is that it is an event brought about by one of God's particular volitions; see *Réponse au livre des Réflexions*, I, OC VIII 696.

In this remarkable passage, Malebranche is expounding one of the familiar themes of his theodicy. As a result of the general laws of soul–body union, it may happen that on a particular occasion I fail to perform an act of charity that God wishes me to perform; the laws of soul–body union have consequences that are in a sense in conflict with God's particular volitions. But no contradiction is involved, for according to Malebranche's theodicy, general laws take priority over particular volitions; God wills me to perform acts of charity provided that such acts are consistent with the laws He has established. Thus, strangely perhaps, there are occasions when God's particular volitions remain without effect. Whatever we may think of the theological adequacy of such a doctrine, one thing is clear: Malebranche is not expounding the thesis that of course general laws need to be executed by particular acts of volition.

The exchange with Arnauld thus fails to supply evidence of Malebranche's explicit commitment to a doctrine of the need for individual volitions to execute the general laws. Nadler seems to hold, however, that Malebranche is at least implicitly committed to recognizing the need for such further acts of individual volition; in particular, he is impressed by those passages where Malebranche speaks of God as acting as a consequence of the laws that He has established. According to Nadler, certain passages, such as the following, supply at least indirect evidence of Malebranche's commitment to the need for individual acts of volition over and above the general laws:

> Now it is clear that God does not at all act by particular volitions in the sense that I have often explained where he acts by general laws. When a thorn pricks me, God makes me feel pain as a consequence of the general laws of the union of mind and body according to which he ceaselessly acts in us. (OC 8:651)

The same expressions are used in the First Elucidation to the *Treatise of Nature and Grace*:

> I say that God acts by general volitions when He acts as a consequence of the general laws that He has established. For example, I say that God acts in me by general volitions when He makes me feel pain at the time that one pricks me; because as a consequence (*en consequence de*) of the general and efficacious laws of the union of mind and body which He has established, he makes me suffer pain when my body is ill-disposed. (OC 5:147)[10]

Nadler takes Malebranche to be saying that when God makes me feel pain, He is simply acting in accordance with the laws of soul–body union; God looks to the laws He has established as a guide or manual, and then gives me the appropriate

---

10. Significantly, Nadler mistranslates the phrase "*en consequence des loix generales et effi-caces*" as "in accordance with the general and efficacious laws"; Nadler, "Occasionalism and General Will," 43. Cf. D. Cunning, "Malebranche to Cudworth on the Constant Activity of God," unpublished paper.

sensations by a particular volition. But Malebranche's meaning, I submit, is quite different. To say that God acts as a consequence of general laws is not to say that God looks to these laws as a guide; it is rather to say that God acts by virtue of the laws He has established. What Malebranche is doing is to clarify the nature of divine causality; it is precisely by willing the laws of nature, plus the initial conditions, that God brings about events in the world. The consequence in question is logical rather than the quasi-causal one that Nadler finds in the text; that is, from a statement of the initial conditions plus the laws of soul–body union, it follows logically that I shall have a sensation of pain on a particular occasion when my flesh is pricked by a thorn. Now in the case of human agency one might be inclined to doubt whether the agent is really committed to willing such a particular act; because of imperfect knowledge the agent might be surprised by the consequences of the general rule and the antecedent conditions. But in the case of God, who is omniscient, such a scruple is removed: God really wills all the particular consequences of His general volitions.

One objection that Nadler raises against the present "minimalist" interpretation is likely to occur to many readers; it concerns Malebranche's subscription to the doctrine that God conserves the world by continuously creating it. This is not just a doctrine to which Malebranche subscribes as a good Cartesian; it forms the basis for one of his chief and most interesting arguments for occasionalism. According to Nadler, the doctrine makes the need for discrete volitional acts on the part of God "especially clear":[11]

> At every moment, God must recreate the universe in order to maintain it in existence. Now this continuous creation of the universe involves a continuous recreation of every object therein. Hence, God must constantly will that our billiard ball exist; otherwise it would cease to exist.[12]

Perhaps the first thing to be said is that the issue of time is in many ways a red herring in this debate. According to Nadler, at every moment Malebranche's God constantly recreates the universe, and though Malebranche may occasionally write in these terms, it is common ground that this is a loose way of speaking; as Nadler himself concedes, Malebranche's God is outside time altogether.[13] God indeed may eternally will in respect of events in time; He may have temporally indexed volitions to the effect that a body b be at place p at time t. But to say this is not of course to say that His volitions, whether general or particular, are events that take place in time. Thus, any discussion of the continuous creation doctrine and its implications for occasionalism must recognize the strict atemporality of the divine volitions. The real issue, then, is not whether God wills in time, but whether the doctrine of continuous creation implies that, to sustain the universe, God must eternally have a series of discrete, individual, and temporally indexed volitions.

11. Ibid., 42.
12. Ibid.
13. Ibid., 44.

One way of responding to this problem would be to question Malebranche's commitment to the doctrine of continuous creation. As we have seen, the chief role played by the doctrine in Malebranche's thought is as a key premise in the argument for occasionalism. According to Malebranche, when the doctrine is properly interpreted, it will be seen that it leaves no room for a realm of secondary causes.[14] For in conserving or recreating bodies, for example, God does not simply will that they be in some place or other and then leave it up to bodies themselves to determine their specific states in accordance with the laws of physics; rather, God's volitions are fully specific with regard to such things as the location and velocity of bodies. Thus, the doctrine of continuous creation enables Malebranche to argue that even orthodox Cartesians, who of course accept the doctrine of continuous creation, are implicitly committed to occasionalism. It might be wondered, then, whether the doctrine of continuous creation forms the basis for an argument against the Cartesians that is merely *ad hominem*; on this view, even if the doctrine of continuous creation does imply a commitment to discrete acts of divine volition, we could not thence infer that Malebranche was committed to recognizing such volitions. The suggestion is intriguing, but there is no direct evidence that the argument is intended to be merely *ad hominem*.

Fortunately a more promising strategy is available; it consists in showing that the doctrine of continuous creation can be reductively analyzed in terms of God's efficacious general volitions. Such a strategy gains plausibility when we consider the point of the doctrine of continuous creation; as Malebranche's spokesman emphasizes, the doctrine does justice to the essential dependence of creatures on God in all their states (DM VII.8, OC 12:157; JS 113). Now other philosophers had emphasized that the doctrine of continuous creation implies that creatures depend on God as a causally necessary condition of their states; in other words, they had conceived of God's continuous creation as a kind of background condition, like the presence of oxygen in the air. Malebranche, by contrast, goes further: creatures depend on God as a causally sufficient condition of all their states. As we have seen, God does not simply will that a particular billiard ball continue to exist in some way or other; He is causally responsible for all its determinate properties, such as its particular location and velocity. It is easy to see how a reductive analysis can accommodate such a claim. To say that all of the billiard ball's states depend on God as a causally sufficient condition is to say that they can all be genuinely explained in terms of God's general volitions (the laws of physics) and the initial conditions which he wills.[15] The doctrine of continuous creation is thus very far from requiring particular discrete volitions corresponding to each state of a creature.[16]

14. Malebranche's fullest statement of the argument for occasionalism from the continuous creation doctrine is found in *Dialogues on Metaphysics and on Religion* VII.

15. In the *Dialogues on Metaphysics* (VII.x), Malebranche even says that that the conservation of creatures is "simply a continuous creation, a single volition subsisting and operating continuously" (OC 12:160; JS 115).

16. It might be thought that Nadler's interpretation is required if Malebranche is to be able to do justice to the theologically orthodox doctrine that God has a providential care for His creatures. However, Andrew Black has shown how this doctrine can be accommodated by an inter-

II

Malebranche's doctrine of efficacious laws thus seems to be decisive evidence against the thesis that God needs to execute the laws by discrete individual acts of volition. But the doctrine of efficacious laws raises its own problems of interpretation, for it may seem to be inconsistent with the central tenet of occasionalism, namely, that God is the one true cause. Recall that, according to Malebranche, "God . . . willed certain laws according to which motion is communicated upon the collision of bodies; and because these laws are efficacious, they act whereas bodies cannot act" (SAT 6.2.3, OC 2:314; LO 449). On the face of it, by claiming that laws, not bodies, are efficacious, Malebranche may seem to be simply reintroducing genuine secondary causes into the world by the back door. That is, instead of attributing causality to particular events or bodies, he is attributing it rather to the laws where these are understood to be general nomological facts. Causality, then, has been clandestinely shifted from particular bodies or events to structural features of the created world.[17] But if this is so, then causal efficacy would still belong to creatures, and this claim would be inconsistent with the fundamental occasionalist tenet that God is the sole true cause.

At first sight, there is a straightforward way of reconciling occasionalism with the doctrine of efficacious laws. The key to solving the problem of consistency seems to be furnished by Malebranche's insistence that efficacious laws are divine volitions. In *Dialogues on Metaphysics* XII.1, Malebranche's spokesman claims that the laws of soul–body union are "but the constant and invariably efficacious volitions of the Creator" (OC 12:279; JS 218). But if efficacious laws are simply divine volitions, then they are not ontologically distinct from God Himself. Thus, there is no danger that the doctrine of efficacious laws will reintroduce genuine causality into the world by the back door. On the contrary, it simply clarifies the nature of God's unique causal activity in the world.

This is a promising suggestion, but unfortunately the issue is not as straightforward as this; it is complicated by the fact that, where divine volition is con-

pretation of occasionalism that holds that within the order of nature God's role is limited to willing the efficacious laws and the initial conditions of the universe. See "Malebranche's Theodicy," 40–4.

17. Some such criticism of occasionalism was made by Ralph Cudworth in his *True Intellectual System of the Universe* (1678), Book I, ch. III, Sect. XXXVI. Cudworth criticizes "Mechanick Theists" who "would have God to contribute nothing more to the Mundane System and Oeconomy, than only the First impressing of a certain Quantity of Motion, upon the Matter, and the After-conserving of it, according to some General Laws." Cudworth argues that these philosophers are, in spite of themselves, committed to his own theory of plastic natures: "Forasmuch as they must of necessity, either suppose these their *Laws* of *Motion* to execute themselves, or else be forced perpetually to concern the Deity in the Immediate Motion of every Atom of Matter throughout the Universe, in order to the Execution and Observation of them. The former of which being a Thing plainly Absurd and Ridiculous, and the Latter that, which these Philosophers themselves are extremely abhorrent from, we cannot make any other Conclusion than this, That they do but unskillfully and unawares establish that very Thing which in words they oppose; and that their *Laws* of *Nature* concerning *Motion*, are Really nothing else, but a *Plastick Nature* . . ." See C. A. Patrides (ed.), *The Cambridge Platonists* (Cambridge: Cambridge University Press, 1980), p. 294. I am grateful to David Cunning for drawing my attention to this passage.

cerned, certain distinctions need to be drawn. In the first place, there is no doubt that, quite generally, Malebranche wishes to distinguish between volitions and their upshots. Consider the case of a human being who raises his or her arm, for example; here Malebranche will say that there is a volition that is the occasional cause of its effect or upshot, namely, the movement of the arm (SAT 6.2.3, OC 2:315; LO 449). Moreover, *prima facie* we need to distinguish between the act of divine volition and its propositional content: a volition is a mental act whereby one wills that something or other be the case. Strictly speaking, then, when I will to raise my arm, I will that my arm go up. If efficacious laws are divine volitions, it seems clear that they must be identified with the propositional contents of these volitions, and not with the acts themselves. As we shall see, each of these distinctions generates problems of interpretation for the doctrine of efficacious laws.

Volition and Upshot: The Problem of Necessary Connection

According to Malebranche's version of occasionalism, it is efficacious laws that bring about particular events in the world. It is clear, then, that efficacious laws belong on the volition side of the divide between divine volitions and their upshots; particular events, on the other hand, are the upshots of these volitions.[18] In this way Malebranche can legitimately claim that laws are not part of the created furniture of the world. But if laws are volitions, and not their upshots, then Malebranche has some explaining to do. For though Malebranche prefers to understand agency in general in terms of the volition/upshot model, he is clear that volitions and upshots may be related in quite distinct ways. In the case of human beings, the volition that one's arm go up is, as we have seen, only the occasional cause of the movement of the arm. In the case of God, by contrast, volitions are genuine causes of their upshots or effects by virtue of the fact that that there is a necessary connection between the two. As Malebranche says in *The Search after Truth*, "the mind perceives a necessary connection only between the will of an infinitely perfect being and its effects" (SAT 6.2.3, OC 2:316; LO 450). Malebranche is famously committed to what we may call the "necessary connection" principle concerning divine causality. Thus, if Malebranche claims that efficacious laws bring about particular events in the world, he is committed to holding that there is a necessary connection between these laws and the events that they produce. And it is not clear that Malebranche can satisfy the demands of the "necessary connection" principle.

To appreciate the force of the problem, let us consider an alternative way of applying the volition/upshot model to the case of divine agency. Suppose that laws of nature were to be regarded, not as divine volitions, but rather as the upshot of divine volitions. In this case there would be a straightforward and elegant way of satisfying the demands of the "necessary connection" principle. To say that there is a necessary connection between God's volitions and their upshots would be to

---

18. The point that for occasionalists laws of nature are identical with God's volitions rather than the effects of them is emphasized by C. J. McCracken, *Malebranche and British Philosophy* (Oxford: Clarendon Press, 1983), p. 91.

say that it is a necessary truth that if God wills the law of inertia, for example, then the law of inertia obtains in our world. Of course this model is unsatisfactory on other grounds. If laws of nature are the upshots of divine volitions, then their home, as it were, is in the world; on this model they are to be identified with those general structural features of the world that are the truth-makers for nomological propositions. But in that case, laws of nature become creatures of a special sort; and thus, according to the fundamental tenet of occasionalism, incapable of genuine causal efficacy. But flawed as it is, the model does have the merit of accommodating the "necessary connection" principle.

Although there are compelling reasons for regarding the laws of nature as volitions, not upshots, this approach cannot so easily accommodate the "necessary connection" principle. Recall that this principle states that there is a necessary connection only between the will of an infinitely perfect being and its effects. But it is natural to object that there is no necessary connection between the laws of nature, taken by themselves, and particular events in the world; that is, descriptions of such particular events do not follow from the laws of nature alone. As Jonathan Bennett remarks in another context, "if a particular clap of thunder were necessitated *by* the laws of physics, there would be thunder everywhere and always."[19]

The proper response to this objection is that our account of divine volitions is incomplete as it stands. According to Malebranche, laws of nature are God's general volitions, and it is true that no such purely general volitions necessitate particular events in the world, such as claps of thunder. But, as we have seen, God does not merely will the laws of nature; He also wills the initial conditions. Thus, the divine volition that is necessarily connected with its effect is not simple, but compound; it is constituted by a general volition regarding the laws of nature and a particular volition regarding the initial conditions of the universe.[20] On the assumption that the laws of nature are not merely probabilistic, all particular events in the universe are indeed logically fixed by this compound divine volition.

Act and Content: The Problem of Efficacy

Malebranche, then, is not merely committed to a volition/upshot model of divine agency; he is also committed to holding that the laws of nature belong on the voli-

19. J. Bennett, *A Study of Spinoza's Ethics* (Cambridge: Cambridge University Press, 1980), p. 113.

20. As Donald Rutherford emphasizes, creation itself must be regarded as the product of a "particular volition" that establishes the initial conditions of the world; see his "Malebranche's Theodicy," S. Nadler (ed.), *The Cambridge Companion to Malebranche* (Cambridge: Cambridge University Press, 2000), p. 171. It is not entirely clear how many volitions (miracles aside) Malebranche wishes to ascribe to God: If, as Malebranche says at DM VII.x, the conservation of creatures is a "single volition subsisting and operating continuously," it is possible to see the natural order of the world as fixed by a single compound volition. In the *Treatise of Nature and Grace* (I.17, OC V 31), however, Malebranche says that God is able to "produce an infinity of marvels with a very small number of volitions." In any case, it is clear that Malebranche wishes to keep the number of divine volitions as low as possible.

tion side of the divide. But if this is the case, the doctrine of efficacious laws is confronted by a new difficulty. Divine volitions are acts that have propositional content, and it is with these propositional contents that laws of nature are to be identified; more strictly, laws of nature are the propositional contents of divine general volitions. But understood in these terms, laws of nature seem to be of the wrong ontological type to be capable of causal efficacy. For propositional contents would appear to be abstract entities, and abstract entities are not the sort of item that can cause anything. Thus, the doctrine of efficacious laws may seem to rest on something like a category mistake. It may, then, be doubted whether Malebranche subscribes to the doctrine in this form.

One way of responding to the objection is to draw on an analogy with Malebranche's theory of ideas. Throughout his career, Malebranche is famously committed to the thesis that all ideas are in God; by virtue of the fact that they possess such properties as infinity, eternity, and necessity, God is the only possible locus for ideas. At least in his later philosophy, Malebranche comes to add a new property to the list: ideas in God are said to be efficacious; that is, they have the power to cause perceptions in finite minds.[21] Scholars who have noted this development in Malebranche's teachings have wondered why he was led to the theory of efficacious ideas. At least part of the answer seems to be that Malebranche felt the need to respond to a challenge thrown down by Regis (see OC 17-1: 293–4). Malebranche is committed to the thesis that in perceiving ideas the mind is united to God, and he had been pressed by Regis to explain the nature of this union. Malebranche seems to have come to the conclusion that the only way of explaining the union was in causal terms. A further motive for the doctrine of efficacious ideas may have been more theological. Malebranche seems to have felt the need to offer a stricter interpretation of the patristic thesis that the mind is an illuminated light *(lumen illuminatum)*, not an illuminating light *(lumen illuminans)*. To this end, he comes to deny that the human mind possesses an inborn Cartesian faculty of pure intellect whereby it apprehends ideas in God; the mind finds in itself only modalities full of darkness. But having deprived it of a faculty of pure intellect, Malebranche needed to offer some account of how a purely passive mind was in touch with the divine ideas: the theory of efficacious ideas fills the lacuna in his thought left by the disappearance of the faculty of pure intellect.[22]

The relevance of the doctrine of efficacious ideas for interpreting the doctrine of efficacious laws should now be clear. It is widely agreed that ideas, for Malebranche, are not psychological items, as they are for Descartes; by virtue of the fact that their locus is God who is outside space and time, they are more like Platonic forms than Cartesian thoughts *(cogitationes)*. Thus, in his later philosophy Malebranche is not reluctant to ascribe genuine causal properties to abstract entities whose locus is God. Malebranche's argument for the attribution of causal

---

21. "A partir de 1695 l'idée qui est infinie, éternelle, nécessaire etc. . . . , reçoit en un sens précis le qualificatif d'efficace qui n'apparaissait jusqu'ici que rarement au hasard de la plume." A. Robinet, *Système et existence dans l'oeuvre de Malebranche* (Paris: Vrin, 1965), p. 259.

22. For further discussion of this issue, see N. Jolley, "Intellect and Illumination in Malebranche," *Journal of the History of Philosophy* 32 (1994), 209–24.

properties to ideas is straightforward: Ideas are in God, and whatever is in God is efficacious; hence, ideas are efficacious (Malebranche to De Mairan, 12 June 1714, OC 19:884). Whatever we think of the merits of this argument, it is nonetheless instructive for our present purposes, for it serves to show that a similar argument can be constructed for the strict efficacy of laws:

1. Laws are propositional contents of divine general volitions.
2. Propositional contents of divine general volitions are in God.
3. Therefore, laws are in God.
4. Whatever is in God is efficacious.
5. Therefore, laws are efficacious.

Like the argument for the efficacy of ideas, this one is vulnerable to philosophical criticism. For instance, we might wish to dispute the premise that whatever is in God is efficacious; indeed, it seems to run together different aspects of the divine nature that Malebranche had earlier insisted on distinguishing. Nonetheless, it is clearly an argumentative strategy to which Malebranche might have appealed to defend his doctrine of efficacious laws against the charge that it is guilty of a category mistake.

Impressed by the strangeness of ascribing causal properties to abstract entities, some scholars have been inclined to doubt whether the theory of efficacious ideas should be taken at face value. Alquié notes that Malebranche sometimes says, not so much that it is ideas that are efficacious, but rather that it is God who acts in us by means of his ideas;[23] in the *Dialogues on Death*, for instance, Malebranche writes that God alone . . . acts on our souls by the idea of extension which he contains (OC 12:409). In other words, in such passages Malebranche is expressing himself more carefully; he is correctly attributing efficacy to the divine will rather than the divine ideas. In a structurally similar way, some readers may wonder whether it is laws themselves that are efficacious. It may be said that talk of efficacious laws is merely a *façon de parler*, and that efficacy strictly belongs not to the laws but to the act of God's volition in willing them.

Alquié's scruples are understandable, but there are powerful considerations on the other side. For one thing, it is not clear that passages like the one from the *Dialogues on Death* really do offer a more careful alternative to the theory of efficacious ideas. To say that God acts on our minds by means of His ideas may mean simply that God acts on our minds precisely *qua* locus of efficacious ideas. Moreover, not merely does Malebranche state the thesis of efficacious ideas in uncompromising terms, as when he says that ideas are only the efficacious substance of the divinity (*Conversations Chrétiennes*, OC 4:79); he also offers a direct argument for the thesis that suggests he is untroubled by the objection that abstract entities cannot have causal properties. As we have seen, Malebranche has the resources to offer a parallel argument for the efficacy of laws themselves. But even if, in the spirit of Alquié, we decide to say that talk of efficacious laws is a *façon de parler*, one thing is clear: such a concession has no tendency to give aid and comfort to the proponents of the Nadler thesis. For what is at issue is whether it is laws them-

---

23. F. Alquié, *Le Cartésianisme de Malebranche* (Paris: Vrin, 1974), 210–1.

selves or God's action in willing the laws to which efficacy properly belongs. Neither thesis has any tendency to imply that that in order to bring about particular events in the world God has to do more than will the laws and the initial conditions.

A striking feature of Malebranche's discussions of causality is that they tend to run the claim that laws are efficacious in tandem with the thesis that God acts by virtue of or in consequence of His laws. This, I believe, is just what we would expect, for Malebranche may well be seeking to assuage the worry that to talk of efficacious laws is to reintroduce secondary causality into the world by the back door. Malebranche seems to be responding to this objection by emphasizing that it is precisely by means of efficacious laws that God, the unique causal agent, acts in the world; the doctrine of efficacious laws is thus in no way inconsistent with the central tenet of occasionalism. But whatever his reasons for running the two doctrines in tandem, it is fortunate for our purposes that he does so; for he thereby makes it clear that God does not need to implement the laws that he has willed through a series of discrete individual volitions.

Midwest Studies in Philosophy, XXVI (2002)

What Kind of a Skeptic Was Bayle?

THOMAS M. LENNON

Pierre Bayle (1647–1706) is not easy.[1] As anyone who has ever looked at his work knows only too well, it is very difficult, certainly at first, to determine Bayle's view on any of the myriad topics he discusses. Even so, there is a conditioned response to his name—in fact, conditioned partly in response to the interpretive difficulty—and that is skepticism. The conditioning started in his own time, continued throughout the Enlightenment, when his influence was at its greatest, and has persisted up to recent literature. It has seldom been clear, however, which of the several senses the term has had when applied to him. With a focus on the recent literature, the aim here will be to define the three most important of these senses and to determine the appropriateness of their application to Bayle.

One relevant kind of skepticism might be termed *Humean Pyrrhonism*. This is the apparently paradoxical view that, sometimes at least, it is reasonable to renounce reason in favor of some other, contrary means of belief formation, if not access to truth. In Hume's case, the well-known alternative access was through natural instinct; in Bayle's case, the alternative access was through religious faith, perhaps a kind of supernatural instinct.[2] It is precisely the validity of this alterna-

---

1. I have benefited from discussion on this topic, over a long period of time, from Harry M. Bracken, Bruce Freed, Giovanni Grandi, Leo Groarke, and Jose R. Maia Neto. References to Bayle are to his *Dictionnaire historique et critique* (1st ed., 1697; 2nd ed., 1702) by article and remark, which will be sufficient for referencing across any editions, and to his *Oeuvres diverses* (1st ed. The Hague, 1727–31; reprinted, Hildesheim: Georg Olms, 1664–90) cited as OD with volume, page number, and column.

2. Thus, Bayle has generally been described as a fideist. But this term has been used with even less precision than *skepticism*, and thus will be avoided here. For some discussion of the term in connection to Bayle, see Richard H. Popkin, *The History of Scepticism from Erasmus to Spinoza* (Berkeley: University of California Press, 1979), pp. xviii–xxi, and Antony McKenna, "Port-Royal

tive access, at least with respect to religion, that is denied by the second relevant kind, which might be termed *religious skepticism*. In Bayle's case, the term indicates that, despite his repeated professions of religious faith, Bayle in fact denied, or was at least logically committed to a denial of, the very faith he was professing. The third relevant kind might be termed *Academic skepticism*, although in Bayle's case its sense must be sharply distinguished from that classically given by Sextus Empiricus. It is not the apparently dogmatic assertion that all that can be known is that nothing can be known, but a methodological prescription, that we act in our knowledge claims only with Ciceronian integrity (*integra . . . potestas iudicandi*).[3] In Bayle's case, it is the homely injunction always to speak the truth as it is seen. The thesis to be argued here is that Academic skepticism best characterizes the relevant positions of Bayle, and that properly understood it accounts for the plausibility of applying the other two senses of skepticism to his work.

The above tripartite division represents something of a Procrustean bed, certainly historically, since there were important overlaps among the three kinds of skepticism, both in the ancient and early modern periods. For example, Anesidemus founded the Pyrrhonian school in opposition to the perceived intrusion of dogmatism into Academic skepticism, but did so as a continuation of the purer strand of skepticism that prized intellectual integrity.[4] Nor was there any sharp distinction between Pyrrhonian and Academic skepticism in the early modern period, certainly not in the terminology that was used in the seventeenth century. By the time of Bayle's work, the terminology was being expanded even further, implicating religious skepticism. The French translator of Shaftesbury was not the only one to notice the term *Pyrrhonian* being applied at that point to free-thinkers.[5] Even so, important conceptual distinctions can be made. Given the thesis to be argued here, it will be useful, therefore, to begin with a schematic characterization of Academic skepticism as limned above.

Imagine a truth machine—a device, or at least a source, that produces nothing but true sentences. One that does so, moreover, not just randomly, which

---

et le scepticisme; histoire d'un détournement," to appear. To describe Bayle in these terms, however, is not necessarily to say that Hume himself was a Pyrrhonian skeptic. For an argument that Popkin's characterization of Hume is mistaken, and that Hume was an Academic skeptic, see John P. Wright, "Hume's Academic Scepticism: A Reappraisal of His Philosophy of Human Understanding," *Canadian Journal of Philosophy* 16 (1986), pp. 407–36.

 3. *Academica* II, iii, 8.

 4. See David Selby, "The Protagonists," in *Doubt and Dogmatism: Studies in Helenistic Epistemology* ed. M. Scholfield, M. Burnyeat & J. Barnes (Oxford: Clarendon Press, 1980) pp. 16–17. Also, Michael Frede, who distinguishes between modern "dogmatic skepticism" (nothing is, or can be, known) and ancient, classical skepticism that includes both Academic and Pyrrhonian skepticism, such that differences between the latter are less significant than between them and modern, dogmatic skepticism. "The Sceptic's Two Kinds of Assent and the Question of the Possibility of Knowledge," in *The Original Sceptics: A Controversy* (Indianapolis: Hackett, 1997). For more on the continuity of ancient Academic and Pyrrhonian skepticism, see Leo Groarke, *Greek Scepticism: Anti-realist Trends in Ancient Thought* (Montreal and Kingston: McGill-Queens University Press, 1990), esp. pp. 111–13.

 5. See John S. Spink, "'Pyrrhonien' et 'sceptique' synonymes de 'matérialiste' dans la littérature clandestine," in *Le matérialisme du XVIIIe siècle et la littérature clandestine*, ed. Olivier Bloch (Paris: J. Vrin, 1882), esp. p. 144.

would be utterly unexceptional, but in relevant response to specific questions. It might be imagined as doing its thing by correcting false sentences that are put to it. Because of Chomsky-Popper-Searle-type questions, the truth machine would not be just a computer with an extraordinarily well-stocked memory; but what then? Many in the seventeenth century thought of nature as just such a machine. One had only to put the question to her in proper terms in order to be infallibly informed. (That nature provides answers to our questions in this or any other way is not an obvious or trivial thought, by the way.) But no one, except Spinoza perhaps, thought that every truth could be wrung from nature. Perhaps just God, then, who, as Bayle put it, can neither deceive nor be deceived.

If the machine says P, should I believe P? No one after some time with the machine would have much inclination to do otherwise. Would I, even after a lifetime of experience with the machine, thereby know that P? Worried about problems of induction from nature, I might hesitate to make such a claim—the machine might break down, after all. I would want to know how the machine works, and that it is working in saying that P. In short, I would want evidence for my belief.

What is true of the machine is true, the Pyrrhonian skeptics argued, of any criterion that might be proposed for determining that the machine is working properly. Just as the machine must be checked to ensure its proper functioning, so the criterion itself must be checked. At this point, well-known problems of vicious, infinite regress emerge. At some point, if we are to arrive at the truth, we must simply see the truth for what it is. And if we restrict the sentences that we produce to just those based on such perceptions, then we, too, are, in our limited fashion, truth machines. This was the defining great realization of Descartes and others such as Foucher and Huet in the tradition of seventeenth-century Academic skepticism. The restriction might mean that we are seldom, perhaps never, in a position to produce sentences. Foucher and Huet would argue this, citing Democritus that the truth lies unperceived at the bottom of a well. Descartes obviously thought otherwise. But they all agree on the conception of themselves as truth machines, disagreeing only on how often it might properly function.

That Descartes belonged to this tradition is, of course, beyond the present argument. Suffice it to say that in his own time Descartes was interpreted as an Academic skeptic of this sort who abandoned his intellectual integrity for an indefensible dogmatism. On this interpretation, Descartes begins with an intention of skepticism but ends, *malgré lui*, as a dogmatist—the exact converse of the canonical interpretation, due primarily to Popkin, that Descartes begins with an intention of dogmatism but, because of well-known circularity problems, ends, *malgré lui*, as a skeptic. The important argument here, in any case, is that Bayle was a part of the Academic tradition as just limned.[6]

In his pioneering papers on early modern skepticism, Popkin seems to have placed not just Descartes, but also Bayle, in a very different tradition. He classi-

6. Popkin, *History of Scepticism*. For more on Foucher and his critique of Descartes, see Watson, *The Downfall of Cartesianism* (The Hague: Martinus Nijhoff, 1967), esp. pp. 18–19. For Huet's critique of Descartes, see his *Censura philosophiae cartesianae* (1st ed., 1689), ch. 8.

fies Bayle as the most notable of those critics of Descartes who showed that Cartesian principles lead not to Academic skepticism, but to Pyrrhonism. In some instances, again most notably Bayle's, this outcome was embraced as the critic's own. "Bayle . . . was to put together and add to the critique of Cartesianism, to carry the skeptical onslaught to all types of theories . . . Bayle not only took over this aspect of seventeenth-century skepticism [i.e., the response to Descartes], but he made it a part of a massive, all-encompassing attack on all attempts to comprehend and explain man's world. Bayle's aim was to undo every effort to find rationality in the universe . . . Bayle' s efforts were to provide the high road to complete Pyrrhonism . . ."[7]

In an earlier paper, Popkin had argued that Bayle's Pyrrhonism was more extreme than any that had ever been on offer. "Bayle centered his attack at the point where the Montaigne tradition [of skepticism] was at its weakest, a skepticism with regard to reason [as opposed to the senses] . . . he went much further, and declared [that Cartesian] *évidence* could not be the mark of truth, since there are *evident* propositions that lead to conclusions that are false."[8] Presumably, because *évidence* is the only possible property that could serve as the requisite mark of truth, and reason is a faculty for recognizing this non-empirical property, reason is undone when the reliability of evidence is undone.

In arriving at the unreliability of *évidence*, however, Bayle seems not to attack reason quite to the extent that Popkin thinks. The modus tollens argument that undoes the reliability of *évidence* seems unchallenged, so presumably reason stands at least to this extent. That is, the skeptic *reasons* that if *évidence* is the mark of truth, then no proposition is both evident and false, but that some propositions are both evident and false, and therefore that *évidence* is not the mark of truth. A possible answer to this objection is the classical gambit of Sextus, that reason is like a purgative that expels itself along with what it has undone. This may be at least part of the point that Bayle is making in a wonderfully quotable but not altogether clear text in which he employs a similar medical metaphor. "We may compare philosophy to certain powders so very corrosive, that, having consumed the proud and spongy Flesh of a wound, they would corrode even the quick and sound Flesh, rot the bones, and penetrate to the very marrow. Philosophy is

---

7. Thus the title, which is a phrase from Bayle, of the collection of his papers on the topic. "The High Road to Pyrrhonism," *The American Philosophical Quarterly* 2 (1965), 1–15; reprinted, *The High Road to Pyrrhonism* (San Diego: Austin Hill Press, 1980), pp. 25–26. Bayle as a defender of Pyrrhonism was an early view of Popkin's. See his "The New Realism of Bishop Berkeley," *George Berkeley*, University of California Publications in Philosophy, vol. 29 (Berkeley and Los Angeles: University of California Press, 1957), pp. 1–9; reprinted, *The High Road to Pyrrhonism*, p. 324.

8. "Pierre Bayle's Place in 17th Century Scepticism," in Paul Dibon, ed., *Pierre Bayle: Le philosophe de Rotterdam* (Amsterdam: Elsevier, 1959), p. 3. Popkin has continued to read Bayle in these terms. For example: "Skeptical challenges to all of these theories (i.e., Scholasticism and its would-be Cartesian, Epicurean and Platonic replacements), . . . became a most radical sceptical undermining of the very possibility of a foundation for knowledge of God and his, or her, creation, especially as developed by someone of the genius of Pierre Bayle." *Scepticism and Irreligion in the Seventeenth and Eighteenth Centuries*, ed. R. H. Popkin & A. Vanderjagt (Leiden: E. J. Brill, 1993), p. 7.

proper at first to confute errors, but if she be not stopped there, she attacks Truth itself."[9] In any case, one wants to know how the relevant consequent of the modus tollens argument is known to be false. In some instances that Popkin does not consider, where Bayle clearly is placing limits on reason, the consequent is known to be false on the basis of reasoning from other propositions that are taken to be true, presumably on the basis of their *évidence*. (Thus does Bayle impugn our ability to arrive at the truth about the composition of matter on the basis that neither infinite divisibility, nor physical points nor mathematical points, which are the only possible accounts, is acceptable.) In the cases of interest to Popkin, they are known to be false on the basis of religious faith, which is also the solution he sees Bayle as offering to the Pyrrhonian crisis precipitated by the overthrow of *évidence*.

Bayle thus emerges as a paradigm case of the Christian Pyrrhonism that Popkin recounts in his classic *History of Scepticism*, although that work breaks off before reaching Bayle. The major thesis of the book is that many early modern skeptics argued the impotence of reason as an indication of the importance of faith. In the rather lame metaphor of one of them, whom Bayle quotes in connection with skepticism and faith, the mind is a sort of field that must be weeded of its rational pretensions in order to receive the seed of faith.[10]

Historically, it is prima facie far from implausible to read Bayle in these terms, especially if one looks at his critics who thought that when such a herbicide is applied to the mind, nothing can take root. In a work to which Popkin alludes, Bayle's contemporary Jean La Placette regarded him as "plunged into a state worse than direct and dogmatic atheism, i.e. Pyrrhonism," which for him was "the total extinction of reason." A consistent Pyrrhonist should be silent and inactive, the most incurable kind of atheist because unamenable by argument.[11] Perhaps the last of those who criticized Bayle as a Pyrrhonist (as opposed to the Enlightenment welcoming him as one) was Jean-Pierre Crousaz.[12] He took Pyrrhonism to be a form of madness due to personality failings: the habit of contradicting, vanity and laziness, depression, rationalization of immoral behavior, etc. "Among the ancient skeptics, none was the equal of Sextus, among the moderns, none is the equal of Bayle."[13]

However, there are a number of problems with including Bayle under this rubric. For one thing, Pyrrhonism as such figures insufficiently often in Bayle for it to play the role Popkin assigns to it. And when Pyrrhonism does appear, it is not

---

9. Art. Acosta, rem. G. The colorful translation of Pierre Daimaizeaux is cited here (London, 1734–38). See also art. Pyrrhon, rem. C: the Pyrrhonist's argument against certainty, if sound, refutes itself by producing something of certainty. "But the reasons for doubting are themselves dubious; we must doubt whether we must doubt—what chaos!"

10. La Mothe LeVayer. See Popkin, *The History of Scepticism*, ch. 5. Bayle, art. Pyrrhon, rem. C.

11. *Réponse à deux objections* (Amsterdam, 1707). Preface (unpaginated), pp. 1, 12–13.

12. *Examen du pyrrhonism ancien et moderne* (The Hague, 1733), p. 1.

13. "A man who had never heard of Bayle and who opened his *Dictionnaire* by chance at the article Euclid, might he not take him to be the author who most abused the spirit of argument, who made the worst use of his subtlety, who carried contradiction farthest, and who most spread doubt on what was taken for most certain." Ibid., p. 56.

as a position that Bayle espouses, but almost invariably as the relevant premise in a reductio ad absurdum, serving as such in virtue of the obvious contempt that Bayle has for it.[14] Popkin focuses his attention on a single text, the pair of remarks B and C from the *Dictionnaire* article Pyrrhon, some few pages from a work of eight to ten million words, itself not nearly the half of what Bayle wrote.[15] To carry Popkin's thesis, this text must be confirmed by what Bayle says elsewhere, or it must be a systematically very powerful argument on behalf of Pyrrhonism. That it is neither is a negative thesis hard to make except by showing that something else is being argued there that is both confirmed elsewhere and that is a very powerful argument. It will be argued below that what is found here, confirmed by every page that Bayle wrote, is Academic skepticism. But first a very brief rehearsal of these famous two remarks.

The article Pyrrhon begins by observing that only in theology and religion is Pyrrhonism to be feared, although in remarks B and C, the fear turns out to be baseless, since its arguments for suspension of belief are overcome by grace, education, ignorance, and the natural inclination to believe one way or other. Even so, in an imagined dialogue between two *abbés*, Bayle develops at length arguments for suspension, beginning with those from natural philosophy. In Berkeleian fashion, he argues that the arguments for the subjectivity of sensible qualities can be extended to the putatively objective mathematical qualities, which cannot be saved by appeal to divine veracity. He then argues the Pyrrhonist case from theology, this time by showing that doctrines such as the Trinity or transubstantiation are at odds with principles that are perceived with *évidence*, viz., that things not different from a third thing are not different from each other, and that a human body cannot be entirely present in two places at the same time. Finally, in what is undoubtedly for Bayle the most cogent consideration, suspension is recommended by the problem of evil. The drama ends with the dismissal of Pyrrhonism as rationally unanswerable but of no significance because trumped by the faith emphasized by Popkin.

Popkin himself thinks that his account of Bayle as presented so far is not without its problems. Most notable is that Bayle's solution to the problem of reason's demise by an apparently blind appeal to faith itself suggests a reinstitution of reason. Even in the article Pyrrhon, Bayle adumbrates what he later makes explicit, that it is sometimes rational to reject reason in favor of faith. As he put it in his very last work, "I have said thousands of times that one cannot act more in conformity with reason than by preferring the authority of Scripture to the philosophical maxims that oppose our mysteries [of faith]."[16] This might suggest

---

14. Craig Brush claims that Bayle makes such use of Pyrrhonism "hundreds of times." *Montaigne and Bayle: Variations on the Theme of Skepticism* (The Hague: Martinus Nijhoff, 1966), p. 283. J.-P. Jossua points out that the work of Montaigne was known well to Bayle and was often cited by him but hardly ever as the work of a skeptic. "Doute sceptique et doute méthodique chez Pierre Bayle," *Revue des sciences philosophiques et théologiques*, 61 (1977), p. 324.

15. Sean O'Cathesaigh, "Bayle's *Commentaire philosophique*, 1686," *Studies on Voltaire and the Eighteenth Century*, no. 260, 1989, p. 159.

16. *Entretiens de Maxime et Thémiste* (posthumous) II, vi; OD IV, 44b.

an appeal to a higher sense of reason, but not according to Popkin. Instead, as Bayle puts it when explaining to his rationalist critic Jaquelot that his rejection of reason is not a renunciation of it, what he does is "to give preference to some evident maxims of reason over some other evident axioms of reason."[17] But Popkin sees no basis for excepting from the skeptical argument the axioms and proofs that make the acceptance of faith rational. He attempts to resolve this inconsistency, or gratuitous exception, by viewing Bayle as structurally anticipating Hume's naturalism. Thus the label given this first form of skepticism above.

Hume, too, is both a doubter ("if reason be considered in an abstract view, it furnishes invincible arguments against itself, [such] that we could never retain any conviction or assurance, on any subject")[18] and a believer ("we lie under an absolute necessity, notwithstanding these difficulties, of thinking, and believing, and reasoning with regard to all kinds of subjects, and even of frequently assenting with confidence and security").[19] Hume resolves the tension between what our reason rejects (affirms) and what we find ourselves nonetheless believing in terms of a genteel naturalism: "the conduct of a man, who studies philosophy in this careless manner, is more truly skeptical than that of one, who feeling in himself an inclination to it, is yet so overwhelm'd with doubts and scruples, as totally to reject it. A true skeptic will be diffident of his philosophical doubts, as well as his philosophical conviction; and will never refuse any innocent satisfaction, which offers itself, upon account of either of them."[20] In Hume's case, it is not supernatural faith or grace that determines belief, but very natural human psychology—taste and sentiment, as he calls it.[21]

There is an important text, to be discussed below, in which Bayle seems to subscribe to precisely the metaphilosophical view expressed by Hume. Accused of Pyrrhonism by Pierre Jurieu, Bayle said, "I recognize myself in what he says about my manner of philosophizing, and I admit that, except for the truths of religion, I regard other disputes as mind-games in which it is a matter of indifference to me whether the pro or the con is proven. If those with whom I must live are happier with Aristotelianism than with Gassendism or Cartesianism, I will leave them be, and my friendship and devotion to them will not thereby be diminished, nor am I put off when contradicted, but instead shift my view innocently and without chagrin whenever some greater probability is presented. This has been throughout the ages the spirit of the Academic philosophers."[22] Despite the similarity of attitude toward philosophy, however, there is a difference between Hume's drawing-room genteelness and Bayle's dead seriousness about what he most

17. Ibid. II, viii; OD IV, 47a.

18. *Dialogues Concerning Natural Religion* ed. N. K. Smith (London: 1947), p. 135; quoted Popkin, p. 14.

19. Ibid., p. 219, n. l; quoted Popkin, p. 15.

20. *Treatise of Human Nature* (Oxford, 1951), p. 273; quoted by Popkin, p. 15.

21. Making out the difference between the natural and the supernatural in this case is far from obvious. What is clear is that there was a historical connection of influence between them. See Thomas M. Lennon, "Taste and Sentiment: Hume, Bayle, Jurieu and Nicole," *Pierre Bayle: la foi dans le doute*, eds. O. Abel & P.-F. Moreau (Geneva: Labor et Fides, 1995), pp. 49–64.

22. *La cabale chimerique* II, xi; OD II, 675a.

profoundly believes. It is hard to imagine someone with the attitude expressed by Hume above suffering what Bayle underwent for his religious beliefs.

Moreover, the exception on behalf of religious beliefs expressed by Bayle above provides an answer to Popkin's question as to what justifies the preference of some maxims of reason over others in the argument for the rationality of faith. It is Scripture itself that does so. There may be a strategy available for dealing with instances when the evident maxims of reason come into conflict with one another, but in other instances the conflict may be intractable. In the case of matter's composition, for example, there seems to be no way to decide between the maxims that yield an exhaustive inconsistent triad of views, none of which is true. But in the case of the problem of evil, for example, Bayle claims that "from actuality to potentiality" is always a valid inference, and thus that, although we cannot rationally solve the problem, we can nonetheless know from the fact of evil in the world that it is possible for evil to have been introduced into the world even though God is infinitely perfect.[23]

What emerges in Bayle is something like a holistic web of belief, of the Quine-Ulian sort, at least in the sense that cognitive anomalies are resolved by rejecting the troublemakers beginning with those farthest from the center. The difference is that the center for Bayle is made up, not just of logical principles, such as the law of non-contradiction, but truths of faith. As he explains to Jaquelot, his rejection of reason is not a total renunciation of it, which he never proposes, but a (temporary) withdrawal before it. The latter is a matter of "being unwilling to admit as a judge in a question of religion a given philosophical maxim. It is to recognize that a dispute in which the maxim is decisive would be an unfair contest because no evident reply can be made to evident objections.[24] It is to wisely avoid such a contest, or to sound the retreat early in order to find a more defensible position, following the lead of reason, which itself commands us by some of its most evident axioms to make use of it in this way. This happens everyday in purely philosophical disputes—one abandons some axioms of reason and places oneself under the protection of others."[25] Such a strategy seems far from Humean Pyrrhonism. Still farther is it from the Pyrrhonism of the Christian skeptics who employed argument to achieve the classical epoche that is resolved only by faith. Bayle's concern here, as throughout, is to resolve doubt, not to propagate it.

The most dramatic argument against reading Bayle in Pyrrhonian terms comes from Harry M. Bracken.[26] His thesis is that in art. Pyrrhon, Bayle does not *embrace* Christian Pyrrhonism, but instead mounts a *reductio ad absurdum* of it,

---

23. Art. Manichéens, rem. D *in fine*.

24. Bayle's claim here is ambiguous: (*1*) generally, if an objection is evident, then there can be no evident reply to it; (*2*) in this particular case, the objection is evident and there is no evident reply. He may be content with either. Both yield unfairness—both make the contest between faith and reason unfair in that what determines our assent, or should do so, is *évidence*, which by definition excludes faith.

25. *Entretiens* II, vi: OD IV, 45a.

26. "Bayle's Attack on Natural Theology: The Case of Christian Pyrrhonism," in *Scepticism and Irreligion in The Seventeenth and Eighteenth Centuries*, ed, Popkin and Vanderjagt, loc. cit., pp. 254–66.

so that the skeptical arguments that he produces there are not offered in his own behalf.[27] In Bracken's view, Christian Pyrrhonism is a natural theology that offers a kind of preamble to faith, viz., the humiliation of reason so that, cleansed of intellectual pride, we can accept the faith. Bayle, of course, is always suspicious of natural theology, but the specific problem that Bracken sees is that this psychological preparation creates a role for a teacher, and a slippery slope to a mediator and finally to an infallible guide of the sort that Rome claimed to be. In short, Christian Pyrrhonism "threatens both the Protestant 'way of examination' and the connected doctrine of inviolable conscience."[28]

The slippery slope seems implausible, however. For one thing, the connected doctrine of the inviolable conscience was clearly formulated by Aquinas and has been reaffirmed by Rome ever since. In addition, the relevant concept would appear to be not that of a teacher, or even of a mediator, but of a meditator. The psychological preparation is something that can be, indeed must be, done on one's own. (Descartes's meditator is a highly relevant example.) But herein lies just the the problem that Bayle would see. Any role of our own in the acquisition of grace, anything less than total dependence on an unconstrained God, amounts to Pelagianism. And this may be what Bracken is getting at when he claims that the Christian Pyrrhonists fail because "their efforts have the unwanted and paradoxical consequence that, far from making us humble, they now seem to equip us with such dogmatic and intellectually arrogant claims as the demonstrable ... falsity of [rational] principles, as well as perhaps the principles such demonstrations require."[29]

There are two advantages to Bracken's approach. One is an explanation of an oddity perceived from Bayle's time to the present, viz. why it is that Bayle puts the skeptical arguments, and the problems they generate, into the mouths of a pair of *abbés*, i.e. Catholics. It is because the arguments were in fact advanced by Catholics, and not by Bayle. In addition, Bracken resolves the inconsistency that Popkin saw in Bayle's argument that it is rational to abandon reason in favor of faith. On Bracken's view, it is not Bayle who argues in this way, but, as he saw it, his Catholic opponents.[30] Moreover, as has been seen, Bayle does not renounce reason in the way Popkin thinks, but merely withdraws in those instances when it contradicts faith.

Before Bracken's critique can be accepted, however, two problems with it must be addressed. First, the Protestant way of examination seems itself open to the exercise of authority according to Bayle. Consider, for example, his argument

27. See especially pp. 256–57.
28. Ibid., p. 256.
29. Ibid., p. 257.
30. Bracken's argument was at least adumbrated in as early as 1964. "Bayle Not A Sceptic?" *Journal of the History of Ideas* 25 (1964). "We may eventually decide that Bayle intended to deny that he was resting faith on ruined reason . . ." (p. 170). At this point, Bracken was already questioning the standard line on the two-abbés passage. He took the target to be those theologians who criticize the more Socinian of their colleagues who rely inordinately on reason with respect to the Trinity, and then take an analogous stance with respect to the Catholics on transubstantiation (p. 177).

that respect for conscience entails that only the church as the church is in a position to define what is heretical.[31] Bracken is not unaware of this drift in Bayle, but attributes it to Bayle's reliance on rational principles. Almost quoting a text cited above, he says, "there is nothing more reasonable than believing what God says."[32] Against an unwelcome reappearance of natural theology, Bracken argues that the reasonableness of belief does not make it any less a mere belief. "Once we have faith, we may be able to say that it is founded on God not being a deceiver, but being able to prove, by principles of natural reason, that God is not a deceiver, is totally irrelevant to generating faith."[33]

There is, moreover, an additional way to support Bracken's position that will appear below. To put it as a slogan, for Bayle faith must be in good faith. This is the requirement expressed by Descartes in response to the objection that he made his own thought the standard of truth, that in this sense he has illicitly made himself an authority. Part of his reply is that there is a sense in which one should make one's thought the standard of truth. "In other words, all the judgments that he makes about some thing must conform to his perception if they are to be correct. Even with respect to truths of the faith, we should perceive some reason which convinces us that they have been revealed by God, before deciding to believe them. Although ignorant people would do well to follow the judgment of the more competent on matters which are difficult to know, it is still necessary that it be their own perception which tells them that they are ignorant; they must also perceive that those whose judgment they want to follow are not as ignorant as they are, or else they would be behaving more like automata or beasts than men. Thus the most absurd and grotesque mistake a philosopher can make is to want to make judgments that do not correspond to his perception of things."[34] Not incidentally, this is one of the best indications of Descartes's Academic skepticism.

A second problem with Bracken's critique is that Bayle himself had great problems with the way of examination. The upshot of the *Dictionnaire* articles Nicolle and Pellison is that the Jansenist Pierre Nicole's arguments against the way of examination are telling (although Bayle also believes that the same or analogous arguments tell against the Catholic way of authority).[35] To be sure, this represents a dramatic departure from the Protestant tradition, but it does not necessarily upset the "closely related primacy, privacy, and inviolability" of con-

31. His full argument is that one cannot condemn the Socinians without asserting that they act against conscience; but to do so is to strip from God his right as "the judge of the reins and hearts" of men, and from the church its right of defining according to the authority of Scripture what is heretical. *Janua coelorum*, OD V, 1; p. 419. That the way of examination allows such exercise of authority is a particularly pressing problem, since, for Bracken, the real issue is the use of skeptical arguments in the destruction of reason in order to make room for the exercise of political power, not just in the seventeenth century, but also and especially in recent times. See "Bayle's Attack," pp. 262–65.

32. Ibid., p. 259.

33. Ibid.

34. Appendix to *Replies V*; *The Philosophical Writings of Descartes*, trans. J. Cottingham, R. Stoothoff, D. Murdoch (Cambridge: Cambridge University Press, 1984), vol. 2, pp. 272–73.

35. For Bayle's own third way, see E. D. James, "Scepticism and Fideism in Bayle's *Dictionnaire*," *French Studies* 16 (1962), esp. pp. 309–11.

science that is "impervious to skeptical attack."[36] It will also be argued below that, despite Bayle's relinquishing the way of examination, conscience still stands for Bayle, at least in so far as it resists Pyrrhonian attempts to bring about epoche. Conscience as the expression of good faith understood in the terms above is infallible with respect to right action.

A next step beyond Bracken's position would be that it is not just against Catholic Pyrrhonism, or even against Catholicism, that Bayle is arguing, but against every form of Christianity and every form of religion. The historical fact of the matter is that in his own time Bayle was taken to be an atheist. The term *atheism* in the period was no less problematic than *skeptic*, one reason being that the two terms were often interchangeable.[37] So Bayle might be a skeptic in the selective sense that he does not believe in the existence of God, or in the existence of God conceived as orthodoxy required. On this interpretation of Bayle, his repeated professions of religious belief were often attributed to dissimulation on his part. For whatever reason, he was not prepared to divulge his real views. This interpretation in terms of religious skepticism flourished during the Enlightenment and has persisted to the present.

H. T. Mason not long ago raised, and answered, an interesting question: "What would Bayle have done if he had discovered in himself a growing scepticism about all religious faith? It seems likely, given his temperament, he would have done exactly what he did."[38] The temperament to which Mason alludes is one of cautious, passive conservatism, which is a temperament not only exhibited by Bayle but, it might be added, recommended by him as well. To support his observation, in fact, Mason might have drawn the contrast between the dispassionate calculation of Bayle and the hotheaded enthusiasm of his opponent Jurieu—a contrast that was clear, for example, from the advice each gave from exile in Holland to the Huguenots still living under French rule. Jurieu urged revolution; Bayle, for Hobbist-like reasons, advised obedience to the king. But that Bayle's personality profile was compatible with dissimulation does not establish that he did dissimulate.

On another level, Mason extends his argument by pointing to Bayle's nonchalant attitude toward his church. Even though Bayle admitted to the Consistory of the Walloon Church that the articles of his *Dictionnaire* were prejudicial to Calvinism in the eyes of some, the modifications he made for the second edition fell far short of the Consistory's expectations. Mason worries over the "the harm to his church," the "disrespect" for it, that Bayle must have known that he was responsible for. It is hard to evaluate the truth of these claims for want of information about Bayle's relation to his church, and still harder to evaluate their relevance to the dissimulation hypothesis in support of the allegation of religious skepticism. For one thing, Bayle's concern is not with the success of his church in

36. "Bayle's Attack," p. 261.
37. For a bibliography on the term in early modern times, see Ernestine van der Wall, "Orthodoxy and Skepticism in the Early Dutch Enlightenment," in Popkin & Vanderjagt, loc. cit., p. 122, n. 3.
38. pp. 205–6.

terms of propagation, but with its faith, to which alone he makes profession in his response to the Consistory and everywhere else. Bayle's attitude toward the former is typically one of pessimistic, indeed cynical, resignation. He felt that nothing he or anyone might deliberately do would change church history very much. Mason's confusion of the two sorts of concerns is like the mistake that Bayle attributes to the Socinians, who are alleged to dilute Christian dogma in order to make it palatable to non-Christians but who thereby end only by being condemned even more and tolerated even less by Christians.[39]

Mason rehearses some of the well-known problems that Bayle raises for the rationality of religion (the problem of evil, the lack of religious basis for toleration, etc.) and ends with a perhaps surprising conclusion. There is not much difference in the end between the skeptical non-believer and the believer of the sort Bayle claims to be, for both agree on the "ultimate incomprehensibility of the universe, its origin and motivation." (Presumably, the only difference is the belief of the latter, an important difference if due to grace, perhaps less so if due to delusion. Mason regards it as so insignificant as to excuse Bayle of any hypocrisy.) In any case, Bayle seems to be an instance of the former, disguising himself with faith in order "to preserve what little tranquility remained to him in a bitter world of exile."[40] Now, it seems a priori implausible that Bayle, who mercilessly attacked his fellow exile Jurieu, for example, should have been led by a desire for tranquility to such a deep and elaborate ruse over such a long period of time. Tending to some other garden would have been a more attractive pastime. Mason offers an additional advantage that appeals to just this possibility. The advantage is that disguise opened the way to "positive work in other domains"; that is, Bayle was thus able to pursue the life of scholarship (for which, it might be added, he also sacrificed marriage and a university appointment). That would have been an advantage, but the historical fact of the matter is, however, that from the time of the two editions of the *Dictionnaire* to the end of his life, Bayle was by choice involved in nothing other than religious controversy.

Mason also offers two kinds of justification for what might otherwise seem a reprehensible pretense. One is that it involved a faith that Bayle anyhow "would have liked to hold"; the other is Bayle's perception of the social utility of religion.[41] Ironically, the distinction between what one would like to be the case, and what one knows, or should know, to be the case, is one that Bayle continuously emphasized, especially with respect to questions of religion. Moreover, appeal to the social utility of religion was a sensitive issue in the period because of the use made of it by Spinoza, Hobbes, and others who were charged with atheism in even stronger terms than was Bayle. It may well be that Bayle saw social utility in religion, but to make social utility his principal interest in religion requires more

---

39. Art. Socin, rem L *in fine*.

40. Howard Robinson had previously floated such a hypothesis. "St. Paul's counsel, that Christians submit to revealed truth, was certainly [*sic*] not taken to heart by Bayle himself . . . It was merely a way of warding off the orthodox." *Bayle the Sceptic* (New York: Columbia University Press, 1931), pp. 214–15, but cf. p. 218.

41. Loc. cit., pp. 214–15.

textual evidence than Mason provides.[42] At this point, it might be best to heed the observation of Elizabeth Labrousse, the power and eloquence of whose statement defy translation. "Il y a de l'odieux dans une curiosité inquisitoriale qui chercherait à etiqueter l'attitude intime de Bayle; au surplus, chez un auteur aussi discret sur soi, aussi hésitant et aussi héroiquement tendu vers une objectivité imperturbable, la question est évidemment insoluble."[43]

Gianluca Mori takes the question of Bayle's belief and the sincerity of his expression of it to be "undecidable, although absolutely legitimate."[44] Whatever its status, the question is one that he tenaciously refuses to pronounce upon. His concern, instead, is with the logic of Bayle's position, and here the question is clearly decided for him. "All the paths of Bayle's philosophical reflection lead to atheism."[45] The case that Mori makes for his claim is very impressive, and full justice cannot be done to it here. It will be sufficient to sketch the case and focus on the specific question of skepticism.

According to Mori, there are three issues that must be faced if Bayle is to be read as other than a religious skeptic, especially if his putative faith is to be of the blind sort he claims it must be. One is the rationalist ethics that appears at every stage of Bayle's career. It is an especially important issue in so far as it provides the key premise in his defense of toleration. His argument was directed against the "literal" interpretation, deriving from Augustine, of Luke 13:23 ("Compel them to enter") that was used to justify the forced conversions of Huguenots. According to Bayle, every interpretation of Scripture that attributes to God, as this literal one does, actions manifestly contrary to the idea we have of His virtue must be false.[46] All that can be offered here, in brief response to Mori's argument, is the distinction that Bayle drew between the domains of ethics and religion, and between them and the domain of salvation.[47] There are good people and bad in all religions, and even among those with no religion. That only those good people in the right religion are saved, although not because they are good

---

42. In art. Spinoza, rem. O, at the end of a long argument that, even if not all the difficulties it raises can be answered, Spinozism is refuted by showing the falsity of its premises and the contradictions in its conclusions, Bayle summarizes as follows: "Let us reduce the whole thing to a few words. The ordinary hypothesis, compared to that of the Spinozists in terms of its clear content, shows us greater evidence; and when the former is compared to the latter in terms of its obscure content, it appears less opposed to natural lights; and besides (*d'ailleurs*), [it promises us an infinite good after this life, and grants us a thousand consolations in this one, whereas the other promises us nothing beyond this world and strips us of trust in our prayers and the remords of our neighbor; the ordinary hypothesis is therefore preferable to the other]." Mason rather overstates the matter when he says on the basis of the bracketed material that for Bayle Christianity is "preferable" to Spinozism "partly because it is less contradictory of 'lumières naturelles,' but also because it is "socially more useful." Loc. cit., p. 209.

43. *Pierre Bayle: Héterodoxie et rigourisme* (The Hague: Martineus Nijhoff, 1964), pp. 607–8.

44. *Bayle: philosophe* (Paris: Honoré Champion, 1999), p. 9.

45. Ibid. p. 189.

46. *Pensées diverses sur le comète* ccxxv; OD 3 III, 138a.

47. See Thomas M. Lennon, *Reading Bayle* (Toronto: University of Toronto Press, 1999), pp. 44–47.

and in the right religion, is the paradox of the Calvinist view of grace. In any case, the tension between the domains was not one he was unaware of. The ethical message of Christ is toleration, a virtue open to all who can reason, but Christianity requires the rejection of reason. None of this was hidden by Bayle. Indeed, that last point is nothing less than celebrated in the *Eclaircissement* to be discussed immediately below. But to say that religion is contrary to reason is not to say that it is contrary to conscience. To repeat a point from above that will be more fully developed at the end below, Bayle's Academic skepticism requires that faith be accepted only with intellectual integrity.

A second issue is the problem of evil, an issue never far from Bayle's consciousness. The short of a very long story is that a God who failed to bring about a miracle to prevent Adam's sin, and thus the whole history of evil, is one contrary to what the natural light shows us God to be.[48] One solution would be that of the Socinians—God was willing to prevent Adam's sin, but, ignorant of future contingents, was unable to do so. Bayle thought that even such surprising ignorance would not solve the problem.[49] Another solution would be that of the Epicurians, namely, the atheism that Mori sees the whole of Bayle's philosophy tending toward anyway. The problem that Mori sees in the solution of Bayle's blind faith in a God who did not bring about that miracle is that it opens Bayle to the worst kind of fanaticism and superstition.[50] Reason has been rejected, but only if reason can be appealed to can the literal interpretation of Luke 13:23 and all its horrors be avoided.

As has been seen, however, Bayle does not offer the Pyrrhonist's wholesale, principled, and permanent renunciation of reason, but a piecemeal, contingent, and temporary withdrawal when, and only when, reason is in conflict either with itself or with faith. In those myriad instances where there is no such conflict, such as the exegesis of Luke's text, reason has free reign. Moreover, even when reason has free reign, there is no foolproof, mechanical way of avoiding the dangers of fanaticism and superstition. Bayle has what he thinks are sound arguments to block those dangers, but there is no guarantee either that they are sound or that they will have the effect he desires.

A third problem concerns the terms in which Bayle expresses his blind faith, which according to Mori undermine the very faith he was supposed to be expressing. Most notable, but not unique, in this regard is the most important text in which Bayle addresses the allegation of religious skepticism against him. The historical background is as follows. Bayle's *Dictionnaire* immediately achieved notoriety because his erstwhile friend Jurieu acquired and published a confidential report to the French authorities by the abbé Renaudot, who was critical of it. The Consistory of the Walloon Church in Rotterdam commissioned its own reports and invited Bayle to deal with certain issues, which he promised to do in a second edition, although in the meanwhile he also published a set of *Reflections* on the

---

48. See Mori, pp. 138–39.
49. But cf. *Réponse aux questions d'un provincial* II, cxlii; OD III, 792b–93.
50. Mori, pp. 82–83, 261 ff.

criticisms and a short *Lettre* describing the proceedings and reaffirming his ortho-doxy.[51] The principal change of interest here, though not the only one, was an *Eclaircissement* on his treatment of Pyrrhonism.

The *Eclaircissement* provides some of the clearest, certainly the most cited, of Bayle's statements of blind faith. "A choice must be made between philosophy and the Gospel: if you wish to believe only what is evident and in conformity with common notions, take philosophy and leave Christianity; if you wish to believe the incomprehensible mysteries of religion, take Christianity and leave philosophy . . . The most valuable faith is that which on divine witness embraces truths most opposed to reason."[52] He supports his position with citations of the epistles of Paul and James and illustrates it with citations of the English physician John Brown, the Scottish mathematician John Craig, the French Jesuit René Rapin, and the libertine Saint-Evremond. The latter quartet is a typically motley array of unlikely references, but there seems to be little problem with the religious faith, or its blind-ness, of the first three.[53] The problem Mori sees concerns the fourth source.

Mori's position is that Bayle in fact throws his lot in with the libertine by espousing the irrationalist conception of faith that makes it liable to an atheist libertine's objections. Worse, he does so with problematic motivation, as evidenced by the *Eclaircissement* citation of a text from Saint-Evremond, which depicts the faith, not of a simple peasant, but of a noble simpleton. "Bayle finds nothing better to characterize his notion of faith than a clearly ironic text from an author whose incredulity was notorious—a text, furthermore, that he had already described as libertine . . ." Mori says at this point that we should not take this as indicating religious skepticism in Bayle. "But let us not say either that he was a naive and spontaneous writer honestly unaware of the explosive effect that his fideist and irrationalist declarations might have on readers among the Protestant community in Holland."[54]

To be sure, Saint-Evremond's text is ironic. But Mori neglects to mention that Bayle himself immediately characterizes it as such. "Let this thought be given a more serious and proper tone and it will become reasonable."[55] That is,

51. OD IV, 742–52, 763–65.

52. Vol. 15, pp. 316–17.

53. Rapin was involved in the skeptical controversies with Cartesianism, but his religious orthodoxy seems not to be the least impugnable among the four. Brown (1605–82) was the author of *Religio medici* (1642, pirated edition) in *The Prose of Sir Thomas Browne* ed. N Endicott (New York: New York University Press, 1968). There is no reason to doubt, and every reason to accept the sincerity of this work and Bayle's representation of it. Craig (d. 1731) was the author of *[Craig's] Rules of Historical Evidence* (s'Gravenhage: Mouton, 1964). There is some slight reason to question Bayle's citation of this work, since according to the editor, it came to be regarded as more damaging to Christianity than the skepticism it was combating. For example, he used his algebraic calculus to compute the Second Coming as no later than 3150 AD, and the probability of the Gospel as then equal to the what it was at the time of Christ, given the testimony of twenty-eight of his disciples. Until more is known of Bayle's work habits, and that may be never (e.g., how did he produce such a volume of work, with an unsurpassed information–volume ratio?), the significance of this trio might not be known. That is, these three might just have happened to be what Bayle was reading at that point.

54. Mori, pp. 262–63. Elizabeth Labrousse would seem to be the target here.

55. *Dictionnaire*, 15, 319.

Saint-Evremond's text read ironically is objectionable, but if it is stripped of its irony and ridicule, it becomes unobjectionable—indeed, a statement of Bayle's own position. He then proceeds to quote a criticism of Saint-Evremond that offers the necessary corrective. In addition, Bayle might in fact have been the naif that Labrousse took him to be, for it is not clear that Bayle much read Saint-Evremond beyond this text, which he in fact nowhere describes as libertine.[56] Moreover, one wants to know what pathology would motivate Bayle to have an explosive effect on his pathetic, exiled co-religionists? A cryptic message of atheism sealed in a bottle and left to drift to another time and place would be one thing, but a local upheaval of the contemporary scene would be quite another. Finally, the fact is that there was no explosion of the sort Mori implies. Or, if the rationalists Jaquelot, Bernard, and Leclerc who engaged Bayle in very lengthy controversy from the time of the *Dictionnaire* until his death are interpreted as being concerned that Bayle's version of the faith was cryptically propagating atheism, if that was the explosion, then it is hard to understand why Bayle should have engaged in the controversy at all, for his aim had been accomplished, or why he defended his position against them in unexplosive, unexceptional terms.

According to Mori, Bayle holds both (*a*) that only a rational examination of faith can give it a foundation for avoiding the slide into fanaticism, and (*b*) that, as a matter of fact, such examination is impossible, and that religion is based on instinct.[57] Now, in art. Pellison, rem. D, Bayle discusses the dispute over the Catholic way of authority and the Protestant way of examination. With both open to essentially the same serious objections, he presents a third party who argues for Mori's latter point. In a rational examination, both sides of the question should be examined, but prejudice keeps (almost) everyone from a serious examination of others' views. The argument is long and impassioned. But the remark ends with Bayle, speaking in *propria persona*, accepting prejudice as a guarantee against heresy for (those lucky enough to be) the orthodox. How else, it might be asked, could the faith of a simple peasant, who no less (or more) than anyone else deserves to be saved, withstand the onslaught of atheistic argument from a clever libertine? This is why faith must be instinctive. The only alternative is some form of Socinianism, according to which the likelihood of salvation would vary with intelligence.

That faith is instinctive does not preclude rational investigation, however. The argument of the third party is that most (*sic*) people cannot read, and that of those who can, most do not read the works of their opponents, relying instead on excerpts that represent them in the worst light, etc. These are not epistemological objections in principle to knowledge, but moral impediments that are surmountable, certainly to some degree, by practice of the very virtues that Bayle preached in the *Dictionnaire* and everywhere practiced. Assessing the credibility of one's

---

56. This is a long story, the short of which is that every one of Bayle's few and generally insignificant references to Saint-Evremond's work can be traced to two secondary sources that he himself mentions. See my "Did Bayle Read Saint-Evremond?" *Journal of the History of Ideas*, in press.

57. Ibid., p. 260.

belief, which is incumbent upon even the simple peasant, is a matter of conscience: one should simply do the best one can. Indeed, not to engage in rational investigation of faith is to make it infantile, amenable to fanaticism and likely to become no more than mechanical, rote recitation.[58] Moreover, although the objections of the libertine cannot be rationally met, the credibility of faith is not thereby upset. In fact, only by the disingenuous refusal to engage would its credibility be threatened. The requirement of *bona fide* engagement cuts both ways, of course. The Pyrrhonists' objections cannot be met; their objections are not in good faith; hence, following St. Paul's epistle to Titus, they should be warned twice and then ignored.[59]

The concept of *bona fide* engagement, of intellectual integrity generally, is central to the third conception of Bayle's skepticism, due entirely to the recent work of Jose R. Maia Neto. In his view, the key to Bayle's skepticism is to be found in art. Chrysippus, rem. G. "Antiquity had two sorts of philosophers. One sort was like the lawyers [at a trial] and the other like those who report a trial. The former, in proving their case, hid as best they could the weak side of their own case and the strong side of their opponents'. The latter, namely the skeptics or the Academics, represented faithfully and without any partiality both the weak and strong sides of the two parties." Maia Neto's argument is that Bayle is a reporter, not a lawyer.

The lawyer-reporter distinction is in fact central to this interpretation, so it will be appropriate to elucidate the above text somewhat. The remark is, in several respects, typical Bayle. It is long, running to two and a half pages *in folio*. The argument, including the crucial distinction, is introduced, not by Bayle, but by Plutarch. With no names mentioned, a swipe is taken at Jurieu. There is a report of a conversation with an unnamed learned theologian. And the moral of the story is applied as an argument against censorship, with the efforts to censor Bayle's *Dictionnaire* as the clear object lesson.[60] Atypically, the remark is actually a commentary and development of the body of the article, which raises the following issue. The Stoic Chrysippus had so extensively represented the arguments of the Academics that the Stoics complained that he could not refute them. He thus seemed to act with honesty, except for the fact that he advised his followers not to represent their opponents' views so strongly as to gain conviction for them. The upshot is that Chrysippus in fact acted out of vanity in outdoing the Academics, Arcesilaus in particular, at defending their own position.

58. See the texts cited by Mori, p. 260. Gianni Paganini seems to have found the right path for Bayle between speculative atheism and blind belief of an exaggerated sort. See his *Analisi della fede e critica della ragione nella filosofia di Pierre Bayle* (Florence: La Nuova Italia, 1980), pp. 175–202, recently reaffirmed in "Apogée et declin de la toutepuissance: Pierre Bayle et les querelles post-cartésiennes," in *Potentia Dei: L'omnipotenza nel pensiero dei secoli XVI e XVII*, eds. G Canziani et al. (Milano: Angeli, 2000), p. 629, fn. 117

59. *Eclaircissement III.*

60. The argument is that books proposing the censorship of other books should also be censored if they faithfully report the books to be censored, with all their strengths, which ex hypothesi must be dangerous to readers, or if they do not do so, they lack credibility. That all he did was report as a historian the salacious material of others was Bayle's response to the charge of obscenity form the Walloon Consistory.

Bayle's interest is in the advice Chrysippus gave his followers, which is of interest here because in relating it, Bayle indirectly endorses Academic skepticism. "He would have those who teach a truth speak but softly of the arguments for the opposing position, and that they imitate lawyers. This is the general attitude of dogmatists; only the Academics gave the arguments of both sides with the same strength. Now, I maintain that this method of dogmatizing is bad, and that it differs very little from the deceptive art of the rhetorician sophists that made them so odious, and which consists in converting the worst case into the best; for one of their main tricks was to hide the advantages of the case they were attacking along with the weakest of the one they were defending, yet without failing to include a few objections selected from those easiest to refute. This is what Chrysippus would have philosophers do." That is, Chrysippus's view was in fact typical of dogmatist special pleading, the antidote to which is Academic honesty and intellectual integrity.[61]

In another typical twist, it might be noted, Bayle goes on to observe that there are hardly any more reporters to be seen, then or previously. "For if someone represents in good faith and without disguise the full strength of the opposite side, he makes himself odious and suspect and runs the risk of being treated as an infamous liar." His sidebar note refers to Charron, who was attacked by the Jesuit Garasse for his view that it is difficult to prove the existence of God. The case is obviously Bayle's own before those who impugned his appeal to faith after the attack on reason.

The evidence that Maia Neto proposes for including Bayle among the academic skeptics seems inconclusive. It is of two sorts, textual and causal. The latter is in terms of influence, particularly from Simon Foucher, the principal reviver of Academic skepticism in the seventeenth century. A problem, however, is that Bayle mentions Foucher only infrequently, and almost never to endorse a position of his. (An exception is the application of the arguments for the subjectivity of secondary qualities to the primary as well, which he himself carries through to a problem about the very existence of bodies. This is in the problematic two-*abbés* passage.) The texts cited by Maia Neto are suggestive but not definitive. One is a statement from the *Projet*, an advance notice Bayle gave of what he intended to do in the *Dictionnaire*. "Most commonly I shall not be the discoverer of [others'] faults, but the reporter of what others have said."[62] This text certainly places Bayle on the right side of the lawyer-reporter divide, but, like the text above, it is not strong enough to place him among the Academics, who, as Maia Neto understands them, do more than merely report others' views. For they also honestly formulate and report their own. In another text, already cited above, Bayle seems to go farther in just this direction. In response to a charge of skepticism from Jurieu, Bayle says, "I recognize myself in what he says about my way of philosophizing,

---

61. Typically, there is a strange twist to Bayle's account. Not only was Chrysippus dishonest, he was indiscreet. He should have kept the view to himself, as politicians do their maxims of state, or at most have spoken it "into the ear of some wise and learned disciple." Irony, reductio ad absurdum, or something else?

62. Quoted by Maia Neto, "Bayle's Academic Scepticism," p. 273.

and I admit that, except for the truths of religion, I regard other disputes as only mind-games in which it is a matter of indifference to me whether the pro or the con is proven. If those with whom I live are happier with Aristotelianism than with Gassendism or Cartesianism, I will leave them be, and my friendship and devotion to them will not thereby be diminished, nor am I put off when contradicted, but instead shift my view innocently and without chagrin whenever some greater probability is presented. This has been throughout the ages the spirit of the Academic philosophers."[63] Says Maia Neto: "Bayle says outright that his way of philosophizing is Academic. He holds only to the Academic commitment to intellectual integrity, that is, he is not committed to any doctrine."[64]

But perhaps the above self-description is not so straightforward. As Jossua pointed out some while ago with respect to this passage, the larger context is Jurieu's attributing the anonymous and, for Jurieu, inflammatory *Avis important aux refugiés* to Bayle. "Let us be wary of this false admission. For Bayle was the author of the *Avis*. More views must be attributed to him than he is willing to admit to."[65] It is not clear that this upsets the self-description, but it does amount to a caution. In addition, however, the skepticism of which Jurieu accused Bayle, and in which presumably Bayle claims to recognize his way of philosophizing, is not Academic but Pyrrhonian. Moreover, it is said to be Pyrrhonian, with a precision unusual for the period, in that it seeks epoche by finding an equally cogent proof for the contradiction of every claim that is thought to be proven. "[Bayle] enters a subject only to find difficulties, and he might be said to have a sixth sense in finding them and a special talent for pressing them. These difficulties obviously cast him into Pyrrhonism; he finds difficulty everywhere and that is why he is unwilling to find the truth anywhere. All difficulties are for him proofs, and he finds them in opposed views. This is why he believes that all views are equally proven."[66] Such epoche artificially reached by juxtaposition of arguments is no part of Academic skepticism.[67]

63. OD II, 676. See also to Jacob Bayle, 29 May 1681. Discussing his view of Cartesianism as "simply an ingenious hypothesis useful for explaining certain natural effects," Bayle says that he is "a philosopher without prejudices, taking Aristotle, Epicurus or Descartes as inventors of conjectures to be followed or not according to preference for this mind-game or that." *Oeuvres diverses* (The Hague, 1737), vol.1, p. 126.

64. Maia Neto, p. 272. OD II, 676.

65. Jossua, p. 441. The authorship of the *Avis* has long been a matter of dispute. Even if now the scholarly opinion is generally that Bayle is responsible for it, the fact is that he never acknowledged his authorship. In any case, Jossua's concern seems well-founded, for in the very text in which the self-identification as an Academic skeptic is supposed to occur, Bayle says that since he is a Protestant there is as great a difference between him and the author of the *Avis* as between heaven and earth. OD II, 675.

66. *Examen d'un libelle contra la religion . . . intitulé* Avis important. . . . (The Hague, 1691), pp. 45–46. The larger issue is one alluded to in passing above, the advice that should be offered to the Huguenots still living under French rule. Although he does not name him, Jurieu is sure that the author is Bayle because of the fine French, erudite references, the taste for newspapers and dictionaries, an exclusive reliance on reductio ad absurdum as a method of proof, and the Pyrrhonian skepticism.

67. Bayle himself, however, relates that according to Sextus Empiricus (the Academic) Arcesilaus held suspension of belief to be naturally good [*secundum naturam*] but according to Pyrron, it was only apparently good [*secundum id quod apparet*]. Art. Pyrrhon, rem A.

Despite the inconclusiveness of Maia Neto's evidence, it might be that his identification of Bayle is exactly right. Indeed, if it is right, then looking for the sort of direct evidence considered so far might be inappropriate. Consider a variation on Mason's question as follows: What would Bayle have done if he was writing, however consciously, from the perspective of Academic skepticism as Maia Neto understands it? Perhaps exactly what he did, especially if he actually held that perspective. For he would have sought to give instances of intellectual honesty, practice it himself and, presumably, promulgate it, and not just say what it is. He would have indicated what it is by exhibiting it himself, which would be a recommendation of it to others. To say what it is, and to recommend it to others *as such* would be to falsify the perspective. The philosophical ideal, on this account, is not one of *oratio recta*, but of example, of edification. This is why Bayle, although he offered himself ample opportunity to do so, nowhere subscribes to Academic skepticism, which would be the contradiction of subscribing to the view that rejects all subscription.[68]

Another look at the conception of ourselves as truth machines might help to focus this notion of skepticism. There is no explanation of why we are able to produce truth, and thus no guarantee, either, that we do. (Homunculus theorists of the sort that Descartes is supposed to be seem to be looking for such an explanation and guarantee—an inner look at the outer look, to ensure that it is a good look.) We may be truth machines, but there is no machinery. The apprehension of truth is non-mechanical, that is, non-formulaic. Were we to accept a formula or mechanism for the production of truth we would be behaving, as Descartes put it in a text cited above, "more like automatons or beasts than men." We should assert something to be true because we see it to be true, not because something else says that it is true.

But why, then, does Bayle reject *évidence*? Isn't the *évident* just what appears to be true? It is, which is why Bayle only rejects it when it contradicts either something else that is *évident*, or what is known to be true on the basis of faith. Bayle's rejection in art. Pyrrhon, rem. B of *évidence*, and a fortiori of every other criterion of truth, is the rejection of the mechanical infallible discovery of truth. To put it another way, to reject *évidence* is only to say that sometimes what seems to be true is not. Descartes, in relying on *évidence* (clarity and distinctness), cannot be saying that we never err, even when we think we are perceiving something clearly and distinctly. We are truth machines only when we function properly, that is, when we restrict our assertions to what we in fact clearly and distinctly perceive to be true. This is why he does not beg the question against Gassendi and Leibniz, who, in requiring of him a way to determine when a perception was clear and distinct, were looking for a criterion and thus begged the question against him.

---

68. Art. Carneades, for example, is a disinterested account that in fact is critical of Foucher's attempt to defend Carneades's moral theory. Similarly, in art. Arcéselas, Bayle is concerned primarily with getting the record straight—for example, on the question of the originality attributed to this Academic skeptic by Diogenes Laertius, which Bayle disputes, since his method of arguing pro and con came from Socrates and Plato, even if Arcesilaus pursued it "with more ardor . . . and showed himself more aggressive and determined than the first inventors," thereby making him "the first disturber of philosophers' public peace." Rem. E.

There is an important difference between the optimist Descartes and the pessimist Bayle, however. For Descartes we are truth machines *tout court* so long as we employ the natural light with integrity. God would be a deceiver were it otherwise. For Bayle, reliance on divine veracity aside from matters of faith is problematic, as his discussion of the extension-sensible quality distinction helps to show. He is willing to employ the natural light, and repeatedly does so, in seeking the *évident*. He simply does not find many instances of it. His skepticism is thus highly contingent and nontheoretical. Only in one domain does he find absolute certainty by employing reason, and that is morality. Instead of the natural light, it is conscience that is infallible. There is an objective truth of any matter, and integrity requires good faith effort to discover it, but we infallibly do what is right only in asserting what we take that truth to be. This is the inviolable conscience, on which Bracken rightly insists, that withstands Pyrrhonist attempts to bring about a permanent epoche. A deceived wife should not sleep with an imposter husband, but she infallibly does what is right when she innocently does sleep with him.[69]

In other domains there is a certainty to be found that is appropriate to the domain. Most notably, history allows something like moral certainty. If Bayle describes himself as a "historical Pyrrhonist" it is because he employs a methodology of doubt about historical facts until they can be proven with the relevant kind of certainty.[70] The *Dictionnaire* itself testifies to Bayle's conviction that a very un-Pyrrhonian certainty can be achieved, that the historical record can, in many cases, be known and corrected. For various reasons, ranging from simple difference in perspective to passion and outright fraud, suspension of belief is often warranted. But sometimes belief is warranted, as when there exists eyewitness testimony from someone with nothing to gain from lying. *Not* to accept such testimony, says Bayle in a clear *reductio ad absurdum*, "opens the door to Pyrrhonism, and nothing can ever be proved."[71]

The literature has come to appreciate Bayle's historical method as a form of Cartesianism, despite the Cartesians' own dismissal of history.[72] "The first rule of the Cartesian method, that of methodical doubt, suspension of judgment, radical and preemptive rejection of the argument from authority, was necessarily the golden rule of [historical] criticism." The motivation was what it was supposed to be for the Cartesians: objectivity and impartiality.[73] To put it another way, Bayle's "historical Pyrrhonism" is an instance, albeit a very important one, of his Academic skepticism.

Finally, it might be asked, how can Academic skepticism be understood as compatible with religious faith? What legitimates this appeal to authority? Isn't

---

69. The wife of Martin Guerre is Bayle's example. For more, see Lennon, *Reading Bayle*, pp. 81–82.

70. See Brush, loc. cit, pp. 253–54.

71. Art. Grotius, rem. H.

72. See especially Labrousse, loc. cit., Chs. 1, 2.

73. Jossua takes over and develops a thesis advanced by Cassirer, who drew on the positivist reading of Bayle by Delvolvé, and especially by Labrousse, whom he cites above. Loc. cit., pp. 389 ff., esp. 391.

Bayle's blind belief a mechanical acceptance of what God says, and thus a sacrifice of intellectual integrity? For what is believed is, far from *évident*, "obscurity itself," as Descartes put it.[74] One answer is that God is independently known to be trustworthy. (That God must be so known is the case that Bayle argues even if one accepts the Catholic way of authority.)[75] God is rather like a truth machine whose mechanism is known, or is at least known to work. A deeper response is that the question has bite only in so far as it tacitly assumes a premise that Bayle rejects, viz., that belief is sometimes not blind because it is absolutely justified by reason(s). But no belief avoids blindness in this mechanical way.

There are many reasons, according to Bayle, why we believe what we do: faith, education, grace, dumb luck, in addition to reason. If Bayle finds himself honestly believing in God, then for him to deny God would be to act without integrity. And conversely, to assert God in the absence of such belief would also be to act without integrity. This is Descartes's "case of an infidel who is destitute of all supernatural grace and has no knowledge of the doctrines which we Christians believe to have been revealed by God. If, despite the fact that these doctrines are obscure to him, he is induced to embrace them by fallacious arguments, I make bold to assert that he will not on that account be a true believer, but will instead be committing a sin by not using his reason correctly."[76] Bayle takes this sort of case to be a matter of conscience, and the *Commentaire philosophique*, which is his defense of toleration, contains many similar illustrations—for example, the man who kills an enemy whom he takes to be his father, and who thus does what is wrong, and conversely, the man who kills his father whom he takes to be his enemy, and thus does what is right. Conscience for Bayle determines rightness in both cases. Descartes's and Bayle's positions converge if assertion is taken to be a moral act.[77] Their Academic skepticism would be the injunction always to assert what one honestly thinks is true, perhaps with a degree of certainty commensurate with perceived certainty, regardless of why one believes it.

---

74. *Replies* II; loc. cit., p. 105.
75. *Commentaire philosophique* I, I; OD II, 370b.
76. *Replies* II; loc. cit., p. 106.
77. Which it may be—even if "words are not deeds," that is, even if words should never be censored. The latter is the case that Harry M. Bracken makes out on Baylean grounds in his *Freedom of Speech: Words Are Not Deeds* (Westport: Praeger, 1994), esp. ch. 1.

Midwest Studies in Philosophy, XXVI (2002)

From Locke's *Letter* to Montesquieu's *Lettres*[1]

EDWIN CURLEY

In his essay on Montesquieu, Isaiah Berlin appropriates a line from Jeremy Bentham, which I wish to reappropriate here, for a different purpose. Bentham had made the following contrast between Locke and Montesquieu: "Locke—dry, cold, languid, wearisome—will live forever. Montesquieu—rapid, brilliant, glorious, enchanting—will not outlive his century."[2]

There is, I think, some truth in this unhappy comparison. It may be unfair to Locke, who surely would not have had the influence he had if reading him were quite as tedious as Bentham suggests; and it is certainly too pessimistic about Montesquieu, whose works have outlived their century after all, and are still being freshly translated and kept in print. Nevertheless, Montesquieu has lost his place in the pantheon. For all his influence on the founders of our republic, historians of philosophy nowadays pay him little attention, whereas Locke still looms large on our horizons.

This is particularly true in the area which is my concern here. Locke dominates English-language historiography of the development of arguments for religious toleration. Montesquieu is barely mentioned.[3] I shall argue that this neglect

---

1. This is a revised version of papers presented at the meeting of the American Society for Eighteenth Century Studies, held in Milwaukee, in March 1999, and at Boston University in December 1999. I've profited from the comments I received on those occasions, and also from discussions with three students of mine, Craig Duncan, Justin Dombrowski, and Ahmad Kayali.

2. From *The Works of Jeremy Bentham*, ed. by John Bowring (Edinburgh, 1843), vol. 10, p. 143; cited by Isaiah Berlin, in "Montesquieu," in *Against the Current*, ed. by H. Hardy (Penguin, 1982), p. 130.

3. To get a measure of this, note the comparative frequency with which Locke and Montesquieu are cited in the following recent works: *Justifying Toleration: Conceptual and Historical Perspectives*, ed. by Susan Mendus (Cambridge University Press, 1988); *On Toleration*, ed.

is unfortunate, that whatever the merits of Locke's arguments, Montesquieu added something distinctive to the conversation, something which needed saying, and which *may* actually have been influential on the politicians who formalized the commitment to toleration which emerged in Western Europe and North America during the Enlightenment.

I shall leave the question of Montesquieu's influence for another day. My purpose here is to give an account of the argument for religious toleration in the *Persian Letters*. But before I celebrate the virtues of Montesquieu, I'm afraid I have a few unpleasant things to say about Locke, whose treatment of the subject seems to me to be generally overrated.

It's a common observation that Locke's treatment of toleration is unhappily limited. His subject is "mutual toleration among Christians,"[4] that is, he speaks as a Christian to other Christians, urging that the various Christian denominations practice toleration toward one another. Or more precisely, since he does not think that a state in which the majority of Christians are Protestant ought to tolerate Roman Catholicism (K/G, 131–135; W, 425–426), he urges that the various kinds of Protestants should practice toleration toward one another. He does suggest in passing that a state whose dominant religion is Christianity ought to tolerate Jews, pagans, and perhaps even Muslims.[5] He does not think that any state ought to tolerate atheists (K/G, 135; W, 426).

Locke argues that church and state ought to be separate both on religious grounds and on the grounds of a theory about the nature of church and state. Let us take the religious argument first:[6] among other things, it appeals to the principle that we should love our neighbors as we love ourselves, and contends, plausibly enough, that we do not act lovingly toward our neighbors if we confiscate their property, imprison them, torture them, mutilate their bodies, or kill them, *even if we claim to do this for the salvation of their souls*. Locke is inclined to suspect the good faith of those who would use state power to do such things. Those who wish to use coercion to change the *beliefs* of those they disagree with do not use it to

by Susan Mendus and David Edwards (Clarendon Press, 1987); *Toleration: An Elusive Virtue*, ed. by David Heyd (Princeton University Press, 1996); *Toleration and the Constitution*, ed. by David A. J. Richards (Oxford University Press, 1986).

4. Locke, *Epistola de Tolerantia, A Letter on Toleration*, ed. by R. Klibansky, tr. by J. W. Gough, Oxford: Clarendon Press, 1968 (abbr: "K/G"). For the convenience of readers who may not have access to this edition, I also cite the reprint of the Popple translation in David Wootton's *Political Writings of John Locke*, Penguin/Mentor, 1993, p. 390 (abbr: "W"). Wootton's edition of the letter seems to me very valuable for its presentation of other Lockean writings relating to toleration and for its interpretive commentary in the introduction.

5. "Indeed, if it should be permitted to speak the truth openly, and as becomes one man to another, neither pagan, nor Mohammedan, nor Jew should be excluded from the commonwealth for the sake of religion." Cf. K/G, 145; W, 431. The status of Muslims is unclear, though. A few pages earlier Locke had contended that a Muslim who owes blind obedience to the Mufti of Constantinople (who in turn is bound to obedience to the Ottoman Emperor) cannot be considered a faithful subject of a Christian magistrate. Such a Muslim would be comparable to a Catholic, whose duty of obedience to the Pope implies allegiance to a foreign prince, which may conflict with his loyalty to his civil sovereign. Cf. K/G, 133, W, 426. But these passages will be consistent if Locke is aware that not all Muslims owe a duty of obedience to the Mufti of Constantinople.

6. For the most part, what I am calling the religious argument falls in K/G 59–65 (W, 390–393).

change the *conduct* of those they agree with, even when their brothers in faith act in ways which might seem highly prejudicial to their salvation. This raises the suspicion that their professed reasons for acting are not their real reasons.

More crucially, Locke does not think that a truly saving faith can be coerced. A saving faith involves an inward persuasion of the mind, which coercion by the state cannot produce. All state coercion can produce is external conformity, which will save no one if it is insincere, even if it happens to be conformity to the true religion (K/G, 67–69; W, 394–395). Moreover, the persecutors' efforts to insure uniformity of belief typically involve subtle matters of dogmatic theology, beyond the comprehension of ordinary men, matters not truly essential to salvation (K/G, 61, 93; W, 391, 407). No opinion can be essential for salvation if it is not expressly taught in the Christian scriptures. When we seek to determine what those scriptures tell us is necessary for salvation, we are not permitted to make inferences from, or interpretations of, the scriptures (K/G, 151–155; W, 434–435). The arcane matters which Christians typically dispute about, and which provide a pretext for persecution, do not have clear scriptural authority. If they did, they would not be matters of dispute.

No doubt this part of Locke's argument sounds very agreeable to modern ears, particularly to the ears of those modern Christians who favor a liberal version of Christianity, which privileges conduct over faith and blurs the doctrinal differences between denominations. But it does rather miss the point of the classical arguments for persecuting nonbelievers. And more generally, I think it fails to see what a radical change in Christianity this doctrine of toleration might require. Thomas Aquinas, for example, would concede that a faith embraced at the point of the sword has no value for salvation: those nonbelievers "who have never received the faith, such as the heathens and the Jews . . . are by no means to be compelled to the faith in order that they may believe, because to believe depends on the will."[7] I take this last to mean that for Thomas the faith which is conducive to salvation must be voluntary in the sense that it is not coerced.

But this does not mean that nonbelievers who have never embraced the faith cannot be coerced for other reasons. They can be compelled to the faith—or perhaps we should say, compelled to conform externally—to prevent them from hindering the faith of believers, whether by blasphemy, by persecution of their own, or by what Thomas ominously calls 'evil persuasions'. If these are acceptable grounds for persecuting those who have never embraced the faith, they would also justify the persecution of those nonbelievers (perhaps a more dangerous group) who *once* embraced the faith, but have gone astray, that is, heretics and apostates.[8]

---

7. *Summa theologiae* II-II, qu. 10, art. 8, "Ought Unbelievers to Be Compelled to the Faith," in *On Law, Morality, and Politics*, ed. by William Baumgarth & Richard Regan, Hackett, 1988, p. 250.

8. In their case, however, Thomas has an additional reason for persecution: he regards acceptance of the faith as involving a commitment which the heretic can be forced to honor. "Just as taking a vow is a matter of will, and keeping a vow a matter of obligation, so acceptance of the faith is a matter of will, whereas keeping the faith once one has received it is a matter of obligation" (ibid., Reply to Obj. 3).

If Locke were to object that coercion can produce only external conformity, not belief, Thomas might reply that compelling the external conformity of nonbelievers, or at least, compelling them not to express their non-Christian beliefs, may still be very useful in preserving the faith of believers. Those who reject the faith will not be permitted to undermine the faith of those who don't. If religious belief is typically acquired by growing up in a community in which it is regarded as normal and natural, then the suppression of dissident views may be very important to the maintenance of the faith. And if we acknowledge Pascal's psychological insight, that external conformity, if practiced long enough, can lead to genuine belief,[9] the coercion need not be only for the benefit of others.

Moreover, even if forced external conformity does not yield favorable results in the first generation of those who have been coerced, it may still do so in subsequent generations. This seems to have happened among the Jews forcibly converted to Christianity in late medieval Spain.[10] In the first generation some, whose commitment to Judaism may not have been that strong to begin with, became sincere Christians; in the second and later generations, many more did. The restrictions placed on the *conversos*, as they were called, meant that it was very dangerous for them to attempt to secretly give their children a traditional Jewish education. And early childhood education seems to be a major factor in determining the religious beliefs a person will hold as an adult.

Jeremy Waldron writes that, although Locke's religious argument has only limited value, insofar as it relies on assumptions a non-Christian ruler could not be presumed to share, "as an *ad hominem* argument addressed to . . . Christian authorities, it is . . . devastating, for it exposes an evident and embarrassing inconsistency between the content of their theory and their practice in propagating it."[11] I take a less sanguine view of the religious argument, which seems to me defective in ways Waldron does not contemplate.

Apart from the considerations mentioned above, Locke completely ignores the scriptural passage persecutors had traditionally relied on as providing the strongest support for their practices, the parable of the great dinner in Luke. Recall the parable of the man who gave a great dinner in Luke 14. He sent a servant to invite his friends to come; when his friends made excuses, he sent the servant out again to bring in the poor, the crippled, the blind, and the lame; when these were not enough to fill the places at the table, he sent the servant out again with instruc-

---

9. Cf. Pascal's wager: "Learn from . . . [the] people who know the road you want to follow and have been cured of the affliction of which you want to be cured [unbelief]. Follow the way by which they began: by behaving as if they believed, taking holy water, having masses said, etc. That will make you believe quite naturally, and according to your animal reactions . . ." (Tr. by Honor Levi, in Pascal, *Pensées and other writings*, with intr. and notes by Anthony Levi, Oxford, 1995, pp. 155–156).

10. On this controversial topic, see B. Netanyahu, *The Origins of the Inquisition in Fifteenth Century Spain*, New York: Random House, 1995, and Henry Kamen, *The Spanish Inquisition: A Historical Revision*, New Haven, CT: Yale University Press, 1998.

11. "Locke: Toleration and the Rationality of Persecution," in Mendus, *Justifying Toleration*, p. 62. Waldron does, however, acknowledge the validity of some of the points I have been making, pp. 80–84.

tions to compel others to come in. Bayle thought it worthwhile to write an entire book disputing the traditional interpretation of this parable.[12] Locke never mentions it.[13]

Locke also seems somewhat naive when he claims that only doctrines which scripture clearly teaches are required for salvation. This is itself a claim which is controversial within Christianity, not a claim, for example, which would be accepted by those Christians who believe, with Pascal, that God deliberately chose not to make the path to salvation too easy to discern.[14]

The Christian scriptures are, in fact, quite ambiguous on the fundamental issue of the conditions for salvation. Some passages suggest that the path to heaven runs through a strict adherence to the commandments, as in the story of the rich man, told with slight variations in all three of the synoptic gospels (cf. Mark 10, Matthew 19, and Luke 18). A man asks Jesus what he must do to inherit eternal life. Jesus advises him to keep the ten commandments and reminds him what they are. The man replies that he has kept those commandments since his youth. Jesus then says to him: "There is still one thing lacking. Sell all that you own and distribute money to the poor, and you will have treasure in heaven" (Luke 18:22). And the man is said to have become very sad on hearing this, "for he was very rich." The path to salvation is not represented as being easy here, but it is represented as possible to find, through loving obedience to some very rigorous commandments, not the acceptance of any christological doctrines.[15]

Other passages make it appear that the path to salvation involves acceptance of some special belief about Jesus, as in the verse Luther called "the Gospel in miniature":

For God so loved the world that he gave his only Son, so that everyone who believes in him may not perish but may have eternal life . . . Those who believe in him are not condemned; but those who do not believe are con-

---

12. See Pierre Bayle, *Philosophical Commentary on these Words of Jesus Christ, Compel them to come in*, tr. by Amie Godman Tannenbaum (Peter Lang, 1987).

13. As Wootton has noted in his introduction to the *Letter* (*Political Writings*, p. 98). This passage is not the only one in scripture which apparently supports the persecution of heretics and other nonbelievers. Mark 9:42 (repeated in Matthew 18:6–7, Luke 17:1–2) is also ominous.

14. Cf. fragment 681 (in Levi's numbering): "[Christianity] says that humanity is in darkness, estranged from God, that he has hidden himself from its knowledge . . . that God has established visible signs in the Church by which those who seek him sincerely should know him; and that he has nevertheless hidden them in such a way that he will only be perceived by those who seek him whole-heartedly . . ." Anthony Levi's index to this translation lists numerous other passages on the theme of God's hiddenness, a doctrine which has become popular recently in apologetic attempts to deal with the problem of evil.

15. Some who believe in salvation by faith would reconcile this passage with their position by calling attention to the fact that after the passage quoted Jesus says, in all three gospels: "Come and follow me." But the passage does not say that following Jesus requires acceptance of christological doctrines. "Follow me" would more naturally be read as meaning: follow my example or my leadership. And in any case, this command comes only after Jesus has said that (assuming obedience to the other commandments) giving all you have to the poor is the only further thing necessary for salvation.

demned already, because they have not believed in the name of the only Son of God.[16]

Texts like this suggest that *some* belief about Jesus is both necessary and sufficient for salvation. These texts do not specify the nature of that belief as precisely as we might wish, but a plausible and historically popular elaboration of this text would say that the believer must accept that he is a sinner, whose sinful nature has been redeemed by God's sacrifice of his only son, himself innocent, who nonetheless suffered on the cross for our sins.

Anyone familiar with the Reformation debates about the relative importance of faith versus works must, I think, acknowledge that it is a matter for controversy, among those otherwise united by their acceptance of the Christian scriptures as the Word of God, just what those scriptures say is the path to salvation. Tolerationists like Locke emphasize the importance of works and the unimportance of faith. Persecutionists, on the other hand, like Luther and Calvin, emphasize the importance of faith and dismiss the possibility of achieving salvation by works as mere wishful thinking, given our fallen nature.

The skeptical reader of Locke might also question whether he is right to hold that Christian love requires us not to use physical mutilation, torture, and killing against nonbelievers. How, Locke asks, can these practices be consistent with Christian love? But suppose that the forcible repression of heretical views can help preserve the faith of those who have not yet strayed. Those are the people whose souls the persecutionists seem to have been most concerned with. Here is Calvin defending the burning of Michael Servetus:

> That clemency which [those who wish to pardon heretics] praise is cruel: it exposes the [poor] sheep to being taken as prey, in order to be merciful to the wolves. [I ask you, is it reasonable that the heretics] should murder souls with the poison of their faulty doctrines and that their bodies should be protected from the legitimate power of the sword? Shall the whole body of Christ be torn apart, that the stench of one rotten member may be preserved intact?[17]

The persecutionists fear that permitting heretics to publicly embrace, articulate, and perhaps defend their views will lead many believers to reject the beliefs in which they have been raised. On the evidence of our experiment with freedom of thought and expression over the past two centuries in this country, their fear was not irrational. If the persecutors are genuinely concerned about the salvation of their flocks, then, holding the theological beliefs they do, they act quite reasonably

---

16. John 3:16, 18. I'm indebted to *The New Oxford Annotated Bible* for the information about Luther's praise of this passage. Similar views may be found in John 6:29–40, 11:25–26, 12:44–50; Mark 16:15–16; and Romans 10:9–13.

17. Calvin, *Defensio orthodoxae fidei contra prodigiosos errores Michaelis Serveti*, in *Opera*, vol. VIII, p. 471, *Corpus reformatorum* vol. XXXV. My translation. Bracketed phrases are from the French translation, cited by Lecler, *Histoire de la Tolérance au siècle de la Réforme* (Paris: Albin Michel, 1994, p. 320).

in treating nonbelievers severely. We are told that a loving God subjects the damned to horrendous eternal torment, as punishment for their lack of faith. Humans may be excused for thinking that any pain they might inflict on nonbelievers, to save believers from that fate, is trifling by comparison, no violation of the obligations of love, and well-justified if it succeeds in achieving its purpose.

D. P. Walker has demonstrated[18] that the traditional doctrine of hell was under assault in Locke's day; by the end of the seventeenth century many more Christians rejected it than had at the beginning of that century. I have the impression that now even more Christians regard this doctrine as an embarrassment. But the conservative defenders of the doctrine are right about this much, at least: the prima facie support for it in the Christian scriptures is strong.[19] As appalling as the doctrine may be from a moral point of view, I doubt that Christians can reject it without rejecting the Christian scriptures as a reliable guide to our proper conduct in this life, and to the fate which awaits us in the life to come, if we fail to please God. And that's a step I don't think Locke was prepared to contemplate.

There has been a tendency, I suggest, for Locke's readers to nod with approval when they consider his religious argument, because they like its conclusion, and to ignore the fact that the argument itself preaches only to those who are already converted. I fear the same thing has happened with his political argument. The main theme of that argument is that church and state are human institutions, which have fundamentally different purposes, purposes which do not, and cannot legitimately, overlap.

As a first approximation, we might understand the argument to proceed as follows. The state may be defined as an association of men who have established among themselves a body which has the power to make laws, whose violation it may punish by death and all lesser penalties, but only for the purposes for which it is instituted, which include the furtherance of its citizens' civil interests—life, liberty, bodily health, freedom from pain, and the possession of property—but which do not include furtherance of its citizens' spiritual interests.[20] It is not, and cannot be, the function of the state to secure our salvation. For the means definitive of the state involve the use of force, and hence are inherently unsuited to the pursuit of spiritual interests. It would be irrational for the state to use coercion to pursue the salvation of its citizens; hence, this cannot be one of the proper functions of government.[21]

18. See *The Decline of Hell* (University of Chicago Press, 1964).

19. E.g., in Matthew 5:22, 29, 30; Mark 9: 42–48; Luke 12:4–5, 16:19–31; Revelations 20.

20. Locke does, however, allow that the state may pursue the spiritual interests of its citizens by noncoercive means, such as teaching and persuasion (K/G, 69; W, 395). So he does not adhere to a separation of church and state strict enough to satisfy most modern adherents of that doctrine.

21. Cf. K/G, 65–71, W, 393–396. This 'first approximation' to an account of the political argument is influenced by Waldron, 63–67. But I do not strictly follow Waldron even here, since the definition of the state I use makes its contractarian character more explicit than it is either in the definition of the *Second Treatise of Government* (ch. 1, par. 3) or in the *Letter Concerning Toleration* (K/G, 65; W, 393–394). In the passage on which Waldron relies from the *Second Treatise*, Locke does not define the state exclusively in terms of the means it has at its disposal. He also

The church, on the other hand, is a voluntary association of men, "joining together of their own accord, for the public worship of God, in such manner as they believe will be acceptable to the Deity, for the salvation of their souls" (K/G, 71; W, 396). The church has an end which might make it a suitable agent for the repression of religious error. But it does not have the necessary means available to it. It can use exhortation, admonition, and advice, but not force, which belongs properly only to the civil magistrate. Its ultimate sanction is excommunication, exclusion from membership, a sanction it must use in a way which does not harm the civil interests of the excluded member (K/G, 77–81; W, 399–400).

Now as Waldron has pointed out, one weakness of the argument just sketched is its dubious assumption about the necessary ineffectiveness of persecution, the assumption that coercion cannot produce genuine faith. From this assumption it infers that persecution to insure correct belief is not an activity the state can rationally or legitimately engage in. As I've presented the religious argument, the same assumption about the ineffectiveness of persecution also appears there, and we've already seen in that context why it's dubious. But there is another way of reading the political argument, which seems to me to give a more accurate account of Locke's reasoning, and may give Locke a better argument.

David Wootton has suggested[22] that Locke's main point is not so much that it is irrational for the state to attempt to coerce people into having correct religious beliefs (because such attempts are necessarily ineffective), as that it would be irrational for the citizens to consent to the state's doing this (because such consent would be imprudent). Locke's contractarian political philosophy requires that the legitimate powers of the state be ones a citizen could rationally consent to. But it is not rational for a citizen to consent to let the state determine his religion for him, even if he supposes that it can. Why is that?

Suppose we assume, for the sake of argument, that there is only one true religion.[23] Arguably, our chances of accepting the true religion are not very good if we follow a policy of letting the government determine our religion for us. There are many religions which the various princes of the world accept. What are the odds that we will be lucky enough to have a prince who accepts the right religion? The fact that a prince has political power gives him no special competence in

includes a description of the ends political power is instituted to achieve ("regulating and preserving of property," etc.). Waldron's elliptical quotation of this definition (p. 65) makes Locke sound more Weberian than he would have appeared had the full definition been quoted.

22. In the introduction to his edition of the *Political Writings*, pp. 99–104. I do not attempt here to take up all the points Wootton makes in defense of Locke, and in particular, I ignore his analysis of what he identifies as Locke's first argument for the irrationality of consenting to state enforcement of religious belief, which relies on the assumption that it is irrational for me to consent to the state's having the right to impose on me an obligation which I cannot be confident of being able to fulfill. I agree that belief cannot simply be commanded. But I do not think this line of argument can be freed of overly optimistic assumptions about the limited effectiveness of state attempts at controlling belief.

23. It's not clear to me that Locke does assume that there is only one true religion. The passage which most strongly suggests that he does occurs at K/G, 71 (= W, 396), but even there it's not clear whether he believes this, or is merely making a concession to his opponent for the sake of the argument. Similarly at K/G, 67, 91 (W, 394, 406).

religious matters. And he may be influenced in his choice by extraneous considerations, favoring the church which will be most useful to him politically. It may be said that the prince can seek advice from those who are knowledgeable in religious matters. But the fact that he must ultimately be the one to choose his advisers makes our reliance on his personal judgment inescapable. The most rational course of action for the citizen, then, is to make his own decision, as best he can, taking responsibility for his own salvation, as he must generally take responsibility for his own temporal well-being.[24]

One difficulty with this argument, it seems to me, is that it relies on the questionable assumption that it is prudent for the ordinary believer to rely only on his own reason in attempting to form a correct judgment about religious truth. The odds that he will have a prince who has chosen the best religion may not be good. But the odds that he himself, on his own, will do better may be even worse. Suppose we assume, as Locke seems to, that the path to salvation is to be found in the Christian scriptures. We may think of that path as broad or narrow. If the path requires the believer only to acknowledge the existence of a God whose nature is not too precisely specified, to accept the immortality of the soul and some general proposition about Jesus which few Christians would question,[25] and to conform to a small number of commandments, which are not too difficult to fulfill and for which there might be plausible nonreligious grounds, then the path is broad. If, on the other hand, it requires some pretty specific beliefs about God and Jesus, beliefs whose truth will not be obvious to the uncommitted, and conformity to a strict moral code, whose requirements are not easy to justify in secular terms, we may call it narrow.

If the path to salvation is broad, it is reasonable to hope that a conscientious inquirer will find it for himself easily enough. If it is narrow, that hope may not be so reasonable, and reliance on some kind of authority may seem more necessary. Locke is a broad path man, as many Christians nowadays are, and as far fewer Christians were in his day. I think that makes his argument easier for the modern reader to accept than it was for seventeenth century readers. In Locke's day most of the major denominations had extensive sets of doctrines whose acceptance was required for membership in the church. For example, the thirty-nine articles of the Church of England took positions on such controversial matters as original sin, the necessity of prevenient grace to do good works, justification by faith, predestination, infant baptism, the rejection of purgatory, the rejection of priestly celibacy, and so on.

Suppose the narrow path folks are right, and religious truth is not easy to find on your own.[26] In our time, we rely on the government to look out for our

24. This paragraph summarizes passages on K/G, 71, 91–101 (W, 396, 405–410).

25. E.g., that he at least articulated the divine revelation more adequately and authoritatively than any other prophet. This seems to me a rather minimal requirement for being a Christian.

26. Locke's assumptions about the accessibility of religious truth may do more to explain his resistance to the toleration of Catholics than his official argument, which contends that Catholics ought not to be tolerated because they owe allegiance to a foreign prince (cf. K/G, 133–135; W, 426). Wootton notes that Locke wrote his *Letter on Toleration* during his exile in Holland, where

well-being in many ways, to make countless decisions for us which can have life or death consequences. We trust it to insure that the medicines sold in our pharmacies are safe and effective, that our food supply is not contaminated, that our water is safe to drink, and our air safe to breathe. We trust it to examine the cars and toys we buy, and to regulate the trains and the airways and the stock markets. Libertarians may resent the amount of government regulation most of us have come to accept. But I would assume that for the most part our acceptance of this regulation is rational, because it would be very difficult for the ordinary citizen to make a rational choice about such matters as the safety and efficacy of our medications and our water and so on. If you think that the path to salvation is narrow, and that locating that path with confidence may be beyond your capacity—and you may well think that—it is not clear that it will be irrational to rely on someone else to locate that path for you, even though you know that that person may not always be impartial.

Consider in this context Locke's requirements for faith in his *Essay Concerning Human Understanding*, IV, xvi, 14, and xviii, 2, 6. Belief on faith requires a determination by reason that the proposer of the proposition believed, be it a person or a book, is the agent of a divine revelation. But determining which candidates for inclusion in the canon properly belong there, and which are properly excluded, what the best text for the canonical books is, how that text is best translated into a modern language, and how to reconcile apparent inconsistencies in scripture—all these matters will require extensive scholarly knowledge, knowledge which few ordinary believers would possess.

So I have serious reservations about the force of Locke's arguments. I don't find his religious arguments nearly as devastating as Waldron does, and I don't think his political arguments can be freed of the questionable assumptions about the accessibility of religious truth which weaken the religious arguments. I think, rather, that the case which needs to be made against religious persecution requires a more direct challenge to the assumptions of the persecutors, a challenge specifically to their assumption that their scriptures teach the path to salvation. And I find that challenge being made by Montesquieu. That, at any rate, is what seems to me most valuable about his contribution to this conversation, in the work I shall concentrate on, his *Persian Letters* (1721).

I take Montesquieu to be a deist.[27] By 'deism' here I understand the idea that human reason, unaided by revelation, *can* establish the existence of God, the existence of an afterlife, and the moral requirements whose fulfillment

---

there was a Protestant state church, and no formal legislation guaranteeing toleration, but "a general and informal toleration in practice," which included Catholics. "Read in a Dutch context, Locke's attack on Catholicism seems strangely indifferent to the fact that no harm had come to the Dutch from their extension of toleration to Catholics" (96). I believe much of Locke's opposition to Catholicism comes from his antipathy toward any religion which assumes that ordinary believers must accept the authority of a church hierarchy.

27. As seems inevitable in these cases, there has been controversy about the precise nature of Montesquieu's religious views. For a good summary of the evidence, see Robert Shackleton's "La religion de Montesquieu," in *Essays on Montesquieu and on the Enlightenment* (Voltaire Foundation, 1988).

God will reward in the afterlife, but that it *cannot* establish, or even make it probable, that any of the sacred texts of the major religions is in fact the record of a divine revelation, which we must take as our guide to salvation. For the deist, anything we can learn only from scripture is unnecessary. The beliefs and practices prescribed by the organized religions on the basis of their scriptures are superfluous.[28] I read the *Persian Letters* as a deistic critique of revelation-based religions. In rejecting revelation, deism undermines an argument for religious persecution which more neutral arguments, arguments which seek to defend toleration without criticizing the fundamental doctrines of any religion, leave untouched.

I make the following assumptions here: (*1*) that the major monotheistic religions are typically exclusivist, in that each characteristically claims that it alone offers the path to salvation; (*2*) that their exclusivism provides their most plausible rationale for religious persecution, since it permits them to represent persecution as an act undertaken to assist others (not necessarily the ones being persecuted) in attaining the supreme good and avoiding the worst of evils; (*3*) that these religions typically base their exclusivism on their sacred texts, which in fact constitute their only plausible reason for claiming to provide the unique path to salvation; and finally, (*4*) that anything which undermines the authority of the sacred texts, also undermines exclusivism, and with it the most plausible rationale for persecution.

My purpose is to consider how the *Persian Letters*[29] contribute to this line of argument. But first a word about the peculiar literary form of this work. It presents itself as a translation, by an anonymous Frenchman, of a series of letters, most of which are supposed to have been written either to or from two Persian visitors to Paris, Usbek and Rica, over a ten-year period, from 1711 to 1720. So it spans the last years of the reign of Louis XIV and the first years of the Regency of the Duke d'Orléans. As the purported translator, Montesquieu claims that Usbek and Rica lodged with him, and spent time with him. Because they considered him as "a man from another world," they hid nothing from him (V, 7; B, 39). But Montesquieu quickly contradicts this claim when he reports that his guests showed him only "*most* of their letters," and that he intercepted some they never would have entrusted to him because the letters were too embarrassing. The collection also contains letters whose presence is quite mysterious, since the Persian visitors were neither their authors nor their recipients. Montesquieu offers no explanation of how he came by them.

---

28. This account falls somewhere in between the simple definition Antoine Furetière gave in his *Dictionnaire universel* (1690), and the much more complex one the Abbé Malet gave in Volume IV of the *Encyclopédie* (1754). Cf. C. J. Betts, *Early Deism in France*, M. Nijhoff, 1984, pp. 3–5.

29. For the French text, I rely on Montesquieu, *Lettres persanes*, ed. by P. Vernière (Paris: Bordas/Garnier, 1992, cited as V). Unless otherwise noted, translations will be those of C. J. Betts, *Persian Letters* (Penguin, 1993, cited as B). I shall refer to individual letters by their number; so "L161" refers to Letter 161.

The idea that the letters were actually written by Persians, then, is a transparent fiction,[30] a device Montesquieu uses to invite us to see ourselves as others might see us, much as Montaigne does in his essay "On Cannibals." After an extended and respectful, but not uncritical, account of the way the cannibals live in their native land, Montaigne reports their reaction to European customs when they were brought to France in 1562. There they met with Charles IX, who had just ascended the throne at the age of 10. The cannibals expressed surprise that "so many grown men, bearded, strong and armed . . . would submit to obey a child . . ." and that the poor would submit to the gross disparity between their lot and that of the wealthy.[31]

Montaigne's essay is often read as endorsing a kind of relativism. Early in the essay he writes: "Each man calls barbarism whatever is not his own practice; for indeed it seems we have no other test of truth and reason than the example and pattern of the opinions and customs of the country we live in" (Frame, p. 152). But in the end Montaigne's essay undermines *this* form of relativism, by showing that it *is* possible for us to use another test of truth and reason, by looking at our own opinions and customs through the eyes of someone from a different culture. It is not inevitable that when we know how things look to members of the other culture, we will reject its perspective. Although Montaigne does not idealize his cannibals, he evidently thinks that they have sound criticisms of some French practices. In his honor, we might call this kind of criticism "cannibal criticism."

Montesquieu uses his Persian visitors to engage in cannibal criticism. They permit him to say to his reader: "yes, this is the way you're accustomed to thinking and acting; and here's how it might look to someone brought up in a different world." This permits Montesquieu to criticize French ways without taking responsibility for making that criticism in his own person. Even during the Regency, when censorship was less severe than it had been under Louis XIV,[32] that distancing must have seemed a useful precaution. But near the end of his life, after his work

30. Montesquieu's preface also contains another contradiction which warns us not to take everything at face value: he says that his function has been "merely that of a translator"; but then he reports that he has taken some pains to "adapt the work" to French customs by editing out Oriental turns of phrase and trivial details "which ought always to die between two friends."

31. Donald Frame, *The Complete Works of Montaigne* (Stanford University Press, 1958, p. 159). In Pierre Villey's edition of the *Essais* (revised by V.-L. Saulnier, Paris: PUF, 2nd edition, 1992), pp. 213–214. But Montaigne says that the cannibals made three points, the third of which he has forgotten. In a forthcoming essay, "An Anatomy of the Mass: Montaigne's 'Of Cannibals,' " George Hoffmann argues that the third point, which Montaigne had not forgotten, but chose to leave implicit, was that "Europeans should condemn them for eating their prisoners of war, when Europeans were willing to go to war in the first place over the right to eat their god." Hoffmann observes that the accusation of theophagy was prominent in sixteenth century Protestant criticism of Catholicism and points to a number of internal signs that this essay was intended to suggest skepticism about the Catholic interpretation of the Eucharist.

32. This was also a period during which the persecution of Protestants and Jansenist Catholics was somewhat relaxed. See René Pomeau, introduction to Voltaire, *Traité sur la tolérance*, Paris: Flammarion, 1989, p. 7.

had come under sharp attack from an ecclesiastical critic,[33] Montesquieu dropped the pretense that he was merely the translator of letters written by others:

> There are some passages which many people have found too bold; but I would ask them to note the nature of the work. The Persians who had to play such an important part in it found themselves suddenly transplanted to Europe, that is, to another universe. There was a period when they had to be represented as full of ignorance and prejudices. One's only concern was to show the origin and development of their ideas. Their first thoughts were bound to be strange: the only thing to do, it seemed, was to attribute to them the kind of strangeness which is compatible with intelligence . . . If [these Persians] sometimes find our dogmas strange, the strangeness is always characterized by their total ignorance of the way in which these dogmas are linked with our other truths. (B, 284, modified; V, 4)

So Montesquieu's claim is: "I am not speaking for myself here; I am only presenting the views of my ignorant, *but intelligent*, Persians."

Montesquieu also uses his Persian visitors to make a more subtle and indirect critique of European ways. Though he portrays them as men who are, in their own way, civilized, sophisticated, and capable of acute observations about European foibles, who leave their native land because they yearn for knowledge and wish to see what wisdom they can find in the West, who are capable of giving an intelligent account of the teachings of European philosophers, and of engaging in perceptive philosophical reflections of their own, he also portrays them as men who have distinct limitations, both morally and intellectually. They have religious beliefs a European reader is likely to regard as superstitious, and their conduct toward women is apt to strike even a European reader of the eighteenth century as barbarous. This is less true at the end of the novel than it is at the beginning. Usbek and Rica do change as a result of their experience of European culture, but Usbek does not change enough to avoid domestic tragedy. During his extended absence, the sexual frustration of the wives he left behind leads them to subvert the discipline of the seraglio; ultimately, his favorite and most trusted wife, discovered in infidelity, commits suicide as the only escape from her unbearable position.[34]

---

33. The critic was the abbé J. B. Gaultier, whose pamphlet, *Les Lettres persanes convaincues d'impiété*, was published in 1751. Montesquieu's reply was the "Reflections on the *Persian Letters*," which he added to the edition of 1754. The *Persian Letters*, along with *The Spirit of the Laws*, was placed on the *Index of Prohibited Books* in 1761.

34. The fate of Roxana, whose suicide concludes the novel in L161, is foreshadowed by that of Anaïs, who invites her husband to murder her, in the story Rica presents Zulema as telling in L141. Although the story is, in a sense, Zulema's, I think that Rica's retelling of it may earn him some credit as being more enlightened about women than Usbek is. It may be that the story of Anaïs is intended as a warning from Rica to Usbek, a warning which comes too late, and would not in any event have been heeded, given the indirectness with which it is conveyed.

Montesquieu invites us, then, not only to laugh *with* his Persians when they mock foolish European customs, but also to laugh *at* them when they are foolish in their own way, and to be appalled by them, when they are cruel. When their foolish ways bring to mind European ways we have unreflectively assumed to be reasonable, his ridicule of the foreigners serves his critique of European ways. Shackleton[35] cites a line from Horace which defines this species of criticism:

Quid rides? Mutato nomine de te
Fabula narratur . . .

As we might translate that:

What are *you* laughing at? Just change the names,
And the story I tell is yours.

The Persian visitors provide a vivid demonstration of the proposition that even highly intelligent and cultivated human beings are capable of believing the most bizarre things when it comes to religion. This kind of criticism—what I'll call *quid rides* criticism—happens quite often in the *Letters*.

Before we look at examples of these two kinds of criticism, though, we must confront the fact that Montesquieu's Persians are not uniformly reliable informants about Muslim belief and practice.[36] For example, in L24 Rica expresses the view that women have been created inferior to men, and that according to the prophets, they are not eligible for paradise. This is at least partly false. There does seem to be Quranic support for the view that women are inferior to men;[37] but the notion that they are not eligible for paradise has no direct support that I can

35. Robert Shackleton, *Montesquieu: A Critical Biography* (Oxford University Press, 1961), p. 30.

36. On this general topic, see Ahmad Gunny's "Montesquieu's View of Islam in the *Lettres persanes*," *Studies on Voltaire*, 1978, pp. 151–166. Gunny argues that, while it would be unrealistic to expect Montesquieu to have as accurate a knowledge of Islam as modern Islamists do, since he relied heavily on Western sources who were often very hostile to Islam, not all of Montesquieu's misrepresentations can be excused as the result of ignorance or the bias of his sources. I would agree with that. But I think it is a mistake to assume that Montesquieu is striving in this work for sociological accuracy. He writes as a satirist, who needs to paint a picture which has enough accuracy to be credible to his audience but is not bound to give a fair representation of the religions he discusses. For more on this theme, see below, n. 51.

37. The most explicit text I am aware of is 4:34, which reads (in the Dawood translation, Penguin, 1999, p. 64): "Men have authority over women because God has made the one superior to the other, and because they spend their wealth to maintain them. Good women are obedient . . . As for those from whom you fear disobedience, admonish them, forsake them in beds apart, and beat them. Then if they obey you, take no further action against them." I should note, however, that as translated by Arberry, this passage does not affirm male superiority quite so bluntly: "Men are the managers of the affairs of women, for that God has preferred in bounty one of them over another, etc." (Macmillan, 1955). The whole subject is one which is heatedly debated among contemporary Muslims and students of Islam. For a helpful discussion of the issues, see John Esposito, *Islam: The Straight Path* (Oxford University Press, expanded edition, 1991, pp. 94–101).

find and is contrary to several quite explicit Quranic texts.[38] To appreciate what is going on here, we need to look at this passage in its context.

Before he articulated the views just described, Rica was writing to Ibben, a Muslim friend in Smyrna, reporting on the French reception of the papal bull *Unigenitus*:

> In order to keep [the French King] in training, so that he will not get out of the habit of believing, [the Pope] gives him certain articles of belief as an exercise from time to time. Two years ago he sent him a long document called the *Constitution* [i.e., *Unigenitus*] and tried to make this king and his subjects believe everything in it, on pain of severe penalties . . . (B, 73, V, 560)

The bull here referred to was a condemnation of certain Jansenist views, advanced by Paschasius Quesnel, in a book entitled *Reflections morales*.[39] Rica reports that the Pope succeeded with the king,

> who submitted at once, setting an example to his subjects. But some of them rebelled, and said that they refused to believe anything in the document. The instigators of this revolt, which has split the court, the whole kingdom, and every family, are the women. The Constitution forbids them to read a book which all the Christians say was brought down to them from Heaven;[40] it is really their Koran. The women, indignant at this insult to their sex, have started a whole movement against the Constitution . . .

Now so far we only have Rica commenting on a dispute among the Christians, and not obviously taking sides (though the tone of his report suggests that we might cite this as an example of cannibal criticism). But at this point he introduces a cross-cultural comparison which seems to put him on the papal side:

> One must confess that this mufti does not reason badly. By the great Ali, he must have been instructed in the principles of our sacred law. For, since women are a creation inferior to ours, and our prophets tell us that they will

38. Cf. the Quran 33:35, 40:39–40, 43:68–70. As Gunny notes, this seems to have been a common Christian misunderstanding in Montesquieu's time, but one which he would have found corrected in some of the sources he used (e.g., in J. Chardin's *Voyages en Perse*, or in Bayle's article on "Mahomet" in his *Dictionnaire historique et critique*). I conjecture that the misunderstanding may have arisen from some of the Quran's descriptions of the joys of Paradise, which, as traditionally translated, seem designed to appeal most strongly to a male audience. Cf. 44:50–57, 55:52–78.

39. For the text of this bull, see Henry Denzinger, *The Sources of Catholic Dogma*, tr. by Roy Deferrari, Herder, 1957, pp. 347–354.

40. This is a reference to the fact that among the Jansenist propositions the Pope condemned was the doctrine that "it is an illusion to persuade oneself that knowledge of the mysteries of religion should not be communicated to women by the reading of Sacred Scriptures. Not from the simplicity of women, but from the proud knowledge of men has arisen the abuse of the Scriptures, and have heresies been born" (Denzinger, p. 352).

not enter into Paradise, why must they meddle with reading a book whose whole purpose is to teach the way to Paradise? (V, 57; B, 73–74)

I take it that Montesquieu's main purpose here is not to give an accurate account of Muslim views, but to criticize the Pope for a prohibition on women's reading scripture, which could be justified only if the Pope subscribed to the (supposed) Muslim views that women are inferior and not eligible for Paradise. So this part of the letter may be counted as an example of *quid rides* criticism.

In any event, Montesquieu does not let Rica's understanding of Islam go unchallenged. In a late letter, L141, Rica writes to Usbek relaying a story he had told to a French lady of the court who objected to the Muslim practice of poly-gyny.[41] Once upon a time there was a Persian woman named Zulema, who knew the whole of the Quran by heart and understood the history of its interpretation better than any of the religious experts. One day one of her companions in the seraglio asked whether she accepted the ancient tradition of these scholars, that Paradise is made only for men. "That's the common opinion," she said.

> There is nothing which has not been done to degrade our sex. There is even a nation spread thought all Persia, called the Jewish nation, which maintains, on the authority of its sacred books, that we have no soul. Such insulting opinions have no other origin than the pride of men, who wish to continue their superiority beyond their life, and don't realize that on the great day every creature will appear as nothing before God, without there being any distinction among them except those which virtue has put there. (V, 297; B, 248)

Just as men who have lived well, and behaved well toward women, will go to "a Paradise full of ravishing celestial beauties," so virtuous women will go to their own place of sensual delights. The details of Zulema's picture of the afterlife of women may lack scriptural support, but in her contention that women as well as men may enjoy the afterlife, she is on sounder scriptural ground than Rica had been earlier. (It's an interesting irony that it is Rica who tells her story.)

Montesquieu may have many targets in his sights in these letters. I suspect that he is amused by the tendency of humans to imagine the joys of the afterlife in a very this-worldly fashion. But his main point, I suggest, in presenting these two contrary Muslim views of the fate of women in the afterlife is to illustrate the fact that the sacred texts of any scriptural religion are typically subject to con-flicting interpretations, that the parties to the disputes are not without their own biases, and that the notion of a "reliable informant" about the beliefs and prac-tices of a religion is inherently suspect. The sacred texts are long, the meaning of individual passages is frequently not transparent, and often there are prima facie contradictions between different passages which different believers will resolve in different ways.

---

41. "She found it objectionable that one man should be shared among ten or twelve women. She was unable to contemplate the happiness of the one without envy and the state of the others without pity" (V, 296; B, 247).

Let's turn now to a sequence of letters whose fictional date is earlier in the story. In L16 Usbek writes to a mullah he has met on his journey in Kum, where he had stopped to worship at the tomb of "the virgin who gave birth to twelve prophets" (L1). When he writes L16, Usbek has left Persia, but is still in Muslim lands, at Erzerum, in what is now Turkey.[42] The mullah to whom he writes is supposed to be the guardian of the sacred tomb. Usbek's first letter begins with extravagant praise of the mullah's wisdom and superior knowledge of the Koran:

> Why do you live among the tombs, divine Mullah? You are much better suited to living among the stars. No doubt you conceal yourself for fear of obscuring the sun . . . Your knowledge is an abyss deeper than the ocean; your mind is more piercing than Zufagar, Ali's sword . . . you read the Koran on the breast of our divine Prophet, and when you find some passage obscure, at his orders an angel spreads his swift wings, and descends from the throne to reveal its secret to you . . . Through you I can communicate intimately with the Seraphim. (V, 39–40; B, 62)

How are we to take this praise? In a previous letter, one of Usbek's Persian friends had asked him to explain something the friend had often heard him say: that men were born to be virtuous, and that justice is as proper to them as existence (L10). The friend writes that he has asked "our mullahs about it, but they drive me to despair with their quotations from the Koran; for I am not consulting them as a true believer, but as a man, as a citizen, and as a father" (V, 27–28; B, 53). So Usbek seems to belong to a circle of friends who do not want to hear appeals to the authority of scripture when they have a question about human nature and its relation to morality. Usbek's reply certainly accepts the presupposition that human reason is capable of answering questions of this kind (L11).

This makes the effusive praise of the mullah in L16 look suspicious. Usbek may be engaging in irony at the mullah's expense. But in the immediate context Montesquieu presents Usbek as apparently entrusting his soul to the care of the mullah. In his first letter to the mullah, Usbek never does get around to posing the question on which he wants advice, but in his next letter he does. He wants to know why "our Lawgiver" issued some of the prohibitions he issued. Why, for example, does he

> deprive us of pig's meat, and all the meats which he calls *impure*? Why is it that he forbids us to touch a corpse, and that, to purify our souls, he com-

---

42. It's worth noting that Montesquieu portrays his Persian (Shiite) Muslim as having contempt for the Turkish (Sunni) Muslims. Cf. L6, in which Usbek writes to a friend back in Ispahan: "I must admit, Nessir, that I felt a secret pain when I lost sight of Persia, and found myself among the faithless Osmanlis. As I penetrated further into this profane land, I had the impression that I was becoming profane myself." Locke, by contrast, frequently uses "Turk" as a synonym for "Mohammedan" (or more properly, "Muslim"). Montesquieu's standard term for referring to Muslims is "Mahométan," a term which is offensive to Muslims, as implying a worship of Mohammed which is inconsistent with their understanding of monotheism. (Betts' translation of the *Lettres*, perhaps seeking to lessen the offensiveness of the text, consistently renders "Mahométan" as "Muslim.")

mands us to constantly wash our bodies? It seems to me that things in themselves are neither pure nor impure. I cannot conceive of any inherent quality
in objects which could make them so . . . (L17; V, 41; B, 63)

Usbek acknowledges that we may have a natural repugnance to some of the things
prohibited, for example, to touching a corpse, or to being around someone who
does not bathe regularly. But he thinks this reaction is not universal, that it depends
on the constitution of our sense organs, and hence, cannot be used as a standard
for distinguishing between the pure and the impure.

   The question of the rationality of these restrictions may not seem to be an
important one, since the modern reader is apt to regard them as merely odd or
quaint, particularly when they are the restrictions of another culture. But
Montesquieu suggests a reason why we cannot dismiss this question as trivial when
he has Usbek conclude L17 with the rhetorical question:

   Divine mullah, would not this [rejection of the traditional distinction
   between purity and impurity] overthrow the distinctions established by our
   divine Prophet, and the fundamental points of the Law, which was written
   by the hands of angels? (V, 42; B, 64)

Montesquieu's point, I take it, is that we can reject the traditional restrictions as
not binding on us only if we are prepared to claim that the sacred texts are not
always authoritative, perhaps by questioning whether the traditions they establish
really go back to the prophet, the supposed intermediary between us and God, or
(more radically) by questioning the prophet's claim to that authoritative status. If
a religious prohibition must be defensible by secular reason before we can regard
it as binding, and if its claim to be a revealed command is not sufficient, then revelation becomes superfluous, and revealed religion is an anachronism.

   The mullah is in a dilemma, I think. He does not want to admit that Usbek's
demand for an explanation is reasonable. But he also does not want to admit
that the command is arbitrary. The strategy he adopts seems rather high-handed.
He begins by accusing his questioner of ignorance of the Muslim religious
tradition:

   You keep on asking us questions people have put to our holy Prophet a thousand times. Why not read the *Traditions* of the learned? Why refuse to
   consult that pure source of all understanding? You would find all your doubts
   resolved. (V, 42–43; B, 64)

Then, perhaps sensing that Usbek must have *some* knowledge of what the tradition says, and must have found that it did *not* resolve his doubts, he attacks his
character:

   Unhappy are you who, forever caught up in earthly things, have never gazed
   fixedly on what is in Heaven, and revere the life of a Mullah without daring
   to take it up or imitate it. (V, 42; B, 64)

This is followed by an assertion of the superior wisdom of those who have devoted their lives to the study of religion:

> Profane men, who never enter into the secrets of the eternal, the light of your minds is like the darkness of the abyss, and your arguments are like the dust your feet raise, when the sun is at its height, in the burning month of Shaaban. Your mind, even at its zenith, cannot reach the nadir of the lowliest imam's. Your vain philosophy is like the flash that heralds storms and darkness; you are in the midst of the tempest and wander at the behest of the winds. (V, 42; B, 64)

At this point, apparently thinking that he has abused his questioner enough and made a bold enough claim for his own moral and intellectual superiority, the mullah offers his answer to Usbek's objection, by recounting a story which explains why pigs are unclean.

When Noah, his family, and the animals were on the ark, there was a waste disposal problem, which Noah dealt with by piling all the animals' droppings on one side of the ark. Eventually this made the ship list dangerously to one side. To remedy that, Noah put the elephant on the other side, as a counterweight. The elephant produced a large heap of excrement, from which a pig was born. So pigs are unclean because they're made of elephant dung. (This theory might seem falsifiable by doing a simple taste comparison, but I think the results would not be conclusive. The wine in the Eucharist, after all, does not *taste* like human blood.)[43]

The mullah goes on to explain, in analogous terms, why rats and cats are also unclean. (He never does explain the prohibition on touching dead bodies or the requirement to bathe constantly.) He concludes by returning to the themes of the beginning of the letter, attributing Usbek's inability to see the reason of these commandments to his ignorance of heavenly matters, as if the composition of pig flesh were a heavenly matter. Then, in a rather surprising reversal, he admits that even the professionally religious do not *always* understand the reasons for things. This admission of some degree of ignorance may serve to inoculate him against questions to which he doesn't have such a plausible answer.

These early letters are an example of what I'm calling *quid rides* criticism. Montesquieu conjures up a Muslim cleric invoking his superior wisdom to gain credit for a ridiculous story which has been invented to explain an irrational custom. It is not clear whether Usbek himself is gullible enough to believe him.[44]

---

43. Never having tasted human flesh, I cannot say whether the taste of the host resembles it. But on the Catholic doctrine that the body of Christ continues to have the accidents of bread, even after its substance has been transformed in the mass, this is not to be expected.

44. Apart from the considerations mentioned in the text, suggesting that Usbek's praise of the mullah is ironic, a later letter to him (L123) shows a rather skeptical Usbek. Gunny notes (p. 163) that in *The Spirit of the Laws* (Bk. XXIV, ch. xxv) Montesquieu shows an awareness that there may be a more rational argument for the prohibition on eating pork, based on considerations of health. Indeed, Montesquieu there cites this as an example of religious prohibition which is appropriate to countries with the kind of climate in which the prohibition originated, but inap-

But the mullah would not be in the position he is in if he did not find many who *are* that gullible. So the exchange is a parable, illustrating the extent of human credulity. Europeans may not see their own credulity reflected in that of the Muslims, provided they have a firm conviction of their own moral and intellectual superiority. But when *quid rides* criticism is combined with cannibal criticism, that conviction may falter. So let us turn to an example of cannibal criticism.

Consider Usbek's complaints about the Christians, after he has been in Europe for a couple of years. In L46 we find him writing to a Persian friend in Venice, about the European disposition to quarrel about religion, particularly about matters of ritual observance:

> I see here people who argue endlessly about religion; but it seems to me that they are competing at the same time to see who can observe it the least. Not only are they not better Christians, they are not even better citizens, which is what concerns me. For in whatever religion one may live, obedience to the laws, love of one's fellow men, and piety towards one's parents are always the first acts of religion. (V, 94; B, 101)

Of course this is very much in the spirit of Locke: the complaint that people quarrel endlessly about unimportant religious issues and neglect what really matters, right conduct. But Montesquieu's acceptance of religious difference is much broader than Locke's: *in whatever religion one may live* . . . And his version of the Lockean complaint contains a challenge to religious authority which I do not think has a parallel in Locke. Later in the letter Usbek imagines a man making the following prayer to God:

> Lord, I cannot understand anything in the disputes which people continually engage in about you. I would like to serve you according to *your* will, but everyone I consult wants me to serve you according to *his* will. When I want to pray to you, I don't know in what language I should speak, or what posture I should adopt . . . There are some who claim I must wash every morning in cold water; others maintain that you will regard me with horror if I do not have a small piece of my flesh cut off. The other day, at an inn, I happened to eat a rabbit. Three men who were nearby made me tremble. All three maintained that I had deeply offended you—one, because the animal was unclean; the second, because it had been strangled; and the third, because it was not a fish. A Brahmin who was passing by, and whom I appealed to as a judge, told me: "They are wrong; for presumably you did not kill this animal yourself." "Yes," I said, "I did." "Ah!" he replied, in a severe voice, "you have committed an abominable action, which God will never forgive you for. How do you know that the soul of your father had not passed into that animal?" (V, 94–95; B, 101–102)

propriate to transfer to other countries. The point here, I think, is that in the Quran the prohibition is issued without any reasons being offered, leaving the teachers of the religion to their own devices when believers seek a reason.

Usbek concludes by proclaiming that he's in a terrible quandary. He would like to please God, but he keeps getting conflicting advice about how to do it. And he cannot find an impartial judge to resolve the conflict. So he decides that the best way is to live as a good citizen in the society God has caused him to be born in, and to be a good father to the family God has given him. The abbé Gaultier, who criticized the *Persian Letters* for their impiety, cited this passage as teaching that "every religion is indifferent, provided that in it one fulfills the duties of society" (V, 96n). This criticism seems perfectly just, from the abbé's point of view. That is precisely the point of the passage.

After Usbek has been in Europe a few more years, we find him taking a bolder stance with respect to the religion of his birth. In L97, which is supposed to have been written in the sixth year of his visit, the addressee is a dervish named Hassein. As in the sequence to the mullah, Usbek begins with flattery. But the tone is decidedly different:

> Oh wise dervish, whose inquisitive mind is so rich in knowledge, listen to what I have to tell you. (V, 200; B, 180)

Note that instead of abasing himself before the dervish, Usbek is now demanding the religious man's attention.

> There are philosophers here who have not, it is true attained the peaks of oriental wisdom. They have not been transported up to the throne of light; they have not heard the ineffable words resounding from angelic choirs, nor felt the fearful onset of divine ecstasy. But left to themselves, deprived of these holy marvels, they follow in silence the path of human reason . . .

In his annotation of this passage, Vernière observes that its language is too close to that of Paul's second letter to the Corinthians (12:1–10) not to be intended to recall it. He also characterizes the reminiscence of Paul as malicious, as it certainly seems to be. The use of familiar Christian language to describe the claims of Muslim mystics suggests an equivalence between Christian and Muslim pretensions which no Christian or Muslim exclusivist can accept.

Usbek's letter goes on to describe with fervor the understanding of nature Western philosopher-scientists have achieved by following reason: how God gave motion to matter, and how this was sufficient, given the operation of a few simple and immutable general laws, to produce the prodigious variety we observe in the universe. However dated that science may be, Montesquieu's essential point seems valid: that science, by relying on reason, can achieve an understanding of nature more wonderful than any of the miracles the religious authorities allege.

> If some man of God had phrased the works of these scientists in elevated and sublime words, if he had mixed with it bold metaphors and mysterious allegories, he would have produced a fine work, second only to the Koran. (V, 202; B, 181)

This apparent preference for the Koran over a stylistically adorned work of science looks ironic, though, since Usbek quickly undermines it:

> If I must tell you what I think, I don't like this ornate style at all. In our Koran there are a great many small things, which always seem so to me, however much they may be enhanced by the force and liveliness of the writing. It seems at first as though the inspired books are just divine ideas, rendered in human language. On the contrary, in our Koran one often finds the language of God and the ideas of men, as if, by a wonderful act of capriciousness, God had dictated the words and man had furnished the thoughts.

This is dangerous stuff. To make sure we don't miss the point, Montesquieu has Usbek conclude the letter with the kind of ritual disclaimer philosophers often use in these situations:

> You will perhaps say that I am speaking too freely about the holiest thing we possess, and you will think that this is the fruit of the independence in which one lives in this country. But no, thanks be to heaven, my mind has not corrupted my heart; as long as I live, Ali will be my prophet.

This shouldn't fool anyone. It certainly didn't fool the abbé Gaultier, who wrote that:

> the author pretends to be talking about Ali, Mohammed and the Koran, but it's St. Paul, the prophets and the sacred books which he's attacking . . . Mohammed and Ali are only men of straw . . . The author wants us to believe that he is still a Christian, and always will be. But his discourse is full of impiety. (V, 203, n1)

These letters seem to me to make a fundamental deistic point very forcefully: that religions which claim to be the vehicle of an exclusive divine revelation typically maintain that their revelation is recorded in a sacred text, written long ago; that because the sacred text was written long ago it embodies the superstitious ideas of past ages, which can be defended now only by some measure of obscurantism; that the principal agent for defending these outmoded ideas is a priestly class, which claims authority over the rest of us because its members purport to lead exemplary lives, dedicated to religion, lives which permit them privileged access to the secrets of the sacred texts and give them the right to guide the conduct of their followers, whose more mundane concerns do not permit them the leisure to master the religious literature so that they can speak on religious issues with authority;[45] these priests may, though they do not always, make some sacrifice of

---

45. Interesting in connection with the issue of priestly authority is L61, in which Usbek reports a conversation with a Christian clergyman who complains about the difficulties of his life: "As soon as we appear [in the outside world] we have to argue. We have to undertake, for instance, the task of proving the usefulness of prayer to a man who does not believe in God, or the neces-

worldly goods in order to secure their religious authority; when they do make that sacrifice, they are compensated by the power they acquire over those of their fellow men who are foolish enough to believe them.

One of the most important of the letters, for the purposes of my argument, is L35, which deploys an interesting variation on the theme of *quid rides* criticism. This purports to be a letter written by Usbek to a cousin, who is a dervish in a monastery in Tabriz. In his letter, Usbek raises questions about the exclusivism of Islam:

> What, sublime dervish, do you think of the Christians? Do you believe that on the Day of Judgment they will be like the faithless Turks, who will be used as donkeys for the Jews, to trot them quickly off down to Hell?[46] I am well aware that they will not go to the dwelling-place of the prophets, and that the great prophet Ali did not come for them. But do you think, because they are not fortunate enough to have mosques in their country, that they are condemned to eternal torments, and that God will punish them for not having practised a religion he did not reveal to them? (V, 75–76; B, 88)

This transposes a standard objection to Christian exclusivism, giving it a special bite by showing a Muslim assuming that Christians, of course, will not go to Heaven, but that it might be a tad unfair for them to go to Hell.

Note that in this case the Muslim does not provoke amusement by uncritically accepting the teachings of his religion—at least as far as the Christians are concerned.[47] He does accept those teachings without criticism as they apply to the Jews and to other Muslims who do not belong to his branch of Islam. But he thinks

---

sity of fasting to another who has spent his life denying the immortality of the soul. It is a laborious enterprise, and the humorists are not on our side. What is more, *we suffer constantly from a certain desire to make other people share our views; it is part of our calling*, so to speak. This is as ridiculous as it would be to see Europeans trying to turn the Africans' faces white, for the sake of human nature. We cause social disturbances and make ourselves suffer in order to spread religious beliefs which are not fundamental, and we resemble the Emperor of China who provoked his subjects to general rebellion by trying to compel them to cut their hair or their nails" (B 127, my emphasis).

46. As Vernière notes, this is an ironic reversal of a view Chardin ascribed to the Turks: that the Jews will go to Hell mounted on the Persians.

47. There is, of course, some disagreement as to precisely what his religion teaches regarding the eligibility of Christians and Jews for Paradise. Some Quranic texts which seem to clearly endorse exclusivism (e.g., 3:19, "The only true faith in God's sight is Islam," or 3:85, "He that chooses a religion other than Islam, it will not be accepted of him, and in the world to come he will surely be among the losers") are open to the interpretation that they mean by "Islam" any form of monotheism which teaches submission to God. On the other hand, the first pillar of Islam involves not only the acceptance of monotheism, but also the acceptance of Mohammed as the prophet of God (i.e., acceptance of the Quran as divine revelation). And the Prophet's attitude toward "the Peoples of the Book" (i.e., Jews and Christians) seems to have changed over the course of his life: favorably disposed in the early days of his mission, when he still hoped to win Jewish and Christian converts, and hostile in the later days, as those hopes were disappointed. On these issues, see Faruq Sherif, *A Guide to the Contents of the Qur'an*, London: Ithaca Press, 1985, pp. 89–94. In any case, Usbek would have some ground for supposing that the official position is exclusivist in a way which would exclude Jews and Christians.

the Christians deserve special consideration because in many respects they are *almost* Muslims:

> If you examine their religion closely, you will find the rudiments, as it were, of our own dogmas. I have often marveled at the secret ways of Providence, which seems to have wanted to prepare them in this way for general conversion.

Usbek goes on to mention a book by a Christian theologian, arguing that Christians are commanded to practice polygamy; he then proceeds to compare the Christian rite of baptism with the Muslim requirement for frequent ablutions, the Christian requirements for frequent prayer to Muslim requirements, and the Christian hope of Heaven to that of the Muslims. Christians often criticize the Islamic conception of the afterlife as being too sensual. Usbek does not mention that criticism, but does claim that the Christian doctrine of the resurrection of the body offers them the hope of similar physical pleasures. And so it goes.

I will not detail here all the similarities Usbek finds between Christianity and Islam.[48] What is most interesting in this letter is that his position offers an apparent middle ground between exclusivism and pluralism, one which would say: "Yes, of course there is one revealed religion which is true, all others being false to one degree or another; but it may not be necessary to accept the true religion to avoid damnation; it may be sufficient to accept a false religion if it is near enough to the true one."[49] But the condescension implied in this view may be more evident to a Christian when it is a Muslim who is saying: "*My* religion, of course, is the true one; but you *may* be saved in *yours* if it comes near enough to mine." Montesquieu's own position is surely more radical: it is possible to be saved in any religion, so long as its moral teachings make you a good man—a good husband, a good father, and a good citizen.

There are many other letters it would be desirable to discuss: L143, with its admission by a Muslim, writing to a Jew, that many of their practices are superstitious:

> What wretched beings men are! They vacillate incessantly between false hopes and ridiculous fears; instead of relying on reason, they make for themselves monsters which frighten them, and phantoms which seduce them.[50]

---

48. We should note, however, that L35 is quickly followed by another letter, L39, which claims to have been written by a Muslim to a Jewish convert to Islam, citing the prodigies which are supposed to have accompanied the birth of Mohammed as proof of his divine mission. Among the parallels with the Christian birth narratives are the genealogies which seek to establish Mohammed's descent from the patriarchs.

49. This position closely resembles the inclusivism adopted by the Catholic Church in the Second Vatican Council, when it abandoned its traditional doctrine that there is no salvation outside the church. See the Second Vatican Council, *Dogmatic Constitution on the Church* (21 November 1964), ch. ii, par. 16.

50. V, 311; B, 259. This is one of a number of passages in the *Letters* which may indicate a reading of Spinoza. Cf. the account of superstition in the preface to the *Theological-Political Treatise*, Bruder par. 1.

Or L24, with its cannibal criticism of the Pope, as a great magician, who can make people believe that three are only one, or that the bread we eat and the wine we drink are not bread and wine (V, 26; B, 73). Or L57, with its cannibal criticism of the practice of casuistry, which enables Christians to get to heaven with the minimum possible compliance with the letter of the law (V, 119–122; B, 120–122).[51] Or L134, where Rica reports a conversation with a learned priest, who is candid enough to admit the tortured interpretations which his fellow ecclesiastics impose on scripture, in an attempt to buttress their own ideas with divine authority (V, 283–285; B, 238–239).[52] Or L85, with its *quid rides* criticism of the Revocation of the Edict of Nantes, presented indirectly as a criticism of the Persian persecution of the Armenians, arguing that it is to the advantage both of the state and of religion that there be a multiplicity of religions in society. Or L29, which offers cannibal criticism of the papacy for its wealth and (now declining) political power, the bishops of the church for collectively establishing requirements which the individual bishops then find it useful to suspend on appeal, and the Inquisition for its brutality and procedural injustice.

At the end of the letter just mentioned, Rica concludes with ironic praise of Islam (at least as practiced in Persia):

Happy the land where the children of the prophets dwell! There such piteous sights are unknown. The holy religion that the angels brought down is defended by its very truth; it does not need these violent methods to preserve itself. (V, 67–68; B, 82)

In a note to this passage, Montesquieu writes that "the Persians are the most tolerant of all the Mohammedans." I call this praise ironic, since in later letters Usbek will make it quite clear that, even in Persia, Islamic rulers have sometimes used violent methods to "persuade" nonbelievers to accept the faith. In L35 Usbek's report of Islamic attempts at forcible conversion is not specific about where this occurred, nor is it critical of those attempts.[53] But in L85 he is talking specifically about Persian persecutions, both of the Armenians (Christians) and of the

---

51. This, incidentally, might be cited as an example of Montesquieu's unfairness to a Christian practice. Applying any legal code requires a certain amount of casuistry, in the sense of a determinination of what exceptions might be made to a general principle, without doing violence to the spirit of that principle. So casuistry has a good side, which Montesquieu's satirical purposes do not permit him to acknowledge. In this instance, I think we can ascribe the unfairness to Montesquieu himself, and not merely to one of his fictional characters. In other passages, this is not so clear. For example, where Usbek accepts a common stereotype of Jews as avaricious (L60), or ascribes to them a "proselytizing spirit" (L85), or where Zulema, as reported by Rica, ascribes to them the view that women have no soul (L141), the point may be that people generally are apt to have inaccurate views of the beliefs and practices of those who embrace religions different from theirs.

52. Another echo of Spinoza. Cf. the *Theological-Political Treatise*, ch. vii, Bruder par. 1.

53. In arguing that it might not be fair for Christians to be condemned to Hell he writes: "They do not resemble the infidels whom our holy prophets put to the edge of the sword, for refusing to believe in the miracles of Heaven" (V, 76; B, 88).

Gabars,[54] and he is critical of the practice, attributing it (perhaps unfairly)[55] to religious zealotry and arguing that it was contrary to the economic interests of the country.

In L85 Usbek seems to regard these uses of force to promote Islam as aberrations, the product of excessive zeal. Other voices in the *Letters* present a different view. As Gunny notes, in L67 the Gabar Aphéridon represents Islam as a religion that has established itself, "not by persuasion, but by conquest" (V, 143; B, 139). Gunny also observes that this is a view of Islamic history which Montesquieu, perhaps speaking in his own voice, seems to endorse in *The Spirit of the Laws*:

> It is a misfortune for human nature when religion is given by a conqueror.
> The Mohammedan religion, which speaks only with a sword, continues to
> act on men with the destructive spirit which founded it.[56]

Is Montesquieu being fair to Islam here? Or is he merely endorsing a common Christian prejudice about Islam?

These are large questions, which I cannot claim any special competence to answer. But I do not think we should say "yes" to either question. The sources on which I rely in this paper suggest that the truth is more complicated. *Often*, though *by no means always*, Islam did win adherents by using force rather than persuasion. Here is the judgment of one prominent Western scholar, who seems generally sympathetic toward Islam, and who seems to characterize the situation accurately:

> A common issue associated with the spread of Islam is the role of jihad, so-called holy war. While Westerners are quick to characterize Islam as a religion spread by the sword, modern Muslim apologists sometimes explain jihad as simply defensive in nature. In its most general sense, jihad in the Quran and in Muslim practice refers to the obligation of all Muslims to strive [*jihad*, self-exertion] or struggle to follow God's will. This includes *both* the struggle to lead a virtuous life and the universal mission of the Muslim community to spread God's rule and law through teaching, preaching, *and where necessary, armed struggle* . . . As Islam penetrated new areas, people were offered three options: (1) conversion, that is, full membership in the Muslim community; (2) acceptance of Muslim rule as "protected" people and payment of a poll tax; (3) battle or the sword if neither the first nor the second option was accepted. The astonishing expansion of Islam resulted *not only* from armed conquest, *but also* from these two peaceful options. In later centuries, in many

---

54. 'Gabar' is a derogatory term meaning 'unbeliever', used by Persian Muslims to refer to the Zoroastrians, who were the dominant religious group in Persia before the Muslim conquest of the seventh century. See George Healy, *The Persian Letters*, Hackett, 1999, p. 112, n1.

55. Vernière's annotation of this passage (V, 178, n1) observes that Montesquieu's source here represents the motivation for Suleiman III's persecution of the Armenians as more financial than religious.

56. *The Spirit of the Laws*, XXIV, iv, p. 462 in the translation by Cohler, Miller, and Stone (Cambridge University Press, 1999).

areas of Africa, the Indian subcontinent, and Southeast Asia, the effective spread of Islam would be due primarily to Muslim traders and Sufi [mystic] missionaries who won converts by their example and preaching.[57]

Moreover, although conversion to Islam was in fact often voluntary, and although the Quran teaches that "there shall be no compulsion in religion," it also teaches its adherents to "make war on the unbelievers and the hypocrites and deal rigorously with them," and to "fight against them [the idolaters or unbelievers] until idolatry is no more and Allah's religion reigns supreme."[58] So although Montesquieu himself (in *The Spirit of the Laws*) and his character (Aphéridon in the *Persian Letters*) may grossly exaggerate when they represent Islam as having become established *only* by the sword, there is a kernel of truth underlying the exaggeration.

I am not, however, certain that Montesquieu is expressing his own most considered view in the passage cited above from *The Spirit of the Laws*. Although that work does not deploy the distancing devices Montesquieu uses in the *Persian Letters*, I suspect that his discussion of religion there is frequently ironic. In this instance, it may be that his intent is to dissuade Christians from forcible conversion by reminding them how strongly they disapprove of that practice when Muslims engage in it. If that is his intent, then it may serve his purpose to embrace the common Christian misconception of Islam, even if he knows that it is an exaggeration.

But there may be a larger point lying beneath the surface of the passage which led us into this discussion, that is, Rica's exclamation in L29:

Happy the land where the children of the prophets dwell! There such piteous sights are unknown. The holy religion that the angels brought down is defended by its very truth; it does not need these violent methods to preserve itself. (V, 67–68; B, 82)

If the true religion does not need to use violence to win and keep adherents, and if the use of such methods by a religion's followers raises questions about the truth of the religion, what does it say about a religion if its God threatens nonbelievers with eternal torment? Are we entitled to infer that such a God cannot be the true God? These are, I think, among the questions which Montesquieu's work raises. They seem to me important questions, which needed to be asked, and which may have done much to smooth the path for a broader toleration than Locke ever contemplated.

57. John Esposito, *Islam: the Straight Path*, pp. 36–37 (my emphases). For a similar account, stressing that the early Arab military campaigns were "wars of Arab conquest, not Muslim conversion," see Thomas Lippman, *Understanding Islam: An Introduction to the Muslim World*, Meridian, 2nd revised edition, 1995, ch. 5.

58. The quotes are from 2:257, 9:73, 2:193 (= 8:40), in the Dawood translation. In the latter two cases, Arberry has a somewhat different translation. I owe these references to Faruq Sherif, who cites many other passages which are in the spirit of the latter two (pp. 113–115). So I do not think the differences in translation can be crucial.

Contributors

Felicia Ackerman, Department of Philosophy, Brown University

Michael J. B. Allen, Department of English, University of California, Los Angeles

Brian P. Copenhaver, Department of History, College of Letters and Sciences, University of California, Los Angeles

Edwin Curley, Department of Philosophy, University of Michigan

Daniel Garber, Department of Philosophy, University of Chicago

Hilary Gatti, University of Rome "La Sapienza"

Tatiana V. Gómez, Department of Philosophy, University of Arizona

Jasper Hopkins, Department of Philosophy, University of Minnesota

Douglas M. Jesseph, Department of Philosophy, North Carolina State University

Nicholas Jolley, Department of Philosophy, University of California, Irvine

Jeff Jordan, Department of Philosophy, University of Delaware

Nancy Kendrick, Philosophy Department, Wheaton College

Thomas M. Lennon, University of Western Ontario

Steven Nadler, Department of Philosophy, University of Wisconsin–Madison

Cary Nederman, Department of Political Science, Texas A&M University

Margaret J. Osler, University of Calgary

Rose-Mary Sargent, Department of Philosophy, Merrimack College

Bruce Silver, Department of Philosophy, University of South Florida

John L. Treloar, S. J., Associate Academic Dean, Jesuit School of Technology at Berkeley

Peter A. French is the Lincoln Chair in Ethics and the Director of the Lincoln Center for Applied Ethics at Arizona State University. He was the Cole Chair In Ethics, Director of The Ethics Center, and Chair of the Department of Philosophy of the University of South Florida. Before that he was the Lennox Distinguished Professor of the Humanities and Professor of Philosophy at Trinity University in San Antonio, Texas, and served as Exxon Distinguished Research Professor in the Center for the Study of Values at the University of Delaware. He is the author of seventeen books including *Cowboy Metaphysics: Ethics and Death in Westerns*; *Corporate Ethics*; *Responsibility Matters*; *Corporations in the Moral Community*; *The Spectrum of Responsibility*; *Collective and Corporate Responsibility*; *Corrigible Corporations and Unruly Laws*; *Ethics in Government*; and *The Scope of Morality*. His most recent book, *The Virtues of Vengeance*, was published in April 2001. He has published dozens of articles in the major philosophical and legal journals and reviews, many of which have been anthologized. **Howard K. Wettstein** is Professor of Philosophy at the University of California, Riverside. He has taught at the University of Notre Dame and the University of Minnesota, Morris, and has served as a visiting professor of philosophy at the University of Iowa and Stanford University. He has published articles on the philosophy of language and the philosophy of religion and is the author of *Has Semantics Rested on a Mistake? and Other Essays* (1992). He is currently finishing a book on the philosophy of language.

MIDWEST STUDIES IN PHILOSOPHY 1976–2004

Vol. I	Studies in the History of Philosophy	February 1976
Vol. II	Studies in the Philosophy of Language *Rev. Ed.*, Contemporary Perspectives in the Philosophy of Language	February 1977
Vol. III	Studies in Ethical Theory	February 1978
Vol. IV	Studies in Metaphysics	February 1979
Vol. V	Studies in Epistemology	February 1980
Vol. VI	Foundations of Analytic Philosophy	1981
Vol. VII	Social and Political Philosophy	1982
Vol. VIII	Contemporary Perspectives on the History of Philosophy	1983
Vol. IX	Causation and Casual Theories	1984
Vol. X	Studies in the Philosophy of Mind	1985
Vol. XI	Studies in Essentialism	1986
Vol. XII	Realism and Anti-Realism	1987
Vol. XIII	Ethical Theory: Character and Virtue	1988
Vol. XIV	Contemporary Perspectives in the Philosophy of Language II	1989
Vol. XV	The Philosophy of the Human Sciences	1990
Vol. XVI	Philosophy and the Arts	1991
Vol. XVII	The Wittgenstein Legacy	1992
Vol. XVIII	Philosophy of Science	1993
Vol. XIX	Philosophical Naturalism	1994
Vol. XX	Moral Concepts	1995
Vol. XXI	Philosophy of Religion	1996
Vol. XXII	Philosophy of the Emotions	1997
Vol. XXIII	New Directions in Philosophy	1998
Vol. XXIV	Life and Death: Metaphysics and Ethics	1999
Vol. XXV	Figurative Language	2001
Vol. XXVI	Renaissance and Early Modern Philosophy	2002
Vol. XXVII	Meaning in the Arts	2003 forthcoming
Vol. XXVIII	The American Philosophers	2004 forthcoming

Volumes XXIII onwards available through Blackwell Publishers. All previous volumes may be available through University of Notre Dame Press.